Diana Amnéus & Katinka Svanberg-Torpman (Eds.)

Peace and Security

Current Challenges in International Law

Studentlitteratur

The papers and inks used in this product are eco-friendly.

Art. No 31478
ISBN 91–44-04265-5

Cover picture: © Ingrid Booz More John (Non violence) and Amy Sancetta/AP (World trade Center) Pressens bild
Cover design by: Francisco Ortega

Printed in Sweden
Studentlitteratur, Lund
Web-address: www.studentlitteratur.se

Printing/year 1 2 3 4 5 6 7 8 9 10 | 2008 07 06 05 04

Dedication

To the memory of Anna Lindh, Swedish Foreign Minister,
who was murdered in September 2003.

Anna Lindh was versed in international law
and devoted to its principles.
She was a Foreign Minister
who really understood the connection
between human rights and
the maintenance of international
peace and security.

Contents

Preface

This book was conceived by the present editors, Ms Diana Amnéus and Ms Katinka Svanberg-Torpman, who are both doctoral candidates in public international law at Stockholm University. The idea was to inspire the production of a number of articles on the theme of international law and international security, a theme that is nowadays daily proving its relevance on the global scene. Research colleagues, legal advisers and other practising lawyers with their academic roots in public international law were asked to contribute. A number of Swedish international law scholars have shared their expertise in this book.

The focus of the book is on the enforcement and protection of legally prescribed principles and values relating to international peace and security. Most of the contributions have a military dimension, either from a United Nations Charter perspective or from the perspective of international humanitarian law applicable to armed conflict. Those of us who have been involved in the planning of the book believe that *Peace and Security* will be useful both to scholars and students in advanced courses on public international law at universities and other institutions. Several contributions include a 'law of war' perspective, and may therefore be of particular interest to students at military academies and defence colleges.

Although the idea of the book originated in the academic environment of the Faculty of Law at Stockholm University, we are happy to welcome Professors Iain Cameron and Inger Österdahl of the University of Uppsala as contributors. The Swedish international legal setting today includes a dynamic combination of experts, and the contributors deliver a mix of research that reflects current developments, for better or worse, in the present world community.

Stockholm, June 2004

Ove Bring
Professor
Carl Lindhagen Chair of International Law
Stockholm University

Contributors

Diana Amnéus (LL.M.) is a doctoral candidate in public international law at the Faculty of Law at Stockholm University. She is writing her thesis on the concept of human security and its implications for international law. She has previously served as a Desk Officer at the Swedish Ministry for Foreign Affairs in the Departments of Public International Law and Global Cooperation. Amnéus also has working experience from the the United Nations High Commissioner for Refugees and the Swedish Red Cross. She is director of a course on women's human rights at the Stockholm School of Theology in Stockholm, and lectures in public international law at Stockholm University. She is co-editor of *Human Rights – on the Frontline of Research,* Amnéus, Diana, Gunner, Göran (2003).

Ove Bring (LL.D), Professor in International Law at the University of Stockholm, is also attached to the Swedish National Defence College. Professor Bring has served as a legal advisor at the Swedish Ministry for Foreign Affairs and written a number of books, *inter alia* on Disarmament, the UN Charter and International Criminal Law, *e.g. Folkrätt för totalförsvaret. En handbok,* 2nd edition (2000); *FN-stadgan och världspolitiken,* 4th edition (2002); *International Criminal Law in Historical Perspective – Comments and Materials* (2001). He is a member of the Permanent Court of Arbitration in the Hague, the Executive Council of the International Law Association and the Governing Council of the San Remo Institute of International Humaniterian Law.

Iain Cameron (LL.D) is Professor of Public International Law at the University of Uppsala. He has published extensively in the fields of international law and constitutional law, particularly on international criminal law and human rights issues. He has acted as an expert adviser to several Swedish official inquiries in the field of international law. His most recent books are *National Security and the European Convention on Human Rights* (2000) and *An Introduction to the European Convention on Human Rights,* 4th edition (2002).

Ola Engdahl (LL.M.) is a doctoral candidate in public international law at Stockholm University and the Swedish National Defence College. The subject of his thesis is *Protection of Personnel in Peace Operations: Safety and Security in the Mission Area.* Ola Engdahl has served as a Legal Adviser to the Commander of the Nordic-Polish Brigade in SFOR, Bosnia-Herzegovina. He lectures in international law at the Swedish National Defence College and is a co-author of *Fredsbevarande operationer och andra kollektiva insatser,* in *Folkrätt för totalförsvaret. En handbok,* Bring, Ove, 2nd edition (2000).

David I. Fisher (LL.D), Associate Professor of International Law and Lecturer in Public International Law, including Human Rights, at Stockholm University. Recent publications include *Mänskliga Rättigheter: En Introduktion,* (2001) and *Defamation via Satellite: A European Law Perspective* (1998).

Marie Jacobsson (LL.D) is the Principal Legal Adviser on International Law at the Swedish Ministry for Foreign Affairs. She holds a doctorate in law from the University of Lund. Jacobsson has published articles in the areas of international law and politics, most recently *Maritime Security: an Individual or a Collective Responsibility* in Nordic Cosmopolitanism: Essays in International Law for Martti Koskenniemi (2003). Jacobsson is a frequent lecturer at various Swedish and foreign universities and institutions.

Anna Körlof (LL.M.) is a doctoral candidate in public international law at Åbo Academy University and the Swedish National Defence College and is presently working on her thesis *Responsibility and Liability of States for Use of Weapons in Armed Conflicts; Concepts of Reparation and Compensation.* She is co-author of *Folkrätt för totalförsvaret. En handbok,* Bring, Ove, Körlof, Anna, 3rd edition (2002).

Cecilia Hellman (LL.M.) is currently working at the Swedish National Defence College as a military lawyer at the Department of Security and Strategic Studies (ISS) and the Centre for Information Operation Studies (CIOS). She is also a member of the Joint Cabinet Working Group on Information Operations. Prior to this she worked at the main office of the Swedish Red Cross in the Department of International Law. She is author to *The Introduction of International Humanitarian Law to Sweden* (2000).

Per Sevastik, LL.D. in Public International Law at Uppsala University and an LL.M. from Harvard Law School. His doctoral thesis is entitled *Informell modifikation av traktater till följd av ny sedvanerätt och praxis. En studie mot bakgrund av FN-stadgans innovativa utveckling* (2002). He has also published *The Binding Force of Treaties under International Law* (1997) and has edited and co-authored *Legal Assistance to Developing Countries: Swedish Perspectives on the Rule of Law* (1997). He is currently working at the Swedish International Development Cooperation Authority (Sida) on issues relating to rule of law, democracy and human rights.

Fredrik Stenhammar (LL.M.) is a doctoral candidate in public international law at the Stockholm University Faculty of Law, and is now writing his thesis on UN smart sanctions. Stenhammar has served in the Ministry for Foreign Affairs, as a law clerk in the Enforcement Department of the Swedish National Tax Board and at Nacka District Court.

Katinka Svanberg-Torpman (LL.M.) is a doctoral candidate in public international law at Stockholm University. The subject of her thesis is *The Security Council and the Right of Internal Self-determination.* She holds a Master's Degree in law from Stockholm University and a Master's Degree in Comparative Law from New York University. Publications include *Introduktion till traktaträtten – en lärobok i traktaträtt,* 3rd edition (2003); *Folkrätten efter den 11 september 2001,* in Terrorismens Tid, Jervas, Gunnar (Ed.) (2003); *Folkrätten och våldsförbudet – när är våld tillåtet?* Försvar i nutid, No. 1 (2003).

Inger Österdahl (LL.D.) is Professor in Public International Law at the University of Uppsala. Her latest publications include *Implementing Human Rights in Africa. The African Commission on Human and Peoples' Rights and Individual Communications* (2002); *Is Intervention Humanitarian? Protecting Human Rights and Democracy Abroad* (Ed.) (2002); *The EU and its Member States, Other States and International Organisations – the Common European Security and Defence Policy after Nice,* Nordic Journal of International Law (2001); *FN-sanktioner och mänskliga rättigheter,* Svensk Juristtidning (2002). Her current research project is entitled: *"Collective or Individual Security? The Transformation of the Collective Security System under the UN".*

Introduction

The world has changed in several ways after the end of the Cold War; the greatest current threats to international peace and security are no longer the traditional inter-state wars. Internal wars have plagued several continents, maps have been rewritten, nationalism has increased, gross violations of international humanitarian law and human rights continue, and the horrific acts of international terrorism that struck the US on 11 September 2001 have changed the world forever.

There has been an upsurge of interest in public international law and its rules on the use of force and international peace and security during the last decade and the law is adapting to several of these new developments in the international arena. The end of the Cold War finally made it possible for the collective security system laid down by the UN Charter to function as intended, now that the Security Council was no longer paralysed by vetoes. As a result the Council has been able to pass an unprecedented number of mandatory resolutions under Chapter VII and has come close to acting as a law enforcer and legislator. International criminal law has also had a breakthrough during the 1990s as a result of the enhanced focus on the enforcement of humanitarian law through the punishment of acts of genocide, crimes against humanity, acts of aggression and war crimes. Two *ad hoc* criminal tribunals, one for the territory of the former Yugoslavia and one for Rwanda, paved way for the adoption of the Statute of the Permanent International Criminal Tribunal (ICC) in 1998.

During the last decade there has been increased focus on the security of people, *e.g.* in internal conflicts, and the UN and other international organisations have increasingly undertaken humanitarian interventions in order to halt widespread or systematic violations of human rights. Another recent trend is the development of a right to self-defence against acts of international terrorism. This is a new development set in motion by the extensive terrorist acts in

September 2001, which prompted the US to declare war on international terrorism and to intervene in Afghanistan. Efforts to combat international terrorism have however, in some cases appeared to infringe individuals' human rights. A new situation has arisen in which the use of smart sanctions and other international measures to combat terrorism have clashed with the human rights regime. Another trend connected with international terrorism that has alarmed governments and defence departments is the possibility of cyberspace attacks paralysing large parts of a country's infrastructure. How should such attacks be regarded in the context of public international law?

This book tries to analyse these recent trends and new phenomena related to international peace and security. We find that the current literature, in particular for students, on public international law has not yet been able to account for these rapid developments and aspects in a satisfactory way. Our aim is to attempt to fill this gap. We hope that both students and scholars will benefit from and enjoy its content.

The order of the chapters in this book have been organised according to how the main set of rules that are dealt with, are listed in the Chapters of the UN Charter. The *first chapter* of the book is introductory and deals with issues of concern regarding the UN Charter and its binding force. Thereafter, in *chapter 2*, the book moves on directly to the UN Charter's rules on pacific settlement of disputes which are the subject of Chapter VI and beyond ('Chapter VI 1/2'). *Chapter 3, 4* and *5* of the book pertain to Chapter VII of the Charter. The first two focus on the Security Council and its mandate regarding the maintenance of international peace and security and on the rules on smart sanctions, respectively. *Chapter 5* deals with developments in the right to self-defence, which is regulated in Article 51 of the UN Charter.

The following chapters are not as obviously connected to the UN Charter as the previous ones and their order is determined by how the subjects interconnect with each other. *Chapter 6* also deals with international terrorism but from a different perspective – that of human rights. The *next chapter, 7* deals with explosive remnants of war and humanitarian law, which is a subject closely connected with human security. *Chapters 8, 9* and *10* deal with the very latest trends and phenomena which have not yet been fully regulated in public international law or regarding which practice is lacking: computer network attacks, the future relationship between the ICC and the Security Council, and theories on the concept of human security and its relationship with humanitarian intervention, respectively. *The last chapter, 11,* deals with the legal, moral and philosophical issues surrounding the recent military intervention in Iraq in March 2003. A more detailed presentation and description of each of the chapters will follow below.

In *Some Reflections on the Interpretation of the UN Charter and its Binding Force* Per Sevastik describes the mechanism that makes the UN Charter binding on all members of the organisation. What actually makes a Chapter VII action – with respect to threats to the peace, breaches of the peace or acts of aggression – mandatory for all members of the United Nations? This chapter discusses step by step the various features of the Charter and how they should be interpreted. The fact that the Charter is seen as a living instrument with constitutional features – partly as a dynamic treaty regime and partly as an organisation holding implied powers – increases the difficulty of explaining the binding force of the UN Charter. Moreover, the undisputed fact that there is no 'custodian of the Charter' capable of making binding decisions when doubts arise as to whether or not certain measures comply with its provisions makes it even more difficult to assess its binding force.

Ola Engdahl's analysis, *The Status of Military Personnel in United Nations Peace Operations – Interplay Between the Laws of Peace and War,* deals with the unprecedented increase in deliberate attacks against personnel in United Nations peace operations. Attempts to strengthen protection of the personnel include, *inter alia,* developments in the area of international humanitarian law. The deteriorating situation for personnel involved in peace operations in the early 1990s, with the operations in former Yugoslavia and Somalia as perhaps the most troublesome, led to the adoption of the Convention on the Safety of United Nations and Associated Personnel in 1994. The Convention provides a protective regime for military and civilian personnel engaged in UN operations. Taking the 1994 Convention as a point of departure, his article investigates the relationships between rules and norms applicable in peace and in war to the protection of personnel engaged in peace operations and discusses trends and developments.

In chapter 3 Katinka Svanberg-Torpman investigates her thesis on *The Security Council as a Law Enforcer and Legislator.* The contribution tries to establish a link between the Security Council's sanctions decisions under Chapter VII and important principles of public international law. In the new millennium the Council has gone even further and started to legislate, using Chapter VII in order to establish new rules of international law. The Chapter attempts to prove that the Council has acted to uphold and implement fundamental norms of public international law such as the prohibition of genocide, war-crimes, acts of international terrorism, respect for human rights and peoples' right to self-determination. Decisions of the Security Council pursuant to Chapter VII have helped to strengthen those norms and contributed to their development in customary international law. Some of the Security Council's decisions have had a clearly legal content, *i.e.,* so called "quasi-judicial decisions". The thesis is that the Security Council through its activity pursuant to Chapter VII has acted both as a law enforcer and legislator.

In *UN Smart Sanctions – Political Reality and International Law,* Fredrik Stenhammar investigates some aspects of the Security Council's increased use of so called smart sanctions, *i.e.,* freezing of foreign held assets, travel bans and arms embargoes. In recent years, such smart sanctions have come to replace traditional sanctions in the form of comprehensive trade embargoes as the main instrument of coercion under article 41 of the UN Charter. However, as evidenced by the experience of recent sanctions regimes, this development is not unproblematic. In particular, a delicate balance has to be struck between the competing interests of maintaining international peace and security on the one hand and respect for individual rights on the other.

Ove Bring and David Fisher's contribution *Post-September 11 – A Right of Self-Defence against International Terrorism?* investigates the newly developing right of self-defence against international terrorism, which was invoked as a response to the terrorist attacks on the USA on 11 September 2001. The unanimously adopted Security Council Resolution 1368 on September 12 (2001) referred in general terms to a state's right to individual and collective self-defence in accordance with the UN Charter. This was in fact the first time the Security Council adopted an anti-terrorist resolution linking the issue of self-defence with the war on terrorism. The authors examine the traditional limits of the right to self-defence and show how a new extensive interpretion has been made in relation to large-scale international terrorism. The world community's support for this interpretation, NATO's activation of the so called musketeer principle laid down in Article 5 of the Washington Treaty and other states' positions are discussed and evaluated.

Iain Cameron takes up a number of burning questions concerning the relationship between means of combating international terrorism and promoting human rights in *Human Rights and Terrorism*. National security is the overriding concern of states, and states often try to push their powers to the limit when dealing with terrorism. This means that anti-terrorism measures frequently raise issues under many international human rights norms. Failure to respect human rights in the struggle threatens the legitimacy of the state. Experience shows that executive demands on the legislature for expanded powers to fight terrorism should be viewed with healthy scepticism. National judicial control over anti-terrorist measures is often deficient for a variety of reasons, and judges should be aware of this and be vigilant in ensuring that security agencies do not exceed their powers.

The contribution *Anti-Personnel Landmines, Explosive Remnants of War and International Humanitarian Law* by Anna Körlof describes the rules of international law relating to the problems of anti-personnel landmines and explosive remnants of war (ERWs). Modern armed conflicts leave behind explosive remnants such as mines, sub-munitions from cluster bombs, artillery shells, grenades, mortars, rockets and missiles, which cause large numbers of civilian victims every year. They often continue to kill and injure civilians decades after the actual conflict is over. This necessitates the rapid and safe clearing of mines and other ERWs, and calls for national and international rules initialising clearing as soon as possible. The author deals with the use of mines and ERWs and the responsibility of states for their removal.

Cecilia Hellman's chapter *Computer Network Attacks and Public International Law* discusses the new emerging threats of Computer Network Attacks (CNA). It has been demonstrated that it is theoretically possible to achieve the same effects by CNA as by traditional military attacks. Can we retaliate with conventional weapon systems against a CNA, and who is really the enemy in cyberspace? Today, single individuals can pose a threat to international peace and security, but does that make them combatants? Hellman analyses both the relevant *jus ad bellum* and *jus in bello* rules that would be raised by CNA, *inter alia,* does a large-scale CNA constitute a breach of the prohibition of use of force laid down in Article 2(4) of the UN Charter; can we claim a right to self-defence against these new, perhaps non-physical attacks; or will we have to adopt new means of regulating these activities? IT-warfare is no longer just a future sci-fi scenario, but is already present reality.

The chapter by Inger Österdahl, *The International Criminal Court and Collective Security,* examines the International Criminal Court's direct relationship with the UN Security Council and indirect relationship with the collective security system as a whole. It is explained that the ICC originates partly from the Nuremberg and Tokyo tribunals and partly from the many resolutions of the Security Council during the post-Cold War period, emphasizing on international humanitarian law and the role of individual criminal responsibility in maintaining or restoring international peace and security under Chapter VII of the UN Charter. The author argues that the direct influence of the UN Security Council on the working of the ICC weakens the independence of the Court as a judicial organ, while the political dimension of the collective security system maintains the upper hand. In addition, the issue whether or not the ICC is able to judge terrorists is discussed in this contribution.

The first part of *Rethinking Security – Humanitarian Intervention in the Age of Human Security – A Responsibility to Protect* by Diana Amnéus aims to introduce the reader to the concept of human security. It presents the background to the concept, its key advocates in the international arena, the human security agendas and discusses its relationship with state security and human rights. The second part deals with the connections between the conceptions of human security and *the responsibility to protect* – a new ground for legitimising humanitarian intervention in extreme cases without a Security Council mandate, introduced by the International Commission on Intervention and State Sovereignty. The Kosovo crisis is examined as the most recent and clear-cut example of a *human security war.* The legal limitations, challenges and implications of these two emerging concepts of international law and security are also analysed and discussed.

In the chapter *The Use of Force and the Case of Iraq* Marie Jacobsson examines the US and UK use of force against Iraq in March 2003, which caused a particularly significant legal, philosophical and moral debate. Most international lawyers agreed that the intervention was contrary to the wording of the UN Charter, but many participants still considered it *legitimate*. The fall of Saddam Hussein was welcomed since his regime and possession of weapons of mass destruction were percieved to pose a threat to international peace and security. The author analyses the different justifications for the intervention in this chapter, *inter alia* the UK argumentation that Security Council Resolution 687 "suspended but did not terminate the authority to use force under resolution 678" and that a "material breach" of Resolution 687 revived the authority to use force under Resolution 678. Jacobsson also scrutinizes the US argumentation relying on the National Security Strategy (the Bush Doctrine), which reflects the new US security thinking after the September 11.

1 Reflections on the Interpretation of the UN Charter and its Binding Force

Per Sevastik

1.1 Introduction

The horizontal structure of international law sometimes makes it difficult to see the binding force of the international legal system. The lack of formal sources in international law creates a presumed setting of 'formal sources', which cannot take the place of the constitutional or vertical structure of municipal law. Throughout the history of international law the lack of formal sources has created a controversy between 'consent' – the 'Voluntarist' school of thought, and *opinio juris* – the belief that a norm is accepted as law. Rules that where perceived as having a 'higher normativity' – *jus cogens* – such as rules against aggression, for example Article 2(4) of the Charter of the United Nations, were safeguarded under customary international law and were conceived as being universally binding as norms from which no derogation was permitted.[1]

International law is thus characterized with the help of a number of theories, which seek, in particular to fill the gap between the constitutional structure of the national legal system and the lack of such structure in the international legal system. The missing constitutionality in the international community made Hart ask the question '[i]s international law really law?'[2]

Disregarding the fact that there is no constitutional machinery of law-making in international law, the Charter of the United Nations has traditionally been regarded as the constitution of the world

1 See Article 53 Vienna Convention on the Law of Treaties 1969; Brownlie, I., *Principles of Public International Law,* fifth edition, Oxford University Press, Oxford, 1998, pp. 1–3, Mendelson, M., *The Formation of Customary International Law,* RdC, Vol. 272, 1998, p. 283; Higgins, R., *Problems and Process,* Clarendon, Oxford, 1994, p. 22.

2 Hart, H., *The Concept of Law,* Clarendon, Oxford, 1961, p. 209.

community. This approach was originally introduced by Alfred Verdross in 1926 when he wrote 'Die Verfassung der Völkerrechtgemeinschaft' and it has been repeated ever since and continues to be discussed by legal writers.[3]

Compared to the Covenant of the League of Nations the Charter makes more obvious reference toward constitutional intent for the Organisation and not merely a treaty.[4] This is so because the Charter establishes permanent organs and lays down procedures for their functioning. But what are the actual constitutional features of the UN Charter, and what are the normative implications of this constitutionality? Most legal writers believe that the UN Charter is a multilateral treaty and that one should look to the 1969 Vienna Convention on the Law of Treaties (VCLT) for guidance in its interpretation. Some also stress that it is also a constitution with constitutional provisions guiding the interpretation of the Charter.[5] In his inaugural speech at the 1945 San Francisco Conference, President Harry Truman made constitutional assimilations comparing the UN Charter to a constitution that grows and develops and expands as time goes on.[6] Since then the concept has regularly been echoed by legal writers. Thus, a strong perception has *ab inito* been that the Charter has been something else than an ordinary treaty.[7] This is particularly evident with respect to the Charter's supremacy clause (Article 103), which stipulates that the provisions of the Charter cannot be contracted out by a conflicting agreement.[8]

3 See for instance; Sloan, B., *The United Nations Charter as a Constitution,* Pace Yearbook of International Law, Vol. 1, 1989, pp. 61–126; Onuf, N., *The Constitution of International Society,* EJIL, Vol. 5, 1994, No. 1, pp. 1–19; Fassbender, B., *The United Nations Charter as Constitution of the International Community,* Columbia Journal of International Law, Vol. 36, 1988, pp. 531–616, and Crawford J., *International Law as an Open System,* Cameron May, London, 2002, pp. 123–135.

4 Sloan, *ibid.* pp. 61–62; Crawford, *ibid.* pp. 125–127.

5 Fassbender, *op. cit.* note 3, pp. 531–619.

6 Travaux préparatoires to the UN Charter, UNCIO doc, 1945 [hereinafter UNCIO], p. 610.

7 Vallat, F., *The General Assembly and the Security Council of the United Nations,* BYBIL, Vol. 29, 1952, p. 66.

8 Suy, E., *The Constitutional Character of Constituent Treaties of International Organisations and the Hierarchy of Norms,* Beyerlein, U., (Ed.) *Recht zwischen Umbruch und Bewahrung, Festschrift für Rudolf Bernhardt,* Springer, Berlin, 1995 p. 267; Suy, E., *The Constitutional Dimension of the Charter of the United Nations Revisited,* Max Planck Yearbook of United Nations Law, 1997, pp. 12; Reisman, M., *The Constitutional Crisis in the United Nations,* AJIL, Vol. 87, 1993, pp. 83–100.

However, a thorough assessment of the doctrinal views leads to the conclusion that the Charter should be perceived as a treaty with constitutional features, including the right of the Security Council under Chapter VII to take binding decisions for all states – implemented by secondary legislation.[9] The United Nations Charter is thus both a multilateral treaty and a constitution of an international organization, which gives the Charter a special legal position. Simply put, the Charter's binding force can be said to derive its validity from the notion of *pacta sunt servanda, i.e.* consent and secondary law found in domestic public law such as the constitutional and administrative law of the member states.

Consequently, the purpose of this article is to describe and discuss step-by-step the various features of the Charter by focusing on interpretation and its binding effect. It begins by discussing the allegorical description of the Charter as a living instrument, followed by the various real ways in which the Charter has been interpreted. In this context some interpretative innovations are described and analysed. These 'innovations' are characterized as textual interpretations and in many cases without any explicit textual support in the Charter. The role of custom within a treaty regime is also briefly discussed. Charter interpretation in general and the formal methods of interpretation in particular are discussed in accordance with the provisions set forth in the VCLT. The doctrine of implied powers and the effectiveness rule are discussed, followed by a discussion describing the binding mechanisms of the Charter and why Security Council decisions, particularly under Chapter VII, are binding on all states. Constitutional implications in theory – monism and dualism – and what they imply in reality are discussed in order to explain the municipal law requirements that are necessary in order to make these decisions effective.

9 Simma, B., (Ed.), *The Charter of The United Nations: A Commentary*, second edition, Vol. I, Oxford University Press, Oxford 2002, p. 15.

1.2 The Charter as a living instrument

As mentioned above, in his inaugural speech in San Francisco in 1945, President Truman made constitutional assimilations with the US Constitution when predicting the application of the UN Charter. The Charter was seen as a living instrument, and every application of the Charter, every use of an article would imply an interpretation, which would eventually start and lead to a new constitutional development.[10]

From its inception the Charter was seen as something more than an ordinary treaty. It was after all the most important post-war peace treaty with the overall objective 'to save succeeding generations from the scourge of war'. The treaty was therefore intended to last over time and expand as time went on. If we ignore the fact that the UN is facing currently one of its most severe crises ever, which has been caused by the split in the international community regarding the inspection and evidence of weapons of mass destruction in Iraq and the subsequent lack of Security Council authorization for the illegal allied invasion and current occupation of Iraq, the 1945 Presidential forecast – seeing the Charter as a 'living instrument' – has turned out to be quite accurate. This is particularly true since the Charter is an instrument reflecting the world in 1945, as it was after the Second World War. Since then the socio-economic structure of the international community has changed considerably. The end of the Cold War and the collapse of the USSR, with repercussions in the east, which redefined the map of Europe, and the enlargement of the European Union, are significant examples of the changes that characterizes this era. Nevertheless, the text of the Charter has basically remained unchanged. The low rate of amendments to the Charter can be explained by the fact that UN members do not wish to assemble a general conference for the purpose of reviewing the present Charter where the outcome may be unknown.[11]

10 Pollux, Edward, Hambro, *The Interpretation of the Charter of the United Nations,* UNCIO, 1945, p. 610; Fassbender, B., *The United Nations Charter as Constitution of the International Community,* Columbia Journal of International Law, Vol. 36, 1998, pp. 594–595.

11 Amendments have been made, see the introductory note of the Charter.

Disregarding the fact that the Charter has been a rather weak instrument with respect to dispute resolution and peace implementation – particularly during the Cold War – it has managed to by pass the deadlock created by the veto. The Charter has on several occasions been interpreted in an 'innovative' fashion, that is, the text of the Charter has remained unchanged but the interpretation of the text and the meaning of the words have been interpreted with sufficient flexibility to provide an operative instrument for maintaining peace and security.[12] 'If in fact, the Charter had remained static, as the virtual absence of formal amendments might suggest, the United Nations would by now have become an obsolete and totally ineffective institution utterly in the backwater of world events.'[13]

1.3 Charter 'innovations' – by means of interpretation

The Charter has on numerous occasions been interpreted in an 'innovative' fashion. These 'innovations' have been facilitated by the so called *compétence de la compétence* that has enabled the various organs of the organisation to interpret the parts of the Charter that are applicable to their particular functions. This, together with the fact that the Charter is also seen as a living instrument with constitutional features, partly as a dynamic treaty and partly also as an organisation holding implied powers, increases the flexibility of the interpretative radius of the Charter. Furthermore, the fact that there is no custodian of the Charter who is capable of making a binding decision where doubts arise as to whether or not a certain measure complies with its provisions, does that the interpretation of the Charter becomes even more flexible. Ultimately, it should be stressed that the member states of the UN are in disposition of the contents of the Charter and can consequently decide when a provision may be interpreted in an innovative fashion.

12 Sloan, *op. cit.* note 3, p. 119.
13 Zacklin, R., *The Amendment of the Constitutive Instruments of the United Nations and Specialized Agencies,* Sijthoff, Leyden, 1968, p. 180.

Thus, the examples referred to below are often classified as 'innovations', indicating that the interpretation of the text of the Charter has not been strictly textual but flexible, implying a change of the language and the meaning of the words.[14]

The first example is concerned with the interpretation of Article 27(3), which enabled the Security Council to adopt non-procedural resolutions despite the abstention of the permanent members. Briefly Article 27 provides that all members of the Security Council have one vote. On procedural matters, Article 27(2) requires that decisions shall be made by an affirmative vote of nine members. Article 27(3) provides that decisions on all other matters shall be made by an affirmative vote of nine, including the concurring votes of the permanent members. However, practice in the area shows that the interpretation of Article 27(3) has developed contrary – *contra legem* – to the literal interpretation of the wording. Abstention by one of the permanent members of the Council can be traced to 1946, which implies that abstention does not prevent the Council, despite the Article's language, to take affirmative action by an Article 27 vote.[15]

Likewise, *mutatis mutandis*, absence from Security Council voting sessions created a practice that was interpreted as tantamount to an

14 However, a distinction is made, between *interpretation* and *informal modification* of treaties. *Informal modification* implies that a treaty – or a provision in a treaty – is changed without following the prescribed general provisions found in the treaty regarding – formal – modification or amendment of treaties. In the case of the UN Charter, Articles 108–109 under Chapter XVIII refer to amendments. In the case of *informal modification,* a provision in a treaty is interpreted in such a way as to extend the interpretative radius of the provision (treaty). Such an interpretation is considered to be *contra legem* in relation to the provision being interpreted and can lead to a *de facto* modification if the requirements of 'consistent practice' and 'common consent' are met. Interpretations that remain within the interpretative radius of the provision (treaty) are considered as being *sub lege* interpretations and do not result in any informal modification (Article 31 VCLT – see below). The issue of informal modification is not discussed in of this article. The issue of informal modification is, however, discussed in Sevastik, P., *Informell modifikation av traktater till följd av ny sedvanerätt och praxis. En studie mot bakgrund av FN-stadgans innovativa utveckling,* Norstedts juridik, Stockholm 2002, pp. 380–391. See also Kontou, N., *The Termination and Revision of Treaties in the Light of New Customary International Law,* Oxford University Press, Oxford 1994; Karl, W., *Vertrag und Später Praxis im Völkerrecht,* Springer Verlag Berlin, 1983 and Zacklin, R., *op.cit* note 13.

15 Repertoire of Practice of the United Nations Organs, Vols. I–V, New York 1955 and Supplements No. 1–2, United Nations New York 1957, 1964; ICJ Pleadings, Legal Consequences of the Continued Presence of South Africa in Namibia (South West Africa) Notwithstanding Security Council Resolution 276, ICJ Reports 1971, p. 39.

abstention, implying that if a permanent member was not present at the moment of voting in the Council – whether deliberately or not – that absence should not prevent the Council from taking affirmative and binding decisions.[16] However, this practice has not developed to the same extent as abstention from voting.[17] In both cases the interpretation has been *contra legem* of the wording of Article 27(3), and has resulted in a *de facto* modification of the provision.[18] This *de facto* modification is considered to be as legally binding as a formally accepted amendment.

The third example, the development of the 'Uniting for Peace' Resolution, can also be described as an 'innovation' that has been created without any apparent textual support in the Charter. Due to the newly emerging practice regarding abstention from voting in the Security Council, the Council was able to act on Korea despite the fact that the Soviet Union boycotted the Council for a period of time. However, it was considered unlikely that the Soviet Union would repeat this practice in the future. After the outbreak of the war the Western states tried to safeguard themselves from prospective vetoes from the Soviet Union by strengthening the General Assembly. It was argued that when the Security Council's 'primary responsibility' (Article 24(2) of the UN Charter) was in jeopardy, the General Assembly would not be precluded from exercising a 'secondary' responsibility – although not referred to in any provision of the Charter – in order to maintain peace and security. This was an argument that was later approved by the International Court of Justice in the *Expenses* case.[19]

16 Bailey, S., and Daws, S., *The Procedure of the UN Security Council,* third edition, Clarendon, Oxford, 1998, p. 257.

17 *Ibid.* p. 257.

18 Zacklin, *op. cit.* note 13, p. 185 *et seq.*

19 ICJ Reports, 1962, p. 151 *et seq*; the following should also be mentioned regarding the Security Council's 'general powers' deriving from the inherent reference in Article 24(2) of the Charter to 'specific powers'. Implicitly the wording of "specific power" raises the question if alongside the reading of "specific powers" there may be some room for a so called *e contrario* interpretation of article 24(2) that would give the Security Council non-textual 'general provisions' – 'general powers' for the maintenance of peace and security. This is a view that has gained considerable support in the doctrine, and was first presented by the first Secretary-General of the United Nations, Mr. Trygve Lie. His view was afterwards reflected in the *Namibia Advisory Opinion*, ICJ Reports, 1971, p. 52. See also Akehurst, M., *A Modern Introduction to International Law,* fourth edition, Allen and Unwin, London, 1982, p. 186.

This extension of the powers of the General Assembly was due to 'Uniting for Peace' Resolution 377(V), adopted on 3 November 1950, which enabled the General Assembly to act without textual support from the Charter. The 'Uniting for Peace' Resolution explicitly signifies that when a veto blocks Security Council action to maintain peace and security under Chapter VII, the General Assembly can take the Security Council's place. The Resolution reasons: *'with a view to make appropriate recommendations to Members for collective measures, including in the case of breach of the peace or act of aggression the use of armed force when necessary, to maintain or restore international peace and security'*.

The 'Uniting for Peace' Resolution also establishes that 'emergency special meetings' shall be assembled either as a procedural decision by the Security Council or upon request by a majority of the members of the UN. Between 1956 and 2000, ten special 'extra sessions' were convened by the UN. The resulting resolutions were either approved by a majority or unanimously by the members of the Security Council. In each case the General Assembly assumed the Security Council's primary responsibilities.[20]

The fourth 'innovation' is the establishment of the War Crimes Tribunal for the former Yugoslavia. The innovation was due to the fact that for the first time the Security Council classified the humanitarian situation in the former Yugoslavia as so grave as to constitute a threat to international peace and security.[21] The Security Council based its action on Chapter VII even though Article 41 does not expressly give the Council the authority to assign criminal responsibility to individuals. However, there is room for such an interpretation within the interpretative frame of Article 24(1) of the Charter in order for the UN to 'ensure prompt and effective action' in support of the Council's primary responsibility for the maintenance of international peace and security.[22]

20 Department of Public Information, www.un.org/ga/documents/liemsps.htm, (10 January 2002).

21 SC Res. 827 (1993) and SC Res. 995 (1994).

22 See Sevastik, P., *op. cit.* note 14, pp. 318–322: Sarooshi, D., *The United Nations and the Development of Collective Security,* Oxford, 1999, pp. 97–98: Österdahl, I., *Threat to the Peace,* Iustus, Uppsala, 1998, pp. 50–51.

Before the horrifying terrorist attacks on the World Trade Center in New York and in Washington D.C. on 11 September 2001, self-defence in accordance with Article 51 of the UN Charter was not a permitted action against international terrorism. Previously, international terrorism was to be combatted through legal measures provided for in international terrorist conventions. Article 51 of the UN Charter provides the right for states to act in self-defence against an armed attack against a member of the United Nations. 'Armed attack' has been interpreted to mean an armed attack from another state and not from a terrorist organization. Furthermore the act of self-defence could only be executed against another state if the threat was overwhelming and if the state was under current attack from another state.

The two unanimous Resolutions – 1368 of 12 September 2001 and 1373 of 28 September 2001 – that were passed after the terrorist attacks against the US extended the interpretation of the term 'armed attack' found in Article 51 of the Charter. The Security Council compared terrorist attacks against states with the wording of Article 2(4), which makes reference to armed attacks between states. This new interpretation was due to the fact that the Security Council unanimously adopted two Resolutions that provided new measures to combat terrorism and placed heinous terrorist attacks on an equal footing with an armed attack against another state. As a consequence of this interpretation the Resolutions made reference to the inherent right of individual or collective self-defence, 'an inherent right' in accordance with the provisions set forth in Article 51 of the UN Charter.

In this fifth example, the term 'innovation' is most accurately used and may also have further implications for the interpretation of the term 'self-defence' in Article 51.[23] As a consequence of these new developments there may also be a development toward an Article 51½-motion – although it may still be too early to say.[24]

23 Hannikainen, L., *The World after 11 September 2001: Is the Prohibition of the Use of Force Disintegrating?* Petman, Y., & Klabbers, J., (Eds.), Nordic Cosmopolitanism: Essays in International Law for Martti Koskenniemi, Martinus Nijhoff Publishers, Leiden, Boston, 2003, pp. 445–466.

24 *Cf.* Bring, O., *FN-stadgan och världspolitiken,* fourth edition, Norstedts juridik, Stockholm, 2002, pp. 315–324; Gray, C., *The Use of Force and The International Legal Order,* International Law, Evans, M. (Ed.), Oxford University Press, Oxford, 2003, p. 604.

The Allied war in Kuwait also gave rise to a so called 'innovation' – the sixth – in that some of the provisions in the Charter were bypassed so as not to prevent the UN from acting to promote peace. The use of force is strictly formalized in the Charter. The Preamble of the Charter states 'that armed force shall not be used, save in the common interest' of the United Nations. These common interests were considered to have been jeopardized by the Iraqi invasion of Kuwait in 1990. This gave rise to an authorized UN military action – the US-led alliance against Iraq. The provisions in the Charter that regulate the use of force are contained in Chapter VII, Articles 39 and 42–48. Security Council Resolutions 665 (25 August 1990) and 678 (29 November 1990) did not, however, follow the procedures set out in these provisions. Armed forces were not made available to the UN in accordance with special agreements signed between the member states and the UN specifying the number and types of forces, their degree of readiness and general location, and the nature of the facilities and assistance to be provided (Article 43). Nor was the Military Staff Committee, provided for in Article 47, established to advise and assist the Security Council on all questions relating to the Council's military requirements for the maintenance of international peace and security.[25] The technical term to explain this phenomenon is *desuetude*, which does not necessarily lead to informal modification.[26]

The seventh example that was also seen as a 'distinctive innovation' is 'peacekeeping'.[27] The Charter does not make any reference to peacekeeping. The concept was developed as a complementary tool to patch up the deficiency created by vetoes, which hampered UN actions to maintain peace and security. 'Peacekeeping' was developed, in particular, during the cold war as a result of the deadlock in the Security Council among the permanent members. The

25 See Sevastik, *op. cit.* note 14, pp. 330–334.

26 *Ibid.* pp. 385–386.

27 Kirgis, F., *The Security Council's First Fifty Years,* AJIL, Vol. 89, 1995, p. 532, referring to Urquhart, B., *The United Nations, Collective Security, and International Peacekeeping,* Negotiating World Order: the Artisanship and Architecture of Global Diplomacy, Henrikson, Alan K. (Ed.), Scholarly Resources, Wilmington, Del., 1986, pp. 59, 62.

inability to maintain international peace and security by means of consensus within the Security Council or by majority decisions within the framework of the General Assembly further developed the mechanisms for conflict prevention outside the interpretative radius of Article 34 of the Charter.[28]

1.4 Customary implications?

Goodrich and Hambro wrote in 1949 that much of the practice deriving from the interpretation of the UN organs would eventually lead to the formation of customary international law.[29] Likewise, Baily and Daws stated that 'much of the practice of the Security Council is based on custom, some of it so deeply rooted and generally respected as to virtually have the force of law'.[30] However, in the examples discussed above the characteristic criteria of customary law – 'general practice accepted as law' – are difficult to distinguish. In the practice that develops within a treaty regime – such as the UN Charter – there is no room for 'persistent objectors' who can object to an emerging rule. The practice that evolves within a regime resembles the customary process, but is distinct from it and might be better described as the impact of '*coutume constitutionelle*', *i.e.* constitutional customary law.[31] The elements used to describe this process are *consistent practice* and the *common consent* of the parties.[32] This practice is contractual and is established by tacit agreement.[33]

This is also probably the case with the last example, which will not be discussed in detail within the confines of this paper. The issue concerns NATO's intervention in Kosovo 1999, which is not

28 See Sevastik, *op. cit.* note 14, pp. 335–338.

29 Goodrich, L., and Hambro, E., *Charter of the United Nations,* Boston, 1949, pp. 547–548.

30 Baily, S., and Daws, S., *op. cit.* note 16, p. 17.

31 Müller, J., *Vertrauensschutz im Völkerrecht*, Heymanns, Köln, 1971, p. 87.

32 This terminology derives from the discussion the ILC had concerning draft article 38, Modification of treaties by subsequent practice regarding the 1969 VCLT, YearBook of the International Law Commission, 1966-II, p. 23.

33 See Kontou, *op. cit.* note 14, p. 125. This is more evident in the case of informal modification of treaties.

considered an 'innovation' *per se* but concerns the issue whether subsequent customary international law was in the process of developing, and permitting unauthorised humanitarian intervention contrary to the provision of Charter Articles 53 and 2(4).[34]

1.5 Charter interpretation – general remarks

The United Nations Conference in San Francisco raised the question of Charter interpretation and discussed it at length without really coming to grips with it. The issue was what would happen if a conflict arose between different UN organs and how such a conflict would be tackled? Belgium, as the initiative-taking state for this discussion, proposed that a provision should be incorporated into the Charter that would give either the International Court of Justice, the General Assembly, a specifically established expert committee, or a commonly established conference interpretative priority.[35] However, this proposal did not win the support of the other member states.

The interpretation of the Charter was further discussed at the San Francisco Conference in the Committee's final report. The question at stake was: how and by what organ or organs of the Organisation should the Charter be interpreted? The discussion resulted in the following conclusion:

> In the course of the operation from day to day of the various organs of the Organization, it is inevitable that each organ will interpret such parts of the Charter as are applicable to its particular functions. This process is inherent in the functioning of any body which operates under an instrument defining its functions and powers. It will be manifested in the functioning of such a body as the General Assembly, the Security Council, or the International Court of Justice. Accordingly, it is not necessary to include in the Charter a provision either authorizing or approving the normal operation of this principle.
>
> Difficulties may conceivably arise in the event that there should be a difference of opinion among the organs of the Organisation concerning the correct interpretation of a provision of the Charter. ... If two Member States are at variance concerning the correct interpretation of the Charter, they are of course free to submit the dispute to the

34 For a more detailed discussion, see Sevastik, *op. cit.* note 14, pp. 339–355.
35 Doc. 664, IV/2/33, 13 UNCIO Docs, pp. 633–638.

> International Court of Justice as in the case of any other treaty. Similarly, it would always be open to the General Assembly or the Security Council, in appropriate circumstances, to ask the International Court of Justice for an advisory opinion concerning the meaning of a provision of the Charter. Should the General Assembly or the Security Council prefer another course, an *ad hoc* committee of jurists might be set up to examine the question and report its views, or recourse might be had to a joint conference. In brief, the Members or the organs of the Organisation might have resource to various expedients in order to obtain an appropriate interpretation. It would appear neither necessary nor desirable to list or to describe in the Charter the various possible expedients.[36]

Practice in this area shows that the UN organs have the competence to interpret their own provisions specifying their competence. This possibility of interpreting their competence derives its validity from the general principle of law *i.e., compétence de la compétence,* which originates from French and German constitutional law.[37] The Security Council, with support from the San Francisco Conference and also from the Advisory Opinion on the Interpretation of the Greco-Turkish Agreement from 1926, has been deemed to have this competence to interpret its own competence in accordance with the Charter. The Permanent Court of International Justice clarified this as follows: 'the principle that, as a general rule, any body possessing jurisdictional power has the right in the first place itself to determine the extent of its jurisdiction ...'.[38]

As a consequence, today, there is no official body that can authorize a binding interpretation – a third party determination. As in so many other international treaties, the Charter does not have any arbitration clause to settle disputes on issues regarding interpretation. The fact that there is no 'custodian of the Charter' capable of making authoritative decisions in cases where doubts arise as to whether or not certain measures comply with its provisions creates further flexibility in the interpretation of the Charter.[39]

36 UNCIO, Report of the Rapporteur of Committee IV/2, Doc. 933, IV/242 (2), pp. 7–8.

37 Degan, V. *General Principles of Law – A Source of General International Law,* FYBIL, 1992, Vol. III, p. 43.

38 PCIJ Series A, No. 9, 1926, p. 31.

39 Schröder, M., *Amendments to and Review of the UN Charter,* Documents of Reform of the United Nations, Taylor *et al.* (Eds.), Aldershot Dartmouth 1997, p. 491.

1.6 Charter interpretation and the VCLT

There are many factors that make the interpretation of the Charter difficult.[40] First of all there are no provisions in the Charter concerning interpretation. Secondly, the Charter is an essentially political multilateral treaty with deficiencies in its drafting – a characteristic which is not unique for the Charter but also found in numerous international treaties. In the Charter's case, this is because politicians were employed to draft the Charter rather than lawyers. Thirdly, the Charter is signed in five authentic versions. Finally, Charter interpretation is crucial since the majority of the member states joined the United Nations after 1945 and were not able to participate at the San Francisco Conference. This is particularly true since the text has remained largely unchanged and the political, social end economic context of the world community has changed considerably after 1945, which has affected the meaning of the words in the text. These factors together make the Charter a difficult instrument to interpret and give rise to constant discussions on this topic.

There are other difficult legal issues linked to interpretation. Closely related to the issue discussed above is the question of new interpretations of the provisions of the Charter that may imply obligations, which are different from those originally undertaken. In this regard new obligations can occur 'under the present Charter' and it is here that Article 103 becomes applicable. Article 103 stipulates that if the members of the UN are in conflict between their obligations under the Charter and their obligations under any other international agreement, their obligations under the Charter shall prevail. Article 103 is therefore, as previously mentioned, referred to as the 'supremacy clause' and is essential if the Charter is to be perceived as the 'constitution' of the international community.[41] This is particularly apparent since Article 103 only becomes effective when a state's obligations under other treaties conflict with obligations under the UN Charter.[42] In the examples discussed above there was apparently no conflict between obligations.

40 Goodrich, and Hambro, *op. cit.* note 29, pp. 547–548.

41 Suy, *op. cit.* note 8, p. 267.

42 See Cameron, I., *Targeted Sanctions and Legal Safeguards*, www.jur.uu.se/sii/articles; for the initial discussions regarding Article 103 see Goodrich, and Hambro, *op. cit.* note 29, pp. 517–519.

In any event, since the Charter is a multilateral treaty – concluded between some 200 member states at present – the logical point of departure for treaty interpretation is to be found in the 1969 Vienna Convention on the Law of Treaties (VCLT). Article 5 of the VCLT applies to any treaty that is the constituent instrument of an international organization. Despite the fact that the VCLT only applies to treaties which are concluded by states after the entry into force of the Convention in 1980 (Article 4 VCLT),[43] Articles 31–33 of the Convention are considered to be part of customary international law and can therefore be applied by analogy to the interpretation of the Charter by each of the UN organs. This was also pointed out regarding the provisions of the Convention in general by the ICJ when it held that the provisions 'in many respects may be considered as a codification of existing customary international law'.[44] The main categories of treaty interpretation can generally be classified as *textual or grammatical, subjective* and *teleological.*[45]

Article 31(1) of the VCLT provides that a treaty shall be interpreted in good faith in accordance with the ordinary meaning to be given to the terms of the treaty in their contexts and in the light of its object and purpose. Article 31 is entitled 'General rule of interpretation' and its singular spelling indicates that the Article contains only one rule and that the interpretative process is one unit and that the text as a whole should be treated as an integral part. The application of the provision is also general in that it does not distinguish between different types of treaties. However, such a distinction is necessary, particularly where the interpretation of the UN Charter as the founding treaty of the international organisation is concerned. However, as already mentioned – and further discussed below – some distinctive constitutional features have to be considered when interpreting the Charter.

Paragraph (2) defines the meaning of 'context', referring in subparagraph (a) to any agreement and in (b) to any instrument related to the treaty and drawn up in connection with its conclusion.

43 Vierdag, E., *The Law Governing Treaty Relations Between Parties to the Vienna Convention of the Law of Treaties and States not Party to the Convention,* AJIL, Vol. 76, 1982, pp. 780–786; Sinclair, I., *The Vienna Convention on the Law of Treaties,* Manchester University Press, Manchester, 1973, pp. 69–76.

44 Namibia case, ICJ Reports (1971), p. 47.

45 Sinclair, I., *supra.* note 43 pp. 1–27.

While this does not necessarily mean that the documents such as those referred to in (a) and (b) are part of the treaty, they should be regarded not merely as a legal basis for the purposes of interpretation, but also as part of the context in which the ordinary meaning of terms is established.[46]

Paragraph (3) makes reference to other elements to be taken into account, together with the content, for the purpose of interpretation: (a) any subsequent agreement between the parties regarding the interpretation of the treaty or the application of its provisions; (b) any subsequent practice in the application of the treaty which establishes the agreement of the parties regarding its interpretation should be included as an 'authentic means of interpretation'; (c), any relevant rules of international law applicable in the relations between the parties.

In paragraph (4) reference is made to the special meaning that is given to a term if it is established that the parties so intended.

According to Article 32, the preparatory work – *travaux préparatoires* – is not a primary means of interpretation but an important supplementary means. This helps the interpreter of the treaty to come to an understanding of what the negotiators had in mind when they negotiated the treaty.

However, *travaux préparatoires* are not as commonly used for the interpretation of constitutional treaties. Constitutional treaties are intended to have a longer lifetime than ordinary treaties. In the case of the UN Charter the *travaux* were discussed in the 1940s and may in parts be out of place in a 21st century context. In the case of the Charter the *travaux* were prepared at Dumbarton Oaks in 1944 and complemented during the Yalta Conference the same year. The Dumbarton Oaks proposal was then discussed at the United Nations Constitutive Conference in San Francisco in 1945.

At the Vienna Conference, the draft articles formed the basis of the conference, which in two sessions – 1968 and 1969 – completed the work of the Vienna Convention on the Law of Treaties. At the Conference the US representative, Myres McDougal, made it clear that the treaty text and 'the common public meaning of words'

46 Aust, A., *Modern Treaty Law and Practice,* Cambridge University Press, Cambridge, 2000, p. 190; Brownlie, I., *Principles of Public International Law,* fifth edition, University Press, Oxford, 1998, pp. 634–635.

ought to be the point of departure for the interpretation of a treaty, but not 'the end of the inquiry'. The text should be treated as an important but not conclusive criterion in order to determine the common intention of the parties. All circumstances that were relevant in a specific case ought to be used. The common meaning of the words, subsequent practice, the *travaux préparatoires* and other elements that might be relevant to the interpretation should be taken into consideration.[47]

1.7 The doctrine of implied powers and the effectiveness rule

The wording of Article 31(1) VCLT, 'in the light of its object and purpose', can be said to open the door to the teleological interpretation from which the doctrine of *implied powers* derives its origin. According to this doctrine, the organisation is not limited to such acts or rights as are specified in the Charter.[48] In other words *implied powers*, 'while not textually provided for by the creators of the organisation, have been recognized or accepted by the member states within a certain period of life of the organisation as auxiliary or subordinate means to accomplish the permanent ends for which the organisation was founded'.[49] The doctrine of *implied powers* does not, however, answer the question of what organ should exercise the powers, but is concerned with the powers of the organisation as a whole.

Thus, in the *Reparation for Injuries* case the ICJ observed in its Advisory Opinion that 'the rights and duties of an entity such as the Organisation must depend upon its purpose and functions as specified or implied in its constituent documents and developed

47 The Vienna Conference 1968 and 1969, on the Vienna Convention on the Law of Treaties, *The Final Report of the Swedish Delegation,* Stockholm, 1970, p. 127.

48 Seyersted, F., *International Personality of International Organizations*, Indian Journal of International Law, Vol. 4, 1964, New Delhi, p. 19; Vallat, *The Competence of the United Nations General Assembly,* RdC, Vol. 97, 1959-II, pp. 281–285; Brownlie, *op. cit.* note 1, pp. 687–689.

49 Chaumont, C., *La signification du principe de specialité des organisations internationales,* Mélanges offerts à Henri Rolin; Problèmes de droit des gens, Paris, 1964, p. 59.

practice'.[50] Likewise, in its Advisory opinion on *Effects of Awards of Compensation made by the United Nations Administrative Tribunal*, the Court made clear that the Charter contains 'no provisions for the establishment of judicial bodies or organs and no indication to the contrary'. The Court held furthermore that the capacity to establish a tribunal to do justice as between the United Nations and the staff members 'arise[s] by necessary intendment out of the Charter'.[51]

In reality the reference to *implied powers* is inherently linked to the principle of effectiveness. In the *Reparation for Injuries* case the Court therefore held that: 'Under international law, the Organisation must be deemed to have those powers which, though not expressly provided in the Charter, are conferred upon it by necessary implication as being essential to the performance of its duties'.[52] The doctrine of implied powers should not, however, be regarded as a universally applied method to resolve all problems related to interpretation in international organisations.

1.8 Binding decisions under Chapter VII

In the initial discussions regarding the establishment of a comprehensive world organisation for the maintenance of international peace and security there was *ab inito* a belief that certain decisions of the organisation relating to the maintanence of peace would have to be binding upon all member states. Although the granting of binding decision-making powers would constitute a grave intrusion upon the sovereignty of the member states – Article 2(7) of the UN Charter – it was nevertheless held to be indispensable in order to maintain international peace. However, this provision was accepted on the understanding that the permanent members of the Security Council would be accorded a veto power when binding decisions were to be taken since it was believed that the implementation of peace actions was impossible without the will of these powers. At the same time, it was recognized that binding decisions endorsed by all the permanent members of the Security Council would have special significance and bind all member states. This implies that the

50 ICJ Reports, 1949, p. 180.
51 *Ibid*, p. 184.
52 *Ibid*, p. 182.

binding force of the Charter involved a limitation of sovereignty for all members of the Security Council except the permanent five. Brierly writes that the powers conferred on the Council by Article 25 are 'greater than have ever before been exercised by any international body' and 'constituted the most far reaching of the innovations which the Charter has introduced into international organization'.[53]

The powers mentioned above are encapsulated in Article 25 of the UN Charter, which prescribes a binding decision-making power in relation to all the member states of the UN. Article 25 should be read in close conjunction with Article 2(5), which obligates all members of the UN to give every assistance in any action taken in accordance with the Charter. Thus, under Article 25 '[t]he Members of the United Nations agree to accept and carry out the decisions of the Security Council in accordance with the present Charter'. At first sight the text of the Article may appear to be unambiguous. However, the notion of 'decision' is not unambiguous at all and all legal commentators have delved into the meaning of the word.[54] Under the confines of the present Articles, however, only decisions under Chapter VII of the Charter – Action with Respect to Threats to the Peace, Breaches of the Peace, and Acts of Aggression – are addressed and in this respect considered to be binding upon all member states.

1.9 Constitutional implications – in theory

The issue regarding the relationship between international law and municipal law gives rise to many practical questions, particularly if there is a conflict between the two. This is also the case regarding the implementation of the Charter.

The organizational structure of the Charter – as both a multilateral treaty and at the same time the constitution (and cornerstone) of the international community – gives the Charter a special position. It is a dichotomy, with both normative and contractual elements. The

53 Brierly, I., *The Law of Nations,* third edition, Oxford University Press, Oxford, 1942, p. 111.

54 Goodrich, and Hambro, *op. cit.* note 29, p. 208; Kelsen, H., *The Law of the United Nations; A Critical Analysis of its Fundamental Problems,* published under the auspices of the London World Affairs, Stevens & Sons, London, 1950, pp. 95–98.

confines concerning conclusion, entry into force, termination, amendments, etc. can be found in the interpretation of the VCLT. Among these rules there is also a fundamental principle that is laid down in the law of treaties: *pacta sunt servanda*, as set out in Article 26. This Article states that all treaties in force are binding upon the parties and must be performed in good faith. Article 27 stipulates that a party may not invoke the provisions of its internal law as justification for its failure to perform a treaty. This means that a state cannot use its constitutional or administrative law as an excuse not to implement a treaty. There are no valid reasons or explanations that a state can use as an excuse in this regard. In principle, the rules of interpretation laid down in the VCLT also apply to the law of international organisations because of the equal standing of the parties.

Some treaties, such as treaties of alliance (*e.g.* NATO) or the Vienna Convention itself, which is considered to be a 'lawmaking' treaty, do not in theory need to have any special effect in domestic law. However, most treaties need to be given some effect in domestic law. This is because some of the treaties may impose an obligation on a state to enact a particular rule as part of its own municipal law. How rules are enacted is of no concern in the context of international law so long as the obligations under the treaty are respected by the member state. How states conduct themselves vis-à-vis international law depends solely on the constitutional setting of each state.

Likewise, the normative aspects of the Charter and the law deriving from it – secondary law – are implemented by the constitutional and administrative law from the respective member state.

With some 200 states in the international community of today there are varieties of constitutional models but only two general schools of thought – with a number of variations – that tackle the issue of international and municipal implementation. The terms used to explain the interrelationship between these doctrinal views are '*monism*' and '*dualism*', and this interrelationship is a topic frequently discussed by legal scholars. In theory these doctrines may be seen as two diverging or opposing models, but in fact the end result is pretty much the same since international law needs to be incorporated into national law.[55]

Briefly, the *monistic* school of thought – derived from natural law theories – assumes that international law and municipal law are unitary legal systems forming part of one and the same legal order. Kelsen, one of the modern advocates of this view, believed that all law derived its validity from one basic source – 'grundnorm' – of customary international law.[56] International law was therefore considered to take precedence over municipal law and could therefore also be directly applicable at the national level. The monist approach implies in essence that a treaty, without internal legislation, can become part of domestic law as soon as it has been concluded and has entered into force – been ratified – for that state.[57]

The decline of natural law thinking and the rise of positivism led, however, to the development of *dualism*. For the dualistic school of thought international law and municipal law are regarded as two separate legal systems, which exist independently of each other. According to this conception, international law can only play a role in the domestic legal order in so far as domestic law adopts an international rule. In essence, international law has to be 'incorporated', *i.e.*, transposed into national law.[58] Technically there are a few options open to states when it comes to incorporating an international treaty into national law (see the discussion below).

1.10 Constitutional implications – in practice

The vast majority of states today are scattered along the borderline between the doctrinal views described above. Among countries, the *United Kingdom* is considered to represent the most highly developed form of dualism while *Switzerland* represents the purest monistic model.

55 Aust, p. 145; Cassese, A. *International Law,* Oxford University Press, Oxford 2001, p. 8.
56 Kelsen, H., *General Theory of Law and State,* (transl. by Anders Wedberg), Harvard University Press, Mass. Cambridge, 1945, pp. 115–116.
57 See Brownlie, *op. cit.* note 1, pp. 31–33.
58 Triepel, H., *Les rapports entre le droit interne et le droit international,* RdC, Vol. 1, 1923, p. 95.

The *US Constitution* reflects both dualist and monistic approaches.[59] In accordance with Article VI(2) of the US Constitution, '[*t*]*reaties made, or which shall be made, under the Authority of the United States, shall be the supreme law of the Land*'. In the case of 'self-executing' treaties, which are not explicitly referred to in the US Constitution since it is a judge-made doctrine, the US Court may decide whether they can be applied directly without the need to implement the legislation by Congress. It is up to the Court to decide whether or not a treaty is self-executing and inherent to the intent of the government. The Court also decides when the treaty is invoked as law.[60] This doctrine differentiates between treaties that could be directly applicable by the courts as 'the law of the land' and treaties that require legislative implementation in order to take effect under municipal law. However, in practice 'self-executing' treaties are undermined since most treaties are executive agreements, made by the President pursuant to statutes requiring an affirmative vote of two-thirds of the legislators present, in both the House and the Senate.[61] Treaties prevail over state law but do not necessarily prevail over conflicting federal statutory law.[62]

Generally speaking, most common law countries other than the US do not permit treaties to be incorporated as municipal law without legislative enactment. The constitutional features of some other countries are briefly discussed in this context. The UK, for example, does not have a written constitution. The regulatory provisions are found in separate Acts of Parliament and in unwritten law, *i.e.*, practice.[63] The power to make treaties is a 'prerogative' power vested in the Crown and exercised by the Secretary of State for Foreign and Commonwealth Affairs. There is no constitutional requirement for

59 Damrosch, Lori Fisler, *The Role of the United States Senate Concerning "Self-Executing" and "Non-Self-Executing" Treaties*, Riesenfeldt, S. and Abbott, F. (Eds.), Parliamentary Participation in the Making and Operation of Treaties: A Comparative Study, Martinus Nijhoff, Dordrecht, 1994, pp. 205–328.

60 Foster & Elam v. Neilson, 27 US (2 Pet.) 253 (1828); Henkin, L., *et al., International Law: Cases and Materials*, third edition, West Publishing Co., St. Paul, Minn., 1993, pp. 212–213.

61 Henkin, L., *et al., Ibid.* pp. 212–213.

62 *Ibid.*

63 *See* www.oefr.unibe.ch/law/icl/uk_indx.html.

Parliament to consent to the Crown's entering into a treaty, and there is a constitutional practice – the Ponsonby Rule of 1924 – requiring that every treaty signed by the Crown subject to ratification should be laid before Parliament for 21 sitting days.[64]

Generally speaking, once again, it can be said that most civil law countries accept the concept of self-executing treaties. For instance, the French Constitution indicates that duly ratified or approved treaties or agreements shall, upon their publication, override laws, subject, for each agreement or treaty, to its application by the party (Article 55 – force of law, principle of reciprocity).[65]

Under the Swiss Constitution, treaty-making power is vested in the Federal Government. It shall sign and ratify treaties and submit them to the Federal Parliament for approval. Article 5, paragraph 4 of the Swiss Federal Constitution requires the Confederation and the cantons to respect international law. There is, however, no constitutional guidance in the event of conflict between international and national legislation. In such cases international law would prevail over national law. 'This follows from the international obligation to apply treaties in good faith – an obligation which, in accordance with the monist tradition of Switzerland has the force of national law.'[66]

In Germany the Constitution – Basic Law, *Grundgesetz*, stipulates in Article 25 that general rules of public international law constitute an integral part of federal law and that they take precedence over statutes and create rights and duties for the inhabitants of the federal territory.[67]

Article 90(1) of the Netherlands Constitution provides that the Kingdom shall not be bound by treaties, nor shall treaties be denounced without the prior approval of the Parliament. An Act of Parliament, Article 90(2), indicates which treaties have to be sub-

64 *See* the Ponsonby Rule, files.fco.gov.uk/treaty/ponsonby.pdf.

65 *See* www.oefre.unibe.ch/law/icl/nl00000_index.html.

66 See Relations Between International and Domestic Law, www.uno.admin.ch/sub_dipl/e/home/Thema/intlaw/relat.html.

67 Tschentscher, A., *The Basic Law (Grundgesetz), The Constitution of the Federal Republic of Germany* (May 23rd), Jurisprudentia Verlag, Wurzberg, 1949.

mitted to the Parliament for approval, given the possibility of tacit approval. According to Article 90(3) provisions of a treaty that conflict with the Constitution, or which lead to conflicts with it, may be approved by the Chambers of the Parliament only if two-thirds of the votes cast are in favour.[68]

Sweden has since early times had a monistic approach.[69] Foreign relations policy was initially within the domain of the monarchy's responsibilities. Section 12 of the 1809 Instrument of Government (IG) gave the monarch exclusive treaty making power. The 1809 Instrument of Government that lasted for 165 years was superseded by the present Instrument of Government 1974. During those 165 years Sweden underwent great constitutional renovation and political changes as parliamentary government gained ground. Shortly after the First World War, a Foreign Affairs Advisory Council was set up and all treaties with foreign states – and other treaties of significance – had to be submitted to the Riksdag (IG 10:1–4). Thus the monistic approach declined during this period and Sweden moved towards the dualistic school of thought. Today international agreements are limited in validity and are not binding on Swedish citizens until they have been incorporated into Swedish Law. This can be done in various ways, for example, by rewriting the agreement as a Swedish statute, promulgating the text in a Swedish translation or, more rarely, retaining the original text of the treaty as a Swedish statue.[70]

Furthermore, the Certain International Sanctions (Act 1996:95) (Lag [1996:95] *om vissa internationella sanktioner*) contains provisions regarding the implementation of international sanctions adopted or recommended by the Security Council of the United Nations under Chapter VII. The law is only activated if an international incident occurs that results in affirmative action taken by the Security Council.

68 www.oefre.unibe.ch/law/icl/nl00000_index.html.

69 Sweden has four fundamental laws: The Instrument of Government, the Act of Succession, the Freedom of the Press Act and, since 1992, the Fundamental Law of Freedom of Expression. The Riksdag Act has a position in-between fundamental law and ordinary law.

70 See, The Constitution of Sweden: The Fundamental Laws and the Riksdag, Stockholm, 2000, pp. 11–14, and pp. 37–39.

According to Article 3, the Government may impose sanctions in accordance with a decision or recommendation of the Council, but such a measure must be submitted to the Riksdag for approval.[71]

1.11 Concluding remarks

As is often the case in international law there are no simple answers, and in most cases the questions are quite complex. This is particularly true when it comes to the subject of interpretation and the determination of the binding force of the UN Charter. The various methods regarding interpretation discussed above are only presumptions, which often conflict with one another and cannot be applied with scientific exactness. The constitutional dimension of the Charter complicates the analysis still further. Political factors play a decisive role in all issues of interpretation in international law, and to disregard them is wishful thinking. Nevertheless, the Charter has on some occasions been interpreted in an innovative fashion. These innovations should be welcomed and perceived as organic developments of the Charter. This trend is not declining, on the contrary, there is still scope for new adaptations of the UN Charter that reflect changing circumstances in the world community, and new developments are likely to give rise to more 'innovations' in the future.

The UN Charter, which may be regarded as the Constitution of the world community, was from the outset constrained by consent and sovereignty. From its inception, however, the granting of binding powers to the UN was held to be indispensable in order to maintain peace. Peace was safeguarded by giving the Security Council binding powers on the condition that the permanent members would have a veto option when binding decisions under Chapter VII were being considered. The Charter contains both contractual and normative elements. The contractual obligations to be met

71 For a presentation on how the law has been used in Swedish practice, see Bring, O. and Mahmoudi, S., *Sverige och folkrätten,* Norstedts, Stockholm 2001, pp. 87–89; Lysén, G., *Folkrättsligt ansvar,* Iustus, Uppsala, 2002, pp. 359–413; Lagen om vissa internationella sanktioner – en översyn. Betänkande av Sanktionslagsutredningen, SOU 1995:28; Internationella överenskommelser och svensk rätt, SOU 1974:100; Folkrätt och straffansvar, DsJu 1984:6.

under the Charter can be found in the Charter itself and the VCLT. The normative obligations deriving from the Charter – secondary law – can only be found in the constitutional provisions of each member state. Thus, how countries address international law is of no concern to international law as long as they comply with it.

References

Books & articles

Akehurst, M., *A Modern Introduction to International Law,* fourth edition, Allen and Unwin, London, 1982.

Aust, A., *Modern Treaty Law and Practice,* Cambridge University Press, Cambridge, 2000.

Bailey, S. and Daws, S., *The Procedure of the Security Council,* third edition, Clarendon, Oxford, 1998.

Brierly, I., *The Law of Nations,* third edition, Oxford University Press, Oxford, 1942.

Bring, O., *FN-stadgan och världspolitiken,* fourth edition, Norstedts juridik, Stockholm, 2002.

Bring, O. and Mahmoudi, S., *Sverige och folkrätten,* Norstedts juridik, Stockholm, 2001.

Brownlie, I., *Principles of Public International Law,* fifth edition, Oxford University Press, Oxford, 1998.

Cassese, A., *International Law,* Oxford University Press, Oxford, 2001.

Chaumont, C., *La signification du principe de specialité des organisations internationales,* Mélanges offerts à Henri Rolin; Problèmes de droit des gens, Paris, 1964.

Crawford, J., *International Law as an Open System,* Cameron May, London, 2002.

Damrosch, L., *The Role of the United States Senate Concerning "Self-Executing" and "Non-Self-Executing" Treaties,* Riesenfeldt, S. and Abbott, F. (Eds.), Parliamentary Participation in the Making and Operation of Treaties: A Comparative Study, Martinus Nijhoff, Dordrecht, 1994.

Degan, V., *General Principles of Law – A Source of General international Law,* Finnish Yearbook of International Law, 1992.

Fassbender, B., *The United Nations Charter as a Constitution of the International Community,* Columbia Journal of International Law, Vol. 36, 1988, pp. 531–616.

Goodrich, L. and Hambro, E., *Charter of the United Nations,* Boston, 1949.

Hannikainen, L., *The World after 11 September 2001: Is the Prohibition of the Use of Force Disintegrating,* Petman, Y. & Klabbers, J. (Eds.), Nordic Cosmopolitanism: Essays in International Law for Martti Koskenniemi, Martinus Nijhoff Publishers, Leiden, Boston, 2003.

Hart, H., *The Concept of Law,* Clarendon, Oxford, 1961.

Henkin, L. et al., *International Law: Cases and Materials,* third edition, West Publishing Co., St. Paul, Minn., 1993.

Higgins, R., *Problems and Process,* Clarendon, Oxford, 1994.

Karl, W., *Vertrag und Später Praxis im Völkerrecht,* Springer verlag, Berlin, 1983.

Kelsen, H., *The Law of the United Nations; A Critical Analysis of its Fundamental Problems,* Stevens & Sons, London, 1950.

Kelsen, Hans, *General Theory of Law and State,* Harvard University Press, Mass. Cambridge, 1945.

Kirgis, F., *The Security Council's First Fifty Years,* American Journal of International Law, Vol. 89, 1995.

Kontou, N., *The Termination and Revision of Treaties in the Light of New Customary International Law,* Oxford University Press, Oxford, 1994.

Lysén, G., *Folkrättsligt ansvar,* Iustus, Uppsala, 2002.

Mendelson, M., *The Formation of Customary International Law,* Recueil des Cours, Vol. 272, 1998, pp. 155–410.

Müller, J., *Vertrauensschutz im Völkerrecht,* Heymanns, Köln, 1971.

Onuf, N., *The Constitution of International Society,* EJIL, Vol. 5, No. 1, 1994.

Pollux, Edwards, Hambro, *The Interpretation of the Charter of the United Nations,* British Yearbook of International Law, Vol. 23, 1946, pp. 54–82.

Reisman, M., *The Constitutional Crisis in the United Nations,* American Journal of International Law, Vol. 87, 1993, pp. 83–100.

Sarooshi, D., *The United Nations and the Development of Collective Security,* Clarendon Press, Oxford, 1999.

Schröder, M., *Amendments to and Review of the UN Charter in Documents of Reform of the United Nations,* Taylor *et al.* (Eds.), Documents on Reform of the United Nations, Aldershot Dartmouth, 1997.

Sevastik, P., *Informell modification av traktater till följd av ny sedvanerätt och praxis. En studie mot bakgrund av FN-stadgans innovativa utveckling,* Norstedts juridik, Stockholm, 2002.

Seyerstedt, F., *International Personality of International Organizations,* Indian Journal of International Law, Vol. 4, 1964, pp. 1–74.

Simma, B. (Ed.), *The Charter of the United Nations: A Commentary,* second edition, Vol. I, Oxford University Press, Oxford, 2002.

Sinclair, I., *The Vienna Convention on the Law of Treaties,* Manchester University Press, Manchester, 1973.

Sloan, B., *The United Nations Charter as a Constitution,* Pace Yearbook of International Law, Vol. 1, 1989, pp. 61–126.

Suy, E., *The Constitutional Character of Constituent Treaties of International Organisations and the Hierarchy of Norms,* Beyerlein, U. (Ed.), Recht zwischen Umbruch und Bewahrung, Festschrift für Rudolf Bernhardt, Springer, Berlin, 1995.

Suy, E., *The Constitutional Dimension of the Charter of the United Nations Revisited,* Max Planck Yearbook of United Nations Law, Vol. 1, 1997.
Triepel, H., *Les rapports entre le droit interne et le droit international,* Recueil des Cours, Vol. 1, 1923, pp. 73–121.
Tschentscher, A., *The Basic Law (Grundgesetz) The Constitution of the Federal Republic of Germany (May 23rd)* Jurisprudentia Verlag, Wurzberg, 1949.
Vallat, F., *The Competence of the United Nations General Assembly,* Recueil des Cours, Vol. 97, 1959-II, pp. 207–287.
Vallat, F., *The General Assembly and the Security Council of the United Nations,* British Yearbook of International Law, Vol. 29, 1952, pp. 63–104.
Vierdrag, E., *The Law Governing Treaty Relations Between Parties to the Vienna Convention of the Law of Treaties and States not Party to the Convention,* American Journal of International Law, Vol. 76, 1982, pp. 779–801.
Zacklin, R., *The Amendments of the Constitutive Instruments of the United Nations and Specialised Agencies,* Sijthoff, Leiden, 1968.
Österdahl, I., *Threat to the Peace,* Iustus, Uppsala, 1998.

Treaties

The Vienna Convention on the Law of Treaties, 1969.

Cases

Certain Expenses case, ICJ Reports 1962.
Foster and Elam *v.* Nielson, Supreme Court of the United States 1829, 27 US (2 Pet.) 253.
ICJ Pleadings, Legal Consequences of the Continued Presence of South Africa in Namibia (South West Africa) Notwithstanding Security Council Resolution 276, ICJ Reports, 1971.
Interpretation of Greco-Turkish Agreement. PCIJ Series A, 1926, No. 9.
Reparation of Injuries, ICJ Reports 1949.

UN documents

Reportoire of Practice of the United Nations Organs, Vols. I–V, New York, 1955 and Supplements No. 1-2, New York, 1957, 1964.
SC Res 827 (1993)
SC Res 995 (1994)
Travaux Préparatoires to the United Nations Charter, (UNCIO Doc.), 1945.
Yearbook of the International Law Commission (YBILC) 1966-II.

Conference papers

The Vienna Conference 1968 and 1969 on the Vienna Convention on the Law of Treaties, The Final Report of the Swedish Delegation, Stockholm, 1970.

Internet material

Cameron, I., *Targeted Sanctions and Legal Safeguards,* www.jur.uu.se/sii/articles.

www.files.fco.gov.uk/treaty/posonby.pdf.

www.oefr.unibe.ch/law/icl/uk_indx.html.

www.oefre.unibe.ch/law/icl/n100000_index.html.

www.un.org/ga/documents/liemsps.html.

www.uno.admin.ch/sub_dipl/e/home/Thema/intlaw/telat.html.

Miscellaneous

Folkrätt och straffansvar, DsJu 1984:6.

Internationella överenskommelser och svensk rätt, SOU 1974:100.

Lagen om vissa internationella sanktioner – en översyn, Betänkande av Sanktionslagsutredningen, SOU 1995:28.

The Constitution of Sweden: The Fundamental Laws and the Riksdag, Stockholm 2000.

2 The Status of Military Personnel in United Nations Peace Operations

Interplay Between the Laws of Peace and War

Ola Engdahl

2.1 Introduction

In the morning of 5 June 1993, units of the Pakistani contingent in the United Nations peace operation in Somalia suddenly came under attack in several places in southern Mogadishu. The premeditation of the assault was evidenced, *inter alia*, by the attack against checkpoint 89, where Pakistani troops were trapped in a confined area and subjected to concentrated fire by hidden gunmen using both heavy machine guns and anti-tank weapons. The attacks continued until late afternoon, leaving 24 soldiers dead and 56 wounded. In response, the Security Council unanimously adopted Resolution 837 demanding the arrest, trial, and punishment of those responsible. The Secretary-General was requested to investigate the incident. The gravity of the situation is illustrated in the investigational report, which states:

> No act could by its very character more perfectly exemplify an international crime than the use of force against United Nations soldiers to prevent them from carrying out their responsibilities. Such use of force is a plain challenge to the ability of the United Nations to maintain international peace and security and hence to that minimum order on which all other collective human interests depend.[1]

1 Report pursuant to paragraph 5 of the Security Council Resolution 837 (1993) on the investigation into the 5 June 1993 attack on United Nations forces in Somalia conducted on behalf of the Secretary-General, UN Doc. S/26351, 24 August 1993. See the annexed executive summary of the report, para. 7.

The purpose of the present article is to analyse the status of military personnel in United Nations peace operations. Attacks against UN personnel have led to the establishment of a new protective regime, dealing with prosecution or extradition of offenders. The difficult environment in which UN military personnel are required to act raises the question of combatant status for these forces under international humanitarian law applicable in war. Attacks against military personnel involved as combatants in armed conflict may arguably be regarded as legitimate acts of war. The status of military personnel in peace operations is thus dependent on the interplay between the laws applicable in peace and those applicable in war.

By way of introduction, an overview of the relevant international humanitarian law will be presented, followed by a brief presentation of past and present peace operations. On the particular question of the legal status of military forces, the practice of bilateral status agreements between United Nations and host nations will be examined. Then the Convention on the Safety of United Nations and Associated Personnel[2] will be appraised, with special emphasis on its scope of application and relation to international humanitarian law. In this respect, the position of the UN will be considered in the light of the Secretary-General's Bulletin on the Observance by United Nations forces of international humanitarian law.[3]

2.1.1 International humanitarian law[4]

The main purpose of international humanitarian law is to provide standards to protect those not participating in war, such as civilians, sick and wounded, prisoners of war and medical personnel. It also lays down rules concerning the means and methods of warfare

2 Convention on the Safety of United Nations and Associated Personnel, 9 Dec. 1994, 34 ILM 482 (1995).

3 Secretary-General's Bulletin, Observance by United Nations forces of international humanitarian law, UN Doc. ST/SGB/1999/13, 6 August 1999.

4 In a strict sense, the international humanitarian law does not comprise all the norms in what is usually referred to as the Laws of War, *e.g.* the law of neutrality. See Greenwood, Christopher, *Historical Development and Legal Basis*, Fleck, Dieter, (Ed.) The Handbook of Humanitarian Law in Armed Conflicts, Oxford University Press, Oxford 1995, p. 9.

for parties to the conflict.[5] Much of the conventional law is, in general, regarded as declaratory of customary international law.[6] At the heart of international humanitarian law is the distinction between civilians and combatants. Civilians and civilian property must not be the object of attacks. Combatants are legitimate military targets, as are the military installations of the warring factions. United Nations military personnel enjoy the same protection as civilians if they act in the area of an armed conflict, as long as they are not engaged as parties to the conflict.[7]

International humanitarian law is only applicable in situations of an armed conflict or in cases of partial or total occupation. A distinction is made between international armed conflicts and non-international armed conflicts. International armed conflicts are defined as 'all cases of declared war or ... any other armed conflict which may arise between two or more of the High Contracting Parties'.[8] Conventional international humanitarian law mainly applies to *international* armed conflicts. However, the evolution of customary international humanitarian law needs, to be taken in consideration.[9] Article 3 common to the four Geneva Conventions lays

5 See Geneva Convention for the Amelioration of the Condition of the Wounded and Sick in Armed Forces in the Field of August 12, 1949, UNTS, Vol. 75, p. 31 (Geneva Convention I), Geneva Convention for the Amelioration of the Condition of Wounded, Sick and Shipwrecked Members of Armed Forces at Sea of August 12, 1949, UNTS, Vol. 75, p. 85 (Geneva Convention II), Geneva Convention Relative to the Treatment of Prisoners of War of August 12, 1949, UNTS Vol. 75, p. 135 (Geneva Convention III), Geneva Convention Relative to the Protection of Civilian Persons in Time of War of August 12, 1949, UNTS, Vol. 75, p. 355 (Geneva Convention IV), Protocol Additional to the Geneva Conventions of 12 August 1949, and Relating to the Protection of Victims of International Armed Conflicts, UNTS, Vol. 1125, p. 3 (Additional Protocol I), Protocol Additional to the Geneva Conventions of 12 August 1949, and Relating to the Protection of Victims of Non-International Armed Conflicts, UNTS, Vol. 1125, p. 609 (Additional Protocol II).

6 Greenwood, *op. cit.* note 4, pp. 24–26 and the authorities cited there.

7 See the Rome Statute of the International Criminal Court, Article 8(2) (b) (iii) and (e) (iii), at www.un.org/law/icc/statute/romefra.htm, viewed 17 June 2003.

8 The Conventions also apply in relation to a Power which is not party to the Conventions if it 'accepts and applies the provisions thereof'. See common Article 2 to Geneva Conventions I–IV.

9 A forthcoming study by the International Committee of the Red Cross examines the development of customary rules of international humanitarian law applicable in international and non-international armed conflicts.

down basic norms applicable to all armed conflicts irrespective of whether they are of an international or non-international nature.[10] Additional Protocol II develops the law further with regard to non-international armed conflicts but its applicability depends *inter alia*, on a threshold of control of territory by dissident armed forces.[11]

The International Criminal Tribunal for the Former Yugoslavia formulated criteria for determination of the existence of an armed conflict. According to the Court:

> an armed conflict exists whenever there is a resort to armed force between States or protracted armed violence between governmental authorities and organized armed groups or between such groups within a state.[12]

International humanitarian law is based on reciprocity and applies equally to all parties to the conflict independent of its legitimacy. A defending state is therefore bound by international humanitarian law just as the aggressor state is. An often quoted statement by Sir Hersch Lauterpacht, reads, '[i]t is impossible to visualize the conduct of hostilities in which one side would be bound by rules of warfare without benefiting from them and the other side would benefit from them without being bound by them'.[13]

10 See Article 3 common to Geneva Conventions I–IV.

11 According to Article 1 of Additional Protocol II, it applies to armed conflicts not covered by Additional Protocol I 'which take place in the territory of a High Contracting Party between its armed forces and dissident armed forces or other organized armed groups which, under responsible command, exercise such control over a part of its territory as to enable them to carry out sustained and concerted military operations and to implement this Protocol'.

12 Prosecutor v. Tadic, Case IT-94-1-AR72, Appeal on Jurisdiction, October 2, 1995, para. 70.

13 Lauterpacht, Hersch, *The Limits of the Operation of the Law of War*, British Yearbook of International Law, Vol. 30, 1953, p. 212.

2.1.2 United Nations peace operations[14]

The concept of traditional peacekeeping has developed in practice and is underpinned by three basic principles:[15] 'consent of the parties, impartiality and the non-use of force except in self-defence'.[16] The concept was introduced in 1956 by the United Nations in response to the Suez crises. A UN force was deployed in Egypt to 'secure and supervise the cessation of hostilities'[17] and served as an interpositionary force between Egypt and Israel. Being a neutral body that both parties could rely on, the UN forces functioned as a tool placed at the disposal of the warring states. In this respect the UN forces contribute to the process of increasing trust between the parties, and in the end to a peaceful solution of the conflict. In operations where a military force has been required to act as a buffer between warring parties, adherence to these basic principles has generally functioned well.[18]

However, by the end of the Cold War the UN assumed greater responsibility both in terms of the number of operations and their level

14 The term 'peace operation' is used for the purpose of this article as an overall term for the activities of the United Nations in the maintenance of international peace and security. It includes operations that range from traditional peacekeeping to peace enforcement operations, based on a UN mandate but not necessarily under its command and control, but stop short of war such as the operations against North Korea and Iraq.

15 A peacekeeping operation will be of a more intrusive nature than what is envisaged under Chapter VI of the UN Charter but less intrusive than enforcement measures under Chapter VII. Peacekeeping operations are therefore referred to at times as operations coming under the imaginary Chapter VI $^{1}/_{2}$. In practice, however, traditional peacekeeping operations are often referred to as 'Chapter VI' operations and those involving enforcement measures as 'Chapter VII' operations. The UN has no forces of its own and each operation is dependant on voluntary contributions by member states.

16 Supplement to An Agenda for Peace: Position paper of the Secretary-General on the occasion of the Fiftieth Anniversary of the United Nations, UN Doc. A/50/60-S/1995/1, 3 January 1995, para. 33.

17 General Assembly Resolution 998 (ES-I) (1956) in Siekmann, Robert C.R., *Basic Documents on United Nations and Related Peace-keeping Forces,* 2nd ed., Martinus Nijhoff, Dordrecht 1989, p. 3.

18 See *e.g.* United Nations Emergency Force II (UNEF II) S/RES/ 340 (1973), United Nations Disengagement Observer Force (UNDOF) S/RES/350 (1974), United Nations Interim Force in Lebanon (UNIFIL) S/RES/425 (1978), and United Nations Peacekeeping Force in Cyprus (UNIFICYP) S/RES/186 (1964).

of ambition.[19] Operations known as 'second-generation peace-keeping' became multifunctional and included a wide variety of actors often with a large civilian component.[20] When the pressure of a bipolar world eased, this led to a change in the nature of armed conflict. From being mainly international, the great majority of armed conflicts since 1990 have been of a non-international character. As a result, UN operations have mainly been mounted in the context of *internal* conflicts, such as those in Somalia,[21] former Yugoslavia,[22] Cambodia,[23] Mozambique,[24] Haiti,[25] and Rwanda.[26] The nature of the conflicts has made it difficult to adhere to the principles of consent, impartiality and use of force in self-defence.[27] The lack of discipline among rival forces, sometimes with the objective of exterminating or otherwise removing people belonging to a particular ethnic, religious or cultural group, which in itself is contrary to international humanitarian law, has worsened the security situation for UN forces.

Another trend that evolved from the mid-1990s was the practice of 'contracting out' operations, to coalitions of the willing, regional

19 In 1988, 11,121 personnel (military, police and civilian) were deployed in UN peacekeeping operations and in December 1994, 77,783 personnel (the highest number so far) were deployed. See *The Blue Helmets. A Review of United Nations Peace-keeping*, 3rd ed., United Nations Department of Public Information, New York, NY 1996, p.4.

20 *Ibid.,* p. 5. Examples are United Nations Angola Verification Mission I – III (UNAVEM I- III), S/RES/626 (1988), S/RES/696 (1991), S/RES/976 (1995); United Nations Observer Mission in El Salvador (ONUSAL), S/RES/693 (1991); United Nations Transitional Authority in Cambodia (UNTAC), S/RES/745 (1992); United Nations Mission in Haiti (UNMIH) S/RES/867 (1993); United Nations Operation in Somalia I-II (UNOSOM I-II), S/RES/751 (1992), S/RES/814 (1993).

21 United Nations Operation in Somalia I-II (UNOSOM I-II), S/RES/751 (1992), S/RES/814 (1993).

22 United Nations Protection Force (UNPROFOR) S/RES/743 (1992).

23 United Nations Transitional Authority in Cambodia (UNTAC), S/RES/745 (1992).

24 United Nations Operation in Mozambique (ONUMOZ), S/RES/797 (1992).

25 United Nations Mission in Haiti (UNMIH) S/RES/867 (1993).

26 United Nations Assistance Mission for Rwanda (UNAMIR), S/RES/872 (1993).

27 According to the Panel on United Nations Peace Operations, these principles have been challenged, in the context of modern peace operations deployed in internal conflicts, by so called spoilers who seek to undermine the peace process. The principles of consent, impartiality and use of force in self-defence should, however, according to the Panel 'remain the bedrock principles of peacekeeping'. Report of the Panel on United Nations Peace Operations, UN Doc. A/55/305 – S/2000/809, 21 August 2000, Part 2, para. 48. See Part 2 paras. 21–22, 48–55 at www.un.org/peace/reports/peace_operations/docs/part2.htm, (19 June 2003).

organisations or individual states, such as in Bosnia-Herzegovina,[28] Kosovo,[29] Rwanda,[30] East Timor,[31] and Afghanistan.[32] Such operations often involve enforcement measures. The Security Council has the right to take enforcement measures against any member of the UN when it finds that a situation poses a threat to international peace and security.[33] UN Security Council resolutions that provide an operation with an enforcement mandate often contain the formula 'the use of all necessary means' to achieve a set of defined tasks.[34]

The principal criteria for traditional peacekeeping operations do not as such apply to peace enforcement operations. In enforcement operations, the *consent* of the host nation is not necessary. In practice, however, it is sought and often received.[35] A Chapter VII mandate provides UN forces with the power to enforce the tasks entrusted to them irrespective of the consent of the host nation. The UN forces therefore maintain a strong position in relation to the host nation. The criterion of consent is the principal divide between war and peace. As long as UN forces are present with the consent of the host nation, they will not simultaneously be engaged in armed conflict with that nation. The consent of the host nation is therefore of fundamental importance to the legal status of the forces. If the UN forces are being drawn into armed conflict with, for example, resistance movements present in the territory of the host nation, the legal position of the forces vis-à-vis the host

28 The NATO-led Implementation Force (IFOR), S/RES/1031 (1995).

29 The NATO-led Kosovo Force (KFOR), S/RES/1244 (1999).

30 The French-led Opération Turquoise in Rwanda, S/RES/929 (1994) assisting the United Nations Mission in Rwanda (UNAMIR).

31 The Australian-led International Force in East Timor (INTERFET) in East Timor, S/RES/1264 (1999).

32 The, initially, UK-led International Security Assistance Force (ISAF), S/RES/1386 (2001).

33 Chapter VII of the United Nations Charter.

34 See *e.g.*, S/RES/794 (1992), para. 10 (Somalia), S/RES/929 (1994) para. 3 (Rwanda).

35 See *e.g.*, East Timor, S/RES/1264 (1999), Haiti S/RES/944 (1994) (peaceful deployment of the US-led multinational force), the Military Technical Agreement between KFOR and the Federal Republic of Yugoslavia and the Republic of Serbia, 38 ILM 1217 (1999), at www.nato.int/kfor/kfor/documents/mta.htm, (17 June 2003) and the General Framework Agreement for Peace in Bosnia-Herzegovina, 35 ILM 75 (1996), at www.nato.int/ifor/gfa/gfa-frm.htm, (17 June 2003).

nation will not be affected. The capability of the host nation to ensure the legal status of the UN forces may, however, be restricted in areas where it does not exercise effective control.

Impartiality of the UN forces is a consequence of the fact that traditional peacekeeping operations are based on the consent of the host nation. Even though impartiality is something to strive for, it is, therefore, not indispensable in an enforcement operation. The very nature of enforcement operations goes beyond *self-defence* limitations on the use of force. It should be noted, however, that the principle of self-defence has been given a wide interpretation by the UN. It has repeatedly been stated that self-defence includes 'resistance to attempts by forceful means to prevent it from discharging its duties under the mandate of the Security Council'.[36]

The operations against North Korea[37] and Iraq,[38] decided under Chapter VII of the UN Charter and definitely enforcement operations, were established *against* the will of the target states (North Korea or Iraq clearly did not consent). In these operations there were identified enemies, and the laws of war applied unequivocally to the use of force by the UN-mandated coalitions. Enforcement operations conducted on the basis of consent of the host nation have the character of robust police operations rather than engagement of military forces in armed conflict.[39]

36 See *e.g.*, Report of the Secretary-General on the implementation of Security Council Resolution 340 (1973), UN Doc. S/11052/Rev. 1, 27 October 1973 in Siekmann, *op. cit.* note 17, p. 190, and Report of the Secretary-General on the implementation of Security Council resolution 425, UN Doc. S/12611, 19 March 1978, in Siekmann, *op. cit.* note 17, p. 215.

37 S/RES/84 (1950).

38 S/RES/678 (1990).

39 A study of the peacekeeping doctrines of the United Kingdom, United States and France demonstrates these states' efforts to come to terms with the problems connected with the new character of conflicts where the consent of the parties is limited. It is possible to distinguish three pillars (with some variations): i) traditional peacekeeping, ii) peace enforcement, iii) war. The first pillar is based on Chapter VI of the UN Charter and the use of force is limited to self-defence. Pillars ii) and iii) are based on Chapter VII of the UN Charter, involving enforcement measures and force is permitted beyond the concept of self-defence. The third pillar (war) is different from the other two in that it involves a designated enemy. See Jakobsen, Peter Viggo, *The Emerging Consensus on Grey Area Peace Operations Doctrine: Will It Last and Enhance Operational Effectiveness?*, International Peacekeeping, Vol. 7, No. 3 Autumn 2000, p. 41.

Although United Nations military forces may not initially act as combatants in an armed conflict, the nature of their tasks and the environment in which they act may have the effect of drawing them into an armed conflict and thus becoming combatants under international humanitarian law. The situation may be very difficult to assess where no government is exercising control over the territory and there is no counterpart to obtain consent from.

2.2 The status of forces agreements

The stationing of UN military forces within the territory of the host nation is governed by the body of law known as the law of visiting forces. A UN operation is considered a subsidiary organ of the United Nations and is therefore also endowed with privileges and immunities under Article 105 of the UN Charter. Status of forces agreements in UN peace operations are in fact influenced by both of these sets of norms.

2.2.1 The law of visiting forces

The law of visiting forces has traditionally regulated the stationing of troops on foreign territory in peacetime. The presence of foreign forces is a rather new phenomenon and, generally speaking, only occurred before 1914 in the form of occupying forces during times of war or peace.[40] The need to regulate the status of foreign forces in peacetime arose, in particular, after the end of the Second World War. The prime example of this body of law is the multilateral Status of Forces Agreement (SOFA) of 1951 defining the status of visiting forces of the North Atlantic Treaty Organisation (NATO).[41]

40 Lazareff, Serge, *Status of Military Forces Under Current International Law*, A.W. Sijthoff, Leyden, 1971, p. 7. During the 18th century there were instances of military forces passing through foreign territory or being stationed for a very brief period of time.

41 Agreement between the Parties to the North Atlantic Treaty Regarding the Status of Their Forces, June 19, 1951, UNTS, Vol. 199, p. 67, at www.nato.int/docu/basictxt/b510619a.htm, (17 June 2003).

A controversial issue of the law of visiting forces concerns jurisdiction. There are two opposing doctrines in this field: the law of the flag and the principle of territorial sovereignty. The essence of the doctrine of the law of the flag is that foreign forces are not subject to the jurisdiction of the host state. The sending state retains exclusive jurisdiction over its forces. According to one writer there is, however, in this respect no 'unqualified statement in favour of the principle of the immunity of jurisdiction'.[42] A customized principle of territorial sovereignty appears instead as the *de lege lata* principle in the absence of an agreement.[43] The receiving state needs to take into account the fact that the personnel of the foreign forces are to some extent representatives of the sending state. This is reflected in the NATO SOFA, which stipulates *concurrent* jurisdiction between the sending and the receiving state in the context of visiting forces.[44]

2.2.2 United Nations privileges and immunities

The Convention on the Privileges and Immunities of the UN, 1946,[45] (General Convention) is based on Article 105 of the UN Charter and provides detailed privileges and immunities for certain categories of personnel, such as 'officials' and 'experts on mission'.[46] These privileges and immunities ('*international* privileges and immunities') have been contrasted with the privileges and immunities enjoyed by states and their diplomatic personnel. The former are primarly founded in treaty law, lack an element of reciprocity and are entirely based on function. Only privileges and immunities that are necessary to fulfil the functions of an international organisation can be expected.[47] The latter, on the other hand, are 'largely based on a theory of equality, supported by the

42 Lazareff, *op. cit.* note 40, p. 17.
43 *Ibid.*
44 See Article VII of the NATO SOFA, www.nato.int/docu/basictxt/b510619a.htm, (17 June 2003).
45 The Convention of the Privileges and Immunities of the UN, 1946, UNTS, Vol. 1, p. 15.
46 See Articles V and VI of the General Convention.
47 See Amerasinghe, Chittaranjan. F., *Principles of the Institutional Law of International Organizations*, Cambridge University Press, Cambridge, 1996, pp. 369–70.

principle of reciprocity, and historically reflected the respect States had for each others's sovereignty.'[48]

Military observers and UN civilian police are mainly regarded as 'experts on mission' and accorded privileges and immunities under the General Convention.[49] Members of national contingents, however, remain in national service and subject to that disciplinary system. Although considered international personnel, and under orders of the commander of the force, their status in the host nation is generally dependent on the privileges and immunities specifically provided for in a SOFA.

2.2.3 United Nations status of forces agreements

In 1956, when the first United Nations peacekeeping operation was launched, the UN forces were present with the consent of the host nation but were intended to play a more active role than traditionally visiting forces had played.[50] Through an Exchange of Letters between the United Nations and the host nation (Egypt), certain privileges and immunities applicable to the members of the operation were agreed upon.[51] The practice from the UNEF operation was generally followed in subsequent operations, and in 1990 the Secretary-General issued a model status-of-forces agreement (UN Model SOFA).[52] It was explicitly stated there that the model agreement was based 'upon established practice and drawing extensively upon ear-

48 Amerasinghe, *op. cit.* note 47, p. 369. It should be noted, however, that the theory of 'functional necessity' also underlies diplomatic privileges and immunities. This was in fact regarded as a theory of increasing importance by the International Law Commission during the preparation of the Vienna Convention on Diplomatic Relations and is mentioned in the preamble to that Convention. See Vienna Convention on Diplomatic Relations, 1961, UNTS, Vol. 500, p. 95.

49 Experts 'performing missions for the United Nations shall be accorded such privileges and immunities as are necessary for the independent exercise of their functions during the period of their missions.' Section 22, Article VI of the General Convention.

50 It may be held that the difference between visiting forces and UN forces depends on the context in which they are deployed. The latter troops are deployed in an 'operational context', although not in a warlike mode, while visiting forces are not charged with any operational tasks in the host nation.

51 Exchange of letters constituting an agreement between the United Nations and the Government of Egypt concerning the status of the United Nations Emergency Force in Egypt, New York, 1957, UNTS, Vol. 260, p. 61.

52 Model status-of-forces agreement for peace-keeping operations. UN Doc. A/45/594, 9 October 1990.

lier and current agreements' and was intended to function as a model for future individual agreements between the UN and host nations.[53]

The United Nations strives to conclude a SOFA with the state that is hosting a peace operation. If, and when, an agreement is concluded it will apply bilaterally between the United Nations and the host nation. Troop-contributing nations are the beneficiaries of the SOFA. A SOFA sets out privileges and immunities for the operation as such, as well as for the members taking part in the operation. To secure the UN's obligations, in relation to the host nation, a Contribution Agreement is concluded between the UN and the contributing nations.[54]

The nature of the privileges and immunities stipulated in a SOFA, that is applicable to a UN operation thus differs from those of the General Convention and the law governing the international civil service. A SOFA draws from the international privileges and immunities as well as the law governing military forces abroad and is adapted to the particular setting of a peace operation.[55] The strength of such an agreement is that it may be designed to meet the specific circumstances of each operation. The weakness is of course that the status provided by a SOFA is dependent on the conclusion of a bilateral agreement.[56]

The most obvious difference compared to the NATO SOFA, as well as the General Convention, is that the sending nations retain the *exclusive* criminal jurisdiction over its forces.[57] On this issue, the

53 *Ibid.*, para. 1.

54 Model Agreement between the United Nations and Member States contributing personnel and equipment to United Nations peace-keeping operations, UN Doc. A/46/185, 23 May 1991.

55 Bowett considers that these status of forces agreements 'represent compromises and shifts between the law of visiting forces on the one hand and the law of international privileges and immunities on the other, against the background of functional necessity'. Typical differences between visiting forces and United Nations forces are, according to Bowett, that '(1) the United Nations Force is not that of an ally: indeed it will generally be completely independent of the local authorities; (2) the Force generally may be actually operating, in the military sense, within the territory of the State and not merely stationed there'. Bowett, Derek W., *United Nations Forces*, Stevens & Sons under the auspices of the Davies Memorial Institute London, 1964, p. 434.

56 Evolving customary law in this regard needs, to be taken into consideration, however.

57 Article 47(b) of the UN Model SOFA A/45/594. Compare Sections 20 and 23 of the General Convention, according to which the Secretary-General has the right and duty to waive the immunity if 'the immunity would impede the course of justice and can be waived without prejudice to the interests of the United Nations'.

Secretary-General Dag Hammarskjöld concluded in his Summary Study of the UNEF operation that:

> The most important principle in the status Agreement ensures that UNEF personnel, when involved in criminal actions, come under the jurisdiction of the criminal courts of their home countries. The establishment of this principle for UNEF, in relation to Egypt, has set a most valuable precedent. Experience shows that this principle is essential to the successful recruitment by the United Nations of military personnel not otherwise under immunity rules, from its Member countries. The position established for UNEF should be maintained in future arrangements.[58]

The fact that UN forces are sometimes deployed before the conclusion of a SOFA, causes ambiguities concerning the forces' legal status. In connection with the authorization of troops to the United Mission in Ethiopia and Eritrea (UNMEE) in 2000 the Security Council requested that the Governments conclude a SOFA with the Secretary-General within thirty days, and recalled 'that pending the conclusion of such agreements, the model status-of-forces agreement of 9 October 1990 (A/45/594) should apply provisionally'.[59]

The privileges and immunities stipulated in the UN Model SOFA have also had an effect on other arrangements regarding the status of forces in peace operations not conducted under UN command and control.[60]

58 Report of the Secretary-General: Summary study of the experiences derived from the establishment and operation of the Force, UN Doc. A/3943 (1958) para. 163.

59 S/RES/1320 (2000) para. 6. See *e.g.* S/RES/1270 (1999) para. 16, on the establishment of the United Nations Mission in Sierra Leone (UNAMSIL), and S/RES/1410 (2002), para. 11, on the establishment of the United Nations Mission of Support of East Timor (UNMISET).

60 See Annex 1-A to the General Framework Agreement for Peace (Dayton Agreement), www.nato.int/ifor/gfa/gfa-ap1a.htm, (13 May 2003); UNMIK/REG/2000/47, On the Status, Privileges and Immunities of KFOR and UNMIK and their Personnel in Kosovo, www.unmikonline.org/regulations/2000/reg47-00.htm (13 May 2003), and Annex A to the Military Technical Agreement between the International Security Assistance Force (ISAF) and the Interim Administration of Afghanistan, www.operations.mod.uk/isafmta.pdf, (13 May 2003).

2.3 The Convention on the Safety of United Nations and Associated Personnel

In the beginning of the 1990s, the United Nations was involved in operations in which the participating personnel were especially exposed to security risks. The deliberate attacks against the personnel in the United Nations operation in Somalia and the United Nations Protection Force in former Yugoslavia, illustrated an increasing lack of respect for UN personnel. Against the background of the volatile environment for United Nations personnel it became clear that the question of the safety and security of UN and other personnel was of particular interest to a growing number of nations and not only those that regularly contributed troops to UN operations. The Convention on the Safety of United Nations and Associated Personnel ('the Convention') may therefore be regarded as a response by the international community to the growing number of attacks against personnel participating in UN operations. The Convention was concluded in a very short space of time. The General Assembly adopted the Convention less than 15 months after the item had been assigned to the Sixth Committee.[61] The rapid consensus on the content of a new international instrument may be interpreted as an indicator of a general *opinio juris* regarding the protection of personnel participating in United Nations operations.

The purpose of the Convention is to put an end to impunity for those who carry out attacks against UN personnel. Member states are obligated to criminalize the acts listed in the Convention and to either prosecute or extradite persons responsible for such crimes. The prosecution and extradition provisions are based in general on other conventions that address similar questions, such as the 1973 Convention on the Prevention and Punishment of Crimes against Internationally Protected Persons including Diplomatic Agents.[62] The negotiations centred on the scope of application of the new

61 For the text of the Convention see the Annex to UN General Assembly Resolution 49/59, 17 February 1995, UN Doc. A/RES/49/59 (1995).

62 See UN Doc. A/AC.242/2 para. 93. The Convention on the Prevention and Punishment of Crimes against Internationally Protected Persons including Diplomatic Agents, 1973, UNTS, vol., 1035, p. 167 (hereinafter IPP Convention). A suggestion to draft an additional protocol to the IPP Convention did not receive sufficient support. See UN Doc. A/C.6/48/SR.29, 15 November 1993, para. 3.

instrument and the solution, clearly a compromise, poses a number of questions.[63]

2.3.1 Scope of application

The Convention applies to United Nations and Associated personnel as defined in Article 1:

(a) 'United Nations personnel' means:
   (i) Persons engaged or deployed by the Secretary-General of the United Nations as members of the military, police or civilian components of a United Nations operation;
   (ii) Other officials and experts on mission of the United Nations or its specialised agencies of the International Atomic Energy Agency who are present in an official capacity in the area where a United Nations operation is being conducted;

(b) 'Associated personnel' means:
   (i) Persons assigned by a Government or an intergovernmental organisation with the agreement of the competent organ of the United Nations;
   (ii) Persons engaged by the Secretary-General of the United Nations or by a specialised agency or by the International Atomic Energy Agency;
   (iii) Persons deployed by a humanitarian non-governmental organisation or agency under an agreement with the Secretary-General of the United Nations or with a specialised agency or with the International Atomic Energy Agency,

   to carry out activities in support of the fulfilment of the mandate of a United Nations operation;

63 The Secretary-General has in fact, upon request, issued a report on the scope of legal protection under the Convention in 2000, UN Doc. A/55/637, 21 November 2000. Based on the recommendations of the Secretary-General to strengthen and enhance the Convention's protection, an Ad Hoc Committee was established to consider these recommendations. The Ad Hoc Committee has so far been convened twice, see the reports of the Ad Hoc Committee on the Scope of Legal Protection under the Convention on the Safety of United Nations and Associated Personnel, UN Doc. A/57/52, 10 April 2002 and UN Doc. A/58/52, 11 April 2003.

2.3.2 Personnel

Paragraph (a) (i) encompasses personnel contributed by the nations participating in a United Nations operation and would therefore probably include the bulk of personnel covered by the Convention. They are commonly viewed as the core group of persons referred to as peacekeepers.[64]

Ambassador Philippe Kirsch, Chairman of the Ad Hoc Committee and its Working Groups, mentioned factors that complicated the negotiations leading up to the adoption of the Convention. The most important of these was that the work on the Convention 'became a surrogate battleground for the more complex issue of the expanded powers of the Security Council'.[65] Traces of this 'battle' are found throughout the Convention. The final definition of 'United Nations personnel' gives the impression that the restrictive approach was victorious. The United Nations, under its Secretary-General, will keep control of the personnel covered by this definition. This restrictive approach is, however, balanced by the definition of 'Associated personnel'.

In terms of the *protection* afforded by the Convention there is no difference between 'United Nations personnel' and 'Associated personnel'. Both categories enjoy the same protection under the Convention. To be included in the category 'Associated personnel' it is, however, not only necessary to have a link with the United Nations but a special link to the United Nations *operation* is also required. The activities of such personnel must support the mandate of the UN operation.

The first group in the category 'Associated personnel' refers to persons who are assigned by a government or intergovernmental organisation with the agreement of the UN. This provision enables military forces that are, not under UN control, to be included in the protective regime of the Convention as 'Associated personnel'. The delegation of the United States, which had a strong interest in including assisting forces under the protection of the Convention,

64 See Bloom, Evan T., *Protecting Peacekeepers: The Convention on the Safety of United Nations and Associated Personnel,* American Journal of International Law, Vol. 89, 1995, p. 623.

65 Kirsch, Philippe, *Convention on the Safety of United Nations and Associated Personnel,* Canadian Council on International Law, Proceedings, 1994, p. 187.

found that the *operations* in Haiti, Rwanda, Bosnia and Somalia would all be covered by the Convention. The Multinational Force supporting the United Nations operation in Haiti (UNMIH) as well as members of NATO supporting the UN operation in former Yugoslavia (UNPROFOR), were mentioned as examples of *associated forces*.[66]

These forces existed before or at the time of the adoption of the Convention. They assisted UN forces, but were not acting under UN command and control. The critical issue in this paragraph is to what extent 'Associated personnel' can act independently. They are not subject to UN command and control, but are required to act in support of a United Nations operation's mandate. Does the requirement to act in support of the mandate of a United Nations operation also mean that the operation must include United Nations personnel? The ambiguous wording of the last sentence of subparagraph (b) may provide scope for these forces to act independently. An earlier version of this sentence read: 'to carry out activities directly connected with a United Nations operation.' The substitution of 'mandate' for 'operation' supports the interpretation that associated personnel must not necessarily be associated with UN personnel. Perhaps the activities could also be associated with the 'mandate'. This interpretation is, however, not fully supported by the paragraph's negotiating history. Several influential delegations held that the association requirement relates to UN personnel and that association with the mandate alone is not enough.[67]

The view of the US delegation that persons included in the Multinational Force (MNF) in Haiti would be considered 'Associated personnel' is not without objections. At the time of deployment of the MNF the United Nations Mission in Haiti (UNMIH) was not yet on the ground. In fact the very purpose of the MNF was to pave the way for the UN mission which had not been deployed due to disturbances in Port-au-Prince earlier.

66 UN Doc. A/49/PV.84 (1994), p. 15.

67 See Lepper, Steven J., *The Legal Status of Military Personnel in United Nations Peace Operations: One Delegate's Analysis,* Houston Journal of International Law, Vol. 18:359, 1996, pp. 386–389.

2.3.3 Operations

The definition of 'Associated personnel' is closely related to the definition of a 'United Nations operation'. The term 'United Nations operation' is, for the purpose of the Convention, defined in Article 1 as:

(c) ... an operation established by the competent organ of the United Nations in accordance with the Charter of the United Nations and conducted under United Nations authority and control:
   (i) Where the operation is for the purpose of maintaining or restoring international peace and security; or
   (ii) Where the Security Council or the General Assembly has declared, for the purposes of this Convention, that there exists an exceptional risk to the safety of the personnel participating in the operation;

There is a major difference between these two categories of operations.[68] The second type needs a political decision in form of a declaration of exceptional risk in order to be protected by the Convention. To date, no such declaration has been made.[69] It is less likely that the operations in the latter category would involve a military component, but if a declaration of risk is made, military personnel may come under the protection of the Convention as 'Associated personnel' in relation to that operation. The Convention applies to the first category automatically. This category includes the whole range from peacekeeping to peace enforcement operations. Military personnel may thus be members of the operation or associated with it.

68 According to the report by the Secretary-General on the Scope of Legal Protection under the Convention on the Safety of United Nations and Associated Personnel, a 'United Nations operation of the first category is clearly any peacekeeping operation conducted under United Nations command and control, to the exclusion of United Nations authorized operations conducted under national command and control. A United Nations operation of the second category mentioned in article (c) (ii) of the Convention is any other United Nations presence in a host country established by a United Nations competent organ – though not necessarily the General Assembly or the Security Council – such as, United Nations political missions, "post-conflict, peace-building offices", and United Nations humanitarian, development and human rights presences.' (Footnotes omitted), UN Doc A/55/637, 21 November 2000, p. 2.

69 One of the main issues dealt with by the Ad Hoc Committee has been the declaration of exceptional risk and proposals to dispense with that requirement.

An illustrative example of an operation that may include 'Associated personnel' is the NATO-led Kosovo Force (KFOR). The personnel of KFOR are assigned by an intergovernmental organisation with the agreement (S/RES/1244) of a competent UN organ. KFOR definitely carries out activities in support of UNMIK's mandate. Being regarded as a peacekeeping operation, UNMIK would qualify as a UN operation falling under category (c) (i).[70] KFOR personnel could therefore be considered 'Associated personnel' under the Convention.

2.3.4 Relationship with international humanitarian law

There is yet another limitation on the applicability of the Convention. It draws a line against the applicability of international humanitarian law on the grounds that these two legal regimes are mutually exclusive. According to Article 2(2) the Convention does not apply to:

> [a] United Nations operation authorized by the Security Council as an enforcement action under Chapter VII of the Charter of the United Nations in which any of the personnel are engaged as combatants against organized armed forces and to which the law of international armed conflict applies.

The purpose of Article 2(2) is to draw a clear line between the application of the Convention and the applicability of international humanitarian law. If UN forces are drawn into an armed conflict, acting as combatants, they cannot at the same time be protected by the Convention, since such a situation might have an eroding effect on the norms of international humanitarian law. The underlying principle of international humanitarian law is that anyone taking part in hostilities as a combatant should have the same kind of legal status, regardless of whether they belong to an aggressor state or a defending party.

Before we exame this issue further, it should be noted that both the Convention and international humanitarian law might protect UN forces acting in the *area* of an ongoing armed conflict. The warring parties must abide by the laws of war and treat the UN forces

70 United Nations Homepage at www.un.org/Depts/dpko/dpko/home.shtml, (22 May 2003).

accordingly. The purpose of Article 2(2) is to regulate situations in which UN forces become *party* to an armed conflict. The Convention does not restrict the protection that UN and associated personnel are entitled to under international humanitarian law.[71] Civilian personnel lose their protection under the Convention once military personnel are engaged as combatants in an international armed conflict. However, their protected status under international humanitarian law will, not change.[72]

Military forces acting on behalf of the United Nations do have a special status according to the Convention, but the authors of the Convention realized that it would not be possible to retain this special protection when those forces acted as combatants in an armed conflict. The result does, however, beg a few questions. Article 2(2) of the Convention consists of a cumulative list of conditions. When these are fulfilled, the Convention becomes non-operative.

The exception from the Convention's scope of application relates to operations 'authorized by the Security Council'. This may imply that only operations *authorized* by the UN but conducted under another organisation's command and control, so called 'contract-out operations', would be excempt from the Convention's scope of application. That would, however, create a very limited exception since such operations would only come under the Convention's regime if the personnel were *associated* with a United Nations operation. This interpretation does not seem to be supported by the

71 See for instance Article 8 of the ICC statute, according to which it is a war crime to attack such personnel when they enjoy protection as civilians under international humanitarian law during both international and non-international armed conflict, ICC Statute, Article 8 (b) (iii) and (e) (iii).

72 There seems to have been some confusion in this respect in the Secretary-General's report on the scope of legal protection under the Convention on the Safety of United Nations and Associated Personnel. Arguing for the dispense of the contractual link between humanitarian non-governmental organisations and the United Nations the Report states in note 5 that, '[i]n conditioning the protection to humanitarian non-governmental organisations on an agreement with the United Nations, the Convention has, in fact, limited the protection to which they are entitled under international humanitarian law in situations of armed conflict'. In support of this view the Report refers to Article 71 of Additional Protocol I to the Geneva Conventions and Article 8 of the ICC Statute. The agreement with the United Nations only relates to protection under the *Convention* and there is no connection in this respect with international humanitarian law. UN Doc. A/55/637, 21 November 2000.

negotiations and creates unnecessary ambiguity concerning the application of the Convention.[73]

Another condition is that it must be an enforcement action authorized by the Security Council under Chapter VII of the UN Charter. According to one author the criterion 'is merely a reflection of the fact that only such operations are likely to involve UN forces as combatants in international armed conflicts'.[74] This is certainly true. Involvement in armed conflict by UN forces in a Chapter VI operation would presumably violate the orders of the commander of the force. Use of force by UN military personnel under such circumstances would arguably not make the Convention non-operative. However, the aim of the Convention is not to protect those who resort to force illegally. Acts, which would otherwise be criminalized under the Convention, could therefore be justified as self-defence against excessive use of force by the UN military personnel.

Another feature of Article 2(2) is that the moment any of the military personnel are engaged as combatants all the personnel lose their protected status under the Convention. Another solution would have been to stipulate that the Convention would continue to be applicable to civilian personnel, but relevant provisions of international humanitarian law would take precedence over the Convention. The Convention's 'all or nothing' approach could have strange effects for instance where a small part of a large-sized UN force is engaged as combatants in a remote part of the area of operation.

Another issue that is not properly dealt with is whether the UN and associated personnel may again be protected by the Convention after the end of the hostilities. A UN operation may continue for several years, and the situation on the ground may change character during this period.

Yet another of the cumulative conditions is that the law of international armed conflict must apply to the situation. The specific reference to the law of *international* armed conflict implies that

73 Shraga, Daphna, *The Applicability of International Humanitarian Law to United Nations Operations*, Emanuelli, Claude (Ed.), Les casques bleus: policiers ou combatants?, Wilson & Lafleur Hée, Montreal, 1997, p. 30.

74 See Lepper, *op. cit.* note 67, p. 398.

there are situations in which UN forces could be engaged as combatants and still be protected by the Convention. Such a situation may arguably arise when UN forces acts against non-state entities.[75] During the negotiations it was suggested that international humanitarian law would apply to situations where United Nations military personnel 'were engaged in combat with organised armed forces having an identifiable command structure, carrying arms openly and controlling part of the territory of the host State'.[76] This criterion is comparable to the 'threshold requirement' in Additional Protocol II to the Geneva Conventions. The fact that the Convention would continue to apply until the conditions of the 'threshold requirement' were met appears to have created an 'overlap' between the Convention and Article 3 common to the four Geneva Conventions. In the current text the 'overlap' between the two separate regimes is even greater. Should this be regarded as a mistake on the part of the drafters or is the wording designed to enhance the protection of the personnel?

The Geneva Convention relative to the treatment of prisoners of war is not applicable to non-international armed conflicts, and if UN military personnel are engaged as combatants in an armed conflict without the current overlap the Convention on the Safety of United Nations and Associated Personnel would not be applicable either.[77] In such situations, only common Article 3 applies – providing very basic protection – or possibly Additional Protocol II to the four Geneva Conventions. The US delegation, up to this point very conscious of the importance of separating the regimes, argued for an overlap with regard to non-international armed conflicts. Influenced by the tragic events in Somalia and the capture of its helicopter pilot, Michael Durant, the US delegation regarded this overlapping 'as a necessary exception to that general rule'.[78]

75 See Bourloyannis-Vrailas, Christiane, M. *The Convention on the Safety of United Nations and Associated Personnel*, International and Comparative Law Quarterly, Vol. 44, 1995, p. 568. She finds this inconsistency unclear and sees no obvious reasons why this situation should be protected by the Convention.

76 Report of the Ad Hoc Committee on the Elaboration of an International Convention dealing with the Safety and Security of United Nations and Associated Personnel, UN Doc. A/49/22, 23 August 1994, Annex 1, para. 13.

77 This is based on the assumption that the involvement of UN forces may not *per se* make an armed conflict an international one.

78 Lepper *op. cit.* note 67, p. 395.

Although the purpose of the drafting is commendable, the result may have repercussions on the respect for international humanitarian law. An opponent involved in a non-international armed conflict would have no reason to capture UN soldiers as prisoners of war, since according to the Convention the opponent would be obliged to release them as soon as they have identified themselves. In a worst-case scenario this would in fact diminish the protection of UN soldiers – why bother to capture UN military personnel if you must immediately release them and might in the long run undermine respect for international humanitarian law.

One of the authors who is critical of the Convention has argued, *de lege ferenda*, that UN forces should have privileges and immunities also when engaged as combatants in an armed conflict. Since they act on behalf of the international community, they should also have special protection in these situations. He therefore suggests that the 'combatant exception' in the Convention should be deleted. He finds it absurd that, while a single attack against the UN and associated personnel is a criminal act, a massive attack leading to an armed response of such intensity that the UN forces will be engaged as combatants, would be lawful. He concludes that the Convention 'encourages would-be attackers to ensure the legality of their actions by increasing the size and intensity of their attack.'[79] These views are criticized by Professor Greenwood for several reasons.[80] First, it is generally accepted within the international community that the principle of equal application is a core feature of the laws of armed conflict. Second, this principle also has pragmatic implications. Everyone who is constrained by law should also benefit from the law. He concludes that to 'depart from that principle would be likely to undermine respect for the law'.[81] Against the background of the NATO air strikes in Bosnia-Herzegovina, Green-

79 Sharp, Walter Gary Sr., *Jus Paciarii, Emergent Legal Paradigms for U. N. Peace Operations in the 21st Century,* Paciarii International, ICC Stafford, Virginia 1999, p. 86. He further claims that, if applying 'existing international law to United Nations forces without any modification allows members of organised armed forces to simply declare a state of hostilities, thereby invoking the application of the law of international armed conflict', p. 86.

80 Greenwood, Christopher, *Protection of Peacekeepers: The Legal Regime,* Duke Journal of Comparative & International Law, Vol. 7:185, 1996, p. 204.

81 *Ibid.*, pp. 204, 205.

wood finds, however, that a higher degree of force may be tolerated in situations involving UN forces before the law of armed conflict becomes applicable.

2.4 The Secretary-General's Bulletin, Observance by United Nations forces of international humanitarian law

As regards the question of the applicability of international humanitarian law to UN forces as such, the position of the UN is that it is not ready to assume all the responsibilities that follow from the Geneva Conventions. The UN is ready to assume the limited obligation to respect the 'principles and spirit' of the four Geneva Conventions and their Additional Protocols, as well as the Convention on the Protection of Cultural Property.[82] There was, until 1999, no authoritative statement on the meaning of the 'principles and spirit' of international humanitarian law. Following a request from the UN's Special Committee for Peacekeeping Operations to develop a code of conduct for UN forces, the Secretary-General issued the 'Secretary-General's Bulletin on Observance by United Nations forces of international humanitarian law' on 6 August 1999.[83] According to the International Committee of the Red Cross

82 See Model Agreement between the United Nations and Member States contributing personnel and equipment to United Nations peace-keeping operations, UN Doc A/46/185, 23 May 1991 para. 28. No such commitment is stated in the UN Model SOFA. However, SOFAs have been concluded after the issuance of the Model Agreement that contain this obligation, *e.g.* the Agreement on the Status of the United Nations Assistance Mission for Rwanda (UNAMIR), 1993, UNTS No. 30482 and the Agreement on the Status of the United Nations Mission in Haiti (UNMIH), 1995, UNTS No. 31695.

83 The Secretary-General's Bulletin, Observance by United Nations forces of international humanitarian law, UN Doc. ST/SGB/1999/13, 6 August 1999. Being part of the UN's internal law, the Bulletin applies to the members of the UN staff. Section 4 of the Bulletin stipulates, however, that troop-contributing nations will retain exclusive jurisdiction for violations of international humanitarian law and violations of the Bulletin's provisions will, therefore, not be handled in the usual administrative processes available to UN staff. See Zwanenburg, Marten, *The Secretary-General's Bulletin on Observance by United Nations forces of international humanitarian law?: A Pyrrhic Victory?,* Revue de Droit Militaire de la Guerre, R250 39, nos. 1–4, 2000, pp. 4, 5.

(ICRC), the most important feature of the Bulletin is the explicit application of some of the core rules of humanitarian law to UN personnel.[84]

The Bulletin applies only to forces under UN command and control, which would seem to exclude operations led by regional organisations but authorized on a mandate from the UN Security Council. It sets out 'fundamental principles and rules of international humanitarian law applicable to United Nations forces conducting operations under United Nations command and control'. Obviously, the reference to 'principles and *rules*' indicates a greater commitment than 'principles and spirit'. These apply to:

> United Nations forces when in situations of armed conflict they are actively engaged therein as combatants, to the extent and for the duration of their engagement. They are accordingly applicable in enforcement actions, or in peacekeeping operations when the use of force is permitted in self-defence.[85]

The first sentence relates to the behaviour of the forces. The military forces must be 'actively engaged therein as combatants'. Compared to the scope of application of the Geneva Conventions, the criterion of being actively engaged in the conflict seems to require something more on the part of the military personnel. The second sentence appears to mean that the Bulletin is applicable when UN forces are actively engaged in an armed conflict notwithstanding the *mandate* of the operation.[86]

According to Section 5.4 of the Bulletin, UN forces 'shall take all necessary precautions to protect the civilian population, individual

84 Comprehensive review of the whole question of peace-keeping operations in all its aspects, United Nations, General Assembly, 54th session, Fourth Committee, item 90 of the agenda, Statement by the International Committee of the Red Cross (ICRC), 1999.

85 The Secretary-General's Bulletin, Observance by United Nations forces of international humanitarian law, UN Doc. ST/SGB/1999/13, 6 August 1999, preamble and Section 1.1.

86 The ambiguous wording could also be interpreted to mean that the Bulletin also applies to every peacekeeping and enforcement operation irrespective of the requirement in the first sentence. That would, however, lead to strange consequences for the status of UN forces if they were to apply international humanitarian law in traditional peacekeeping operations. See Bothe, Michael and Dörschel, Thomas, *The UN Peacekeeping Experience,* Fleck, Dieter (Ed.) The Handbook on The Law of Visiting Forces, Oxford University Press, Oxford 2001, p. 501.

civilians and civilian objects against the dangers resulting from military operations'. However, in the same section it says: '[m]ilitary installations and equipment of peacekeeping operations, as such, shall not be considered military objectives'. Given the reciprocal character of international humanitarian law, respect for these norms might be undermined if military forces under United Nations command, which are actively engaged as combatants in armed conflict, regarded their military installations as protected objects. The reason for including this provision is supposedly on account of the 'peaceful nature' of such equipment when used in peacekeeping operations.[87] It appears, however, to be a reflection of the difficult position of the United Nations: on the one hand willing to comply with the principles and rules of international humanitarian law, and on the other, reluctant to give up its protected status.

2.5 Conclusions

The trend appears to be towards a more consolidated approach to legal protection of UN peace operation personnel in general. Evidence of this trend is the ongoing deliberations on the scope of legal protection of the 1994 Convention on the Safety of United Nations and Associated Personnel and the Security Council's practice of demanding the conclusion of a SOFA for new operations. In the UN operation in East Timor, relevant criminal law provisions of the 1994 Convention have been included in the applicable SOFA between the UN and East Timor.[88] The Special Committee of Peacekeeping Operations has requested the UN Secretariat to consider the status of civilian police personnel and whether they could be accorded privileges and immunities as military contingents in the case of operations in which they have executive tasks.[89] Further evi-

87 Shraga, Daphna, UN Peacekeeping Operations: *Applicability of International Humanitarian Law and Responsibility for Operations-Related Damage*, American Journal of International Law, Vol. 94, 2000, p. 408, footnote 6.

88 Agreement between the Democratic Republic of East Timor and the United Nations concerning the status of the United Nations Mission of Support in East Timor, 2002, on file with the author.

89 UN Doc A/57/767, 28 March 2003, para. 112.

dence of this trend is the fact that attacks against UN personnel are in themselves considered war crimes.[90] However, the connection with international humanitarian law for military personnel in UN operations still seems to be an ambiguous area. With regard to the scope of application of the Convention, a national court will, in the last analysis, have to decide whether a UN soldier was illegally detained or held as a legitimate prisoner of war, or if the killing of a UN soldier was an act punishable by law or a legitimate act of war. A local court may be called upon to take such decisions, irrespective of the applicability of the Convention. The ambiguous formulation of the Convention's scope of application may, however, have complicated the matter. In this respect the Secretary-General's Bulletin is evidence of the ambivalent position of the UN with regard to the applicability of international humanitarian law to UN forces.

References

Books & articles

Amerasinghe, Chittaranjan F., *Principles of the Institutional Law of International Organizations,* Cambridge University Press, Cambridge, 1996.

Bloom, Evan T., *Protecting Peacekeepers: The Convention on the Safety of United Nations and Associated Personnel,* American Journal of International Law, Vol. 89, 1995, pp. 621–631.

Bothe Michael and Dörschel, Thomas, *The UN Peacekeeping Experience,* Fleck, Dieter (Ed.), The Handbook on The Law of Visiting Forces, Oxford University Press, Oxford, 2001.

Bourloyannis – Vrailas, Chistiane, M. *The Convention on the Safety of United Nations and Associated Personnel,* International and Comparative Law Quarterly, Vol. 44, 1995, pp. 560–590.

Bowett, Derek. W., *United Nations Forces,* Stevens & Sons under the auspices of the Davies Memorial Institute London, 1964.

Greenwood, Christopher, *Historical Development and Legal Basis,* Fleck, Dieter (Ed.), The Handbook of Humanitarian Law in Armed Conflicts, Oxford University Press, Oxford, 1995.

Greenwood, Christopher, *Protection of Peacekeepers: The Legal Regime,* Duke Journal of Comparative & International Law, Vol. 7:185, 1996, pp. 185–207.

90 See the ICC Statute, Article 8 (b) (iii) and (e) (iii).

Jakobsen, Peter Viggo, *The Emerging Consensus on Grey Area Peace Operations Doctrine: Will It Last and Enhance Operational Effectiveness?*, International Peacekeeping, Vol. 7, No. 3, 2000, pp. 36–56.
Kirsch, Philippe, *Convention on the Safety of United Nations and Associated Personnel*, Canadian Council on International Law, Proceedings, 1994, pp. 182–187.
Lauterpacht, Hersch, *The Limits of the Operation of the Law of War*, British Yearbook of International Law, Vol. 30, 1953, pp. 206–243.
Lazareff, Serge, *Status of Military Forces Under Current International Law*, A.W. Sijthoff, Leyden, 1971.
Lepper, Steven J., *The Legal Status of Military Personnel in United Nations Peace Operations: One Delegate's Analysis*, Houston Journal of International Law, Vol. 18:359, 1996, pp. 359–464.
Sharp, Walter Gary Sr., *Jus Paciarii, Emergent Legal Paradigms for U. N. Peace Operations in the 21st Century*, Paciarii International, ICC Stafford, Virginia, 1999.
Shraga, Daphna, *The Applicability of International Humanitarian Law to United Nations Operations*, Emanuelli, Claude (Ed.), Les casques bleus: policiers ou combatants?, Wilson & Lafleur Hée, Montreal, 1997.
Shraga, Daphna, *UN Peacekeeping Operations: Applicability of International Humanitarian Law and Responsibility for Operations-Related Damage*, American Journal of International Law, Vol. 94, 2000, pp. 406–412.
Siekmann, Robert C.R., *Basic Documents on United Nations and Related Peacekeeping Forces*, 2nd ed., Martinus Nijhoff, Dordrecht, 1989.
The Blue Helmets. A Review of United Nations Peace-keeping, 3rd ed., United Nations Department of Public Information, New York, 1996.
Zwanenburg, Marten, *The Secretary-General's Bulletin on Observance by United Nations Forces of International Humanitarian Law: A Pyrrhic Victory?*, Revue de Droit Militaire de la Guerre, R250 39, nos. 1–4, 2001, pp. 1–15.

Treaties

Agreement between the Parties to the North Atlantic Treaty Regarding the Status of Their Forces, 19 June, 1951, UNTS, Vol. 199, p. 67.
Agreement on the Status of the United Nations Assistance Mission for Rwanda (UNAMIR), 5 November 1993, UNTS No. 30482.
Agreement on the Status of the United Nations Mission in Haiti (UNMIH) 15 March 1995, UNTS No. 31695.
Convention on the Privileges and Immunities of the UN (1946), UNTS, Vol. 1, p. 15.
Convention on the Prevention and Punishment of Crimes against Internationally Protected Persons including Diplomatic Agents (1973) UNTS, Vol. 1035, p. 167.
Convention on the Safety of United Nations and Associated Personnel, ILM, 9 December 1994, Vol. 34, p. 482 (1995).

Exchange of letters constituting an agreement between the United Nations and the Government of Egypt concerning the status of the United Nations Emergency Force in Egypt, New York, 8 February 1957, UNTS, Vol. 260, p. 61.

General Framework Agreement for Peace in Bosnia-Herzegovina, ILM, 1996, Vol. 35, p. 75, www.nato.int/ifor/gfa/gfa-frm.htm, (17 June 2003).

Geneva Convention for the Amelioration of the Condition of the Wounded and Sick in Armed Forces in the Field of August 12, 1949, UNTS, Vol. 75, p. 31 (Geneva Convention I).

Geneva Convention for the Amelioration of the Condition of Wounded, Sick and Shipwrecked Members of Armed Forces at Sea of August 12, 1949, UNTS, Vol. 75, p. 85 (Geneva Convention II).

Geneva Convention Relative to the Protection of Civilian Persons in Time of War of August 12, 1949, UNTS, Vol. 75, p. 355 (Geneva Convention IV).

Geneva Convention Relative to the Treatment of Prisoners of War of August 12, 1949, UNTS Vol. 75, p. 135 (Geneva Convention III).

Military Technical Agreement between the International Security Force (KFOR) and the Governments of the Federal Republic of Yugoslavia and the Republic of Serbia, ILM, 1999, Vol. 38, p. 1217, www.nato.int/kfor/kfor/documents/mta.htm (17 June 2003).

Military Technical Agreement between the International Security Assistance Force (ISAF) and the Interim Administration of Afghanistan, ILM, 2002, Vol. p. 1032, www.operations.mod.uk/isafmta.pdf (13 May 2003).

Protocol Additional to the Geneva Conventions of 12 August 1949, and Relating to the Protection of Victims of International Armed Conflicts, UNTS, Vol. 1125, p. 3 (Additional Protocol I).

Protocol Additional to the Geneva Conventions of 12 August 1949, and Relating to the Protection of Victims of Non-International Armed Conflicts, UNTS, Vol. 1125, p. 609 (Additional Protocol II).

Rome Statute of the International Criminal Court, 1998, www.un.org/law/icc/statute/romefra.htm (17 June 2003).

Cases

Prosecutor v. *Tadic*, Case IT-94-1-AR72, Appeal on Jurisdiction, 2 October, 1995.

UN documents

Resolutions

GA/RES 998 (ES-I) of 4 November 1956.

A/RES/49/59 (1995).

S/RES/84 , 7 July 1950

S/RES/186, 4 March 1964

S/RES/340, 25 October 1973
S/RES/350, 31 May 1974
S/RES/425, 19 March 1978
S/RES/626, 20 December 1988
S/RES/678, 29 November 1990
S/RES/693, 20 May 1991
S/RES/696, 30 May 1991
S/RES/743, 21 February 1992
S/RES/745, 28 February 1992
S/RES/751, 24 April 1992
S/RES/794, 3 December 1992
S/RES/797, 16 December 1992
S/RES/814, 26 March 1993
S/RES/867, 23 September 1993
S/RES/872, 5 October 1993
S/RES/929, 22 June 1994
S/RES/944, 29 September 1994
S/RES/976, 8 February 1995
S/RES/1031, 15 December 1995
S/RES/1244, 10 June 1999
S/RES/1264, 15 September 1999
S/RES/1270, 22 October 1999
S/RES/1320, 15 September 2000
S/RES/1386, 20 December 2001
S/RES/1410, 17 May 2002

Reports

Comprehensive Review of the Whole Question of Peacekeeping Operations in All Their Aspects. Report of the Special Committee on Peacekeeping Operations, UN Doc. A/57/767, 28 March 2003.

Model Agreement between the United Nations and Member States Contributing Personnel and Equipment to United Nations Peace-Keeping Operations. Report of the Secretary-General, UN Doc. A/46/185 23, May 1991.

Model Status-of-Forces Agreement for Peace-Keeping Operations. Report of the Secretary-General, UN Doc. A/45/594, 9 October 1990.

Report of the Ad Hoc Committee on the Elaboration of an International Convention Dealing with the Safety and Security of United Nations and Associated Personnel, UN Doc. A/49/22, 23 August 1994.

Report of the Ad Hoc Committee on the Scope of Legal Protection Under the Convention on the Safety of United Nations and Associated Personnel, UN Doc. A/57/52, 10 April 2002.

Report of the Ad Hoc Committee on the Scope of Legal Protection Under the Convention on the Safety of United Nations and Associated Personnel, UN Doc. A/58/52, 11 April 2003.

Report of the Ad Hoc Committee on the Work Carried out During the Period from 28 March to 8 April 1994, UN Doc. A/AC.242/2, 13 April 1994.

Report of the Panel on United Nations Peace Operations, UN Doc. A/55/305 – S/2000/809, 21 August 2000, www.un.org/peace/reports/peace_operations/docs/part2.htm (19 June 2003).

Report of the Secretary-General on the Implementation of Security Council Resolution 340 (1973), UN Doc. S/11052/Rev. 1, 27 October 1973.

Report of the Secretary-General on the Implementation of Security Council Resolution 425 (1978), UN Doc. S/12611, 19 March 1978.

Report of the Secretary-General: Summary Study of the Experiences Derived from the Establishment and Operation of the Force, UN Doc. A/3943, 9 October 1958.

Report pursuant to Paragraph 5 of the Security Council Resolution 837 (1993) on the Investigation into the 5 June 1993 Attack on United Nations Forces in Somalia Conducted on Behalf of the Secretary-General, UN Doc. S/26351, 24 August 1993. Annex, Report of an Investigation into the 5 June 1993 Attack on United Nations Forces in Somalia by Professor Tom Farer.

Scope of Legal Protection under the Convention on the Safety of United Nations and Associated Personnel. Report of the Secretary-General, UN Doc. A/55/637, 21 November 2000.

Miscellaneous

Comprehensive Review of the Whole Question of Peace-Keeping Operations in All Their Aspects, United Nations, General Assembly, 54th session, Fourth Committee, item 90 of the agenda, Statement by the International Committee of the Red Cross (ICRC), (1999).

General Assembly Official Records 49th, Session 84th, Meeting 9 December 1994, UN Doc. A/49/PV.84.

Secretary-General's Bulletin, Observance by United Nations Forces of International Humanitarian Law, UN Doc. ST/SGB/1999/13, 6 August 1999.

Summary Record of the Sixth Committee UN Doc. A/C.6/48/SR.29, 15 November 1993.

Supplement to An Agenda for Peace: Position Paper of the Secretary-General on the Occasion of the Fiftieth Anniversary of the United Nations, UN Doc. A/50/60-S/1995/1, 3 January 1995.

UNMIK/REG/2000/47 On the Status, Privileges and Immunities of KFOR and UNMIK and their Personnel in Kosovo, www.unmikonline.org/regulations/2000/reg47-00.htm (13 May 2003).

3 The Security Council as a Law Enforcer and Legislator

Katinka Svanberg-Torpman

3.1 Introduction

This chapter will deal with the questions of whether the Security Council has used its broad enforcement powers under Chapter VII of the UN Charter in the service of public international law and whether the Council has assumed a role as a quasi-judicial body imposing quasi-judicial decisions to enforce and create norms in public international law. The term 'quasi-judicial decisions' applies when the Council makes decisions of a judicial nature that would usually be made by a judicial organ.[1] This raises the question whether the Council is on the verge of becoming a world police and a legislator?

The end of the cold war finally allowed the Security Council to work as intended, without being paralysed by vetoes from two rival superpowers. Global optimism spread with hope for the dawn of 'a new world order based on a far-reaching respect for public international law and an effective collective security system', to quote former US president George Bush, Sr.[2] This change brought a surge of decisions from the Security Council that was unprecedented in its

1 Quasi-judicial decisions are acts by a non-judicial body which entail legal consequences, *e.g.*, void and nullity decisions and declarations, declarations of illegality, the setting up of international tribunals, decisions to extradite suspected criminals, legislative acts, etc., Gowlland-Debbas, Vera, '*The Security Council Enforcement Action and Issues of State Responsibility*', International and Comparative Law Quarterly, Vol. 43, 1994, pp. 55–98; Higgins, Rosalyn, *International Law and the Avoidance, Containment and Resolution of Disputes,* Académie de Droit International, Recoeil des Cours, Part V, Vol. 230, Martinus Nijhoff Publishers, Dordrecht, 1991, p. 337; Danelius, Fredrik, *FN:s säkerhetsråds befogenheter – något om utvecklingen i teori och praktik*, Tandlös eller tiger – sju uppsatser om FN, Ed. Ahlin, Per, Juristförlaget, Stockholm, 1995, p. 71.

2 Cited in US Government Bill 1991/92, p. 14. The global optimism in the early 1990s is also mirrored in the summit meeting of the Security Council S/PV 3046 (31 January 1992) and in the former UN Secretary General's *Agenda for Peace*, Boutros-Ghali, Boutros, United Nations, New York, 1992.

history. Among the new demands on the Security Council is the capacity to respond under Chapter VII to today's challenges and to adopt a modern understanding of what can constitute a threat to the peace at the turn of the new millennium. During this period of increased activity the Council appears to have widened its interpretation of the mandate given to it under Chapter VII, particularly when it comes to its perception of a threat to the peace according to Article 39. Traditional threats of an international character have given way to intervention in internal situations, sometimes even without any armed conflict at all. What is striking is that the Security Council seems to have acted to uphold and implement norms of public international law, thereby using a finding of a threat to the peace under Article 39 to sanction, and even contribute to the creation of, certain fundamental norms in public international law, *i.e.*: core principles of humanitarian law and human rights, a right to internal self-determination (in the form of a right for a racial majority to representative government, or a right to democracy) and the prohibition of international terrorism.[3] The legislative acts of the Council come in two forms: the Council can contribute to forming customary international law by its decisions to enforce an emerging norm, or it can make use of its powers under Chapter VII to adopt resolutions with a direct normative content that come close to legislation.[4] The Council has used sanctions of a quasi-judicial nature to uphold and implement the four norms listed above, which indicates that the Council increasingly aspires to a judicial role.

This Chapter will first discuss the mandate of the Security Council under Chapter VII: A case study is then used to categorize conflicts according to the norm which is found to have (predomi-

3 This Chapter focuses on these norms, but there are other norms also that the Council could be argued to have intervened to uphold, such as prohibition of possession of weapons of mass destruction, or the implementation in good faith of a state's international legal obligations, such as *bona fide* implementation of international agreements or Security Council Resolutions. The Council has moreover intervened to remedy situations of anarchy and chaos in disintegrating states.

4 'The power to legislate, that is, to bring into being abstract rules, not addressed just to a particular state', Szazs, Paul, *Centralized and Decentralized Law Enforcement: The Security Council and the General Assembly Acting under Chapters VII and VIII*, Delbrück, J. (Ed.), Allocation of Law Enforcement Authority in the International System, Duncker & Homblot, Berlin, 1995, pp.17–38, at p. 33.

nantly) triggered Council action under Article 39. Finally, conclusions are drawn from the case study to verify if and in what ways the Security Council can truly be said to have acted as a law enforcer and legislator in public international law.

3.2 The competence of the Security Council under Chapter VII of the UN Charter

3.2.1 Article 39

The primary purpose of the United Nations is to maintain international peace and security by means of collective enforcement measures in accordance with Article 1(1) of the UN Charter.[5] It is the Security Council that has primary responsibility for maintaining international peace and security see Article 24(1). Chapter VII of the Charter is the heart of the collective security system because it provides the Security Council with mandate and enforcement powers that enable it to shoulder its responsibility by imposing binding decisions on states, which they are bound to comply with according to Article 25. The means at its disposal are recommendations, provisional measures, and mandatory non-military and military sanctions.[6]

Article 39 contains the key provisions of Chapter VII that enable the Council to apply enforcemant measures. Article 39 reads:

> The Security Council shall determine the existence of any threat to the peace, breach of the peace, or act of aggression and shall make recommendations, or decide what measures shall be taken in accordance with Articles 41 and 42, to maintain or restore international peace and security.

The first part of Article 39 is a prerequisite for action and the interpretation of the terms 'threat to the peace, breach of the peace, or act of aggression' is crucial. Should 'peace' in the first part of the

5 Frowein, Jochen Abr., *Chapter VII. Action with Respect to Threats to the Peace, Breaches of the Peace, and Acts of Aggression*, The Charter of the United Nations – A Commentary, Simma, Bruno (Ed.), 1st ed. Oxford University Press, Oxford, 1994, pp. 605, 608.

6 See Articles 39, 40, 41 and 42. For a discussion on sanctions, see the contributions by Cameron and Stenhammar.

paragraph be taken to mean international peace? The most convincing interpretation is found in the last part of Article 39 where reference is made to "maintain or restore *international peace*" (emph. added), which is the primary responsibility of the Security Council as well as the main purpose of the United Nations.[7] This limits application to situations which at least involve a threat to international peace.[8] Some authors suggest that this interpretation is incorrect or outdated. They argue that the drafters of the Charter disputed the issue[9] and even if they intended to link 'peace' to international peace, an organic, dynamic interpretation of the Charter indicates that international law 'has expanded its field of application and encroaches more and more on the domain of formerly exclusive jurisdiction'.[10] It should be noted that such an interpretation could also be reconciled with the traditional interpretation, since the phrase 'a threat to the peace' does not, on the face of it, need to be international. The framers of the Charter considered that domestic situations, such as large-scale violations of

7 Such an interpretation would be in accordance with Article 31 (1) of the Vienna Convention on the Law of Treaties from 1969. It reads: 'A treaty shall be interpreted in good faith in accordance with the ordinary meaning to be given to the terms of the treaty in their context and in the light of its object and purpose'. This provision is considered to be a codification of customary international law, see *e.g.*, the following rulings by the ICJ: *Case Concerning Oil Platforms*, (Prel. Obj.) ICJ Reports 1996, para. 23 at p. 812, *Case Concerning the Arbitral Award of 13 July 1989* (Judgement), ICJ Reports 1991, para. 48 at p. 20–21, *Case Concerning the Gabcíkovo-Nagymaros Project* (Judgement), 25 Sep. 1997, ICJ Reports, para. 46, Advisory Opinion on the *Legality of the Use by a State of Nuclear Weapons in Armed Conflict*, 8 July 1996, ICJ Reports, 1996, para. 19. Even the history of the drafting of the Charter supports such an interpretation, as the Charter was drafted at a time when international law was primary concerned with international conflicts (leaving matters which are essentially within the domestic jurisdiction of states outside the scope of the Organisation in accordance with Article 2(7) first sentence.

8 See *e.g.*, Frowein, Jochen Abr., *supra* note 5, at pp. 608–609, Kelsen, Hans, *The Law of the United Nations*, 1st ed., Stevens & Sons, London, 1950, p. 731, Schweigman, David, *The Authority of the Security Council under Chapter VII of the UN Charter*, Kluwer Law International, Boston, 2001, pp. 33–36.

9 Goodrich, Leland M./Hambro, Edward/Simons, Anne Patricia, *Charter of the United Nations*, 3rd ed., Columbia University Press, New York, 1969, p. 296.

10 Österdahl, Inger, *Threat to the Peace – The Interpretation by the Security Council of Article 39 of the UN Charter*, Iustus förlag, Uppsala, 1998, p. 20. As the case study will show, the Security Council has frequently during the 1990s referred to 'a threat to peace and security in the region', omitting the word 'international'. On the other hand, the reference to 'the region' indicates that the Council still maintains a nexus to international consequences even if it is often just cosmetic.

human rights, could threaten international peace and security.[11] When dealing with Chapter VII the framers found that too precise definitions might 'endanger the Council's free discretion', and proposals to insert a definition of what constitutes an aggression were rejected on the same ground.[12] The finding that a threat to the peace does not need to be international in character is widely supported in the doctrine, where it is stated that the Security Council has a very wide margin of appreciation in making determinations under Chapter VII and has almost unfettered discretion.[13] The practice of the Security Council underpins such conclusions, as do findings by international courts.[14]

11 The subcommittee held that 'assuring or protecting such fundamental rights [human rights] is primarily the concern of each State. If, however, such rights and freedoms were grievously outraged so as to create conditions which threaten peace ... then they cease to be the sole concern of each state'. Travaux préparatoires to the UN Charter, UNCIO Doc., Vol. 6, (1945), p. 705.

12 'Too rigid a distinction between threats to the peace and attempts against the peace, or acts of aggression, an enumeration in which one finds countless nuances, appeared to the Committee to be in contradiction with the previous decision to avoid a definition of aggression and with the general spirit of the Charter' *Verbatim Minutes of the First Meeting of Commission III,* UNCIO Doc., Vol. 11, 1945, pp. 12, 18.

13 To quote Kelsen, Hans, *supra* note 8, p. 731: 'In contradiction to other provisions of the Charter, Article 39 does not speak of a threat to, or breach of international peace. Hence the peace referred to in this passage need not necessarily be a status in the relation between states. However, the purpose of the enforcement action to be taken under Article 39 is determined as the maintenance of restoration of international peace and security ... The Security Council may very well decide that a situation which has not the character of a conflict between two states is a threat to the international peace and take enforcement action against a state or a group of people involved in this situation, though the state is not in conflict with another state and the group has not the character of a state.' Moreover, he finds that Article 39 could be used to implement human rights if the Council considers them a threat to the peace, *ibid.*, p. 730. See also Schweigman, David, *supra* note 8, p. 186, Frowein, Jochen Abr., *supra* note 8, p. 609, Shaw, M. N., *The Security Council and the International Court of Justice: Judicial Drift and Judicial Function,* in The International Court of Justice: Its Future Role after Fifty Years, (Eds.) Muller, A. S., Raic, D., Thuránszky, J. M, The Hague, Martinus Nijhoff, 1997, p. 226, Zemanek, Karl, *Is the Security Council the Sole Judge of its Own Legality?* Liber Amicorum Mohammed Bedjaoui, (Eds.), Yakpo, Emile, Boumedra, Tahar, 1999 p. 635, Schachter, Oscar, *United Nations Law,* American Journal of International law (AJIL) Vol. 88, 1994, pp. 1–23, p. 12, Malanczuk, Peter, *Akehurst's A Modern Introduction to International Law,* 7th revised ed., Routledge, London 1997 p. 426, Higgins, Rosalyn, *Problems & Process – International Law and How We Use It,* Clarendon, Oxford 1994 p. 255, Reisman, Michael W., *Peacemaking,* Yale Journal of International Law Vol. 18, 1993, pp. 415–423, p. 418, Kooijmans, P. H., *The Enlargement of the Concept 'Threat to the Peace',* The Development of the Role of the Security Council, (Ed.), Dupuy, René-Jean, Martinus Nijhoff, Dordrecht, 1993 pp. 111–121.

14 See *infra* in 3.2.2 and the case study in section 3.5.

3.2.2 The legal limits of decisions by the Security Council under Article 24 of the UN Charter

The competence of the Security Council to make decisions under Article 39 is not completely unlimited. The minimum requirements are laid down in Article 24(2):

> In discharging these duties [primary responsibility for the maintenance of international peace and security, see Article 24(1)] the Security Council shall act in accordance with the Purposes and Principles of the United Nations. The specific powers granted to the Security Council for the discharge of these duties are laid down in Chapters VI, VII, VIII and XII.

The first sentence refers to Chapter I of the Charter where the purposes (Article 1) and principles (Article 2) of the Organisation are set out. Article 1 reads:

> 1. To maintain international peace and security, and to that end: to take effective collective measures for the prevention and removal of threats to the peace, and for the suppression of acts of aggression or other breaches of the peace, and to bring about by peaceful means, and in conformity with the principles of justice and international law, adjustment or settlement of international disputes or situations which might lead to a breach of the peace;
>
> 2. To develop friendly relations among nations based on respect for the principles of equal rights and self-determination of peoples, and to take other appropriate measures to strengthen universal peace;
>
> 3. To achieve international co-operation in solving international problems of an economic, social, cultural, or human character, and in promoting and encouraging respect for human rights and fundamental freedoms for all without distinction as to race, sex, language, or religion; and
>
> 4. To be a centre for harmonizing actions of nations in the attainment of these common ends.

A strong case can be made that maintaining international peace is the *primary purpose* of the Organisation and that it takes priority over the other purposes.[15] This was evident from the discussion of a

15 'The order of listing, together with the content of subsequent Charter provisions, gives support to the view that the maintenance of peace and security is the primary purpose of the organisation and takes priority over other purposes', writes Goodrich/Hambro/Simons, *supra* note 9, see also, Wolfrum, Rüdiger, *Chapter I. Purposes and Principles,* The Charter of the United Nations – A Commentary, Simma, Bruno (Ed.), 1st ed. Oxford University Press, Oxford 1994, pp. 49, 51.

amendment proposed by the Egyptian delegate, *i.e.* to insert 'in conformity with the principles of justice and international law' in the first part of paragraph 1.[16] The amendment was rejected because it was said that when the Security Council acts in its enforcement capacity it should not be bound by such restrictions.[17] The American delegate compared the Council's actions under Chapter VII with that of a policeman while its actions under Chapter VI were more of the function of a jury.[18] The question of whether the Council is subjected to international law is continuously debated among scholars.[19] However, an organic interpretation indicates that in today's world, where human rights and self-determination are gaining ground at the expense of the more traditional norm of state sovereignty, these other purposes of the UN cannot be ignored.[20] The case study will show how these norms have indeed influenced the decisions of the Council and it will be argued that the Council has intervened under Chapter VII to enforce them.

The principles of the United Nations are found in Article 2. Only some of the principles are relevant to the conduct of the Organiza-

16 Verbatim Minutes of first meeting of Commission I, UNCIO Doc. 1006, Vol. 6, 1945, pp. 1, 12.

17 'The inference ... that in the maintenance of peace and security as a supreme purpose, and in the stopping of aggression, we do not have to consider the principles of law and justice', as the Panamanian delegate remarked. *Ibid.,* p. 29.

18 The American delegate stated: 'It is our view that the people of the world wish to establish a Security Council, that is, a policeman who will say, when anyone starts to fight, "stop fighting". Period.... That is the function of a policeman, and it must be just that short and abrupt; that is, unless at that place we add any more, then we would say "Stop fighting unless you claim international law is on your side". That would lead to a weakening and a confusion in our interpretation.' *Ibid.,* p. 18.

19 Kelsen, Hans, *The Law of the United Nations. A Critical Analysis of its Fundamental Problems,* London, Stevens and Sons, 1951, p. 294, answers the question in the negative, while Bedjaoui, Mohammed, *infra* note 32, p. 31, answers it in the affirmative, as do Dupuy, Pierre-Marie, *Droit international public,* Paris, Dalloz-Sirey, Coll. Précis Dalloz, 1992, p. 127 and Reinisch, August, *Developing Human Rights and Humanitarian Law Accountability of the Security Council for the Imposition of Sanctions,* AJIL, Vol. 95, 2001, pp. 851–872, 857.

20 The framers themselves emphasized that the Charter was intended to be a 'world constitution', capable of adapting to a changing society, UNCIO Doc. 4783, Vol. 6, 1945, p. 15. The British delegate stated: 'We do not want to lay down rules which may, in the future, be a trap for the innocent and a sign-post for the guilty', *Ibid.,* p. 26. For a constitutional interpretation of the UN Charter, see the contribution by Sevastik in Chapter 1. See also Bedjaoui, Mohammed, *infra* note 32.

tion, and again only some of them are applicable when defining the legal limits of the work of the Security Council. Article 2(1) concerns the principle of sovereign equality of UN members. This probably refers to equality before the law, but this is not the same thing as equality under the UN Charter, as the members states have accepted inequality in the form of the special rights of the permanent members.[21] Article 2(7) bars the organisation from intervening in matters that are essentially within the domestic jurisdiction of states, although it explicitly exempts Security Council enforcement measures under Chapter VII.[22] In the doctrine it has been convincingly argued that the principle of good faith in Article 2(2) extends to the organs of the UN. [23] The Council could be accused of abuse of rights, if its determinations under Article 39 were made *mala fide*. Since the concept of good faith is of a rather general and broad nature and the Council has a very wide margin of appreciation in its determinations under Article 39, it might be hard to ascertain if the Council has in fact acted *mala fide*.

Article 24(2) refers to the *specific powers* granted to the Security Council in certain Chapters of the Charter, among them Chapter VII. This raises the question whether the powers of the Council are thus limited or if the Council is vested with implied powers that

21 Bring, Ove, *FN-stadgan och världspolitiken*, 4th ed. Norstedts juridik, Stockholm 2002, pp. 41–42.

22 Article 2(7) reads: 'Nothing contained in the present Charter shall authorize the United Nations to intervene in matters which are essentially within the domestic jurisdiction of any state or shall require the Members to submit such matters to the settlement under the present Charter, but this principle shall not prejudice the application of enforcement measures under Chapter VII.'

23 Article 2(2) provides that: 'all members, in order to ensure to all of them the rights and benefits resulting from membership, shall fulfil in good faith the obligations assumed by them in accordance with the present Charter.' This principle is considered to apply also to the organs of the UN, see Müller, Jörgen P., *Article 2(2),* in The Charter of the United Nations – A Commentary, (Ed.) Simma, Bruno, *supra* note 5, pp. 89–97, Schweigman, David, *supra* note 8, pp. 173–178. Brownlie argues that the Council is ultimately bound by the principle of good faith and cannot act arbitrarily for collateral and independent purposes, such as the overthrow of a government or the partition of a state, Brownlie, Ian, *The Decisions of Political Organs of the United Nations and the Rule of Law,* Essays in Honour of Wang Tieya, (Ed.) Mc Donald, R. St. J, Clarendon Press, Oxford, 1994, pp. 91–102, at p. 96.

would fill any gaps in the provision of powers for the Council?[24] Most evidence points in this direction and it was confirmed in the *Certain Expenses Case:*

> [The United Nations'] purposes are broad indeed, but neither they nor the powers conferred to effectuate them are unlimited ... when the Organisation takes action which warrants the assertion that it was appropriate for the fulfilment of one of these stated purposes of the United Nations, the presumption is that such action is not *ultra vires*.[25]

Each organ of the UN is vested with the power to judge its own competence, *i.e. compétence de la compétence* and no organ is competent to interpret the Charter in a manner that is binding on other organs.[26] The *Lockerbie* case before the ICJ in the 1990s put the spotlight on the intriguing question whether the decisions of the Council, a political body, can be judicially reviewed.[27] Schweigman argues tentatively that the Court can exercise a power of incidental judicial review.[28] However, in its provisional measures the ICJ found that a Security Council Resolution with binding force under Chapter VII has pre-eminence and bars the Court from further review.[29]

24 Frowein observes: 'A restriction of the powers of the SC based on Article 24(2) second sentence, which in the eyes of the authors of the Charter would appear "legalistic", would run counter to the purpose of the UN Charter. Article 24(1) therefore serves as the basis for comprehensive powers for the SC, going beyond the enumeration in para. 2, and thereby fulfils the function of closing any gaps in the provision of powers for the SC.' Frowein, Jochen Abr., *supra* note 5, p. 403.

25 The case deals with the issue whether the expenses of the first peace-keeping missions (UNEF in Suez and the Congo operation) were expenses of the organisation within the meaning of the Charter, *Certain Expenses of the United Nations*, Adv. Op., ICJ Rep. (1962) at p. 167.

26 Müller, *supra* note 23, cites the *travaux préparatoires*, UNCIO Doc. XIII, Committee IV/2, 1945, pp. 633 and 653, in support of his view that this was the intention of the framers and emphasing that the UN has adhered to this principle in practice, Bedjaoui, Mohammed, *infra* note 32, pp. 9–12.

27 *Questions of Interpretation and Application of the 1971 Montreal Convention Arising from the Aerial Incident at Lockerbie* (prov. Measures), Libya v. US, Order of April 1992, *Case Concerning Interpretation and Application of the 1971 Montreal Convention Arising from the Aerial Incident at Lockerbie*, (Preliminary objections), Libya v. US, 27 Feb. 1998. The proceedings concerned the objection by Libya to the Security Council sanctions imposed on Libya with a view to the extradition of suspected terrorists, see *infra* in the case study in 3.5.4.

28 Schweigman, David, *supra* note 8, p. 305.

29 'The Court has at present no choice but to accept the pre-eminence of that resolution', as pointed out by judge Oda. Declaration by Judge Oda, *Lockerbie (Prov. Measures) supra* note 27, at 129. This was the majority view of the Court.

3.2.3 Jus Cogens

Is the Security Council bound by norms of *jus cogens*?[30] The *jus cogens* norms are at the top of the normative hierarchy in international law and override other obligations. The concept of *jus cogens* is somewhat disputed, but there seems to be general agreement on a few norms that without doubt belong to this category, *i.e.* the outlawing of aggression, genocide, slavery and piracy. But also the following norms are widely accepted as qualifying: self-determination, the prohibition of racial discrimination (apartheid) and other fundamental human rights as well as core principles of humanitarian law.[31] A good case can be made that the United Nations, and thus the Security Council, is bound by *jus cogens* norms notwithstanding Article 103.[32] In particular, the prohibition of genocide, the right of self-determination, and fundamental human rights are protected as they are also found in the United Nations' purposes in Article 1. The question whether the Council under Chapter VII can act in contradiction of *jus cogens* was dealt with in the *Bosnia* case, where the Council was accused by Bosnia-Herzegovina of contributing to acts of genocide by maintaining a weapons embargo against the territory of Former Yugoslavia.[33] But what if there is a collision between Council action under Chapter VII and norms of *jus cogens*?

30 A definition of *jus cogens* is found in Article 53 of the 1969 Vienna Convention on the Law of Treaties, which stipulates that a treaty is void if it conflicts with a norm of *jus cogens*. Svanberg, Katinka, *En Introduktion till traktaträtten*, 3rd ed. Jure, Stockholm, 2003, pp. 34–35.

31 Hannikainen, Lauri, *Peremptory Norms (Jus Cogens)*, International Law, Lakimiesliiton kustannus, 1988. *E.g.*, Malanczuk, Peter, *supra* note 13, p. 58, Reinisch, August, *Developing Human Rights and Humanitarian Law Accountability of the Security Council for the Imposition of Sanctions*, AJIL, Vol. 95, 2001, pp. 851–872, 860, suggests that the Council is bound by core provisions of humanitarian law and basic human rights because of those peremptory status.

32 Article 103 in the UN Charter gives pre-eminence to the Charter obligations if they conflict with states' other treaty obligations. Doehring, Karl, *Unlawful Resolutions of the Security Council and Their Legal Consequences*, 1 Max Planck Yearbook of United Nations Law, Martinus Nijhoff Publishers, Dordrecht, 1997, vol. 1, pp. 91–109, at pp. 101–108, Bedjaoui, Mohammed, *The New World Order and the Security Council: Testing the Legality of its Acts*, Martinus Nijhoff Publishers, Dordrecht, 1994, p. 34.

33 The ICJ sidestepped the issue when it rejected the Bosnian request with regard to self-defence, *Case Concerning Application of the Convention on the Prevention and Punishment of the Crime of Genocide* (Prov. Measures) ICJ Reports 1993. Judge Lauterpacht found in his separate opinion, *ibid.*, at p. 440, that Article 103 cannot extend to *jus cogens*.

Could this not be seen as a question of conflicting norms of *jus cogens*. An example would be when the Council uses force to combat aggression and this conflicts with fundamental human rights or humanitarian law. Which norm takes precedence over the other? The question is interesting, but the best way seems to avoid such a collision altogether and to demand that the Council must respect all *jus cogens* norms in its actions under Chapter VII.[34]

3.2.4 Conclusions as to the competence of the Security Council to make decisions under Chapter VII

The Security Council is vested with very broad powers under the Charter for the maintenance of international peace and security. This was intended by the framers of the Charter, as the ultimate goal of the organisation is the maintenance of peace, which is clear from both the preamble and Article 1(1). The specific enforcement powers accorded to the Council to maintain and restore international peace and security are set out in Chapter VII. Under Article 39 the Security Council has the widest possible margin of appreciation to determine if there exists a threat to the peace, a breach of the peace or an act of aggression, and what measures should be taken accordingly. The Security Council does not have unlimited discretion in its decisions; it must act in accordance with the purposes and principles of the UN. However, this does not restrict the Council very much. Since the maintenance of international peace appears to be the overriding purpose of Article 1, this supports the interpretation that it overrides others in cases of conflict. And when it comes to the principles in Article 2, only the principle of sovereign equality, and possibly that of good faith, apply. The principle of good faith implies that the Council cannot act arbitrarily, that is, completely outside its mandate of maintaining international peace

34 Bedjaoui, Mohammed, *supra* note 32, pp. 34–35, finds that the Security Council cannot brush aside such fundamental norms as humanitarian law, human rights and the right to self-determination and 'ignore such cardinal prescriptions'. On the other hand, Lysén maintains that the Council has to respect human rights, because they belong to the purposes of the Charter, *except* in cases of emergency, and then only if the Council acts in accordance with the principles of necessity and proportionality, Lysén, Göran, *Targeted UN Sanctions: On the issue of legal sources and their application and also some procedural matters*, www.jur.uu.se/sii/articles, 29 January 2003.

and security, and it may be argued that the Council is subject to general international law.[35] But the Council is the judge of its own competence and it is vested with implied powers that bridge any gaps in the interpretation of its powers under the Charter. The Charter does not provide for judicial review of the decisions of the political UN organs. In cases of incidental judicial review the ICJ has been very reluctant to pronounce on the issue of whether the Council has overstepped its competence. Even if Article 103 provides that Charter obligations prevail over other international agreements, the Council is probably bound by norms of *jus cogens*, especially those that are embodied in the purposes in Article 1 of the UN Charter.

3.3 The authority of the Security Council to act as an enforcer and legislator of international law

It has been established that the Security Council has almost unfettered discretion to define what constitutes a threat to the peace under Chapter VII. The rest of this article will consider whether the Security Council has assumed a role as a quasi-judicial body, using its extraordinary powers under the Charter to sanction norms of international law.[36] Such a role for the Council may seem problematic at first sight, as the Council is a political organ and was never intended to be a court of law.[37] But the wide discretion afforded to the Council supports the thesis that the Council can use its broad powers in the service of international law.[38] From the foregoing it is

35 Bedjaoui, Mohammed, *supra* note 32, pp. 29–36.

36 The case study indicates that the Security Council has used "a threat to the peace" in a rather fictitious way to be able to apply Chapter VII to enforce or contribute to the creation of central norms in public international law. The norms in question are fundamental human rights, core principles of humanitarian law, self-determination, the outlawing of international terrorism and non-proliferation of weapons of mass destruction.

37 See *supra* at note 27.

38 Bedjaoui finds that the idea that the Council creates and imposes its own law raises two questions: whether such an interpretation is correct and whether the Council is bound by international law in its law-making mode. He answers both in affirmative. Bedjaoui, Mohammed, *supra* note 32, p. 1.

evident that there is nothing to prevent the Council taking positive action to uphold and implement fundamental principles set forth in the UN Charter. On the contrary, such action is in line with Article 24(2), as this would be action for and not against the purposes and principles of the Charter. But the question remains whether the Council can act only in a quasi-judicial capacity if there actually exists a threat to the peace, or whether it can construe such a threat to be able to intervene? Scholars' opinions are divided on the issue. According to at least one view, which may be called *formalistic*, a "real" threat to the peace must exist for the Council to be able to intervene for the other purposes of the UN,[39] while others point to the wide and almost unfettered discretion of the Council to make such determinations.[40] One way to bridge this gap appears in Hannikainen's observation that:

> According to the current interpretation of the Charter, those obligations which are most essential for the maintenance of international peace and security are the *same* as the basic obligations arising from the main purposes of Article 1 of the Charter; the prohibition of acts of aggression, the respect for self-determination of peoples and the (elementary) respect for human rights without distinction, especially without distinction of race.[41]

The question is highlighted in situations where the Council has intervened even though there is no armed conflict, such as in cases of internal self-determination, cases of international terrorism or gross

39 The first view is presented among others by Téson, Fernando R., *Collective Humanitarian Intervention*, Michigan Journal of International Law, Vol. 17, 1995 p. 323; Doehring, Karl, *Unlawful Resolutions of the Security Council and Their Legal Consequences*, Max Planck Yearbook of United Nations Law, Vol. 1, Martinus Nijhoff Publishers, Dordrecht, 1997, pp. 91–109; Fielding, Lois, E., *Taking the Next Step in the Development of New Human Rights: The Emerging Right of Humanitarian Assistance to Restore Democracy*, Duke Journal of Comparative & International Law, Vol. 5 (1994/95) at p. 374; Jama, Leila, Lisa, *Humanitarian Intervention: An Examination of the United Nation's Role in Modern Age of Civil Conflicts,* Florida Journal of International Law, Vol. XII No. 3, 2000, p. 521, 528.

40 Kelsen, Hans, *The Law of the United Nations, supra* note 8, p. 736, Bedjaoui, Mohammed, *supra* note 32, 1994, pp. 52–53, 128. Gowlland-Debbas, Vera, 1994, *supra* note 1, pp. 55–98, at p. 63.

41 Hannikainen, Lauri, *supra* note 31 at p. 284.

violations of human rights. Criticism has been levelled at what is regarded as a too formalistic interpretation, according to which the Council must *construe* a threat to the peace to be able to intervene under Chapter VII, instead of being directly authorized to intervene against violations of basic norms of international law that threaten people's lives.[42] But does it really matter if the Council calls a situation a threat to the peace to be able to intervene in order to uphold fundamental norms of international law when they are in conformity with the purposes and principles of the UN Charter?[43] And if one is inclined toward the more formalistic view – that the Council would act *ultra vires* if it intervened under Chapter VII without the existence of a real threat to international peace – it could always be argued that most situations contain international implications that raise the possibility of such a threat, however remote.[44] Hannikainen appears to put his finger on the most appropriate interpretation, *i.e.* that the Security Council's aim of maintaining international peace and security converges with the other fundamental purposes found in the Charter.

Gowlland-Debbas stresses: 'In its findings which relate to violations of international law, the Council has, moreover, singled out the kinds of breaches which touch on the very fabric of the international legal

42 Supporters of humanitarian intervention often propose that the Security Council has a right and a duty to intervene to alleviate human suffering on a grand scale and stop violations of basic human rights, Téson, Fernando R., *supra* note 39, p. 332, Fielding, Lois E., *supra* note 39, p. 374, Jama, Lisa Leila, *supra* note 39, p. 521, 528. It may be noted that these authors include intervention for internal self-determination in the concept of human rights, as self-determination has a dual character and is also a human right, as is the prohibition of apartheid, while terrorist acts can be regarded as crimes against humanity, Cassese, Antonio, *Terrorism is Also Disrupting Some Crucial Legal Categories of International Law,* European Journal of International Law (EJIL), Discussion Forum on internet, Ejil.org/forum-WTC/ny-cassese.html, (25 October 2001).

43 It could be argued that such an extended role for the Council might endanger international peace as the Council might play a role that runs counter to that envisaged in the Charter, making war and not peace under the guise of justice, see *e.g.,* Mahmoudi, Said, *International Use of Force: Quo Vadis,* Juridisk tidskrift, No. 2, 2003/2004, pp. 341–358, p. 346.

44 It could for example be argued that gross violations of human rights or the unseating of a democratic government would give rise to instability in the region or that refugee flows will affect neighbouring countries, or that democracies are prone to be more peaceful, etc.

order.'[45] It may be argued that the Security Council actually realizes the framers' idea of a policeman acting to uphold and implement fundamental norms of international law. But the Council has advanced its position in assuming the role of a court of law, and even of a legislator contributing to the creation of international legal norms.[46] One argument in favour of such a role for the Council is the fact that the UN Charter is a world constitution, which is supposed to have a vigorous life of its own, laying down provisions that are flexible enough to adapt to a changing world, as the framers of the Charter intended. The wide powers given to the Security Council should be seen in this light, paving the way for an interpretation under which the Security Council extends its role from the executive to the legislative branch. This is explained by the extraordinary powers assigned to the Council in the Organization, since it is the only organ with military enforcement capacity. As long as the Security Council acts within the very broad mandate given to it by the Charter under Chapter VII, it has the authority to take 'any and all actions that it considers useful and suitable for dealing with the situation and its consequences ... even [of] primary judicial nature', according to Szazs,[47] and Koskenniemi concludes that 'what the Council says *is* the law'.[48]

45 She refers to the obligations in the former Draft Articles on State Responsibility, Article 19, *Yearbook of the International Law Commission,* 1980, Vol. II, Part 2, concerning acts constituting international crimes, *i.e.,* the prohibition of aggression, the right of self-determination of peoples, such as the prohibiting of colonial domination, or a serious breach on a widespread scale of an obligation of essential importance for safeguarding the human being, such as the prohibition of slavery, genocide and apartheid. Gowlland-Debbas, Vera, 1994, *supra* note 1, p. 64. The Draft Articles on international crimes have recently been abandoned.

46 Bedjaoui, Mohammed, *supra* note 32, p. 29 writes: 'The Council can create law through its practice, but only "United Nations law" applicable within the sphere of activity of the Organization. Only States can create customary rules or practices contrary to the Charter...'

47 Szazs, Paul, 1995, *supra* note 4, p. 33

48 Koskenniemi, Martti, *The Police in the Temple Order, Justice and the UN: A Dialectical View,* Vol. 6, EJIL, 1995, pp. 325–248, at p. 327. John, Foster Dulles wrote that the Security Council is a law unto itself, in *War or Peace,* Macmillan, New York, 1950, pp. 194–195.

3.4 Interpretation of Security Council Resolutions

Not much has been written about the interpretation of Security Council resolutions. The ICJ has ruled on the method for interpretating Security Council resolutions in its advisory opinion on Namibia:

> The language of a resolution of the Security Council should be carefully analysed before conclusion can be made as to its binding effect. In view of the nature of the powers under Article 25, the question whether they have been in fact exercised is to be determined in each case, having regard to the terms of the resolution to be interpreted, the discussion leading to it, the Charter provisions invoked and, in general, all circumstances that might assist in determining the legal consequences of the resolution of the Security Council.[49]

In the doctrine it is also suggested that reference be made, by way of analogy to Article 31, concerning the interpretation of treaties in the Vienna Convention on the Law of Treaties from 1969. Article 31(1) prescribes that a treaty shall be interpreted in good faith in accordance with the ordinary meaning to be given to the words in light of its object and purpose.[50] But such an analogy should be made with some care as a resolution differs from a treaty in that a treaty is an international agreement negotiated between equal parties, while a mandatory Security Council resolution is a binding decision that UN members are obliged to carry out. The text of a Security Council resolution is often the result of a compromise based on political considerations, and for that reason it is often drafted in cautious, watered-down language. Thus, the intention of the drafters plays a more prominent role as a source for establishing the real meaning of the text than in treaties, in which case there is only limited recourse

49 *Advisory Opinion on Legal Consequences for States of the Continued Presence of South Africa in Namibia (South West Africa) Notwithstanding Security Council Resolution 276 (1970)*, Advisory Opinion, ICJ Reports 1971.

50 On methods of interpretation see Wood, Michael C., *The Interpretation of Security Council Resolutions*, Max Planck Yearbook of United Nations Law, Vol. 2, 1998 p. 73, 75–76, Frowein, Jochen Abr., *Unilateral Interpretation of Security Council Resolutions – a Threat to Collective Security in Liber Amicorum Günter Jaenicke – Zum 85 Geburtstag*, 1998, p. 97, Thirlway, H., *The Law and Procedure of the International Court of Justice 1960–1989*, British Year Book of Internationel Law, Vol. 67, 1996, p. 29, McHugo, John, *Resolution 242: A Legal Reappraisal of the Right-Wing Israeli Interpretation of the Withdrawal Phrase with Reference to the Conflict between Israel and the Palestinians*, ICQL Vol. 51, 2002 pp. 851–882.

to the preparatory works, as they are supplementary means of interpretation according to the Vienna Convention on the Law of Treaties Article 32. Since not all material concerning the drafting of Security Council resolutions is publicly available, "the Official Records of the Security Council debate should be the evidence of the most immediate context for all practical purposes", writes McHugo.[51]

3.5 Case study

3.5.1 Introduction

A word of caution is appropriate when trying to discern 'precedents' in the case study that is intended to underpin the theory of this Chapter. A fundamental difference between a political, as opposed to a judicial organ is that the former is under no legal obligation to follow its precedents, nor is it under any obligation to act or treat like cases alike,[52] and it does not need to explain the precise legal basis for its decisions.[53] But bearing this in mind, the case study indicates that when the Security Council was able to take action under Chapter VII, it did so fairly consistently to enforce and support the creation of fundamental norms in international law.[54] The case study is organized with reference to the norms of international law that the Council has most frequently cited when imposing sanctions under Chapter VII.[55] Three different headings are used, self-determination, humanitarian intervention and international terror-

51 McHugo, John, *supra* note 50.

52 Damrosch, Lori Fisler, *Enforcing Restraint,* New York, Council on Foreign Relations, 1993, p. 302, has argued that the Council should treat like cases alike.

53 Szazs, Paul, 1995, *supra* note 4, p. 33. The Council does not need to adhere to a doctrine of *stare decisis*.

54 Speaking with Gowlland-Debbas: 'The Council, with certain exceptions, has not limited itself to a finding of fact, but has linked its determinations under Article 39 to determinations of the alleged existence of a violation of international law, either explicitly, or by parallel determinations in the same resolution, for the purpose of extending to such breaches the special regime of Chapter VII.' Gowlland-Debbas, Vera, 1994, *supra* note 1, p. 63.

55 It is not exhaustive, because other norms and principles in international law could also be said to have been enforced by the Council, see *supra* note 3. The possession of weapons of mass destruction is discussed briefly in note 180.

ism, and some cases fit under several headings. The case study deals almost exclusively with internal conflicts and situations where there is no armed conflict.

3.5.2 Self-determination

3.5.2.1 Internal self-determination [56]

Southern Rhodesia (1965–1979). In 1965 the racist white minority regime declared independence for the British colony, but this was denied by Great Britain. On the contrary, this started a spur of activity by the Security Council, which adopted an unprecedented number of Resolutions under Chapter VII, imposing harsh non-military sanctions against the seceding colony, which were in force for 15 years.[57] The Council's intervention in a purely internal situation, even without the occurrence of a civil war, was a new development. The Council explicitly referred to Articles 39 and 41 as grounds for action under Chapter VII in defence of the right of peoples to internal self-determination, including the majority's right to a represent-

56 Internal self-determination means the right of peoples to assert the genuine expression of their will through free choice of government, Cassese, Antonio, *Self-Determination of Peoples – A Legal Reappraisal,* 1995. To begin with, internal self-determination was interpreted to be limited to a right of a majority to have a government representing the whole people without distinction as to race, creed or colour. In *The Declaration on Principles of International Law concerning Friendly Relations and Co-operation among States in Accordance with the Charter of the United Nations* (GA Res. 2625 (XXV) 24 Oct. 1970, hereinafter the FRD) the GA stated that *Principles of International Law concerning Friendly Relations* and their content are considered to be customary international law. For the first time ever a principle of internal self-determination is formulated in its so called savings clause in para. 7: 'Nothing in the foregoing paragraphs shall be construed as authorizing or encouraging any action which would dismember or impair, totally or in part, the territorial integrity or political unity of sovereign and independent States conducting themselves in compliance with the principle of equal rights and self-determination of peoples as described above and thus possessed of a government representing the whole people belonging to the territory without distinction as to race, creed or colour.' During the 1990s there is evidence that the right to internal self-determination has evolved to include the right to democracy, Franck, Thomas, *The Emerging Right to Democratic Governance,* AJIL, Vol. 86, 1992, pp. 46–91.

57 These were the most severe non-military sanctions ever imposed by the Council until Iraq (SC. Res. 660–687, 1990–91) and included a comprehensive economic embargo, as well as diplomatic, cultural- and travel sanctions.

ative government without distinction as to race, creed and colour.[58] This conclusion is supported by the number and variety of quasi-judicial sanctions against the colonial regime and its acts, including non-recognition, nullification and voiding declarations. Resolution 216 (1965) set the tone for continuous condemnation, underscored by non-recognition: '*Decides* to call upon all states not to recognize this illegal racist minority regime in Southern Rhodesia and to refrain from rendering any assistance to this illegal regime.'[59]

South Africa (1977–1994). The apartheid policy of the South-African white minority regime became a target of Security Council sanctions in 1977. As in Southern Rhodesia, it was an internal situation without internal armed conflict. The Council imposed a weapons embargo explicitly under Chapter VII in Resolution 418: '*Determines,* having regard to the policies and acts of the South African Government, that the acquisition of arms ... constitutes a threat to the maintenance of international peace and security.'[60] In subsequent resolutions the Council widened the weapons embargo, but not under Chapter VII. It also took quasi-judicial measures against South Africa in the form of non-recognition and the declarations of the invalidity of the South African elections and Constitution (Resolution 554 (1984)) and non-recognition of the bantustans[61] (Reso-

58 McDougal, Myres S., Reisman, Michael W., *Rhodesia and the United Nations: The Lawfulness of International Concern,* AJIL, Vol. 62, 1968, pp. 1, 11–17, Emerson, Rupert, *Self-Determination,* AJIL, Vol. 65, 1971, pp. 459, 466; Gowlland-Debbas, Vera, *Collective Responses to Illegal Acts in International Law – United Nations Action in the Question of Southern Rhodesia,* Martinus Nijhoff Publishers, Dordrecht (1990); Gowlland-Debbas, (1994) *supra* note 1, p. 58, Hannikainen, Lauri, *supra* note 31, p. 415, Cassese, Antonio, 1995, *supra* note 56, p. 131.

59 Although the first resolutions did not invoke Chapter VII, the coming resolutions explicitly cited Chapter VII and repeated this finding: 'Determines that the present situation constitutes a threat to international peace and security' and called the regime 'illegal'. Quasi-judicial sanctions under Chapter VII were imposed in SC Res. 277 (1970), 288 (1970), 423 (1978): 'Determines that the illegal regime is a serious threat to international peace and security'. See also SC Res. 445 (1979), 448 (1979). SC Res. 217 (1965) does not appear to fall under Chapter VII, but like Resolution 216 declares its non-recognition of the regime and the nullity of its decision and acts.

60 Resolution 417 (1977) openly referred to 'the right of self-determination by all the people of South Africa as a whole, irrespective of race, colour and creed', thus an indirect reference to FRD para. 7, cited *supra* in note 56.

61 Bantustans were so called 'homelands', *i.e.* enclaves where the black population were forced to live.

lution 402, 403, 417 (1977)), although those resolutions were not adopted under Chapter VII. It is a moot point whether the sanctions against the South-African apartheid regime were motivated on human rights grounds since self-determination has a two fold character, being also a human right.[62] Thus the denial of the right to internal self-determination for a racial majority could at the same time be regarded as human rights violations, infringing the prohibition against apartheid and racial discrimination.[63] However, some of the resolutions openly refer to self-determination in the words of paragraph 7 of the Friendly Relations Declaration (FRD),[64] for instance Resolution 417: 'Affirming the right to the exercise of self-determination by all peoples of South Africa as a whole, irespectible of race, colour and creed.'[65]

Haiti (1991–1994). The democratically elected president Aristide was ousted by a military junta coup in 1991, the same year he won a landslide victory with over 90% in the UN-supervised elections. Tens of thousands of Haitians fled to the US, which led the Organisation of American States (OAS) to ask the Security Council to impose an embargo on Haiti.[66] Resolution 841 (1992) imposed an oil and weapons embargo under Chapter VII. As no internal armed conflict was raging in Haiti, the Council was very cautious in stating the ground for action under Chapter VII. In the paragraphs leading up to its finding of a threat to the peace under Chapter VII, it cited a number of reasons, *i.e.* the mass displacement of population, and it deplored the fact that the legitimate president had not been reinstated, it also cited the request for measures by the legiti-

62 See article 1 of the International Covenant on Civil and Political Rights, 16 Dec. 1966, article 1 in International Covenant on Economic, Social and Cultural Rights, 16 Dec. 1966.

63 International Convention on the Suppression and Punishment of the Crime of Apartheid, 1974, International Convention on the Elimination of All Forms of Racial Discrimination, 1963.

64 See *Declaration on Principles of International Law Concerning Friendly Relations and Co-operation among States in Accordance with the Charter of the United Nations* (FRD), 24 Oct. 1970, 'the so called savings clause' in para. 7, cited *supra* in note 56.

65 SC Res. 417 (1977), se also SC Res. 556 (1984), 581 (1986). None of these refers to Chapter VII.

66 OAS members are committed to democracy through the adoption of the Santiago Commitment to Democracy and Renewal of the Inter-American System, OAS/GAOR, 21st Reg. Sess. OEA/Ser.P/AG.doc. 2734/91 (4 June 1991).

mate Haitian representatives, as well as the OAS and the GA: '*Determining* that, in these unique and exceptional circumstances, the continuation of this situation threatens international peace and security in the region.' However, in Resolution 917 (1994) the Council is more explicit: 'Reaffirming that the goal of the international community remains the restoration of democracy in Haiti and the prompt return of the legitimately elected president.'[67] The resolution imposed a comprehensive economic embargo. When the military junta did not implement an agreement signed by them to successively step down, the Council authorized the use of force in Resolution 940 (1994):

> *Acting* under Chapter VII of the Charter, *authorizes* Member States to form a multinational force under unified command and control and, in this framework, to use all necessary means to facilitate the departure from Haiti of the military leadership, consistent with the Governors Island Agreement, the prompt return of the legitimately elected president and the restoration of the legitimate authorities of the government in Haiti [...]

The U.S. had offered to lead a military intervention, but the junta stepped down from power as the multinational forces were en route to Haiti.

Haiti's political situation became volatile after flawed elections in May 2000, which were boycotted by the opposition. Civil unrest broke out in Haiti as discontent with president Aristide spread. The situation became chaotic in the beginning of 2004 when rebels demanded Aristide's resignation and marched on Port au Prince. Anarchy erupted and looting took place. Aristide at first refused to resign, claiming that he was Haiti's democratically elected president with a right to serve the rest of his term, but finally he went into exile.[68] The Security Council dealt with the new Haitian crisis in Resolution 1529 (2004), which establishes a multinational interim force with a mandate to uphold security in Haiti.[69] The resolution

67 The mention of a threat to the peace was still accompanied by the same reference to exceptional and unique circumstances.

68 He has accused the US of forcing him to step down from power.

69 Op. para. 2 a): "To contribute to a secure and stable environment in the Haitian capital and elsewhere in the country, as appropriate and as circumstances permit, in order to support Haitian President Alexandre's request for international assistance to support the constitutional political process under way in Haiti."

was adopted under Chapter VII but it is cautiously worded as it links the threat to the peace to the risk of refugees:

> Determining that the situation in Haiti constitutes a threat to international peace and security, and to stability in the Caribbean especially through the potential outflow of people to other States in the sub region,
>
> Acting under Chapter VII of the Charter of the United Nations.

However, in the light of both the preamble and operative paragraph 1, it is the political crisis and its humanitarian consequences that implicitly made the Council intervene.[70] The preamble takes note of Aristide's resignation and the swearing in of the new president in accordance with the constitution. This turn of events makes an interesting twist, as Aristide's reinstallation in 1994 is viewed as a precedent of Security Council action under Chapter VII for democracy. It could be argued that Resolution 1529 is a continuation of the Council's commitment to democracy in Haiti, with a demand for full application of democracy and the non-acceptance of a new coup d'état. On the other hand, it could be seen as the opposite, because Aristide claims that the US forced him to flee.

Sierra Leone (1997–2002). After a civil war a democratically elected government came to power in 1996, but was ousted by a military coup in 1997 in cooperation with the RUF, a violent guerrilla movement. The Security Council adopted Resolution 1132 (1997), with an oil and weapons embargo as well as travel restrictions for the junta. A blockade was authorized to be implemented by the regional peace-keeping force ECOMOG of ECOWAS (Regional Organisation of West African States), which had cooperated with the ousted government and deployed troops in Sierra Leone. The resolution explicitly referred to Chapter VII and VIII. Paragraph 1

70 The "situation" referred to is described in the preamble: "Deeply concerned by the deterioration of the political, security and humanitarian situation in Haiti and deploring the loss of life that has already occurred, Expressing its utmost concern at the continuing violence in Haiti, as well as the potential for a rapid deterioration of the humanitarian situation in that country, and its destabilizing effect on the region". Op. para. 1 reads: "1. Calls on Member States to support the constitutional succession and political process now under way in Haiti and the promotion of a peaceful and lasting solution to the current crisis."

reads: 'Demands that the junta take immediate steps to relinquish power in Sierra Leone and make way for restoration of the democratically elected Government and a return to constitutional order.' Subsequently an agreement was reached with the junta that would reinstate the democratically elected government.[71] But when the junta failed to implement the agreement, troops from ECOMOG overran the junta and reinstalled the democratic government. The Security Council partly terminated the sanctions in Resolution 1156 (1998), welcoming the return of the democratically elected president in what seems to be an *ex post facto* recognition. The sanctions were then transferred to the junta and the RUF, which continued to operate in Sierra Leone.[72] The conflict ended following democratic elections in 2002.

Burundi, Angola, Central African Republic (CAR), Liberia. In these cases too democracy has been part of the reason for Security Council actions under Chapter VII, besides other causes, such as humanitarian concerns, which have also been a determining factor for intervention. In Burundi an attempted coup against the Convention of Government was condemned under Chapter VII in Resolution 1072 (1996). In Angola the refusal of the rebel movement UNITA to implement the results of the democratic elections in 1992 triggered non-military sanctions against UNITA.[73]

In 1993 the CAR had a democratic government, but the country was shaken by military mutinies in 1996 and the president asked for regional help. A commitment was made to hold new democratic elections, and a regional force, MISAB, arrived to monitor implementation. MISAB was authorized to use limited force under Chapter VII.[74]

71 The Conakry Agreement, UN Doc. S/1997/958 (1997). The agreement was negotiated between the junta and ECOWAS and was recognized by the democratically elected president Kabbah.

72 SC Res. 1171 (1998), an embargo on diamonds originating in the area under the control of the RUF was imposed in SC Res. 1306 (2000).

73 SC Res. 804 (1993), 851 (1993) leading up to the sanctions in Resolution 864 (1993).

74 SC Res. 1125 (1997).

Resolution 788 (1992) imposed a weapons embargo against Liberia because of the civil war and the non-implementation of the peace accord, which 'hindered the creation of conditions conductive to the holding of free and fair elections'.[75]

3.5.2.2 External self-determination [76]

3.5.2.2.1 Denials of secession[77]

Congo (1960–1964). When the rich province of Katanga wanted secession from the newly independent Congo (a former Belge colony), the Security Council deployed peace-keeping troops to restore law and order, thus denying secession.[78] The mandate was somewhat unclear, but in fact the peace-keepers took enforcement action in Katanga.[79]

Bosnia (1992–1995). A civil war between three ethnic groups, Bosnian Muslims, Serbs and Croats, ravaged the newly independent Republic of Bosnia. The Bosnian Serbs and Croats obviously wanted their own enclaves that would presumably merge with Croatia and Serbia. Those claims were opposed by the Council, which applied the principle of *uti possidetis*[80] to the internal borders of Bosnia.[81] The Dayton Agreement, which ended the conflict, stipulated that Bosnia must remain one state.[82]

75 Paras. 7 and 8 referred to Chapter VIII of the Charter.

76 External self-determination means the right of a people to rule themselves without outside interference and may give rise to claims of secession.

77 External self-determination in the form of secession has only been accepted for colonial peoples under alien domination and occupied territories, but secession as a right for other peoples and minorities has constantly been denied in public international law. This denial has been upheld by the Security Council, which has actively intervened under Chapter VII to combat secession.

78 There was also outside interference as Belgian troops supported Katanga, which was ruled by the former white colonists.

79 SC Res. 143 (1960), 145 (1960), 146 (1960), 161 (1961), 169 (1961) completely rejecting the claim that Katanga was 'a sovereign independent nation'.

80 Meaning the inviolability of borders.

81 No territorial gains were accepted, see *e.g.* SC Res. 819 (1993) cited *infra* at note 92. The safe havens of certain Muslim areas protected by UNPROFOR can also be seen in this light, SC Res. 824 (1993), 998 (1995) as well as condemning the method of ethnic cleansing, see *infra* on humanitarian intervention in 3.5.3.

82 The Dayton Agreement, reprinted in ILM, Vol. 35, 1996, p. 75, provides that Bosnia should continue its legal existence as a state with its present internationally recognized borders and with a democratic government shared by the three ethnic groups, see Art. 1.

3.5.2.2.2 Recognition of secession

East Timor is an example in public international law of the principle that an occupied territory has a right to independence.[83] East Timor was occupied by Indonesia at the moment it became independent from Portugal in 1975, and the Security Council and the General Assembly condemned the Indonesian occupation.[84] Finally, in 1999, an agreement was reached between Indonesia and Portugal under the auspices of the UN, which led to a popular consultation for the East Timorese people on the choice of independence or autonomy, organized by the UN. The outcome of the consultation was independence which triggered a wave of violence, provoked by the Indonesian militia that led to mass displacement of the East Timor population. The Security Council then determined that the continuing situation in East Timor constituted a threat to peace and security (thus omitting the word international in the context of peace) and authorized a multinational force to restore law and order in Resolution 1264 (1999). The Council established a UN transitional administration in East Timor explicitly under Chapter VII: 'empowered to exercise all legislative and executive authority including the administration of justice and to maintain law and order.'[85] In practice East Timor came under UN trusteeship.[86] East Timor became independent after UN-organized and supervised elections in 2002.

83 The Colonial peoples right to self-determination led to an evolution of the norm of self-determination in customary international law to include a related group, *i.e.*, an occupied people. The Colonial Declaration, cited *infra* in note 174, para. 1, as well as FRD, cited *supra* in note 56, in para. 2b, condemns that a people is under "alien subjugation, domination and explotation". That an occupied people has a distinct right to self-determination was confirmed in the Definition of Aggression, GA Res. 3314 (XXIX), 1974, in art. 7 and in Protocol Additional to the Geneva Conventions of 12 August 1949, Relating to the Protection of Victims of International Armed Conflicts, (Protocol I), 1977, art. 1(4).

84 SC Res. 384 (1975), 389 (1976).

85 SC Res. 1272 (1999). Humanitarian concerns contributed to Council intervention under Chapter VII.

86 Ruffert, Matthias, *The Administration of Kosovo and East-Timor by the International Community*, International and Comparative Law Quarterly, Vol. 50, 2001, pp. 613–630.

Former Yugoslavia (FRY) (1991–95). The disintegration of the Federal Republic of Yugoslavia resulted in a war between the republics, when Croatia and Slovenia in 1991, and Bosnia in 1992, wanted independence, which Serbia as the dominating authority denied. The dissolution brought about the recognition of the republics as independent states in 1992, thus internationalizing the conflict.[87] One important factor that contributed to the premature recognition was the severe atrocities that were committed during the civil war.[88] In the vast number of resolutions on former Yugoslavia the Council took a cautious approach, never explicitly referring to a breach of the peace, but to a threat to the peace. After the recognition of the former republics, the Council imposed severe non-military sanctions on FRY,[89] demanded respect for international borders[90] and demanded the cessation of all interference from outside Bosnia-Herzegovina.[91] In the resolutions on Bosnia the Council applied the principle of 'no fruit of aggression' to the territory of Bosnia between the fighting ethnic groups, reaffirming that 'any taking or acquisition of territory by the threat or use of force ... is unlawful and unacceptable'.[92] In the conflicts in former Yugoslavia the Council took limited enforcement action[93] and applied innovative non-military sanctions, such as the establishment of the Criminal Tribunal for former Yugoslavia (ICTY),[94] although the crime of aggression is not part of the Tribunal's statute. In the case of former

87 The Council recognized Croatia in SC Res. 753 (1992), Slovenia in SC Res. 754 (1992) and Bosnia in SC Res. 755 (1992).

88 Bring, Ove, FN-stadgan och världspolitiken, *supra* note 21. On the atrocities committed, see *infra* in 3.5.3.

89 After the internationalization the weapons embargo against the territory of Yugoslavia in Resolution 713 (1991) was reimposed in Resolution 727 (1992) on 'all areas' that have been part of Yugoslavia. Resolutions 757 (1992), 787 (1992), 820 (1993) established an extensive embargo against the Federal Republic of Yugoslavia for its interference, 'including by units of the Yugoslav People's Army' in Bosnia. They comprehend severe non-military sanctions, as well as economic, diplomatic, scientific and cultural measures.

90 SC Res. 752 (1992) demanded that units from the Yugoslav and Croatian army must cease all outside interference in Bosnia-Herzegovina, SC Res. 994 (1995) sets out: '*Affirming* its commitment to search for an overall negotiated settlement of the conflicts in the former Yugoslavia ensuring the sovereignty and territorial integrity of all States there within their internationally recognized borders and *stressing* the importance it attaches thereof,' see also *e.g.* SC Res. 988 (1995).

91 SC Res. 757 (1992), SC Res. 752 (1992).

92 Se *e.g.* SC Res. 819 (1993).

Yugoslavia the Security Council appears for the first time to have recognized an extension of the principle of external self-determination to the breaking up of federations.[95]

3.5.2.2.3 Autonomy

Kosovo (1998–2003). Kosovo is a region in Serbia with a 90 per cent Albanian population, where severe repression of the Kosovar-Albanians was maintained since 1989.[96] During 1998 and early 1999 a liberation movement (UCK) rose in Kosovo and clashes with the Serbian police escalated. The Serbian government sent in the army to take control, which resulted in a mass exodus of Kosovar-Albanians seeking refuge from their grave humanitarian plight. In accordance with Chapter VII, Resolution 1160 (1998) states that a peaceful resolution of the situation in Kosovo should be based on the territorial integrity of FRY, but also expresses support for an enhanced status for Kosovo, including a greater degree of autonomy and meaningful self-administration.[97] NATO intervened with a large-scale military bombing campaign to stop Serbian attacks. The intervention did not receive a UN authorization due to Russian and Chinese opposition.[98] The war resulted in the defeat of Serbia and its army had to leave Kosovo. The UN took over as an international interim administration with a Chapter VII mandate in accordance with Resolution 1244, 'under which the people of Kosovo can enjoy substantial autonomy within the Federal Republic of Yugoslavia, and which will provide transitional administration while establish-

93 The Council established a peace-keeping operation (UNPROFOR) with a limited enforcement mandate, referring to 'a threat to the peace', in SC. res. 743 (1992). Its mandate was enforcement in self-defence and protection of humanitarian assistance and safe areas protecting the civilian population. Moreover, NATO was empowered to conduct air-strikes to protect the safe areas, enforce the embargo and the no-fly zones, see SC Res. 781 (1993), 820 (1993) and 836 (1993). The more frequent use of air-strikes contributed to the Dayton Accord in 1995.

94 SC Res. 808 (1993), SC Res. 827 (1993).

95 It has been argued that the grave human rights and humanitarian law violations that followed contributed to the decision to secede. In Kosovo the human rights violations contributed to its autonomous status.

96 There was wholesale denials of their minority rights. For example, they were not allowed officially to use their language, and hospitals and higher education were closed down.

97 Resolution 1199 (1998) reaffirms this principle in its preamble.

98 For further details, see the contribution by Amnéus, Chapter 10.3.1.

ing and overseeing the development of provisional democratic self-governing institutions …'[99] Thus Kosovo was denied secession, and the principle that regions and minorities do not enjoy this right was upheld, but the severe repression paved the way for a modification of this principle under which Kosovo was recognized as a territory with a right to autonomy and self-government.

3.5.3 Humanitarian intervention[100]

Northern Iraq (1991). In the wake of the Gulf war the Kurds in Northern Iraq began an uprising against the regime of Saddam Hussein, but it was brutally put down and thousands of Kurds took refuge in the mountains bordering Turkey where they were in acute distress, threatened by starvation and diseases. The Security Council adopted the groundbreaking Resolution 688 (1991), which for the first time applied Chapter VII for humanitarian purposes in a domestic situation. Its preamble read: 'the repression of the Iraqi civilian population in many parts of Iraq, including most recently in Kurdish populated areas, which led to a massive flow of refugees towards and across international frontiers and to cross border

99 SC Res. 1244 (1999) para. 10. The preamble reaffirms both the principle of territorial integrity of FRY and the call in previous resolutions for substantial autonomy and meaningful self-administration for Kosovo, and in the next paragraph 'Determining that the situation in the region continues to constitute a threat to international peace and security, Determined to ensure the safety and security of international personnel and the implementation by all concerned of their responsibilities under the present resolution, and acting for these purposes under Chapter VII…'

100 Humanitarian intervention could be defined as intervention to alleviate large-scale human suffering. The Security Council has intervened under Chapter VII to sanction violations of human rights and humanitarian law, and to aid populations in distress. Falk, Richard, *The Complexities of Humanitarian Intervention: A New World Order Challenge, Michigan Journal of International Law, Vol.* 17 No. 2, 1996, p. 491, Corten, Oliver, Klein, Pierre, *Droit d'íngérence ou obligation de réaction,* 2nd ed., Bruylant, Bruxelles, 1996, p. 1. Another view is that humanitarian intervention applies first and foremost to gross violations of human rights, see *e.g.*, Téson, Fernando R., *Humanitarian Intervention – an inquiry into law and morality,* 1988, Irwington & Hudson, New York, p. 5. *The Responsibility to Protect – Report of the International Commission on Intervention and State Sovereignty,* International Development Research Center, Ottawa, 2001, speaks about two concepts, *i.e.* humanitarian intervention, which implies the use of force, and humanitarian assistance, which implies non-forceful measures. Here humanitarian intervention is used in a broader sense, including unarmed but forceful intervention by the Council under Chapter VII.

incursions, which threaten international peace and security in the region'. However, the Resolution did not authorize the use of force, but insisted that Iraq allow access to international humanitarian organisations for the distribution of humanitarian relief. Iraq had to comply, because the Gulf War allies decided to establish safe havens that were inaccessible to Iraqi forces. This military operation was not linked to any mandate under Resolution 688.

Somalia (1992–1995). Somalia is often quoted as the prime example of humanitarian intervention. A civil war between several warlords ripped Somalia apart and caused the government and state structures to collapse. This state of affairs and a drought contributed to an acute famine in 1992. The Security Council adopted a number of Resolutions under Chapter VII, which connected the threat to peace to the acute humanitarian crises: 'Deeply disturbed by the magnitude of the human suffering caused by the conflict and concerned that the situation in Somalia constitutes a threat to international peace and security.'[101] In November 2002 the plight of the Somali people has worsened, with 3,000 people starving to death every day. The US proposed launching a humanitarian military intervention with a UN mandate. Its offer was realized in Resolution 794 (1992), the preamble of which includes the sentence: '*Determining* that the magnitude of the human tragedy caused by the conflict in Somalia, further exacerbated by the obstacles being created to the distribution of humanitarian assistance, constitutes a threat to international peace and security'. In paragraph 10 it 'authorizes the Secretary-General and Member States cooperating ... to use all necessary means to establish as soon as possible a secure environment for humanitarian relief operations in Somalia'. The next Resolution 814 (1993) was exceptional in that it authorized a nation-building project in Somalia under UN auspices and with a Chapter VII mandate, as well as a strong UN peace-keeping force with a robust peace enforcement mandate to implement the nation-building. Also, individual criminal responsibility for violations of humanitarian law was imposed but never exacted. After a severe attack on UNOSOM II that killed 24 Pakistani peace-keepers,

101 See *e.g.* SC Res. 767 (1992), 775 (1992), establishing UNOSOM, a limited peace-keeping operation. The first Resolution 733 (1992) imposed a weapons embargo citing 'the heavy loss of human life' in the preamble.

Resolution 837 (1993) was adopted, which authorized the investigation, arrest and detention of the persons responsible for such attacks.[102] In fact this became the turning point for the UN operation, as the UN became perceived as a party to the conflict in its hunt for one of the faction-leaders, General Aideed, who was held responsible for the attacks. The UN finally pulled out in 1995.[103]

Former Yugoslavia (1991–1999). Grave human rights violations and violations of humanitarian law occurred during the Balkan conflict, especially in Bosnia and Kosovo.[104] In Bosnia the Security Council appears to have viewed these violations as one of several reasons for treating the situation as a threat to the peace.[105] Resolution 757 (1992) deplored the forcible expulsion of the population and attempts to change its ethnic composition, reaffirmed the need for effective protection of human rights and ethnic minorities, and condemned interference in the delivery of humanitarian assistance.[106] Resolution 770 (1992) explicitly recognized the link between the prevention of the delivery of humanitarian assistance and a threat to the peace.[107] It expressed the determination to establish as soon as possible the necessary conditions for the delivery of humanitarian assistance and demanded unimpeded access

102 Resolution 837 does no more than clarify the authority of UNOSOM as defined in Resolution 814. Resolution 794 had already emphasized that individual criminal responsibility would be imposed for the crimes that had been committed in connection with the distribution of humanitarian aid. For details of the attack, see the contribution by Engdahl, Chapter 2.

103 The Americans decided to pull out when their soldiers became targets in the conflict and eight American soldiers were killed in the hunt for Aideed.

104 Such as ethnic cleansing, mass killings, deportation, rape, forced labour, concentration camps, hindering the distribution of humanitarian assistance.

105 Resolution 757 (1992) cited violations of human rights and prevention of distribution of humanitarian assistance as reasons, among others (*i.e.* the war, external interference) for the conclusion that the situation in Bosnia constituted a threat to international peace and security within the meaning of Chapter VII. It established economic sanctions against FRY.

106 Helgesen writes that the humanitarian concerns were played up by the Council as the conflict dragged on, and points to the fact that it became known that concentration camps and ethnic cleansing campaigns existed, Helgesen Vidar, *Til krig for menneskerettighetene, Institutt for offentlig retts skriftserie nr. 2/1999*, p. 76.

107 '*Recognizing* that the situation in Bosnia and Herzegovina constitutes a threat to international peace and security and that the provision of humanitarian assistance in Bosnia and Herzegovina is an important element in the Council's effort to restore international peace and security in the area.'

under Chapter VII and authorized the use of force to that end.[108] Resolution 781 (1992) expanded the use of force mandate to the enforcement of a ban on military flights as an essential element for the safe delivery of humanitarian assistance. Another feature was the mandate to UNPROFOR to carry out peace enforcement operations under Chapter VII in self-defence.[109] This concept was stretched when the Council declared a number of Bosnian towns as safe areas that were supposed to be free from armed attacks and other hostile acts. UNPROFOR had a mandate to use force in self-defence to deter attacks against the safe areas.[110] NATO was empowered to use air power in and around the safe areas under Resolution 836 (1993).[111] Resolution 771 (1992) was concerned with humanitarian law violations,[112] and cited the 1949 Geneva Conventions to establish that grave breaches give rise to individual criminal responsibility. The resolution also emphasized that all military forces must comply with it under Chapter VII. Individual criminal responsibility was subsequently imposed by the innovative creation of an international criminal tribunal set up by the Security Council under Chapter VII.[113] The tribunal for the territory of former Yugoslavia (ICTY) is competent to try war crimes, acts of genocide and crimes against humanity.[114]

108 *Ibid.* para. 2.
109 See SC Res. 815 (1993).
110 SC Res. 824 (1993).
111 Unfortunately the safe areas were not sufficiently well-protected and the town of Screbrenica was overrun in 1995 and an estimated 7,000 Bosnian Muslims were killed.
112 Including mass expulsion and deportations of civilians, imprisonment and abuse of civilians in detention centres, deliberate attacks on non-combatants, hospitals and ambulances, impeding the delivery of food and medicine, wanton destruction of property.
113 SC Res. 808 (1993) which expressed the Council's 'grave alarm at ... violations of international humanitarian law occurring within the territory of the former Yugoslavia, including reports of mass killings and the continuing practice of "ethnic cleansing" and determined that this situation constituted a threat to international peace and security. It then decided in op. para. 1 to establish 'an international tribunal...for the prosecution of persons responsible for serious violations of international humanitarian law committed in the territory of former Yugoslavia since 1991'. The tribunal was established by Resolution 827 (1993). The tribunal appears to be a non-military sanction under article 41.
114 Bring, Ove, *International Criminal Law in Historical Perspective – Comments and Materials,* Juridiska fakulteten, No. 66 skriftserien, Stockholm, 2001, p. 55.

In addressing **Kosovo** the Security Council referred to humanitarian concerns and violations of humanitarian law, especially the massive exodus of refugees as a result of the 'excessive and indiscriminate use of force' by Serbian security forces. The Resolution expressed that the Council was 'deeply concerned by the rapid deterioration in the humanitarian situation in Kosovo, *alarmed* at the impending humanitarian catastrophe ... and *emphasizing* the need to prevent this from happening'.[115] Resolution 1199 (1998) demanded that FRY take immediate steps to improve the humanitarian situation, facilitate the return of refugees and give unimpeded access to humanitarian organizations. The subsequent NATO bombings without a UN mandate were alleged to be justifiable on the grounds of humanitarian intervention.[116] The ICTY's jursidiction also extends to crimes committed in Kosovo.

Rwanda (1994). The death of the presidents of Rwanda and Burundi in a plane crash in April 1994 triggered a genocide carried out by the Hutu majority against the Tutsi. An estimated one million persons were slaughtered in the following months and approximately two million fled to neighbouring countries. In the summer the Tutsi-dominated movement (RPF) managed to take control over large parts of Rwanda. The UN responded rather weakly, at first decreasing the forces (UNAMIR) already in place.[117] It then established a weapons embargo explicitly under Chapter VII in part B of Resolution 918 (1994); part B concluded that the situation in Rwanda constituted a threat to peace and security in the region. Part A increased the number of peace-keepers and extended their mandate, although without a clear reference to Chapter VII. It cited a number of humanitarian conditions: 'Deeply disturbed by the magnitude of the human suffering caused by the conflict and concerned that the continuation of the situation in Rwanda constitutes

115 SC Res. 1199 (1998), see also Resolution 1160 (1998), which imposed a weapons embargo on FRY under Chapter VII, but only referred to the 'excessive use of force by the Serbian police'.

116 See the contribution by Amnéus, Chapter 10.3.1.

117 SC Res. 912 (1994). The Secretary-General later appointed an Independent Commission of Inquiry that came to the conclusion that the UN failed to prevent the genocide, *Report of the Independent Commission of Inquiry into the Actions of the United Nations During the 1994 Genocide in Rwanda*, S/1999/340 (15 Dec. 1999).

a threat to peace and security in the region ...'. The resolution also recalled that acts of genocide constitute a crime punishable under international law.[118] Since UNAMIR did not have a robust Chapter VII mandate and could only take action in self-defence to protect humanitarian assistance operations and protected areas, and as it was lagging,[119] France offered to lead an enforcement operation mandated by the Council to enforce UNAMIR's humanitarian goals. The proposal was approved and Resolution 929 (1994) is exceptional in that it does not refer to any international implications but states that it is the humanitarian crisis that constitutes a threat to international peace and security: 'Determining that the magnitude of the humanitarian crisis in Rwanda constitutes a threat to peace and security in the region ...'. The French were given a Security Council mandate to use all necessary means and intervened military to establish a safe area in the south of Rwanda in what is known as Operation Turquoise.[120] The French initiative met with criticism because of France's earlier links with the Hutus,

118 'Deeply concerned that the situation in Rwanda, which has resulted in the death of many thousands of innocent civilians, including women and children, the internal displacement of a significant percentage of the Rwandan population, and the massive exodus of refugees to neighbouring countries, constitutes a humanitarian crisis of enormous proportions.' The resolution also speaks of acts of genocide: 'Expressing once again its alarm at continuing reports of systematic, widespread and flagrant violations of international humanitarian law in Rwanda, as well as other violations of the rights to life and property; Recalling in this context that the killing of members of an ethnic group with the intention of destroying such a group, in whole or in part, constitutes a crime punishable under international law'. Resolution 925 (1994) notes: 'with gravest concern the reports indicating that acts of genocide have occurred in Rwanda and recalling in this context that genocide constitutes a crime punishable under international law.'

119 SC Res. 925 (1994) provided for a peace-keeping mission without a Chapter VII mandate, but the force was lagging because it was hard to assemble enough troops from Member States.

120 The mandate is outlined in op. para. 2: 'Welcomes also the offer by Member States (S/1994/734) to cooperate with the Secretary-General in order to achieve the objectives of the United Nations in Rwanda through the establishment of a temporary operation under national command ...contributing, in an impartial way, to the security... of displaced persons, refugees and civilians at risk in Rwanda.'
Op. para. 3. 'Acting under Chapter VII of the Charter of the United Nations, authorizes the Member States cooperating with the Secretary-General to conduct the operation referred to in paragraph 2 above using all necessary means to achieve the humanitarian objectives set out in subparagraphs 4 (a) and (b) of Resolution 925 (1994)'.

and it was soon withdrawn as the RPF won the civil war.[121] In November, in the aftermath of the conflict the Security Council set up an international tribunal for Rwanda, modelled on the ICTY. The language establishing this Tribunal went one step further than previous resolutions as Resolution 955 (1994) focused entirely of the purely internal situation and the serious crimes that took place in Rwanda, omitting any nexus to armed conflict:

> Expressing once again its grave concern at the reports indicating that genocide and other systematic, widespread and flagrant violations of international humanitarian law have been committed in Rwanda, Determining that this situation continues to constitute a threat to international peace and security...[122]

Sierra Leone (1997–2001). The RUF rebels became known for their atrocities, for example, the widespread policy of maiming civilians in campaigns of terror and their ruthless attacks on UN peace-keepers, as well as hindering humanitarian assistance. Resolution 1171 (1998) imposes an arms embargo and travel restrictions on the RUF under Chapter VII, stressing in this connection, among other reasons: 'the urgency for all rebels to put an end to the atrocities ...'. After the RUF's repeated attacks on the peace-keepers and capture of hundreds of them, Resolution 1289 (2000) revised the mandate of UNAMSIL to a robust Chapter VII mandate, in paragraph 10:

> authorizes UNAMSIL to take the necessary action to fulfil the additional tasks set out above, and affirms that, in the discharge of its mandate, UNAMSIL may take the necessary action to ensure the security and freedom of movement of its personnel and, within its capabilities and areas of deployment, to afford protection to civilians under imminent threat of physical violence, taking into account the responsibilities of the Government of Sierra Leone.[123]

In Resolution 1315 (2000), the Security Council requested with reference to Chapter VII that the Secretary-General create a special

121 RPF opposed the French intervention and five countries in the Security Council abstained from the resolution.

122 The Tribunal will try cases concerning the following crimes: genocide, crimes against humanity (without any nexus to the existence of armed conflict, which is innovative), and serious violations of article 3 common to the Geneva Conventions and Additional Protocol II, see Bring, Ove, (2001) *supra* note 114, p. 55.

123 The number of peace-keepers was increased to 17,000 by SC res. 1346 (2001).

domestic court to prosecute persons who bear the greatest responsible for the commission of crimes against humanity, war crimes and other serious violations of international humanitarian law, as well as crimes under relevant Sierra Leonean law.[124]

Congo[125] (formerly Zaire) (1996–2003). The camps in eastern Zaire, which hosted about one million Hutu refugees from Rwanda, became bases for the Hutu militia. This led to a conflict with the Tutsis in Zaire. With support from Rwanda, an uprising led to a rebel movement made up of different groups gaining control of large parts of the country in a struggle to oust the Zairean dictator Mobuto. The humanitarian situation deteriorated in the refugee camps and the humanitarian organisations had to withdraw. The Security Council responded first with Resolution 1078 (1996): 'Determining that the magnitude of the present humanitarian crisis in eastern Zaire constitutes a threat to peace and security in the region.' It cited the humanitarian situation with the need to secure distribution of humanitarian aid as well as the large-scale movements of refugees and internally displaced persons. But it was in the following Resolution 1080 (1996) that the Council adopted measures under Chapter VII by establishing a multinational force that was authorized *to use all necessary means* to achieve humanitarian objectives. These were set out in paragraph 3:

> the establishment of a temporary multinational force to facilitate the immediate return of humanitarian organisations and the effective delivery by civilian relief organisations of humanitarian aid to alleviate the immediate suffering of displaced persons, refugees and civilians at risk in eastern Zaire, and to facilitate the voluntary, orderly return of refugees ... as well as ... displaced persons.

The multinational force was found superfluous since the situation improved with the overthrow of the Mobuto government.

A new war with interference from the neighbouring countries plagued the country (now renamed Congo) for many years to come, until finally a peace accord was implemented and the UN sent in a peace-keeping force. However atrocities continued in the province

124 *Report of the Secretary-General on the Establishment of a Special Court for Sierra Leone*, S/2000/915 (4 Oct. 2000). See the contribution by Österdahl, Chapter 9.
125 Zaire was renamed Congo by the new regime.

of Ituri, in the city of Bunia, where acts of genocide were committed against the civilian population, as well as other grave violations of human rights, including sexual violence. The Council adopted Resolution 1484 (2003), stating that this situation constituted a threat to the peace and gave an enforcement mandate to UN forces to remedy the humanitarian situation in Ituri and Bunia.[126]

Albania (1997). Civil strife broke out in Albania because of discontent with the government and the widespread economic crisis that resulted when many people lost their savings in pyramid schemes. A state of anarchy led to large flows of refugees, especially to Italy. The Security Council adopted Resolution 1101 (1997): 'Determining that the present situation constitutes a threat to peace and security in the region.' The preamble is silent about the reasons for this determination, but they appear to be the humanitarian situation and the need for the distribution of humanitarian assistance, as its operative paragraph 2 establishes a multinational force to 'facilitate the prompt delivery of humanitarian assistance, and to help create a secure environment for the missions of international organisations in Albania, including those providing humanitarian assist-

126 '*Determining* that the situation in the Ituri region and in Bunia in particular constitutes a threat to the peace process in the Democratic Republic of the Congo and to the peace and security in the Great Lakes region, *Acting* under Chapter VII of the Charter of the United Nations, 1. *Authorizes* the deployment until 1 September 2003 of an Interim Emergency Multinational Force in Bunia in close coordination with MONUC, in particular its contingent currently deployed in the town, to contribute to the stabilization of the security conditions and the improvement of the humanitarian situation in Bunia, to ensure the protection of the airport, the internally displaced persons in the camps in Bunia and, if the situation requires it, to contribute to the safety of the civilian population, United Nations personnel and the humanitarian presence in the town'. Resolution 1493 (2003) explicitly refers to Chapter VII of the UN Charter: '2. *Strongly condemns* the acts of violence systematically perpetrated against civilians, including the massacres, as well as other atrocities and violations of international humanitarian law and human rights, in particular, sexual violence against women and girls, *stresses* the need to bring to justice those responsible, including those at the command level, and *urges* all parties, including the Government of the Democratic Republic of the Congo, to take all necessary steps to prevent further violations of human rights and international humanitarian law, in particular those committed against civilians'; The multinational force was replaced by the UN force MONUC, see SC Res. 1501 (26 Aug. 2003).

ance'. The mandate to use force was limited to the security and freedom of movement of the multinational force.[127]

Liberia (2003): A prolonged civil war disabled Liberia in the 1990s. It ended with democratic elections where the infamous warlord Charles Taylor was elected president. He was later indicted by the Sierra Leone Criminal Court for supporting the RUF. The new millennium witnessed a resurgence of violence in Liberia as another civil war broke out when two rebel movements, LURD and MODEL, demanded Taylor's resignation.[128] The plight of the civilian population caused the Security Council to intervene through Resolution 1497 (2003), which authorized a multinational force with a Chapter VII mandate to alleviate human suffering.[129]

127 The authorization to use force is set out in operative para. 4, explicitly citing Chapter VII. Resolution 1114 (1997) confirms that the situation in Albania constitutes a threat to international peace and security in the region. It prolongs the multinational force's mandate over the elections. Resolution 1529 (2004), concerning Haiti (cited *supra* and *infra*) and Resolution 1497 (2003), concerning Liberia (cited *infra*), resemble Resolution 1101, as the Resolutions all attempt to remedy a humanitarian crisis brought about by a collapsing government followed by a state of anarchy and violent lawlessness.

128 Taylor stepped down and was given sanctuary in Nigeria instead of being extradited to the Sierra Leone criminal court.

129 '*Deeply concerned* over the conflict in Liberia and its effects on the humanitarian situation, including the tragic loss of countless innocent lives, in that country, and its destabilizing effect on the region. *Stressing* the need to create a secure environment that enables respect for human rights, including the well-being and rehabilitation of children, protects the well-being of civilians, and supports the mission of humanitarian workers, [...]

Determining that the situation in Liberia constitutes a threat to international peace and security, to stability in the West Africa sub region, and to the peace process for Liberia, *Acting* under Chapter VII of the Charter of the United Nations,
1. *Authorizes* Member States to establish a Multinational Force in Liberia to support the implementation of the 17 June 2003 ceasefire agreement, including establishing conditions for initial stages of disarmament, demobilization and reintegration activities, to help establish and maintain security in the period after the departure of the current President and the installation of a successor authority, taking into account the agreements to be reached by the Liberian parties, and to secure the environment for the delivery of humanitarian assistance, and to prepare for the introduction of a longer-term United Nations stabilization force to relieve the Multinational Force;' The multinational force was replaced by a large UN force with a Chapter VII mandate in SC Res. 1509 (2003) to maintain law and order in Liberia and according to para.3(j): 'to protect civilians under imminent threat of physical violence, within its capabilities; (k) to facilitate the provision of humanitarian assistance, including by helping to establish the necessary security conditions.'

Haiti (2004). Resolution 1529 (2004), cited *supra*, was adopted in response to the political and humanitarian situation in Haiti caused by the rebellion against president Aristide.[130] It can be convincingly argued that the Council intervened to respond to the humanitarian situation.[131] Haiti is one of the world's poorest nations and the chaotic situation could engulf Haiti in a humanitarian disaster, with starvation and refugee flows as a result. Indeed, the determination that the situation in Haiti is a threat to international peace and security is linked to the possibility of refugee flows coming from Haiti.[132] The mandate given to the multinational force is concerned with the protection of the distribution of humanitarian assistance and of aid workers.[133]

Resolution 1529 resembles Resolution 1497 (2003) concerning Liberia, which was adopted after the democratically elected president had resigned due to the demands of rebel movements advancing on the capital. Resolution 1497 was adopted because of the impending humanitarian catastrophe in the existing chaotic situation.[134]

There are other cases where the Council taking action in response to humanitarian concerns were one of several contributing factors-for its intervention.[135]

3.5.4 International terrorism

Libya (1992–2003). Three years after the bombing of Pan Am flight 102 over Scotland a US district court indicted two Libyan nationals, presumed to be state agents, for the deed. Following the charges against Libya, the UK and US issued a declaration insisting on the surrender of the accused and Libya's acceptance of responsibility for the

130 See *supra* for background to the conflict in Haiti in 3.5.2.
131 *Id.*, The preamble is explicit, quoted *supra* in note 70.
132 See Resolution 1529 (2004) cited *supra* in 3.5.2 in note 69.
133 Op. para. 2a) and b) reads: "*To contribute to a secure and stable environment in the Haitian capital and elsewhere in the country,* as appropriate and as circumstances permit, in order to support Haitian President Alexandre's request for international assistance to support the constitutional political process under way in Haiti; (emph. added)
(b) *To facilitate the provision of humanitarian assistance and the access of international humanitarian workers to the Haitian people in need;*" (emph. added). The anarchy in Haiti hindered the distribution of humanitarian aid to the population.
134 There is also similarity to the case of Albania, see *supra* in note 127.
135 Angola and East Timor are further examples of countries where human rights abuses were one important factor that contributed to Security Council action.

actions of its officials. Libya refused but expressed its readiness to settle the dispute under Article 33 of the UN Charter and by arbitration under the Montreal Convention, claiming that a state is not obliged to extradite its own nationals.[136] The US, UK and France brought up the matter in the Security Council, which in Resolution 731 (1992) strongly urged Libya to respond to their request 'so as to contribute to the elimination of international terrorism'.[137] Libya decided to institute parallel proceedings at the ICJ, but this did not prevent the Council from imposing sanctions under Chapter VII, which it did in Resolution 748 (1992).[138] That was the first Resolution ever to decide that international terrorism is a threat to international peace and security. In the preamble the Council reaffirmed that:

> In accordance with the principle in Article 2(4), of the Charter of the United Nations, every State has the duty to refrain from organizing, instigating, assisting or participating in terrorist acts in another State or acquiescing in organised activities within its territory directed towards the commission of such acts, when such acts involve the threat or use of force.
>
> In this context that failure by the Libyan government to demonstrate by concrete actions its renunciation of terrorism and in particular, its continued failure to respond fully and effectively to the requests in resolution 731 (1992) constitute a threat to international peace and security.

Thus the Council imposed an aerial embargo, an arms embargo and diplomatic sanctions against Libya, explicitly citing Chapter VII.[139] In Resolution 883 (1993) the Council tightened the embargo, once again determining that Libya's failure to comply with Resolutions 731 and 748 by not extraditing its nationals constituted 'a threat to international peace and security'.[140] Finally, in 1998 a compromise was reached when Libya agreed to extradite the suspects to the Neth-

136 The Montreal Convention for the Suppression of Unlawful Acts Against the Safety of Civil Aviation (23 Sep. 1971) spells out the principle of *aut dedere aut judicare, i.e.* that suspected terrorists should either be tried by the state on whose territory they are found or should be extradited. In customary international law a state is under no obligation to extradite its own nationals, Österdahl, Inger, *supra* note 10, p. 78.

137 SC Res. 731 (1992) para. 3. This resolution was not mandatory.

138 (Lockerbie case), *ICJ Reports* 1992, see *supra* in note 27. The Court held that resolutions of the Council took precedence.

139 SC Res. 748 (1992) op. para. 4–6.

140 These included the freezing of Libyan assets abroad, additional economic sanctions and a tightened aerial embargo, see SC Res. 883 para. 5–6.

erlands where they were tried under Scottish law. The Council then decided to suspend the sanctions in Resolution 1192 (1998) and lifted them permanently through Resolution 1506 (2003).

Sudan (1996). An attempt to assassinate Egypt's President Mubarak was made in the capital of Ethiopia in 1995. The surviving captured assailants supplied the information that Sudan was involved and was harbouring the three Egyptians who were the key planners of the operation.[141] Ethiopia requested that Sudan extradite them, but Sudan replied that it was unable to locate them. The Security Council adopted Resolution 1044 (1996) referring to the request by the Organisation of African Union (OAU) to extradite the suspects on the basis of an Extradition Treaty between Ethiopia and Sudan. It called upon Sudan to desist from 'activities of assisting, supporting and facilitating terrorist activities and from giving shelter and sanctuary to terrorist elements'.[142] It found that: 'the suppression of acts of international terrorism, including those in which States are involved is an essential element for the maintenance of international peace and security'.[143] However, the Resolution was not adopted under Chapter VII. In Resolution 1054 (1996) the Council found that Sudan's non-compliance with Resolution 1044 'constitutes a threat to international peace and security' and acting under Chapter VII imposed non-military sanctions against Sudan, including diplomatic sanctions and travel restrictions for Sudanese officials. When Sudan still failed to comply, the Council extended the sanctions under Chapter VII to an aerial embargo under Resolution 1070 (1996). The Resolution reaffirmed the importance of suppressing international terrorism and again determined that the non-extradition constituted a threat to international peace and security.

Afghanistan (1998–2002). In 1998 the US formally indicted Usama bin Laden because of his alleged involvement in the bombings of the US embassies in Kenya and Tanzania that year. The US asked the Taliban regime in Afghanistan to extradite Bin Laden, whose al-Qaeda terrorist network operated from bases on its territory. At first the Secu-

141 Schweigman, David, *supra* note 8, writes that Sudan was also said to have supplied them with travel documents and weapons.
142 Op. para. 4.
143 Pre. para. 5.

rity Council adopted Resolution 1189 (1998), which is addressed to all states and, without citing Chapter VII, reaffirms that international terrorism is illegal and specifies conduct that is outlawed.[144] When the Taliban refused to extradite bin Laden, the Council adopted Resolution 1267 (1999. It imposed non-military sanctions under Chapter VII on the Taliban,[145] determining that the failure of the Taliban authorities to respond to the non-binding request to cooperate to bring suspected terrorists to justice set out in Resolution 1244 (1999) constituted a threat to international peace and security. The resolution demanded:

> Stressing its determination to ensure respect for its resolutions, Acting under Chapter VII of the Charter of the United Nations,
>
> 1. Insists that the Afghan faction known as the Taliban ... comply promptly with its previous resolutions and in particular cease the provision of sanctuary and training for international terrorists and their organizations, take appropriate effective measures to ensure that the territory under its control is not used for terrorist installations and camps, or for the preparation or organisation of terrorist acts against other States or their citizens, and cooperate with efforts to bring indicted terrorists to justice;
>
> 2. Demands that the Taliban turn over Usama bin Laden without further delay to appropriate authorities in a country where he has been indicted, or to appropriate authorities in a country where he will be returned to such a country, or to appropriate authorities in a country where he will be arrested and effectively brought to justice [...]'

Bin Laden and al-Qaeda were held responsible for the devastating terrorist attacks against the US on 11 September 2001, in which nearly 3,000 people were killed.[146] The Security Council determined in Resolution 1368 on 12 September 2001, that the terrorist attacks were a threat to international peace and security: '*Unequivocally condemns* in the strongest terms the horrifying terrorist attacks which

144 'Stressing that every Member State has the duty to refrain from organizing, instigating, assisting or participating in terrorist acts in another State or acquiescing in organized activities within its territory directed towards the commission of such acts', and in op. para. 5: 'Calls upon all States to adopt, in accordance with international law and as a matter of priority, effective and practical measures for security cooperation, for the prevention of such acts of terrorism, and for the prosecution and punishment of their perpetrators'.

145 In the form of an aerial embargo and the freezing of assets.

146 Bin Laden has later claimed responsibility for the attacks.

took place on 11 September 2001 in New York, Washington, D.C. and Pennsylvania and *regards* such acts, like any act of international terrorism, as a threat to international peace and security'. The Security Council also affirmed the inherent right to self-defence, which is why the military response by the U.S. and its allies towards Afghanistan (whose targets were al-Qaeda as well as the Taliban regime which persistently refused to extradite Bin Laden) was seen in this context. The Council itself, on the other hand, focused on comprehensive non-military sanctions aimed at rooting out international terrorism. Thus, Resolution 1373 (2001) is revolutionary as it enacts sweeping legislation under Chapter VII.[147] A new and disputed measure is that the sanctions also target individuals worldwide, if

147 '*Acting* under Chapter VII of the Charter of the United Nations,
1. *Decides* that all States shall:
(a) Prevent and suppress the financing of terrorist acts;
(b) Criminalize the wilful provision or collection, by any means, directly or indirectly, of funds by their nationals or in their territories with the intention that the funds should be used, or in the knowledge that they are to be used, in order to carry out terrorist acts;
(c) Freeze without delay funds and other financial assets or economic resources of persons who commit, or attempt to commit, terrorist acts or participate in or facilitate the commission of terrorist acts; of entities owned or controlled directly or indirectly by such persons; and of persons and entities acting on behalf of, or at the direction of such persons and entities, including funds derived or generated from property owned or controlled directly or indirectly by such persons and associated persons and entities;
(d) Prohibit their nationals or any persons and entities within their territories from making any funds, financial assets or economic resources or financial or other related services available, directly or indirectly, for the benefit of persons who commit or attempt to commit or facilitate or participate in the commission of terrorist acts, of entities owned or controlled, directly or indirectly, by such persons and of persons and entities acting on behalf of or at the direction of such persons;
2. *Decides also* that all States shall:
(a) Refrain from providing any form of support, active or passive, to entities or persons involved in terrorist acts, including by suppressing recruitment of members of terrorist groups and eliminating the supply of weapons to terrorists;
(b) Take the necessary steps to prevent the commission of terrorist acts, including by provision of early warning to other States by exchange of information;
(c)Deny safe haven to those who finance, plan, support, or commit terrorist acts, or provide safe havens;
(d) Prevent those who finance, plan, facilitate or commit terrorist acts from using their respective territories for those purposes against other States or their citizens;
The footnote continues on next page.

they are on a list of suspected terrorists supplied by the sanctions committee.[148]

Spain (2004). A large-scale terrorist attack was committed on the 11th of March 2004 in Madrid, when a number of bombs were detonated simultaneously onboard trains in the morning rush-hour, killing more than 200 people and injuring 1,500. The Basque terrorist organisation ETA was immediately suspected by the Spanish Government, but it denied involvement. The next day, the Security Council adopted Resolution 1530 (2004) which:

> *Condemns* in the strongest terms the bomb attacks in Madrid, Spain, perpetrated by the terrorist group ETA on 11 March 2004, in which many lives were claimed and people injured, and regards such act, like any act of terrorism, as a threat to peace and security;

The text is notable in that for the first time it considers an operation by a national terrorist-group a threat to peace and security. It is also the first time that a resolution immediately singles out the alleged

The footnote (147) continued from previous page.

(e) Ensure that any person who participates in the financing, planning, preparation or perpetration of terrorist acts or in supporting terrorist acts is brought to justice and ensure that, in addition to any other measures against them, such terrorist acts are established as serious criminal offences in domestic laws and regulations and that the punishment duly reflects the seriousness of such terrorist acts;

(f) Afford one another the greatest measure of assistance in connection with criminal investigations or criminal proceedings relating to the financing or support of terrorist acts, including assistance in obtaining evidence in their possession necessary for the proceedings;

(g) Prevent the movement of terrorists or terrorist groups by effective border controls and controls on issuance of identity papers and travel documents, and through measures for preventing counterfeiting, forgery or fraudulent use of identity papers and travel documents;

----

5. *Declares* that acts, methods, and practices of terrorism are contrary to the purposes and principles of the United Nations and that knowingly financing, planning and inciting terrorist acts are also contrary to the purposes and principles of the United Nations;

8. *Expresses* its determination to take all necessary steps in order to ensure the full implementation of this resolution, in accordance with its responsibilities under the Charter;

148 These are severe quasi-judicial measures because there is no legal remedy for sanctions by the Council; see the contribution by Cameron in Chapter 6. Resolution 1390 (2002) supplements and defines the list of targeted individuals and entities that are alleged to be suspected terrorists.

terrorist group.[149] It may be noted that the operative paragraph omits the words "international" before peace and security, but they occur in the preamble: "*Reaffirming* the need to combat by all means, in accordance with the Charter of the United Nations, threats to international peace and security caused by terrorist acts,". The preamble refers in the first paragraph to Resolution 1373 (2001) and the 3rd operative paragraph emphasizes states' obligations under Resolution 1373 to cooperate to bring to justice the persons responsible for this terrorist attack.[150] The text of the resolution met with severe criticism from both UN Secretary-General Kofi Annan and several Security Council members. This was because of its premature allegation that the ETA was responsible, which was promted by the resigning Government of Spain, despite the fact that there was no proof of ETA involvement, and the Spanish police subsequently found evidence that pointed in another direction, namely towards international terrorists.[151]

3.6 Conclusions

The principle of self-determination is a striking example of how the Security Council has applied, and even contributed to the evolution of, a norm and its different subsets. Today two new categories of peoples aspire to self-determination, *i.e.*, a people in a state claiming a right to democracy and an oppressed minority claiming a right of secession.

149 The ETA immediately aroused suspicion in Spain because they had been found to have planned attacks on train stations some months before. The Spanish Government asked the Council to name the ETA in resolution 1530. But on 12 March 2004 there was nothing that tied the ETA to the attack, and an ETA spokesman denied involvement. Al-Qaeda is suspected of having carried out the attack in retaliation for Spain's support for the war against Iraq in 2003. It should be noted that Resolution 1368 (12 Sep. 2001), which was adopted following the 11th September attacks, did not name al-Qaeda.

150 '3. *Urges* all States, in accordance with their obligations under resolution 1373 (2001), to cooperate actively in efforts to find and bring to justice the perpetrators, organizers and sponsors of this terrorist attack;'

151 In a tape a representative from al-Qaeda claimed responsibility and the police secured evidence that led to Moroccan citizens. The Spanish police tracked down several of the suspected who blew themselves up in the building where they were hiding. At the time of this writing the investigation of the attacks is still ongoing.

In the case of **internal self-determination** the Council has twice contributed to the evolution of the norm, going from recognition of internal self-determination for a racial majority to encompass the right to democracy. And it did so at a time when the norm was emerging and the Council's intervention under Chapter VII thus became part of its evolution in customary international law.[152] It is supported by the fact that the Council intervened under Chapter VII even without the existence of armed conflict.[153] The Council first applied Chapter VII to remedy situations where internal self-determination was denied to a majority because of race.[154] The Council imposed quasi-judicial sanctions explicitly under Chapter VII to determine the illegality of the minority regimes and their decisions aimed at excluding the black majority from government. In the 1990s the Security Council expanded the normative content of internal self-determination to include the right to democracy.[155] In this era democracy more and more started to be perceived as a right in international law.[156] When it comes to democracy the Security Council is cautious, applying the norm only to cases where a

152 Franck, Thomas, 1992, *supra* note 56, cites the case of Haiti as support for the emergence of a right to democracy. Hannikainen, Lauri, 1988, *supra* note 31, p. 415, cites Southern Rhodesia and South Africa with respect to the formation of the norm of internal self-determination according to race, *see also* Gowlland-Debbas, 1994, *supra* note 1, p. 58 and Svanberg-Torpman, Katinka, *The Security Council's Action under Chapter VII for Internal Self-Determination*, forthcoming; but see Byers, Michael, Chesterman, Simon *'You, the People': Pro-Democratic Intervention in International Law*, in Democratic Governance and International Law, Fox, Gregory H., Roth, Brad R., (Eds.), Cambridge University Press, Cambridge, 2000, pp. 259–293, 289–290 who writes on p. 290: 'If the argument is that customary international law has changed ... more evidence than a Security Council determination that such a coup constitutes a threat to peace and security must be established.'

153 Such as in Haiti, Southern Rhodesia and South Africa.

154 The case of Southern Rhodesia paved the way for the adoption of FRD's 'savings clause' in para. 7, cited, *supra* in note 56.

155 Haiti was the first country in which the Security Council intervened to restore democracy. This may be regarded as an extension of the norm of internal self-determination to include democracy, *i.e.* the right of a people to chose a government representing the whole people, Franck, Thomas, *supra* note 56, Roth, Brad R., *Governmental Illegitimacy in International Law,* Oxford University Press, Oxford, (2000), p. 383.

156 See Franck, Thomas, *supra* note 56. In this famous article he gives an account of how a right to democracy has developed. Cassese, Antonio, *The Right of Peoples to Self-Determination, supra* note 56, points to a number of declarations and GA resolutions assessing a right to democracy. This position has been contested, see *e.g.* the discussion in Fox, Gregory H., Roth, Brad R. (Eds.), *supra* note 152.

military coup has ousted a government democratically elected in elections supervised by the UN or other international observers, or where the results of such elections were never implemented.[157] The Council applied the same methods as in the racial cases, using non-military sanctions, including declarations of invalidity with a view to reinstalling the 'legal' democratic regime.[158] When it comes to democracy the Council has even been prepared to use military sanctions.[159] It could also be tentatively argued that the Council in the new millennium has went a further step and intervened subsequent the resign of democratically elected presidents, when they are found to have abused their powers and lost popular support, being under pressure to resign from a revolting population and advancing groups of rebels as they are losing control over large parts of the country.[160] The purpose of Council intervention is to establish conditions of law and order, a criterion necessary for the holding of new elections. Thus, a democratically elected president cannot shield himself from accountability behind a veil of state sovereignty.

In the case of **external self-determination** the Security Council has stayed the course in customary international law, denying secession except for well-defined categories such as peoples under occupation or alien domination.[161] In the 1990s the Council started to soften its position, seemingly applying the concept of alien domination to a new category of peoples, *i.e.* to minorities making up the majority in a republic inside a federation, which are severely oppressed by the authorities and are fighting to secede. The Council has transferred its methods for ascertaining the will of people under colonial domination, to this new category, demanding a referendum before independence and observance by the new states of the

157 The first was the case in Haiti and Sierra Leone, while the last was the case in Angola and Liberia.

158 Targeted sanctions have been used against the undemocratic party, but weapons embargoes and economic sanctions have also been applied to the whole of the state.

159 In Haiti see SC Res. 940 (1994), in Sierra Leone it commended *ex-post facto* the military force used by ECOMOG to reinstall the democratic regime.

160 Liberia and Haiti are the primary examples, but also Albania fits. However, it could not be disregarded that the Council's interventions were primarily motivated on humanitarian grounds, in a situation of chaos, civil war and anarchy, to fill the vacuum after the presidents resignation.

161 In Congo and in Bosnia the denial of secession was upheld. East Timor is an example of occupation.

principle of *uti possidetis,* thus ensuring that they retain their previous borders and denying further fragmentation. The Council has extended the prohibition of the use of force to include disintegrating federations and has applied the principles of inviolability of international borders and no fruits of aggression to the emerging republics of the former Yugoslavia. Moreover, the Council has declared null and void the annexation and occupation of territory, and the acquisition of territory by the use of force in the case of the seceding republics and their territory as well, in the latter case in order to stop further fragmentation. The Council has also revived methods similar to the trusteeship system established in Chapter XII of the UN Charter, under which the UN was authorized under Chapter VII to set up an interim administration to guide a territory towards independence or autonomy.[162] Moreover, the Council appears to be prepared to give a severely oppressed and abused minority living in a well-defined territory inside a state, less than sovereign rights in the form of self-government.

The Security Council has been very active when it comes to intervention for **humanitarian purposes**. Indeed, this is the most frequently cited motive for action in the case study. It is obvious that the Security Council has acted as an enforcer of humanitarian and human rights law and has intervened under Chapter VII to protect the rights of the human person.[163] The Council has intervened in internal situations where the humanitarian crisis in itself often has been cited as constituting a threat to international peace and security, or such a threat has been construed even though considered remote.[164] It is the single factor in the case studies that most frequently provoked a military response from the Council in the form of humanitarian interventions. In other cases humanitarian concerns were one of the decisive factors cited by the Council for Chapter VII action. The cases reveal that there are basically four types of humanitarian concerns that will trigger sanctions:

162 *E.g.* in East Timor and Kosovo. The trusteeship system applied to non-self-governing territories placed under UN trusteeship; see Chapter XII of the UN Charter.

163 Österdahl, Inger, (1998) *supra* note 10 at pp. 112–118, who, however, criticizes the Council for acting arbitrarily and in an *ad hoc* manner in connection with these measures.

164 It should be pointed out that already the founders of the UN Charter themselves were aware of the fact that massive violations of human rights could amount to a threat to the peace; see *supra* note 11.

1) A *massive humanitarian crisis* characterized by great and large-scale human suffering caused by starvation, refugee flows and persecution. These situations are the ones that make the Council respond most robustly by military means to alleviate human suffering, *e.g.* through peace enforcement aimed at protecting the delivery of humanitarian assistance, the establishment of safe havens and the maintenance of law and order. The Council has also used a number of non-military sanctions such as weapons embargoes and other economic sanctions, often before and/or parallell with military sanctions. A typical case is a state in anarchy and chaos where the constitutional order has broken down and civil war or civil strife is raging.[165]
2) *Genocide* has also made the Council respond by military means in the case of Rwanda, but the Council has been cautious in citing genocide as a ground for intervention, probably because it would prompt the Council to react more forcefully. However the *ad hoc* tribunals are competent to try acts of genocide.
3) *Violations of international humanitarian law* are often cited as one of several factors underpinning a Chapter VII decision. The Council has responded by launching peace enforcement operations and invoked international criminal responsibility for humanitarian law violations. This has been done either by the creation of an international criminal tribunal or by demanding that the perpetrators are otherwise brought to justice.
4) *Grave human rights violations.* Among cited violations are murder, ethnic cleansing, forced labour, rape, apartheid, executions, illegal detentions etc. The Council has responded, for example, by insisting on international criminal responsibility, establishing safe areas, launching limited peace enforcement operations, and imposing non-military sanctions aimed at the guilty party, etc.[166]

165 Hence, we can see a link between constitutional order, form of government and humanitarian concerns. It has been argued that human rights are best promoted by genuinely democratic governments, Wippman, David, *Practical and Legal Constraints on Internal Power Sharing*, in International Law and Ethnic Conflict, Ed. Wippman, David, Cornell University Press, New York, 1998, pp. 211, Franck, Thomas, *supra* note 156.

166 Criminal responsibility was invoked only for the gravest crimes qualifying as crimes against humanity or acts of genocide, and when the Council managed to get the crimes punished by a criminal tribunal.

The Security Council's interventions against **international terrorism** are an excellent example of its assumptions of the role of legislator by means of quasi-judicial activity. In the last decade the Council has sought to enforce the extradition of suspected terrorists by sanctions under Chapter VII. Non-extradition is found to constitute a threat to the peace, even though the state in question is under no obligation in international law to extradite its nationals.[167] The broad powers of the Security Council to define what constitutes a threat to the peace were upheld by ICJ in the *Lockerbie* case, where the Court found that the Council's binding Resolutions under Chapter VII had pre-eminence, as the Council has wide discretion to decide what constitutes a threat to international peace and security.[168] The Security Council continued its fight against international terrorism and broadened its scope as it started to declare what conduct on the part of states amounts to co-responsibility for international terrorism in Resolution 1189 (1998).[169] After the terrorist attacks on 11 September 2001 the Council went even further and began legislating under Chapter VII in Resolution 1373 (2001). This time it went all the way and demanded under Chapter VII that all states must implement a set of provisions relating to terrorism *per se*, which are to be enforced by non-military sanctions. Another new feature that underscores the Council's legislative function is that the sanctions also target individuals if they appear on a list supplied by the sanctions committee.[170] Resolution 1530 (2004) concerning Spain, made it clear that even large-scale terrorist attacks allegedly committed by domestic terrorist groups qualify as threats to international

167 Österdahl, Inger, 1998, *supra* note 10, p. 76.

168 Lockerbie Case, prov. Measures, ICJ Reports, *supra* note 27, Schweigman, David, 2001, *supra* note 8.

169 Bring, Ove, *En rätt till väpnat självförsvar mot internationell terrorism?*, Juridisk Tidskrift, No. 2, 2001/2002, pp. 241–251, Svanberg, Katinka, *Folkrätten efter den 11 september 2001*, Terrorismens tid, Jervas, Gunnar, (Ed.), SNS förlag, Stockholm, 2003, pp. 143–154, at p. 145.

170 This confirms the impression that the Council has assumed the dual role of both a legislator and of a court of law. Individuals who appear on the list have their assets frozen as they are suspected of being international terrorists. This is a quasi-judicial measure with severe consequences, because there is no legal remedy available to challenge a Chapter VII decision by the Council, see contribution by Cameron.

peace and security. Such a development could be explained by the globalization of terrorism, with terrorist networks operating world, cooperating and sharing expertise and members with domestic groups, the victims of which could be of any nationality.

3.7 Final remarks

The case study shows that the Security Council has been influenced by legal considerations when adopting sanctions under Chapter VII. In fact it can be argued that the Security Council's decisions to apply Chapter VII have been motivated by a wish to sanction fundamental norms in public international law.[171] These norms are to a large extent the same as the purposes of the UN enumerated in Article 1 of the UN Charter. Furthermore, fundamental human rights and basic humanitarian law, as well as certain elements of the norm of self-determination are rules of *jus cogens*. It could also be argued that the upholding of those fundamental norms in public international law converges with the Security Council's mandate to maintain international peace and security.[172] Johnstone underlines the Council's ability to have recourse to a legal discourse:

> While first and foremost an executive body responsible for the maintenance of international peace and security, it is also a venue for heated, unsystematic but often principled debate about appropriate standards of international behaviour and the extent and limits of the Council's authority to regulate that behaviour.[173]

There are basically four ways in which the Council has used its powers under Chapter VII in the service of public international law:

171 This is evidenced by the fact that the Council no longer links decisions under Chapter VII to traditional findings of international threats to the peace, *i.e.* implying international conflicts, but have intervened in internal situations, thus motivated by other considerations, *i.e.*, to sanction certain norms in public international law that have come in focus during the era after the end of the cold war; most often they are fundamental norms aimed at the protection of the individual.

172 See *supra* at note 41.

173 Johnstone, Ian, *The Security Council Deliberations: The Power of the Better Argument,* European Journal of International Law (EJIL), Vol. 14, 2003, pp. 437–480, at p. 438.

1) The role as a *law enforcer.* It has sanctioned fundamental norms that already exist in public international law. This is evidenced by the fact that the Council cites various treaties and declaratory acts (which are evidence of customary international law) to underpin its findings. It cites important treaties and declarations, such as the Genocide Convention, the IV Geneva Conventions of 1949 and their two Protocols, FRD, the Colonial Declaration, the Santiago Commitment, human rights law and the principle of self-determination, etc.[174] This shows that the Council consciously bases its findings under Chapter VII on norms in international law.

2) *The Council contributes to the creation of norms in customary law.* The Council's decisions under Chapter VII contribute to the evolution of norms in public international law through their formulation and implementation in mandatory resolutions under Chapter VII. The enforcement decisions of the Council become part of the creation of norms and evidence of their crystallization into customary law. In fact the Council's sanctions constitute evidence both of an *opinio juris* and of *usus* in the international community because sanctions must be complied with by states. However, states could deny the Council this law-making function by making objections and reservations *e.g.* in the debates of the Council, the General Assembly and other international fora.

3) *The role of legislator.* Resolution 1373 is innovative as it is an enactment of sweeping legislation addressed generally to all states outside the context of a particular situation, while it creates

174 *Ibid.*, pp. 458–459. Convention on the Prevention and Punishment of the Crime of Genocide, 1948, The IV Geneva Conventions on Humanitarian Law, 1949, and Protocol I and II Additional to the Geneva Conventions, 1977, The Santiago Commitment to Democracy and Renewal of the Inter-American System, OAS/GAOR, 21st Reg. Sess. OEA/Ser.P/AG. doc. 2734/91, 4 June 1991, Declaration on the Granting of Independence to Colonial Countries and Peoples, GA Res. 1514 (XV), 1960, the International Convention on the Elimination of All forms of Racial Discrimination, 1963, FRD, see *supra* in note 56.

new rules of international law.[175] It is an important precedent that seems to represent a culmination of the Security Council's quasi-judicial activities under Chapter VII.[176]

4) *The role of a court of law* through the use of quasi-judicial sanctions. These are statements of law that become binding by the application of Chapter VII, or they are means of a judicial nature serving the purpose of international law. Examples are illegality, nullity and void decisions and declarations, the setting up of international criminal tribunals, extradition decisions, the demarcation of boundaries, arms control regimes, claims commissions and compensation claims.[177]

A warning is often voiced when discussing the Council's increasingly frequent use of Chapter VII for broader purposes than the traditional one of upholding international peace and security. It is pointed out that the Council is first and foremost a political body swayed by political considerations and thus biased, and as a result of this unable to create anything like a doctrine of *stare decisis*. But the case study indicates that even if the Council is constrained by its voting rules, it is evident that when it has been in a position to do so in view of the political situation it has treated like cases alike, thereby making use of its powers under Chapter VII in the service of public international law.

Its quasi-judicial capacity is nothing new in its history, as proved by the cases of Southern Rhodesia and South Africa. On the contrary, a quasi-judicial role is immanent in its broad powers under

175 'Resolution 1373, while inspired by the attacks of September 11, 2001, is not specifically related to these ... and lacks any explicit or implicit time limitation, a significant portion of the resolution can be said to establish new rules of international law – rather than mere commands relating to a particular situation and, moreover, even creates a mechanism for monitoring compliance with them', Szazs, Paul, *The Security Council Starts Legislating*, AJIL Vol. 96, no 4, 2002, pp. 901–905, at p. 902.

176 'If used prudently, this new tool will enhance the United Nations and benefit the world community, whose ability to create international law through traditional processes has lagged behind the urgent requirements of the new millennium, *ibid.*, p. 905.

177 The last three measures were adopted against Iraq in resolution 687 (1991) imposing severe conditions that Iraq had to accept as terms of surrender after the Gulf war.

Chapter VII, as Kelsen noted already a long time ago.[178] However, the development of international law in the decade following the end of the cold war has paved the way for an extended quasi-judicial role, with greater emphasis on individual and peoples' rights at the expense of state sovereignty.[179] The spur of activity in which the Council has been engaged at the turn of the new millennium has equipped it with a chance to enlarge its quasi-judicial capacity, stretching it to encompass purely legislative acts. And there are other norms waiting on its doorstep to be sanctioned, such as the possession of weapons of mass destruction.[180]

178 Kelsen stresses that there is no overlap between article 2(4) and 39 and lists a number of other possible situations that the Security Council might find to be a threat to the peace such as a states refusal to comply with various Charter provisions, *i.e.* refusal to execute the decisions of the ICJ (Article 94), non acceptance of plans for regulation of armaments (Article 26), non-compliance with the Council's call to settle a dispute by peaceful means (Article 33(2)), non-compliance with various recommendations by the General Assembly or the Council under Article 10, 11(2), 14, 36(1), 37(2), 38, Kelsen, Hans, *The Law of the United Nations*, 1950 *supra* note 8.

179 Mahmoudi, Said, *International Use of Force: Quo Vadis,* Juridisk tidskrift, Vol. 15, 2003/4, No. 2, pp. 341–344. In his speech at the Stockholm Genocide Conference in January 2004 the UN Secretary-General Kofi Annan made clear his position that there is a link between massive and systematic violations of human rights and threats to international peace and security and that state sovereignty cannot bar the "responsibility to intervene" in such cases, Annan, Kofi, *The Secretary-General Address to the Stockholm International Forum*, Stockholm, Sweden, 26 Jan. 2004, www.preventinggenocide.com/files/UN-Speech_26_jan.pdf.

180 Possession of weapons of mass destruction in contravention of international obligations is an emerging category regarding which the Council appears prepared to act under Chapter VII. The only case up to date is Iraq. In Iraq the possession of weapons of mass destruction became illegal by virtue of Resolution 687 (1991), that imposed a severe set of measures monitored by harsh non-military sanctions against Iraq after the Gulf war. It demanded in para. 8 that Iraq "unconditionally accept" the destruction of its weapons of mass destruction, including non-possession of nuclear weapons (para. 12). The non-possession imposed on Iraq was a consequence of its aggression against Kuwait. In resolution 687 the Council also forced Iraq to allow inspections by UN weapon inspectors to check whether Iraq was fulfilling its obligation not to possess any weapons of mass destruction. Iraq persistently refused to cooperate with the inspectors and finally in 1998 expelled them. The Council adopted Resolution 1441 in 2002, which demands Iraq's unconditional compliance with new tougher inspections '*Recognizing* the threat Iraq's non-compliance with Council resolutions and proliferation of weapons of mass destruction and long-range missiles poses to international peace and security'. Other possible cases in the future are North Korea, whose renunciation of the non-proliferation treaty and expulsion of the UN weapons inspectors could make the Council respond with non-military sanctions and Iran, where the IAEA called for inspections because of the country's alleged nuclear weapons programme.

References

Books & articles

Bedjaoui, Mohammed, *The New World Order and the Security Council: Testing the Legality of its Acts*, Dordrecht, Martinus Nijhoff Publishers, 1994.

Bring, Ove, *En rätt till väpnat självförsvar mot internationell terrorism?, Juridisk Tidskrift, No. 2,* 2001/2002 pp. 241–251.

Bring, Ove, *FN-stadgan och världspolitiken*, 4th ed. Nordstedts juridik, Stockholm 2002.

Bring, Ove, *International Criminal Law in Historical Perspective – Comments and Materials,* Juridiska fakulteten, No. 66 skriftserien, Stockholm, 2001.

Boutros-Ghali, Boutros, *An Agenda for Peace, United Nations, New York,* 1992.

Brownlie, Ian, *The Decisions of Political Organs of the United Nations and the Rule of Law,* Essays in Honour of Wang Tieya, Mc Donald, R., St. J., (Ed.), 1994.

Byers, Michael, Chesterman, Simon, *'You, the People': Pro-Democratic Intervention in International Law,* Democratic Governance and International Law, Fox, Gregory H., Roth, Brad, R., (Eds.), Cambridge University Press, Cambridge, 2000, pp. 259–293.

Cassese, Antonio, *Self-Determination of Peoples – A Legal Reappraisal,* Cambridge University press, Cambridge, 1995.

Cassese, Antonio, *'Terrorism is Also Disrupting Some Crucial Legal Categories of International Law',* European Journal of International Law, Discussion Forum on internet. Ejil.org/forum-WTC/ny-cassese.html, visited 25 October 2001.

Corten, Oliver, Klein, Pierre, *Droit d'ingérence ou obligation de réaction,* 2nd ed., 1996.

Damrosch, Lori, Fisler, *Enforcing Restraint,* New York, Council on Foreign Relations, 1993.

Danelius, Fredrik, *FN:s säkerhetsråds befogenheter – något om utvecklingen i teori och praktik,* Tandlös eller tiger – sju uppsatser om FN, Ahlin, Per, (Ed.) Juristförlaget, Stockholm, 1995.

Doehring, Karl, *Unlawful Resolutions of the Security Council and Their Legal Consequences,* Max Planck Yearbook of United Nations Law, Vol. 1, 1997, pp. 91–109.

Dulles, John, Foster, *War or Peace,* Macmillan, New York, 1950.

Dupuy, Pierre-Marie, *Droit international public,* Paris, Dalloz-Sirey, Coll.Précis Dalloz, 1992.

Emerson, Rupert, *Self-Determination,* American Journal of International Law, Vol. 65, 1971, p. 459.

Falk, Richard, *The Complexities of Humanitarian Intervention: A New World Order Challenge,* Michigan Journal of International Law, Vol. 17, 1996, p. 491.

Fielding, Lois E., *Taking the Next Step in the Development of New Human Rights: The Emerging Right of Humanitarian Assistance to Restore Democracy,*

Duke Journal of Comparative & International Law, Vol. 5 (1994/95) p. 329.

Franck, Thomas, *The Emerging Right to Democratic Governance*, Vol. 86, American Journal of International Law, 1992, pp. 46–91.

Frowein, Jochen Abr., *Chapter VII. Action with Respect to Threats to the Peace, Breaches of the Peace, and Acts of Aggression*, The Charter of the United Nations – A Commentary, Simma, Bruno (Ed.), 1st ed. Oxford University Press, Oxford, 1994.

Frowein, Jochen Abr., *Unilateral Interpretation of Security Council Resolutions – a Threat to Collective Security in Liber Amicorum Günter Jaenicke – Zum 85 Geburtstag*, 1998.

Goodrich, Leland M., Hambro, Edward, Simons, Anne Patricia, *Charter of the United Nations*, 3rd ed., Columbia University Press, New York, 1969.

Gowlland-Debbas, Vera, *The Security Council Enforcement Action and Issues of State Responsibility*, International and Comparative Law Quarterly, Vol. 43 pp. 55–98.

Gowlland-Debbas, Vera, *Collective Responses to Illegal Acts in International Law – United Nations Action in the Question of Southern Rhodesia*, Martinus Nijhoff Publishers, Dordrecht, 1990.

Hannikainen, Lauri, *Peremptory Norms in International Law*, Lakimiesliiton kustannus, Helsinki, 1988.

Helgesen, Vidar, *Til krig for menneskerettighetene*, Institutt for offentlig retts skriftserie, No. 2, 1999.

Higgins, Rosalyn, *International Law and the Avoidance, Containment and Resolution of Disputes*, Académie de Droit International, Recueil des Cours, Part V, Vol. 230, Martinus Nijhoff Publishers, Dordrecht, 1991.

Higgins, Rosalyn, *Problems & Process – International Law and How We Use it*, Clarendon, Oxford, 1994.

International Law Commission, Draft Articles on State Responsibility, Article 19, *Yearbook of International Law Commission*, 1980, Vol. II, Part 2.

Jama, Lisa Leila, *Humanitarian Intervention: An Examination of the United Nations' Role in the Modern Age of Civil Conflicts*, Florida Journal of International Law, Vol. XII, No. 3, 2000, pp. 521–541.

Johnstone, Ian, *The Security Council Deliberations: The Power of the Better Argument*, European Journal of International Law, Vol. 14, 2003, pp. 437–480.

Kelsen, Hans, *The Law of the United Nations*, 1st ed., Stevens & Sons, London, 1950.

Kooijmans, P.H., *The Enlargement of the Concept 'Threat to the Peace'* in *The Development of the Role of the Security Council: Colloque de l'Academie de Droit International de la Haye 1992*, The Development of the Role of the Security Council, (Ed.), Dupuy, Réne-Jean, 1993.

Koskenniemi, Martti, *The Police in the Temple Order, Justice and the UN: A Dialectical View*, European Journal of International Law, Vol. 6, 1995, pp. 325–248.

Lysén, Göran, *Targeted UN Sanctions: On the issue of legal sources and their application and also some procedural matters,* www.jur.uu.se/sii/articles, (29 January 2003).

Mahmoudi, Said, *International Use of Force: Quo Vadis,* Juridisk tidskrift, No. 2, 2003/2004, pp. 341–358.

McDougal, Myres S., Reisman, Michael, W., *Rhodesia and the United Nations: The Lawfulness of International Concern,* American Journal of International Law, Vol. 62, 1968, pp.1, 11–17.

McHugo, John, *Resolution 242: A Legal Reappraisal of the Right-Wing Israeli Interpretation of the Withdrawal Phrase with Reference to the Conflict between Israel and the Palestinians,* International & Comparative Law Quarterly, Vol. 51, 2002, pp. 851–882.

Malanczuk, Peter, *Akehurst's A Modern Introduction to International Law,* 7th revised ed., Routledge, New York, 1997.

Reinisch, August, *Developing Human Rights and Humanitarian Law Accountability of the Security Council for the Imposition of Sanctions,* American Journal of International Law, Vol. 95, 2001, pp. 851–872.

Reisman, Michael W., *Peacemaking,* Yale Journal of International Law, Vol. 18, 1993 pp. 415–423.

Roth, Brad, R., *Governmental Illegitimacy in International Law,* Oxford University Press, Oxford, 2000.

Ruffert, Matthias, *The Administration of Kosovo and East-Timor by the International Community,* International and Comparative Law Quarterly, Vol. 50, 2001, pp. 613–630.

Schachter, Oscar, *United Nations Law,* American Journal of International Law, Vol. 88, 1994, pp. 1–23.

Schweigman, David, *The Authority of the Security Council under Chapter VII of the UN Charter,* Kluwer Law International, Boston, 2001.

Shaw, M.N., *The Security Council and the International Court of Justice: Judicial Drift and Judicial Function,* The International Court of Justice: Its Future Role after Fifty Years, Müller, A.S., Raiç, D., Thuránszky, J.M, (Eds.), The Hague, M. Nijhoff Publishers, 1997.

Simma, Bruno (Ed.), *The Charter of the United Nations – A Commentary,* 1st ed., Oxford University Press, Oxford, 1994.

Svanberg, Katinka, *En introduktion till traktaträtten,* 3rd ed., Jure, Stockholm, 2003.

Svanberg, Katinka, *Folkrätten efter den 11 September 2001,* Terrorismens tid, Jervas, Gunnar, (Ed.), SNS förlag, Stockholm, 2003, pp. 143–154.

Szazs, Paul, *The Security Council Starts Legislating,* American Journal of International Law, Vol. 96, No. 4, 2002, pp. 901–905.

Szazs, Paul, *Centralized and Decentralized Law Enforcement: The Security Council and the General Assembly Acting under Chapters VII and VIII,* in Delbrück, J. (Ed.), Allocation of Law Enforcement Authority in the International System, Duncker & Hombolt, Berlin, 1995, pp. 17–38.

Téson, Fernando R., *Collective Humanitarian Intervention,* Michigan Journal of International Law, Vol. 17, 1995, p. 323.

Téson, Fernando R., *Humanitarian Intervention – an Inquiry into Law and Morality*, Irwington & Hudson, New York, 1988.

The Responsibility to Protect – Report of the International Commission on Intervention and State Sovereignty, International Development Research Center, Ottawa 2001.

Thirlway, H., *The Law and Procedure of the International Court of Justice 1960–1989*, British Year Book of Internationel Law, Vol. 67, 1996.

Wippman, David, *Practical and Legal Constraints on Internal Power Sharing*, in International Law and Ethnic Conflict, Ed. Wippman, David, Cornell University Press, New York, 1998

Wood, Michael, *The Interpretation of Security Council Resolutions*, Max Planck Yearbook of United Nations Law, Vol. 2, 1998, p. 73.

Zemanek, Karl, *Is the Security Council the Sole Judge of its own Legality?* Liber Amicorum Judge Mohammed Bedjaoui, Yakpo, Emile, Boumedra, Tahar, (Eds.), Kluwer, The Hague, 1999.

Österdahl, Inger, *Threat to the Peace – The Interpretation by the Security Council of Article 39 of the UN Charter*, Iustus förlag, Uppsala 1998.

Treaties

The Convention on the Prevention and Punishment of the Crime of Genocide, 1948.

The Geneva Conventions on Humanitarian Law I–IV, 1949.

Protocols I and II Additional to the Geneva Conventions, 1977.

The International Convention on the Elimination of All forms of Racial Discrimination, 1963.

The International Convention on the Suppression and Punishment of the Crime of Apartheid, 1974.

The International Covenant on Civil and Political Rights, 1966.

The International Covenant on Economic, Social and Cultural Rights, 1966.

The Montreal Convention for the Suppression of Unlawful Acts Against the Safety of Civil Aviation, 1971.

The Vienna Convention on the Law of Treaties, 1969.

Cases

Advisory Opinion on Certain Expenses of the United Nations, ICJ Reports, 1962.

Advisory Opinion on Legal Consequences for States of the Continued Presence of South Africa in Namibia (South West Africa) Notwithstanding Security Council Resolution 276 (1970), ICJ Reports, 1971.

Advisory Opinion on the Legality of the Use by a State of Nuclear Weapons in Armed Conflict, ICJ Reports, 1996.

Case Concerning Application of the Convention on the Prevention and Punishment of the Crime of Genocide (Provisional Measures), Bosnia-Herzegovina v. Yugoslavia, ICJ Reports, 1993.
Case Concerning Interpretation and Application of the 1971 Montreal Convention Arising from the Aerial Incident at Lockerbie, (Preliminary objections) *Libya* v. *US*, ICJ Reports, 1998.
Case Concerning Oil Platforms, (Preliminary objections), Iran v. US, ICJ Reports, 1996.
Case Concerning Arbitral Award of 13 July 1989, Guinea-Bissau v. Senegal, ICJ Reports 1991.
Case Concerning the Gabcíkovo-Nagymaros Project, Hungary v. Slovakia, ICJ Reports, 1997.
*Questions of Interpretation and Application of the 1971 Montreal Convention Arising from The Arial Incident at Lockerbie (*Provisional Measures), Libya v. US, ICJ Reports, 1992.

UN documents

The Declaration on the Granting of Independece to Colonial Countries and Peoples, GA Res. 1514 (XV), 1960.
Declaration on Principles of International Law Concerning Friendly Relations and Co-operation among States in Accordance with the Charter of the United Nations, GA Res. 2625 (XXV), 24 October 1970.
Report of the Independent Commission of Inquiry into the Actions of the United Nations During the 1994 Genocide in Rwanda, S/1999/340 (15 December 1999).
*Report of the Secretary-General on the Establishment of a Special Court for Sierra Leone, S/2*000/915 (4 Oct. 2000).
Summit Meeting of the Security Council, UN Doc. S/PV 3046 (31 January 1992).
The Conakry Agreement, UN Doc. S/1997/958 (1997).
The Definition of Aggression, GA Res. 3317 (XXIX), 1974
Travaux Préparatoires to the UN Charter, UNCIO Documents, San Francisco, 1945.

Security Council Resolutions

Afghanistan
Resolutions 1189 (1998), 1244 (1999), 1267 (1999), 1368 (2001), 1373 (2001), 1390 (2002)
Albania
Resolutions 1101, (1997), 1114 (1997)
Angola
Resolutions 804 (1993), 851 (1993), 864 (1993)

Burundi
Resolution 1072 (1996)
Central African Republic (CAR)
Resolution 1125 (1997)
Congo (Zaire)
Resolutions 143 (1960), 145 (1960), 146 (1960), 161 (1961), 169 (1961), 1078 (1996), 1080 (1996), 1484 (2003), 1493 (2003), 1501 (2003)
East Timor
Resolutions 384 (1975), 389 (1976), 1264 (1999), 1272 (1999)
Former Yugoslavia
Resolutions 713 (1991), 727 (1992), 743 (1992), 752 (1992), 757 (1992), 770 (1992), 781 (1993), 787 (1992), 808 (1993), 815 (1993), 819 (1993), 820 (1993), 824 (1993), 827 (1993), 836 (1993), 988 (1995), 994 (1995), 998 (1995)
Haiti
Resolutions 841 (1992), 917 (1994), 940 (1994), 1529 (2004)
Iraq
Resolutions 687, (1991), 688 (1991), 1441 (2002)
Kosovo
Resolutions 1160 (1998), 1199 (1998), 1244 (1999)
Liberia
Resolutions 788 (1992), 1497 (2003), 1509 (2003)
Libya
Resolutions 731 (1992), 748 (1992), 883 (1993), 1192 (1998)
Rwanda
Resolutions 912 (1994), 918 (1994), 925 (1994), 929 (1994), 955 (1994)
Sierra Leone
Resolutions 1132 (1997), 1156 (1998), 1171 (1998), 1289 (2000), 1306 (2000), 1315 (2000), 1346 (2001)
Somalia
Resolutions 733 (1992), 767 (1992), 775 (1992), 794 (1992), 814 (1993), 837 (1993)
South Africa
Resolutions 402 (1977), 403 (1977), 417 (1977), 418 (1977), 554 (1984), 556 (1984), 581 (1986)
Southern Rhodesia
Resolutions 216 (1965), 217 (1965), 277 (1970), 288 (1970), 423 (1978), 445 (1979), 448 (1979)
Spain
Resolution 1530 (2004)
Sudan
Resolutions 1044 (1996), 1054 (1996), 1070 (1996)

Miscellaneous

Annan, Kofi, *The Secretary-General's Address to the Stockholm International Forum*, Stockholm, Sweden, 26 Jan. 2004, www.preventinggenocide.com/files/UN-Speech_26_jan.pdf.

Santiago Commitment to Democracy and Renewal of the Inter-American System, OAS/GAOR, 21st Reg. Sess. OEA/Ser.P/AG.doc. 2734/91 (4 June 1991).

Svanberg, Katinka, *The Security Council's Action under Chapter VII concerning the Norm of Internal Self-Determination,* forthcoming.

The Dayton Agreement, reprinted in International Legal Materials (ILM), Vol. 35, 1996.

4 UN Smart Sanctions

Political Reality and International Law

Fredrik Stenhammar

4.1 Introduction

An important aspect of the collective security system created by the Charter of the United Nations (UN) is that Chapter VII provides the Security Council with the power to impose *sanctions* to preserve or restore international peace and security.[1] Short of armed force, non-military sanctions are the most potent means of pressure available to the Security Council. In recent years, traditional UN sanctions in the form of comprehensive trade embargoes against states have increasingly been perceived as not having the desired effects on the behavior of the target state in comparison with the disruptions that these sanctions cause in civilian life.[2] Beginning with Haiti in 1994, and most recently with regard to Afghanistan and al-Qaeda in the aftermath of the terrorist attack in New York on 11 September 2001, the Security Council has therefore come to rely more on so called *smart* or *targeted* sanctions, mainly financial sanctions, travel sanctions and arms embargoes. Smart sanctions are designed to strike directly at the regime elite, whilst reducing the detrimental consequences for the civilian population. If a parallel is drawn to warfare, targeted sanctions could be regarded as analogous to laser-guided, "smart", bombs, as opposed to comprehensive sanctions and carpet-bombing.

In the last few years, a lot of attention has been devoted to smart sanctions, not only in international law, but also in the field of

1 Charter of the United Nations, UNTS, Vol. 1, p. XVI, 1945.

2 On the humanitarian criticism of sanctions, see, *e.g.*, Bruderlein, Claude, *Coping with the Humanitarian Impact of Sanctions: An OCHA Perspective*, United Nations Office for the Coordination of Humanitarian Affairs, 1998, www.reliefweb.int/ocha (2000-09-15) [Hereinafter OCHA-Report].

political science and peace and conflict research.[3] This chapter is limited to an examination of some aspects of the smart sanctions instrument as it has developed in the practice of the Security Council. I will concentrate on two types of measures aimed directly at individuals and private entities, namely the freezing of foreign-held assets and travel bans, which, I think, amply illustrate the various legal problems connected with the use of the powerful international sanctions instrument against non-state actors and individuals. In addition, I will say a few words about arms embargoes, which, even though generally considered as smart sanctions, raise issues of quite a different nature.

4.2 Defining the terms

4.2.1 Sanctions in international law

The word *sanction* does not appear in the UN Charter, and the concept is not entirely unambiguous in international law.[4] In the abstract, it refers to means by which compliance with international law is assured. For example, it can be said that in the absence of consent, the only sanction available to an injured state under international law is self-help.[5] Often, however, the term is used in a technical sense, signifying specific measures taken by a state or group of states, in an effort to impose its will on another state.

On a conceptual level, sanctions can be divided into *retorsions*, or lawful acts designed to hurt another state, and *reprisals*, or *per se* illegal acts rendered lawful by the other state's prior breach of interna-

3 For an extensive bibliography, see Eriksson, M., *Bibliographic Paper on International Sanctions,* 2003, www.smartsanctions.se (2003-05-10). Notably, three consecutive conference series have been devoted to the development of smart sanctions. These are known as the Interlaken Process, the Bonn-Berlin Process and the Stockholm Process. See, respectively, www.smartsanctions.ch, www.bicc.de and www.smartsanctions.se.

4 See, *e.g.*, Combacau, J., *Sanctions*, Bernhardt, R., (Ed.), Encyclopedia of Public International Law, North-Holland, Amsterdam, Vol. 4, 2000, pp. 311–315.

5 Malanczuk, P., *Akehurst's Modern Introduction to International Law*, 7th ed., Routledge, London, 1997, p. 4.

tional law.[6] Because of the coupling of the term reprisals with armed force, which, in principle, is illegal under the UN Charter, *countermeasures* have become the preferred term for in themselves unlawful, but non-forcible, acts justifiably taken in response to a breach of international legal duty by another state.[7] Certain customary rules apply to countermeasures, notably the principle of proportionality.[8] This topic is part of the law on state responsibility.

As distinguished from countermeasures, *sanction* is the established term for a non-forcible measure taken by an international organisation against one of its members to ensure compliance with its statutes.[9] An often quoted example of this is Chapter VII of the UN Charter. However, in the strict sense, UN sanctions are not reactions to a prior internationally wrongful act in the way that countermeasures are. UN sanctions are reactions to a threat to the peace, a breach of the peace or an act of aggression, as determined by the Security Council. Only in the last instance does that necessarily mean that it is an internationally wrongful act.[10] Hence, whilst countermeasures are characteristic of the horizontal, decentralized nature of international law, UN sanctions have a specific legal basis, *viz.* a determination by the Security Council under the UN Charter. The Security Council has, moreover, imposed sanctions not only on members of the UN, but also on non-state actors such as UNITA (National Union for the Total Independence of Angola), as well as on private individuals. Its competence to do this has never been

6 See Partsch, K.J., *Retorsion,* in Bernhardt, R., (ed.), Encyclopedia of Public International Law, North-Holland, Amsterdam, Vol. 4, 2000, pp. 232–233, and Partsch, K.J., *Reprisals*, ibid., pp. 200–205.

7 See, *e.g.,* Articles 47–53 of *The International Law Commission's Draft Articles on Responsibility of States for Internationally Wrongful Acts,* Report of the International Law Commission on the work of its Fifty-third session, G.A.O.R., 56th sess., Suppl. No. 10 (A/56/10). www.un.org/law/ilc/texts/State_responsibility/responsibilityfra.htm. See also Crawford, J., *The International Law Commission's Articles on State Responsibility,* University Press, Cambridge, 2002.

8 See, *e.g., Case Concerning the Gabcíkovo-Nagymaros Project* (Hungary/Slovakia), ICJ Reports 1997, p. 7, at paras. 83–85.

9 See, *e.g.*, Shearer, I.A., *Starke's International Law,* 11th ed., Butterworths, London, 1994, pp. 24–27.

10 See Crawford, J., *The Relationship between Sanctions and Countermeasures,* Gowlland-Debbas, V., (Ed.), United Nations Sanctions and International Law, Kluwer, The Hague, 2001, pp. 57–68, at p. 58.

seriously questioned by states.[11] It would appear to be in conformity with the wording of the relevant Charter provisions, although it is doubtful whether this was intended by its authors. The relationship between UN sanctions and international law on countermeasures is a complex subject, which will not be further explored here. In this connection, it may, however, be mentioned that when a state, or a regional organisation such as the European Union (EU), commits *per se* illegal acts against a perceived breach of legal duty by a non-member state, these acts are often referred to as sanctions rather than countermeasures, presumably to reinforce the appearance of legality.

4.2.2 Non-military sanctions under the UN Charter

According to Article 41 of the Charter, UN sanctions may include "complete or partial interruption of economic relations and of rail, sea, air, postal, telegraphic, radio, and other means of communication, and the severance of diplomatic relations". The most significant item on this non-exhaustive list is interruption of economic relations, usually referred to as *economic sanctions*.

Economic sanctions may be divided into trade sanctions, blocking imports and exports to and from a state, and financial sanctions, although the distinction between these categories is not overly clear. The concept of financial sanctions includes a wide range of financial measures aimed at immobilizing all financial resources at the disposal of a state, and at preventing new resources being made available to it.[12] Besides the freezing of assets and the denying of access to foreign financial markets, financial sanctions include restricting international transfer payments and trade in property abroad, along with the blocking of development aid and

11 See, *e.g.*, Österdahl, I., *FN-sanktioner och mänskliga rättigheter* eller *Hur kunde det bli på detta viset?*, SvJT 2002, pp. 894–916, at p. 899.

12 Jeker, R.M., *Lessons Learned and Definitions*, 2nd Interlaken Seminar on Targeting United Nations Financial Sanctions, 29–31 March, 1999, Interlaken, Switzerland; Convened by the Swiss Federal Office for Foreign Economic Affairs in Cooperation with the United Nations Secretariat, www.smartsanctions.ch (2000-09-25), pp. 67–74 at p. 67 [Hereinafter Interlaken II].

restrictions on international loans and credits.[13] Together, trade sanctions and financial sanctions constitute a comprehensive economic sanctions regime, the most illustrative example of which is that imposed on Iraq through, principally, Resolutions 661 (1990) and 687 (1991).

Next on the Article 41 list is the interruption of communications. Among sanctions directed at communications, the generic and not very precise term *travel sanctions* represents the following four categories of measures: *general transport sanctions* impeding all large-scale cross-border traffic; *travel bans* restricting the international travel of designated groups or individuals; *aviation sanctions* impeding international flights to and from a particular state (these may in turn be divided into commercial passenger transport and air cargo transport sanctions); and *air cargo traffic controls, i.e.* enforcement measures to stop breaches of embargoes.[14]

4.2.3 Smart sanctions

There is, as yet, no accepted definition of the concept *smart sanctions*, also referred to as targeted or designer sanctions. The UN Secretary-General, along with some writers, has designated the following measures as targeted sanctions: the freezing of financial assets of regime members and elites who support them; the suspension of credits and grant aid; the denial and limitation of access to foreign financial markets; trade embargoes on arms and luxury goods;

13 Van Brabant, K., *Can Sanctions be Smarter? The Current Debate*, Report of a conference held in London, 16–17 December 1998, sponsored by the UK Department of International Development, First Part, Overseas Development Institute, 1999, www.smartsanctions.ch (2000-09-25) p. 18 [Hereinafter ODI-Report I]; Newcomb, R.R., *Targeting Financial Sanctions*, Expert Seminar on Targeting UN Financial Sanctions, 17–19 March, 1998, Interlaken, Switzerland; Convened by the Swiss Federal Office for Foreign Economic Affairs, Department of Economy, www.smartsanctions.ch (2000-09-25), pp. 113–119 at p. 117 [Hereinafter Newcomb, Interlaken I].

14 *Report from Working Group I: Travel Sanctions*, First Expert Seminar: Smart Sanctions, the Next Step: Arms Embargoes and Travel Sanctions, Bonn, 21–23 November 1999; Organized by the Bonn International Institute for Conversion in Cooperation with the Foreign Office of the Federal Republic of Germany, www.bicc.de (2000-10-15) pp. 1–2 [Hereinafter Bonn-Berlin I].

flight bans and the denial of international travel, visas and educational opportunities to regime members and their families.[15]

This is a rather motley collection of measures, though all are presumably within the framework of Article 41. In particular, the reasons for categorizing suspension of credits and grant aid, trade embargoes on arms and luxury goods, and flight bans as targeted could perhaps be debated. Lately, the concept of smart sanctions would appear to have crystallized into three categories: financial sanctions, travel sanctions and arms embargoes.[16] It would seem that the critical quality distinguishing a smart sanction from a 'dumb' one is that it is designed to hit at the interests of individuals or groups in positions of power directly, rather than the entity they control.[17] If the character of the target is regarded as the determining factor, arms embargoes would seem to have more in common with general sanctions than with smart sanctions, in that they are aimed at states or state-like entities. Nevertheless, the categorization of arms embargoes as smart sanctions would seem to be established, presumably as only governments are thought to have a legitimate interest in acquiring arms.

4.2.4 The role of the Security Council

According to Article 24(1) of the UN Charter, the Security Council has primary responsibility for the maintenance of international peace and security. After a determination under Article 39 that a situation constitutes a threat to, or breach of, the peace or an act of aggression, the Security Council can order provisional measures under Article 40, sanctions under Article 41 or military action under Article 42, against the responsible entity. A result of the dis-

15 *Report of the Secretary-General to the Security Council on the Protection of Civilians in Armed Conflict*, UN Doc. S/1999/957, 1999, para. 54, note 11; *Adverse Consequences of Economic Sanctions on the Enjoyment of Human Rights*, Working Paper prepared by Mr. Marc Bossuyt, United Nations Economic and Social Council, E/CN.4/Sub.2/2000/33, 2000, pp. 14-15; Cortright, D. & Lopez, G.A., *The Sanctions Decade: Assessing UN Strategies in the 1990s*, Lynne Rienner Publishers, Boulder, 2000, p. 240 [Hereinafter Cortright & Lopez]; Rydell, R., *Monitoring United Nations Arms Embargoes*, p. 4 [Hereinafter Rydell].

16 Para. 2 of SC Res. 1390 (2002) (Afghanistan/al-Qaeda) is the most recent example of Security Council practice on smart sanctions.

17 ODI-Report I, *supra* note 13, p. 15.

tinction between non-forcible and forcible measures, illustrated by the sanctions against Rhodesia, appears to be that a trade embargo can be imposed under Article 41, but its enforcement through a naval blockade requires resort to Article 42.[18] This issue is, however, largely moot, since the Security Council seldom refers explicitly to the operative article, but confines itself to saying that it is "acting under Chapter VII of the Charter".[19] In this way, the Security Council presumably signals that it is acting in the spirit of Chapter VII, if not according to its letter.[20]

The Security Council is a political organ which, when using its power under Chapter VII, is capable of creating *in casu* rules of international law. According to Article 39, it is entirely at the discretion of the Security Council to make a determination of when there is a threat to international peace that warrants the imposition of sanctions. This is necessarily a predominantly political consideration, and Security Council practice ranges from clear-cut cases of military aggression to genocide, and to rather less obvious cases, such as prevention of international terrorism and restoration of democracy. Non-military UN sanctions have, so far, been imposed in 15 cases, all but two after the end of the Cold War.[21]

The competence of the Security Council is limited by Article 24(2), which prescribes that it shall act in accordance with the purposes and principles of the UN Charter. These are spelled out in Articles 1 and 2 of Chapter I. Arguably, the main purpose of the UN is set out in Article 1(1), namely to maintain international peace and security. Besides maintaining international peace and security, another purpose, according to Article 1(3), is "to achieve international cooperation ... in promoting and encouraging respect for human rights and for fundamental freedoms for all without distinction". Although the language is non-committal, the better view would seem to be that this Charter

18 See SC Res. 221 (1966) (Southern Rhodesia); Frowein, J. & Krisch, N., *Article 41*, Simma, B., (Ed.), The Charter of the United Nations – A Commentary, 2nd ed., 2002, pp. 735–748 at p. 740.

19 See, *e.g.*, SC Res. 841 (1993) (Haiti) and SC Res. 1160 (1998) (Federal Republic of Yugoslavia/Kosovo).

20 Bring, O., *FN-stadgan och världspolitiken*, 4th ed., Norstedts, Stockholm, 2002, p. 279.

21 Afghanistan/al-Qaeda, Angola/UNITA, Federal Republic of Yugoslavia/Kosovo, Haiti, Iraq, Liberia, Libya, Rwanda, Sierra Leone, Southern Rhodesia, Somalia, South Africa, Sudan and the former Yugoslavia.

provision is to be understood to mean that the Security Council, when discharging its duties, is obliged to respect customary international norms with respect to human rights.[22] In addition, some authors suggest that, although sanctions are non-forcible measures, the customary rules of international humanitarian law, notably the principles of proportionality, necessity and distinction between combatants and civilians, are applicable to UN sanctions regimes.[23] It is a matter of controversy whether there is any mechanism within the UN system to ensure that the Security Council acts in accordance with either the purposes and principles of the Charter or with human rights and humanitarian law. This is a question of UN constitutional procedure which, as such, is separate from the issue of the legal limits of the Security Council's powers.[24] As it is, the composition of the Security Council, and the veto power held by its permanent members, set the natural boundaries for its actions. Since the end of the Cold War there has been a tendency, on the part of the Security Council, towards a broadened interpretation of the mandate, and also to a preference for smart rather than comprehensive sanctions, which would appear to be continuing.

The purpose of UN sanctions, according to Article 39 of the UN Charter, is to maintain or restore international peace and security. In practical terms, the sanctions should bring to an end a threat to international peace and security. From this one may conclude that UN sanctions should form an incentive for a state to modify its behaviour and abide by international law, by taking or refraining from certain actions.[25] When the state's compliance has been assured, or when changed circumstances have rendered the threat obsolete, sanctions should, accordingly, be terminated. Along these lines, it is sometimes

22 See, *e.g.*, Gasser, H.-P., *Collective Economic Sanctions and International Humanitarian Law*, ZaöRV 56/4 pp. 871-904, 1996, at p. 880 *et seq*.

23 On this, see, *e.g.*, Reisman, W.M., and Stevick, D.L., *The Applicability of International Law Standards to United Nations Economic Sanctions Programmes*, EJIL, Vol. 9, 1998, pp. 86–141, at p. 126 *et seq.*; Szasz, P., *The Law of Economic Sanctions*, Schmitt, M.N., & Green, L.C. (Eds.), The Law of Armed Conflict: Into the Next Millennium, Naval War College, Newport, 1998, pp. 455–481 at p. 474.

24 See further below, Chapter 4.5, on the question of whether the International Court of Justice has powers of judicial review over the Security Council.

25 Beyerlin, U., *Sanctions*, Wolfrum, R. (Ed.), United Nations: Law, Policies and Practice, Vol. 2, Revised English Edition, Martinus Nijhoff, Dordrecht, 1995, pp. 1111–1128, at p. 1112.

pointed out that UN sanctions are not punitive but coercive in character.[26] The helpfulness of this statement is doubtful, however. For example, it is not obvious why the Claims Commission against Iraq, rather than coercive, should not be considered as punitive or reparative.[27] Issues of reparation for damages caused by wrongful acts are dealt with in the law of state responsibility, which, arguably, does not differentiate between punitive and reparative damages in the way that national legislation sometimes does.

The member states' obligation to enforce sanctions ordered by the Security Council follows from Article 25. It is a treaty obligation that applies regardless of whether there are any legal grounds for unilateral countermeasures by the individual member state.[28] Nevertheless, the Security Council sometimes chooses to use non-binding language in sanctions resolutions, presumably to avoid responsibility for enforcement.

4.3 Three categories of smart sanctions

4.3.1 Asset freezes

As such, asset freezes are not new. They are regular features of UN sanctions regimes as well as of unilateral countermeasures. It has even been asserted that foreign financial assets ultimately lay hostage in the hands of the host government.[29] The presumed novelty of targeted asset freezes is that they are not only aimed at government-owned assets, but also at the personal assets of individuals, groups and companies within the governing elite. As mentioned, the Security Council first used targeted asset freezes against Haiti in 1994. The general sanctions imposed against Haiti in 1993 had been found to have a limited effect on the behavior of the regime,

26 *Verification in All its Aspects, Including the Role of the United Nations in the Field of Verification*, Report of the Secretary-General, UN Doc. A/50/377, 1995, para. 179; Combacau, *supra* note 4, p. 339; Gasser, *supra* note 22, p. 879.

27 SC Res. 687 (1991) (Iraq).

28 *Pacta sunt servanda*, as evidenced by Article 26 of the Vienna Convention on the Law of Treaties, UNTS, Vol. 1155, p. 331, 1969, is a general principle of international law.

29 Cárdenas, E.J., *The 1982 Freeze of British Assets in Argentina: A Retrospective Overview*, Journal of International Banking Law, Vol. 2, 1991, pp. 81–83, at p. 82.

despite contributing to a progressive deterioration of civil society. In response, the Security Council tried to target the regime elite specifically in a second round of sanctions.[30] This was the second time that individuals were made the direct targets of UN sanctions. Before, in 1992, sanctions whose purpose was to achieve the extradition of the two Lockerbie bombing suspects had been imposed on Libya.[31] The language of the Haiti resolution was not technically binding. In paragraphs 3 and 4, the Security Council "strongly urges all states to freeze without delay" the funds and financial resources "[o]f all officers of the Haitian military, including the police, and their immediate families; [o]f the major participants in the *coup d'état* of 1991 and in the illegal government since the *coup d'état,* and their immediate families; [o]f those employed by or acting on behalf of the Haitian military, and their immediate families".[32] Subsequently, in 1998, senior officials and adult members of their immediate families were singled out, as the sanctions against UNITA were tightened.[33] The most recent example of targeted asset freezes in Security Council practice are the sanctions against Afghanistan and al-Qaeda in the wake of the terrorist attack in New York in September 2001.[34] From only restricting the movement of funds across borders in the beginning of the 1990s, financial sanctions have evolved into the more sophisticated, and more realistic, asset freeze, which restricts all movement of the targets' funds, even domestically in the sanctioning state.[35] Presumably, freezing assets is not the same thing as confiscation, and should therefore be distinguished from sequestration, as practised during the world wars. Compare, however, the order in Resolution 1483 (2003) to transfer funds to the Iraqi Development Fund, para. 23.

Parallels can be drawn between smart sanctions in the form of asset freezes on the one hand and the international efforts to combat money laundering on the other. The most significant of these

30 SC Res. 841 (1993) imposed a fuel and arms embargo on Haiti. SC Res. 917 (1994), imposed comprehensive sanctions and a freeze on the regime elite's foreign held assets. See, *e.g.* Cortright & Lopez, *supra* note 15, p. 99.

31 SC Res. 748 (1992) (Libya).

32 SC Res. 917 (1994) (Haiti), paras. 3–4.

33 SC Res. 1173 (1998) (Angola/UNITA), para. 11.

34 SC Res. 1390 (2002) (Afghanistan/al-Qaeda), para. 2.

35 Compare SC Res. 661 (1991) (Iraq), para. 4 with SC Res. 1173 (1998) (Angola/UNITA), para. 11.

efforts, from the sanctions point of view, is the Financial Action Task Force on Money Laundering (FATF), operating under the auspices of the Organisation for Economic Cooperation and Development (OECD), whose purpose is to develop policies to combat money laundering.[36] The FATF has issued a list of 40 recommendations, meant to set minimum standards for the improvement of national legal systems, the enhancement of the role of the financial system, and the strengthening of international cooperation, all of which is also relevant to financial sanctions.[37] Money laundering means the conversion of money of illicit origin, *e.g.* drug sales, into apparently legitimate assets[38] which could be described as a three-stage process. In the *placement stage,* cash is converted into different forms of assets, *e.g.* through a bank deposit or a purchase. In the *layering stage,* different transactions are made to conceal the source and ownership of the assets. Finally, in the *integration stage,* the assets are assimilated into the legitimate economic circuit. Usually, none of the actions taken are *per se* illegal, but a number of ordinary actions add up to an illegal result.[39] The so called offshore financial centres or tax havens play an important role in the money laundering process. Offshore centres are jurisdictions with large financial sectors conducting business solely with non-resident customers. Important traits of offshore centres are strict banking secrecy and a minimum of rules interfering with private business. As regards implementation of financial sanctions, the attitudes in the offshore centres vary considerably.

The UN may also have lessons to learn from American experience in the field of targeted financial sanctions. The US law enforcement agencies started early to focus on finances as a means to combat organized crime. Since 1940, there has been a specialized body

36 On the membership of the FATF, see www.oecd.org/fatf.

37 *Financial Action Task Force on Money Laundering, The Forty Recommendations,* www.oecd.org/fatf (2000-11-01); *Financial Action Task Force on Money Laundering,* Report of 6 February 1990, *ibid.*, p. 15.

38 Örnemark Hansen, H., *Penningtvätt: Ett urvattnat begrepp?*, Norstedts, Stockholm, 1998, p. 11.

39 Blum, J.A., Levi, M., Naylor, R.T. & Williams, P., *Financial Havens, Banking Secrecy and Money-Laundering,* United Nations Office for Drug Control and Crime Prevention, 1998, p. 4.

within the US Treasury Department, the Office of Foreign Assets Control (OFAC), which administrates both unilateral measures and multilateral sanctions directed against foreign regimes as well as criminals such as terrorists and drug barons.[40]

4.3.2 Travel bans

A travel ban means, with standard formulations borrowed from Resolution 1127 (1997) (Angola/UNITA), that states are requested to "prohibit the entry into or transit through their territories of all senior ... officials and of adult members of their immediate families".[41] This may sound like a rather harmless measure, but travel bans feature regularly in UN sanctions regimes and are considered to signal disapproval by symbolically isolating a state or entity.[42] In addition, the Expert Panel on the Angola sanctions has pointed out that there is a close link between the ability to travel abroad and the possibility of procuring arms and funds.[43] Usually, travel sanctions are just complements to more extensive regimes. In some cases, however, notably as regards Libya, travel sanctions have been the main form of pressure.

As evidenced by the difficulties experienced by the EU in enforcing the travel sanctions against UNITA, several problems need solving. Portugal, France and Belgium are important centres of UNITA activity in Europe. Having entered Europe through one of these

40 See Newcomb, Interlaken I, *supra* note 13, www.treas.gov/ofac.
41 SC Res. 1127 (1997) (Angola/UNITA).
42 See, *e.g.*, Conroy, R., *Implementation Problems of Travel Bans: Practical and Legal Aspects*, Final Draft, 2000 [Hereinafter Conroy Bonn-Berlin I] p. 1. So far, travel bans have been imposed in the following cases: Iraq, SC Res. 1137 (1997); Libya, SC Res. 748, (1992); Haiti, SC Res. 917 (1994); Sudan, SC Res. 1054 (1996); Angola/UNITA, SC Res. 1127 (1997); Sierra Leone, SC Res. 1132 (1997), SC Res. 1171 (1998); Afghanistan/al-Qaeda SC Res. 1390 (2002). Aviation sanctions have been imposed in the following cases: Iraq, SC Res. 670 (1990); Former Yugoslavia, SC Res. 757 (1992); Haiti, SC Res. 917 (1994); Angola/UNITA SC Res. 1127 (1997); Afghanistan, SC Res. 1267 (1999).
43 *Report of the Panel of Experts on Violations of Security Council Sanctions Against UNITA*, annexed to UN Doc. S/2000/203, 2000, para. 131 [Hereinafter Expert Panel Report]; *Letter Dated 16 October from the Chairman of the Monitoring Mechanism on Angola Sanctions Addressed to the Chairman of the Security Council Committee Established Pursuant to Resolution 864 (1993) concerning the Situation in Angola*, annexed to UN Doc. S/2000/1026, 2000 p. 7 [Hereinafter Mechanism Interim Report].

states, several UNITA officials are known to travel freely within the EU, benefiting from the free movement of persons.[44] In the US, where some UNITA activists have acquired permanent residence or citizenship, it has proved difficult to close down UNITA's unofficial embassies without intruding on the civil liberties protections of due process and freedom of expression.[45]

From the humanitarian point of view, the major criticism against travel bans has been that they may impede the targets' legitimate need of access to professional medical care in foreign states.[46] As personal contact with leaders is often necessary to achieve a peaceful solution to a conflict, travel bans also need to include exceptions to allow travel for this purpose, either explicit as in the case of UNITA, or implicit as in the case of Sudan.[47]

4.3.3 Arms embargoes

As regards arms embargoes, the following locution is often used by the Security Council: "[A]ll states shall prevent the sale or supply ... of arms and related materiel of all types, including weapons and ammunition, military vehicles and equipment, police equipment, and spare parts for the aforementioned".[48]

At best, arms embargoes may succeed in preventing the aggravation of armed conflicts, thereby mitigating a threat to international peace and security, at worst they are symbolic gestures, employed when the political will to take real action is lacking. The arms embargo imposed on Rwanda in 1994 is sometimes quoted as an example of this token use of arms embargoes.[49] However, with the vast number of arms in circulation and the presumed linkage between the availability of arms and the prevalence of armed conflicts, and especially violations of the laws and customs of war, arms

44 *Ibid.*
45 Conroy, Bonn-Berlin I, *supra* note 42, p. 11.
46 Cortright, D., Lopez, G., & Conroy, R., *Are Travel Sanctions Smart?: A Review of Theory and Practice*, Final Draft, 2000, p. 7 [Hereinafter Cortright *et al.*, Bonn-Berlin I].
47 SC Res. 1127 (1997) (Angola/UNITA); SC Res. 1054 (1996) (Sudan).
48 See, *e.g.*, SC Res. 841 (1993) (Haiti), para. 5.
49 SC Res. 918 (1994) (Rwanda); Cortright & Lopez, 2000, *supra* note 15, p. 195.

embargoes are becoming increasingly important.[50] Not even arms embargoes are immune to criticism, however. For example, it has been argued that the arms embargo against the former Yugoslavia, applying equally to all the breakaway republics, amounted to a violation of the Bosnian right to self-defence, since the Serbian regime in Belgrade remained in control of the well-equipped Yugoslav Army.[51] The International Court of Justice has yet to pronounce on this question. In the case of South Africa, the arms embargo had the undesired effect of bolstering the indigenous arms industry.[52]

Arms embargoes can benefit from the various international efforts at export control and curbing illicit arms trafficking. For example, the *Wassenaar Arrangement on Export Controls for Conventional Arms and Dual-Use Goods and Technologies* has produced a *List of Dual-Use Goods and Technologies* and a *Munitions List.*[53] Both of these rather detailed lists are kept updated and may be of use within the context of UN arms embargoes, either as direct references or as models for equivalent UN lists. The Monitoring Mechanism on Angola Sanctions has also sought the cooperation of the Wassenaar Arrangement in the tightening of the system of end-user certificates.[54]

A sometimes neglected reason for the poor record of arms embargoes may be that, by the time the Security Council becomes involved, the conflict zone is already awash with arms and that the target therefore has no immediate need for more arms. Perhaps the arms embargo against the Federal Republic of Yugoslavia in 1998 that failed to modify the Belgrade regime's behavior in Kosovo represents an example of this.[55] Earlier imposition of sanctions would probably not have made any difference as regards Kosovo, but perhaps it would have in Rwanda.[56]

50 *Statement by the President of the Security Council*, UN Doc. S/PRST/1999/28, 1999.
51 See the submissions of Bosnia in the *Case Concerning the Application of the Convention on the Preventions and Punishment of the Crime of Genocide* (Bosnia-Hezegovina v. Yugoslavia), Preliminary Objections, International Court of Justice, Judgment of 11 July 1996, www.icj-cij.org (2000-11-15).
52 Bring, *supra* note 20, p. 266.
53 The Wassenaar Arrangement on Export Controls for Conventional Arms and Dual-Use Goods and Technologies, 1995, www.wassenaar.org (2001-04-25).
54 Mechanism Interim Report, *supra* note 43, p. 5.
55 SC Res. 1160 (1998) (Federal Republic of Yugoslavia).
56 See Cortright & Lopez, 2000, *supra* note 15, p. 195.

4.4 Some problematic issues related to smart sanctions

4.4.1 Access to information and the creation of blacklists

If smart sanctions are to have the desired effect, it is crucial that the Security Council has access to good information on the individuals and groups comprising the targeted elite.[57] More often than not, targets hold their assets under false names, through front companies, or, in jurisdictions where this is still possible, anonymously. There is usually a veil of bank secrecy and lawyer-client privilege to hide the identity of the owner. Accurate information regarding the targets' financial situation, *i.e.* where and how assets are held, and on the major financial partners and preferred routes of money transfers, must be gathered, analysed and shared. This is a process involving both the UN and the member states.[58] Banks and other private actors on the financial market are traditionally reluctant to disclose information about their customers. In addition, states are often suspicious of the ability of the UN to keep secrets, and may accordingly choose to protect their sources rather than to pursue objectives that are not felt to have much relevance to their own national interests.[59] UN intelligence capabilities have attracted attention as regards UN peacekeeping.[60] However, the prospect of a UN intelligence service may seem neither very realistic nor, indeed, desirable.[61] As it is, the Security Council relies on information on the targets gathered by national intelligence agencies and supplied to it by the member states. Aside from logistical problems, the use of national intelligence for UN sanctions is a delicate business. This is illustrated by the case of the three Swedish Somalis put on the al-Qaeda sanctions list due to their involvement with the al-Barakaat money-transfer company, presumably as a result of information

57 *Statement by the President of the Security Council*, UN Doc. S/PRST/1999/28, 1999.

58 Schönenberger, C., *Evasion and Control of Financial Sanctions – Practical Considerations*, Interlaken I, pp. 125–126; Newcomb, R.R., *Targeted Financial Sanctions: The U.S. Model*, Interlaken II, pp. 29–57 [Hereinafter Newcomb, Interlaken II] at pp. 37–38.

59 Conroy, Bonn-Berlin I, *supra* note 45, pp. 7–8.

60 See, *e.g.*, *Letter Dated 17 April 2000 from the Chairman of the panel on United Nations Peace Operations to the Secretary-General*, annexed to UN Doc. A/55/305-S/2000/809, 2000, (a.k.a. the Brahimi Report) para. 51.

61 See Expert Panel Report, *supra* note 43, para. 176.

supplied by US authorities.[62] Since information concerning individuals is gathered and registered, applicable norms relating to civil rights, such as integrity and privacy, have to be taken into account.[63]

A list of individuals and groups to whom the sanctions apply cannot be included in the resolution, as changes in the list would then require a revised resolution, something that is often politically impossible. The resolution must, however, be precise about the categories of persons included, and preferably also set out the procedure by which the list is reviewed.[64] In practice, the relevant sanctions committee compiles or at least endorses a list of targets, often referred to as a blacklist.[65] The list needs to be sufficiently detailed, *i.e.* containing names, alternative spellings, birth dates, passport numbers, pictures *etc.* to allow identification in practice by bank employees, immigration officials and others.[66] Confusion of identities in applying the sanctions not only disrupts the life of innocent people, it also allows the true targets time to continue their economic activities and therefore seriously impedes the efficacy of the sanctions regime. The blacklist needs to be continuously reviewed and updated, not least since targets are likely to attempt to change their identities. A major problem as regards travel bans is that targeted individuals are often able to acquire valid travel documents under false names. When they are part of the government this is to be expected. The situation as regards holders of passports other than that of the sanctioned state also requires some attention.

62 See, *e.g.*, Golden, T. *5 Months After Sanctions Against Somali Company, Scant Proof of Qaeda Tie*, New York Times, 2002-04-13. A case concerning them is currently pending before the European Court of First Instance, see below, section 4.4.5.

63 *E.g.*, Article 17 of the International Covenant on Civil and Political Rights, UNTS, Vol. 999, p. 171, 1966; Article 8 of the European Convention for the Protection of Human Rights and Fundamental Freedoms, ETS No. 5, 1950; For an analysis of the applicability of human rights norms to the fight against terrorism, see the chapter Human Rights and Terrorism by Iain Cameron.

64 *Report of Expert Working Group I*, Final Expert Seminar on Smart Sanctions, the Next Step: Arms Embargoes and Travel Sanctions, organized by the Bonn International Center for Conversion (Bonn-Berlin) in cooperation with the German Foreign Office, Berlin, 3–5 December 2000, www.bicc.de (2001-04-25), p. 7 [Hereinafter Bonn-Berlin II].

65 For example, the al-Qaeda Sanctions Committee's regularly updated list can be viewed on the UN homepage, www.un.org/docs/sc/committees.

66 Conroy, Bonn-Berlin I, *supra* note 42, p. 11; Newcomb, Interlaken II, *supra* note 58, p. 42.

Notably, several of the targeted UNITA officials hold non-Angolan passports with the help of which they travel freely.[67]

Supposedly, the sanctions blacklists indicate that the individuals in question are the targets of UN sanctions, without, as such, implying guilt of violations of civil or criminal law. However, this distinction is blurred, particularly as regards terrorism and not least since the Security Council has ordered states to criminalize the financing of terrorism.[68] In these cases, blacklisting of an individual certainly resembles punishment or at least determination of guilt without trial, something that would fly in the face of the norms of the Rechtsstaat.[69]

4.4.2 Clarity of language

The need for clear and consistent language in Security Council resolutions is another matter of importance in the context of smart sanctions.[70] This applies, firstly, to the objective of the sanctions, *e.g.* either to ensure that Iraq does not have the ability to manufacture weapons of mass destruction, or to topple Iraqi President Saddam Hussein, or perhaps both.[71] But, and this may even be more important, the requirement of unambiguous language also applies to the actual measures ordered. It is of special importance to arms embargoes that prohibited goods be defined with precision, *e.g.* whether an arms embargo includes a prohibition against the provision of military services such as military training, logistical support, expertise and intelligence. The failure to address the issue of military services when sanctions were imposed against Sierra Leone reportedly enabled the Revolutionary United Front (RUF) to hire Ukrainian mercenaries.[72] The provision in Resolution 883 (1993), prohibiting export to Libya of goods or services for the purposes of

67 Expert Panel Report, *supra* note 43, para. 137.
68 SC Res. 1373 (2001) para. 1 (a).
69 See further, Andersson, T., Cameron, I. & Nordback, K., *EU Blacklisting: The renaissance of Imperial Power, but on a Global Scale,* European Business Law Review, Vol. 14, 2003, pp. 111–141, [Hereinafter Andersson *et al.*] at p. 124.
70 See, *e.g.*, ODI-Report I, *supra* note 13, p. 20.
71 SC Res. 687 (1991) (Iraq). See Cortright & Lopez, 2000, *supra* note 15, p. 56.
72 SC Res. 1132 (1997) (Sierra Leone). See also SC Res. 1171 (1998) (Sierra Leone). Cortright and Lopez, 2000, *supra* note 15, p. 174.

constructing or maintaining airfields raised some questions – did it include, as a logical interpretation would suggest, shovels and paint?

Ambiguity provides opportunities for abuse and makes it difficult for states to implement the sanctions regime in good faith. There is also the matter of predictability, which cannot be ignored, at least if the subjects are individuals. Uniformity in interpretation could perhaps be increased by the use of standardized technical language as "building blocs".[73] However, it may be difficult to reach compromises in the Security Council, and the language of resolutions is often abstract. A certain amount of flexibility is probably necessary, since it may not be politically possible for the Security Council to change the resolution.

The scope of an asset freeze needs to be specified, and the precise meaning of the freeze spelled out, *e.g.* if any transactions are to be allowed. For example, when the target is a private individual, an asset freeze without humanitarian exceptions would, if stringently applied, mean that the person would be unable to buy food, medicines *etc.* Resolution 1267 (1999) concerning Afghanistan and al-Qaeda allows the sanctions committee to authorize exceptions "on a case-by-case basis on the grounds of humanitarian needs".[74] The UN Security Council regularly defines the scope of asset freezes as follows: "Funds or other financial resources, including funds derived or generated from property owned or controlled directly or indirectly".[75] This can be compared to the US regulations, which have considerably wider scope, including "all property and interests in property".[76] In the US, the OFAC purports to spell out the precise meaning with the following formula: "[N]o property ... may be transferred, paid, exported, withdrawn or otherwise dealt in", "[e]xcept as authorized by regulations, rulings, instructions, licenses, or otherwise".[77]

73 This has been one of the approaches of the three governmental initiatives to develop smart sanctions, see *supra* note 3.

74 Para. 4 (b).

75 See, *e.g.*, SC Res. 883 (1993) (Libya); SC Res. 1267 (1999) (Afghanistan/al-Qaeda).

76 See, *e.g.*, U.S. Executive Order 12724 Blocking Iraqi Government Property and Prohibiting Transactions with Iraq, 9 Aug. 1990.

77 *Ibid.*

4.4.3 Implementation at UN and state level

The decision to impose smart sanctions needs to be communicated quickly from the Security Council to the member states. The lists of targeted persons must be known and available to the employees of financial institutions and officials of immigration and border control authorities.[78] Delays between the decision and its implementation allow the targets time to move and hide their assets elsewhere. Recently, the sanctions committees have taken up the OFAC practice of publishing the blacklists on the internet.[79] Already, the often-prolonged Security Council debates preceding the adoption of sanctions give the targets ample time to conceal their assets. This time span is perhaps the Achilles' heel of an asset freeze.

There is no permanent sanctions mechanism at the UN level. Instead, sanctions committees reflecting the composition of the Council itself are created by the Security Council on an ad hoc basis.[80] This system has several important consequences.[81] Perhaps the most important of these from a lawyer's perspective is that a sanctions committee is an essentially political organ consisting of diplomats on rotational duty, working on instructions from their governments. Hence, the sanctions committee is, by its nature, not a legal body equipped to undertake legal examinations of individual cases. Its meetings are held *in camera*, its decisions are taken by consensus, and documentation is sparse.[82] Sanctions committees are often understaffed, and tend to become swamped with exemption applications and claims of breaches.[83] When the sanctions regime it was created to supervise is terminated, the sanctions committee is disbanded. This means that there is little opportunity for building so called institutional memory, and, presumably, that it is difficult to develop uniform practice among the sanctions committees.

78 Cortright *et al.*, *supra* note 46, Bonn-Berlin I, p. 7; Expert Panel Report, para. 161.

79 See www.un.org/docs/sc/committees and www.treas.gov/ofac.

80 Doxey, M.P., *United Nations Sanctions: Lessons of Experience,* Interlaken II, pp. 207–219 at p. 215 [Hereinafter Doxey, Interlaken II].

81 See, *e.g.*, Bondi, L., *Arms Embargoes*, Bonn-Berlin I, Final Draft, 2000, [Hereinafter Bondi, Bonn-Berlin I] p. 10.

82 Doxey, Interlaken II, *supra* note 80, p. 211.

83 Bondi, Bonn-Berlin I, supra note 81, pp. 10-11; Doxey, supra note 80, Interlaken II, p. 215.

The Security Council has taken steps to deal with some of the practical problems related to the sanctions committees.[84] Proposals include greater transparency, use of expert advice, and improved communication and coordination with member states and regional organizations.[85] Strengthening the UN is not uncontroversial, however, and an institutionalized sanctions agency is still far away. Many states do not want the UN to have stronger enforcement capabilities, or are at least not willing to provide the necessary funding. Any reform empowering the UN Secretariat at the expense of the Security Council is unlikely to win the approval of the permanent members of the Council.

In addition to the sanctions committees, the Security Council has in some cases created special bodies to monitor the implementation of the sanctions. These are, typically, small groups of experts with mandates limited in time, whose main task is to report to the sanctions committees on the implementation of the sanctions.[86] In 1995, the Security Council through Resolution 1013 (1995) established the International Commission of Inquiry (ICOI) to provide independent reporting on embargo violations and illicit arms trafficking in Rwanda. Despite its obvious shortcomings – it consisted of a four-person team with a six-month mandate and the whole project has been described as "extremely optimistic" – the ICOI was a major innovation as regards sanctions monitoring.[87] These bodies have been given different names – commission, panel, mechanism or group – but their tasks have been similar. It would seem that the Security Council has concluded that a sanctions committee in its present form is not able adequately to monitor the implementation of smart sanctions, and that other means must be sought.[88]

84 *Note by the President of the Security Council: Work of the Sanctions Committees*, UN Doc. S/1999/92, 1999.

85 Rydell, *supra* note 15, Bonn-Berlin I, p. 10.

86 SC Res. 1013 (1995) (Rwanda); SC Res. 1237 (1999) and SC Res. 1295 (2000) (Angola/UNITA); SC Res. 1363 (2001) (Afghanistan/al-Qaeda).

87 Berman, E., *Sanctions Against the Genocidaires: Experience of the 1998 UN International Commission of Inquiry*, Bonn-Berlin I, p. 7 [Hereinafter Berman].

88 Strengthening the role of these monitoring bodies was one of the topics of the Stockholm Process on the Implementation of Targeted Sanctions. See Wallensteen, P., Staibano, C. & Eriksson, M., (Eds.), *Making Targeted Sanctions Effective – Guidelines for the Implementation of UN Policy Options,* 2003, www.smartsanctions.se (2003-05-10) [Hereinafter Stockholm Report] p. 96.

Arguably, Security Council resolutions, to use EC law terminology, lack direct effect, and are thus not directly applicable to individuals and non-state actors.[89] For the sanctions to take effect, national implementation legislation is required. In this regard, the situation differs greatly between the member states.[90] At present, few states have enacted specific legislation enabling Security Council resolutions to be effected through secondary legislation.[91] The others, presumably, are reduced to using domestic legislation in other fields, or the time-consuming primary legislative process.[92]

4.4.4 The role of international organizations

As they are not members of the UN, international organisations are not bound by either Security Council resolutions or the UN Charter, except insofar as it codifies customary international law. However, as laid down in Article 103 of the UN Charter, membership of an international organisation does not absolve a state from its duties under the UN Charter.[93] In addition, a legal basis for cooperation between the UN and other international organisations is enshrined in Article 53(1). The implementation imperative could therefore be said to apply indirectly to regional organisations with legislative competence, such as the European Communities (EC) and, to some extent, the Economic Community of West African States (ECOWAS). The EC has, on occasion, cooperated with the UN on the implementation of sanctions. For example, in 1992, the EC together with the Organisation for Security and Cooperation in Europe, OSCE (at the time the Conference on Security and Cooperation in Europe) began to organize Sanctions Assistance Missions

89 This holds true at least in dualist jurisdictions such as Sweden. See Andersson *et al.*, 2003, *supra* note 69, p. 114.

90 Rydell, Bonn-Berlin I, *supra* note 15, p. 15; Doxey, *supra* note 80, Interlaken II, p. 216.

91 Carver, J.P., *Making Financial Sanctions Work: Preconditions for Successful Implementations of Sanctions by the Implementing State*, Final Report, pp. 87–104 at p. 91, Interlaken I. As regards Sweden, see Lag (1996:95) om vissa internationella sanktioner. (Certain international sanctions act.)

92 Strengthening the implementation capacity of the member states was one of the purposes of the Stockholm Process; see the Stockholm-Report, pp. 55–66.

93 See further Bohr, S., *Sanctions by the United Nations Security Council and the European Community*, EJIL, Vol. 4, 1993, pp. 256–268, [Hereinafter Bohr] at pp. 264 and 268.

for the sanctions against the former Yugoslavia. These Missions consisted of customs officers, acting as advisers to local authorities in neighboring countries, but without any enforcement mandates of their own. It has also been suggested that establishing cooperation between the UN and organisations such as INTERPOL and the International Organisation of Supreme Audit Institutions (INTOSAI), made up of national audit agencies, might benefit the implementation of sanctions.[94]

4.4.5 The lack of remedies

The consequences for an individual of becoming the target of UN sanctions are far-reaching. Several civil rights are at issue, mainly procedural rights and rights of property. There is at present no international legal remedy available for an individual who has been hit by smart sanctions, other than petitioning the sanctions committee, directly or by way of diplomatic protection through his government.[95] The hearing of the matter is at the discretion of the committee. The al-Qaeda Sanctions Committee has, however, adopted guidelines for the removal of individuals from the sanctions list.[96] As has been pointed out, there is nothing to prevent resort to national courts, *e.g.* by bringing a civil action against a bank that has effected a freeze.[97] How the question of the validity of international measures would be handled in a national court, in other words whether a national court would qualify as an effective remedy, is of course another matter.[98] Another tricky question is

94 Expert Panel Report, *supra* note 34, Bonn-Berlin I, para. 174; Rydell, *supra* note 15, p. 16.

95 See, *e.g.*, the report by Cameron, I., *Targeted Sanctions and Legal Safeguards*, 2002, presented within the framework of a project initiated by the Swedish Government, www.jur.uu.se/sii (2003-01-15); *Report of Expert Working Group I*, Bonn-Berlin II, p. 12.

96 See *Report of the Security Council Committee established pursuant to Resolution 1267 (1999)*, annexed to UN Doc. S/2002/1423, 2002 [Hereinafter Afghanistan Committee Report]. The guidelines were last amended on 10 April 2003 and can be found on the Committee site at www.un.org/docs/sc/committees (2003-11-06).

97 See, *e.g.*, Lysén, G., *Targeted UN Sanctions: On the Issue of Legal Sources and their Application and also some Procedural Matters*, 2002, www.jur.uu.se/sii (2003-05-10), p. 4.

98 Compare Article 13 of the European Convention on Human Rights and Fundamental Freedoms, ETS No. 9, 1952.

whether an individual affected by smart sanctions can claim reparation. This is a matter of both responsibility and remedy.[99] Further, in those states that allow judicial review, individuals may challenge domestic legislation implementing Security Council resolutions before national courts. Even though the resolution as such cannot be challenged, this would be a form of indirect review of Security Council action.[100] In a comparable situation in the EC context, the German Constitutional Court, the *Bundesverfassungsgericht,* has declared that it reserves the right to review the compatibility of EC legislation with the German *Grundgesetz.* [101] This stance is said to have been instrumental in the inclusion of human rights norms in EC law.[102] A similar finding by a national court as regards UN sanctions is not inconceivable and would, undoubtedly, harm the credibility of UN sanctions.

The Swedish Somalis on the al-Qaeda sanctions list have instead chosen to bypass the national courts and challenge the EC implementation acts on technical grounds before the European Court of First Instance, where the case is currently pending.[103] The European Court of Justice has, in the *Bosphorus* case, had before it the question of the impact of UN sanctions on third parties.[104] With reference to an EC regulation implementing Resolution 820 (1993)

99 Compare the finding of the International Court of Justice in the *Difference Relating to Immunity from Legal Process of a Special Rapporteur of the Commission on Human Rights,* Advisory Opinion, 29 April 1999, www.icj-cij.org (2004-01-22).

100 Canor, I., *'Can Two Walk Together, Except They Be Agreed?' The Relationship between International Law and European Law: The Incorporation of United Nations Sanctions against Yugoslavia into European Community Law Through the Perspective of the European Court of Justice,* Common Market Law Review, Vol. 35, 1998, pp. 137–187, 161.

101 *Internazionale Handelsgesellschaft v. EVGF,* Bundesverfassungsgericht, 29 May 1974, 2 C.M.L.R. p. 540, 1974, a.k.a. Solange I; *Re the Application of Wünsche Handelsgesellschaft,* Bundesverfassungsgericht, 22 Oct. 1986, 3 C.M.L.R. p. 225, 1987, a.k.a. Solange II; *Brunner v. European Union Treaty,* Bundesverfassungsgericht, 12 Oct. 1993, C.M.L.R., Vol. 1, 1994, p. 57, a.k.a. Solange III.

102 Hartley, T.C, *The Foundations of European Community Law,* 4th ed., University Press, Oxford, 1998, pp. 236–238.

103 *Aden and others v. Council and Commission of the European Communities,* European Court of First Instance, Case T-306/01. See the Order by the Court of 7 May 2002, T-306/01R, ECR II-2387, 2002. At the time of writing, the main hearing has been held but final judgment not yet delivered.

104 *Bosphorus Hava Yollari ve Ticcaret AS v. Minister for Transport, Energy and Communications, Ireland and the Attorney General,* European Court of Justice, Case C-84/95, ECR 3953, 1996.

ordering sanctions against the former Yugoslavia, the Irish Government had impounded an aircraft owned by the Yugoslav national airline, but leased and operated by a Turkish airline company. The Court found that the importance of the aims of the sanctions, *i.e.* to stop the war and end the massive violations of human rights and international humanitarian law in Bosnia, justified "negative consequences, even of a substantial nature, for some operators".[105] Hence, the sanctions applied to the Yugoslav-owned aircraft even though it was leased to a third party with no connection to the conflict. The question of the compatibility of UN sanctions with human rights could also come before the European Court of Human Rights. The question of remedies in connection with international measures against terrorism are dealt with in more detail by Iain Cameron in Chapter 6.

The *Lockerbie* cases before the International Court of Justice (ICJ), emanating from the sanctions against Libya, raised the controversial question whether or not the ICJ is a constitutional court in the sense that it has power of judicial review over Security Council resolutions.[106] The case has been settled out of court and consequently been removed from the International Court's list, somewhat to the regret of international lawyers. In this context, suffice it to say that the increased use of sanctions targeting individuals highlights the need for a solution to the issue of the legality of Security Council measures. Otherwise, states may simply fail to implement the sanctions when questions regarding their lawfulness arise, as was the

105 SC Res. 820 (1993), implemented into Community law by Council Regulation of 26 Apr. 1993, Concerning Trade between the European Economic Community and the Federal Republic of Yugoslavia (Serbia and Montenegro) (990/93/EEC), O.J. L102/14, 1993; Para. 23 of the *Bosphorus* judgment, *supra* note 104.

106 *Case Concerning Questions of Interpretation and Application of the 1971 Montreal Convention Arising from the Aerial Incident at Lockerbie* (Libyan Arab Jamahiriya v. United Kingdom), (Libyan Arab Jamahiriya v. United States of America), Preliminary Objections, International Court of Justice, 27 Feb. 1998, www.icj-cij.org (2000-11-15). On the issue, see, *e.g.*, Martenczuk, B., *The Security Council, the International Court and Judicial Review: What Lessons from Lockerbie?*, EJIL, Vol. 10, 1999, pp. 517–547; Gowlland-Debbas, V., *The Relationship between the International Court of Justice and the Security Council in the Light of the Lockerbie Case*, AJIL, Vol. 88, 1994, pp. 643–677.

case when the Organisation of African Unity, in 1998, announced that it would no longer enforce the sanctions against Libya.[107]

4.4.6 The inherent rigidity of sanctions

Being the products of political compromises, sanctions regimes often lack proper pre-assessment and a clearly formulated strategy for amendment and termination. Accordingly, they suffer from an inherent rigidity, illustrated, *e.g.*, by the Iraq case. Some of the more recent regimes, *e.g.* against Afghanistan and Sierra Leone, have been limited in time, or at least conditioned on review at regular intervals.[108] For example, Resolution 1333 (2000) tightening sanctions against Afghanistan contained a twelve-month limit, and Resolution 1306 (2000) regarding Sierra Leone provided for periodic reviews. Limiting or conditioning sanctions is not uncontroversial, however. In addition, it may in fact be counter-productive, as it may weaken the incentive for the targets to comply with the will of the Security Council. It has been suggested that targeted sanctions would benefit in terms of effectiveness from a combination of incentive and deterrence, *e.g.* a precise time-plan and the formulation of intermediate objectives, which, when achieved, would lead to subsequent modifications in the sanctions regime.[109] This is not uncontroversial either, however, and would, undoubtedly, pose some logistical problems.

4.5 Concluding remarks

To conclude, smart sanctions have, so far, been imposed in half a dozen cases. There is no general agreement as regards either their effectiveness or the amount of collateral damage caused. It has also become apparent that they suffer from flaws, some of which are

107 Organization of African Unity, Assembly of Heads of State and Government, "The Crisis between the Great Socialist People's Libya Arab Jamahiriya and the United States of America and the United Kingdom", 8–10 June 1998, AHG/DEC.127 XXXIV, Cortright & Lopez 2000, *supra* note 15.

108 See *Report of Expert Working Group I: Travel- and Aviation-Related Sanctions (Travel and Aviation Bans)*, Bonn-Berlin II, Final Version, 2001, p. 16.

109 Bruderlein, C., Carrot and Stick Approach for the Implementation of Financial Sanctions, Interlaken I, pp. 127–128; Cortright *et al.*, Bonn-Berlin I, *supra* note 46, p. 50.

rather serious. Nevertheless, it would seem that smart sanctions are here to stay. The practice of the Security Council and the UN member states indicates that smart sanctions can be accommodated within the existing legal framework of UN sanctions. There are, however, some important aspects setting targeted sanctions apart, notably the fact that the subjects of sanctions are often not states or even state-like entities, but private entities and individuals. It can safely be said that the conceptual basis in international law for targeting international measures at individuals is underdeveloped. If smart sanctions are regarded as economic warfare and an alternative to trade sanctions which affect the whole civilian population, it would seem justified to cast the sanctions net fairly wide and accept a certain level of collateral damage. This approach may well be in order when the target is, if not a state, at least a state-like entity such as UNITA. On the other hand, an analogy to law enforcement and the requirements of due process of law, which are arguably more appropriate in the case of individuals, would demand restrictive application and high standards of evidence. Whichever approach is chosen, a delicate balance has to be struck between the competing interests of achieving the objective of the sanctions and respecting individual rights.[110]

110 Afghanistan Committee Report, *supra* note 102, paras. 11–12.

References

Books & articles

Andersson, T., Cameron, I. & Nordback, K., *EU Blacklisting: The Renaissance of Imperial Power, but on a Global Scale,* European Business Law Review, Vol. 14, 2003, pp. 111–141.

Beyerlin, U., *Sanctions,* Wolfrum, R. (Ed.), United Nations: Law, Policies and Practice, Vol. 2, Revised English Edition, Martinus Nijhoff, Dordrecht, 1995, pp. 1111–1128.

Bohr, S., *Sanctions by the United Nations Security Council and the European Community,* EJIL, Vol. 4, 1993, pp. 256–268.

Bring, O., *FN-stadgan och världspolitiken,* 4th ed., Norstedts, Stockholm, 2002.

Canor, I., *'Can Two Walk Together, Except They Be Agreed?' The Relationship between International Law and European Law: The Incorporation of United Nations Sanctions against Yugoslavia into European Community Law Through the Perspective of the European Court of Justice,* CML R., Vol. 35, 1998, pp. 137–187.

Cárdenas, E.J., *The 1982 Freeze of British Assets in Argentina: A Retrospective Overview,* Journal of International Banking Law, Vol. 2, 1991, pp. 81–83.

Combacau, J., *Sanctions,* Bernhardt, R. (Ed.), Encyclopedia of Public International Law, North-Holland, Amsterdam, Vol. 4, 2000, pp. 311–315.

Crawford, J., *The International Law Commission's Articles on State Responsibility,* University Press, Cambridge, 2002.

Crawford, J., *The Relationship between Sanctions and Countermeasures,* Gowlland-Debbas, V., (Ed.), United Nations Sanctions and International Law, Kluwer, The Hague, 2001, pp. 57–68.

Frowein, J. & Krisch, N., *Article 41,* Simma, B. (Ed.), The Charter of the United Nations – A Commentary, 2nd ed., 2002, pp. 735–748.

Gasser, H.P., *Collective Economic Sanctions and International Humanitarian Law, ZaöRV* 56/4, 1996, pp. 871–904.

Gowlland-Debbas, V., *The Relationship between the International Court of Justice and the Security Council in the Light of the Lockerbie Case,* AJIL, Vol. 88, 1994, pp. 643–677.

Malanczuk, P., *Akehurst's Modern Introduction to International Law,* 7th ed., Routledge, London, 1997.

Martenczuk, B., *The Security Council, the International Court and Judicial Review: What Lessons from Lockerbie?,* EJIL, Vol. 10, 1999, pp. 517–547.

Partsch, K.J., *Reprisals,* Bernhardt, R. (Ed.), Encyclopedia of Public International Law, North Holland, Amsterdam, Vol. 4, 2000, pp. 200–205.

Partsch, K.J., *Retorsion,* Bernhardt, R. (Ed.), Encyclopedia of Public International Law, North-Holland, Amsterdam, Vol. 4, 2000, pp. 232–233.

Reisman, W.M., and Stevick, D.L., *The Applicability of International Law Standards to United Nations Economic Sanctions Programmes,* EJIL, Vol. 9, 1998, pp. 86–141.

Shearer, I.A., *Starke's International Law,* 11th ed., Butterworths, London, 1994.

Szasz, P., *The Law of Economic Sanctions*, Schmitt, M.N., and Green, L.C. (Ed.), The Law of Armed Conflict: Into the Next Millennium, Naval War College, Newport, 1998, pp. 455–481.

Örnemark Hansen, H., *Penningtvätt: Ett urvattnat begrepp?*, Norstedts, Stockholm, 1998.

Österdahl, I., *FN-sanktioner och mänskliga rättigheter* eller *Hur kunde det bli på detta viset?*, SvJT 2002, pp. 894–916.

Cases

Aden and others v. *Council and Commission of the European Communities*, European Court of First Instance, Case T-306/01, Order by the Court of 7 May 2002, T-306/01R, ECR II-2387, 2002.

Bosphorus Hava Yollari ve Ticcaret AS v. *Minister for Transport, Energy and Communications, Ireland and the Attorney General*, European Court of Justice, Case C-84/95, ECR 3953, 1996.

Brunner v. *European Union Treaty*, Bundesverfassungsgericht, 12 Oct. 1993, C.M.L.R., Vol. 1, 1994, p. 57, (*Solange III*).

Case Concerning Questions of Interpretation and Application of the 1971 Montreal Convention Arising from the Aerial Incident at Lockerbie (Libyan Arab Jamahiriya v. *United Kingdom*), (*Libyan Arab Jamahiriya* v. *United States of America*), Preliminary Objections, International Court of Justice, 27 Feb. 1998, www.icj-cij.org (2000-11-15).

Case Concerning the Gabríkovo-Nagymaros Project (Hungary/Slovakia), International Court of Justice, ICJ Reports 1997, p. 7.

Difference Relating to Immunity from Legal Process of a Special Rapporteur of the Commission on Human Rights, Advisory Opinion, International Court of Justice, 29 April 1999, www.icj-cij.org (2004-01-22).

Internazionale Handelsgesellschaft v. *EVGF*, Bundesverfassungsgericht, 29 May 1974, C.M.L.R., Vol. 2, 1974, p. 540, (*Solange I*).

Re the Application of Wünsche Handelsgesellschaft, Bundesverfassungsgericht, 22 Oct. 1986, C.M.L.R., Vol. 3, 1987, p. 225, (*Solange II*).

Submissions of Bosnia in the Case Concerning the Application of the Convention on the Preventions and Punishment of the Crime of Genocide (Bosnia-Herzegovina v. Yugoslavia), Preliminary Objections, International Court of Justice, Judgment of 11 July 1996, www.icj-cij.org (15 November 2000).

UN documents

Blum, J.A., Levi, M., Naylor, R.T. & Williams, P., *Financial Havens, Banking Secrecy and Money-Laundering*, United Nations Office for Drug Control and Crime Prevention, 1998.

Bruderlein, Claude, *Coping with the Humanitarian Impact of Sanctions: An OCHA Perspective*, United Nations Office for the Coordination of

Humanitarian Affairs, 2 Dec. 1998, www.reliefweb.int/ocha (15 September 2000).

International Law Commission, Draft Articles on State Responsibility, Provisionally Adopted by the Drafting Committee on Second Reading, Fifty-second Session, UN Doc. A/CN.4/L.600, 21 August 2000.

Letter Dated 16 October from the Chairman of the Monitoring Mechanism on Angola Sanctions Addressed to the Chairman of the Security Council Committee Established Pursuant to Resolution 864 (1993) concerning the Situation in Angola, annexed to UN Doc. S/2000/1026, 2000.

Letter Dated 17 April 2000 from the Chairman of the Panel on United Nations Peace Operations to the Secretary-General, annexed to UN Doc. A/55/305-S/2000/809, 2000.

Note by the President of the Security Council: Work of the Sanctions Committees, UN Doc. S/1999/92, 1999.

Report of the Security Council Committee established pursuant to Resolution 1267 (1999), annexed to UN Doc. S/2002/1423, 2002.

Report of the Panel of Experts on Violations of Security Council Sanctions Against UNITA, annexed to UN Doc. S/2000/203, 2000.

Report of the International Law Commission on the work of its Fifty-third session, G.A.O.R., 56th sess., Suppl. No. 10 (A/56/10). www.un.org/law/ilc/texts/State_responsibility/responsibilityfra.htm.

Report of the Secretary-General to the Security Council on the Protection of Civilians in Armed Conflict, UN Doc. S/1999/957, 1999.

Statement by the President of the Security Council, UN Doc. S/PRST/1999/28, 1999.

The Adverse Consequences of Economic Sanctions on the Enjoyment of Human Rights, Working Paper prepared by Mr. Marc Bossuyt, United Nations Economic and Social Council, E/CN.4/Sub.2/2000/33, 2000.

Verification in All its Aspects, Including the Role of the United Nations in the Field of Verification, Report of the Secretary-General, UN Doc. A/50/377, 1995.

Conference papers

The Interlaken process

Expert Seminar on Targeting UN Financial Sanctions, 17–19 March, 1998, Interlaken, Switzerland; Convened by the Swiss Federal Office for Foreign Economic Affairs, Department of Economy, Final Report, www.smartsanctions.ch (2000-09-25) [Interlaken I].

Bruderlein, C., *Carrot and Stick Approach for the Implementation of Financial Sanctions*, pp.127–128.

Carver, J.P., *Making Financial Sanctions Work: Preconditions for Successful Implementations of Sanctions by the Implementing State*, pp. 87–104.

Jeker, R.M., *Chairman's Conclusions*, pp. 25–27.

Newcomb, R.R., *Targeting Financial Sanctions*, pp. 113–119.

Schönenberger, C., *Evasion and Control of Financial Sanctions – Practical Considerations*, pp. 125–126.
2nd Interlaken Seminar on Targeting United Nations Financial Sanctions, 29–31 March, 1999, Interlaken, Switzerland; Convened by the Swiss Federal Office for Foreign Economic Affairs in Cooperation with the United Nations Secretariat, Final Report, www.smartsanctions.ch (2000-09-25) [Interlaken II].
Doxey, M.P., *United Nations Sanctions: Lessons of Experience*, pp. 207–219.
Newcomb, R.R., *Targeted Financial Sanctions: The U.S. Model*, pp. 29–57.

The Bonn-Berlin process

First Expert Seminar: Smart Sanctions, the Next Step: Arms Embargoes and Travel Sanctions, Bonn, 21–23 November 1999; Organized by the Bonn International Center for Conversion in Cooperation with the Foreign Office of the Federal Republic of Germany, Papers and Reports, www.bicc.de [Bonn-Berlin I].

Berman, E., *Sanctions Against the Genocidaires: Experience of the 1998 UN International Commission of Inquiry*, Final Draft, 2000.
Bondi, L., *Arms Embargoes*, Final Draft, 2000.
Conroy, R., *Implementation Problems of Travel Bans: Practical and Legal Aspects*, Final Draft, 2000.
Cortright, D., Lopez, G. & Conroy, R., *Are Travel Sanctions Smart?: A Review of Theory and Practice*, Final Draft, 2000.
Rydell, R., *Monitoring United Nations Arms Embargoes*.

Final Expert Seminar on Smart Sanctions, the Next Step: Arms Embargoes and Travel Sanctions, organized by the Bonn International Center for Conversion (Bonn-Berlin) in cooperation the German Foreign Office, Berlin, 3–5 December 2000, www.bicc.de [Bonn-Berlin II].

Report of Expert Working Group I: Travel- and Aviation-Related Sanctions (Travel and Aviation Bans), Final Version, 2001.

The Stockholm process

Eriksson, M., *Bibliograhpic Paper on International Sanctions*, www.smartsanctions.se (2003-05-10).
Wallensteen, P., Staibano, C. & Eriksson, M. (Ed.), *Making Targeted Sanctions Effective – Guidelines for the Implementation of UN Policy Options, Results from the Stockholm Process on the Implementation of Targeted Sanctions*, 2003, www.smartsanctions.se (2003-05-10).

Other

Van Brabant, K., *Can Sanctions be Smarter? The Current Debate*, Report of a conference held in London, 16–17 December 1998, sponsored by the UK Department of International Development, First Part, Overseas Development Institute, 1999, www.smartsanctions.ch (25 September 2000).

Miscellaneous

Cameron, I., *Targeted Sanctions and Legal Safeguards*, 2002, presented within the framework of a project initiated by the Swedish Government, www.jur.uu.se/sii (15 January 2003).

Financial Action Task Force on Money Laundering, *Report of 6 February 1990*.

Financial Action Task Force on Money Laundering, *The Forty Recommendations*, www.oecd.org/fatf (1 November 2000).

Lysén, G., *Targeted UN Sanctions: On the Issue of Legal Sources and their Application and also some Procedural Matters*, 2002, www.jur.uu.se/sii (5 October 2003).

5 Post-September 11

A Right of Self-Defence against International Terrorism?

Ove Bring and David I. Fisher

5.1 Introduction

We tend to remember certain dates in world history because they dramatically alter the world stage: 28 June 1914 (the shots in Sarajevo), 1 September 1939 (the outbreak of World War II), 7 December 1941 (Pearl Harbor). It is very likely that 11 September 2001 will occupy a similar place in history, as the day when the Westphalian state structure was pierced by transnational terrorist networks; or, seen from a different vantage point, as the day when the open civil society of the West was challenged by insulate, politically frustrated terrorist cells. The battle against international terrorism has, since the 1960s, been codified in interstate agreements that have sought to lay the groundwork for universal jurisdiction over terrorists, *i.e.*, an adaptation of national legislation so that a suspect can either be prosecuted in the country where he is arrested or be extradited to another country for prosecution there. On the whole, police and judicial measures have been deemed satisfactory. Simply stated, the response to terrorism has been entrusted to the mechanisms of national civil society. Recent years have seen the birth of many conventions providing for international legal co-operation to combat terrorism,[1] but after 11 September, interstate efforts rose to a higher international law level, thereby assuming a new dimension.

1 Convention on Offences and Certain Other Acts Committed on Board Aircraft (Tokyo 1963), Convention for the Suppression of Unlawful Seizure of Aircraft (The Hague 1970), Convention for the Suppression of Unlawful Acts Against the Safety of Aircraft (Montreal 1971), Convention on the Prevention and Punishment of Crimes against Internationally Protected Persons, Including Diplomatic Personnel (New York 1973), European Convention for the Suppression of Terrorism (Strasbourg 1977), Convention Against the Taking of Hostages (New York 1979), Convention on the Physical Protection of Nuclear Materials (Vienna

Footnote continues on next page.

5.2 The UN response to the attacks on the World Trade Center and the Pentagon

For the first time ever, a terrorist act was not only deemed an act against a state or community interest, but also as an act against a state as such. UN Secretary-General Kofi Annan, as well as UN High Commissioner for Human Rights Mary Robinson, has gone so far as to depict the act as an attack on civilisation itself, as a crime against humanity.[2] The day after the attack, 12 September, the UN Security Council unanimously adopted a Resolution in the matter (Resolution 1368). Already the preamble revealed that the response to the terrorist threat would no longer be limited to traditional legal methods. The Security Council declared itself: '*Determined* to combat by all means threats to international peace and security caused by terrorist acts'.

The Council did not use the phrase 'all necessary means', which in the UN parlance denotes military measures, but the phrase 'by all means', which can include both peaceful co-operation and military action.

The next preambular paragraph referred in general terms to a state's right to individual and collective self-defence in accordance with the UN Charter. This was actually the first time the Security Council adopted an anti-terrorist resolution linking the issue of self-defence to the battle on terrorism. The Resolution's first operative paragraph stated that the attacks of 11 September, as well as

Footnote continued from previous page.

1980), Protocol for the Suppression of Unlawful Acts of Violence at Airports (Montreal 1988), Convention for the Suppression of Unlawful Acts Against the Safety of Maritime Navigation (Rome 1988), Protocol for the Suppression of Unlawful Acts Against the Safety of Fixed Platforms on the Continental Shelf (Rome 1988) and UN Convention for the Suppression of Terrorist Bombings (New York 1997), Convention for the Suppression of the Financing of Terrorism 1999.

2 The concept of 'crimes against humanity' has its origin in the 1945 London Charter governing the Nuremberg tribunal. Besides its ethical dimension, the concept has a very specific legal meaning. The most recent definition is found in Article 7 of the Statute of the International Criminal Court (ICC). That instrument speaks of acts committed 'as part of a widespread or systematic attack directed against any civilian population'. Whether the attack of 11 September constitutes such a 'widespread or systematic attack' is an open question.

other (large-scale) attacks, constituted a 'threat to international peace and security', a locution necessary under Article 39 to open the door for the Security Council's legitimation of military action. These formulations propelled the international campaign against terrorism to a higher level of multilateral action, not merely judicial and police co-operation but also recognition of the need for a military dimension in future efforts.

As to the traditional, legal scheme of co-operation, the UN member states were urged to 'redouble their efforts' under the existing interstate anti-terrorist conventions and to bear in mind the Security Council's previous resolutions mandating legal measures against terrorism. Among the previous resolutions, two had required the extradition of Usama bin Laden.[3]

On 28 September the Security Council unanimously adopted Resolution 1373, which dramatically enhanced the requirement of interstate co-operation. The Resolution was adopted within the framework of Chapter VII of the UN Charter – a signal to member states that it embodied a legally binding Security Council decision. Member states were obliged to adapt domestic laws and regulations to the far-reaching requirements of the resolution. Among other things, the Security Council decided in operative paragraph 2(e) that all states *shall*:[4]

> Ensure that any person who participates in the financing, planning, preparation or perpetration of terrorist acts or in supporting terrorist acts is brought to justice and ensure that ... such terrorist acts are established as serious criminal offences in domestic laws and regulations.

Member States were also urged to become parties to the 1999 Convention for the Suppression of the Financing of Terrorism and to report to the UN within 90 days on the measures they had taken under the Resolution.

3 On 19 December 2000 the Security Council adopted Resolution 1333, requiring, *inter alia*, that 'the Taliban comply without further delay with the demand of the Security Council ... in resolution 1267 (1999), that requires the Taliban to turn over Usama bin Laden to appropriate authorities in a country where he has been indicted, or to appropriate authorities in a country where he will be returned to such a country, or to appropriate authorities in a country where he will be arrested and effectively brought to justice'.

4 *N.b.* compulsory language.

Regarding the military dimension under international law, the Security Council once again concluded in the preamble that international terrorism is a threat to international peace and security and reaffirmed, in this context, the right of states to individual and collective self-defence. Clearly, a point had been reached where the traditional regime of prosecution or extradition would no longer suffice: It would have to be augmented by a military dimension. The remainder of this chapter will address the problem of self-defence against large-scale international terrorism by military means.

5.3 The traditional right of self-defence

When the UN Charter was drafted in Dumbarton Oaks and later adopted in San Francisco in 1945, threats posed by international terrorism were given little – if any – thought. The rules for collective security were centred on threats from aggressive states, much as in 1648 when the Westphalian peace treaties at Münster obliged the parties to restrain peace-breakers through collective sanctions. At that time, the drafters had the Ottoman Empire in mind. In San Francisco, the goal was to shield oneself against the threat of new Hitlerite states; hence the global system of security where the Security Council can initiate action under Chapter VII. At the same time, Article 51 recognized that states, individually or jointly, must be able to defend themselves against attacks, until the Security Council has convened and decided to mobilize the resources needed to resolve the crisis. Article 51 expresses it thus:

> Nothing in the present Charter shall impair the inherent right of individual or collective self-defence if an armed attack occurs against a Member of the United Nations, until the Security Council has taken measures necessary to maintain international peace and security.

The term 'inherent right' of self-defence is usually understood to imply a customary law principle whose exact scope is defined not by the UN Charter but by custom and practice. The requirement of proportionality (military measures standing in proportion to the threat posed) is a cornerstone of the customary law regime, as manifested, *inter alia*, in the celebrated *Caroline* case (1842).[5]

That Article 51 has only been envisaged for *state-state* relations naturally complicates its application in the *state-terrorist network* relation. Article 51 does however apply inasmuch as the '9-11' terrorist attacks are not merely regarded as criminal acts against buildings and people, but indeed also as attacks on the US as a state, as an 'armed attack' against a 'Member of the United Nations', to quote the language of the Article. NATO and the EU avoided however using the UN Charter's term 'armed attack', since that would have required that the hijacked, fully tanked planes could be classified as military weapons upon striking the WTC towers. NATO spoke instead of 'attacks ... against the United States' in its first communiqué.[6] The EU Council of Ministers spoke of 'an attack not only on the United States but against humanity itself'.[7] The EU thus avoided binding itself to Article 51's reference to 'armed attack'. Underlying the EU and NATO formulations was probably the view that the wording of Article 51 and traditional international law were insufficiently adapted to the new threat scenario.

On the other hand, it is clear that traditional international law entitles a state under 'armed attack' to take military countermeasures in self-defence. The US referred to the situation as an 'armed attack', implying an act of war. The armed attack was deemed to justify acts of war by the US within its right of self-defence. The traditional international law concept of 'war' is not however relevant in this context (the situation is often different under national constitutional law, where the concept 'war' could be of some significance). Whether the terrorists, through their attack, could be

5 A violation in 1837 of American territory by British-ruled Canada required, according to an American diplomatic note, that Great Britain, in order to invoke self-defence, must show that the Canadian authorities 'even supposing the necessity of the moment authorized them to enter the territory of the U.S. at all, did nothing unreasonable or excessive, since the act, justified by the necessity of self-defence, must be limited by that necessity and kept clearly within it'. Robert Y. Jennings, 'The Caroline and McLeod Cases', American Journal of International Law, Vol. 32, 1938, p. 89. See also Ove Bring, *FN-stadgan och världspolitiken: Om folkrättens roll i en föränderlig värld,* 3rd ed. Norstedts Juridik, Stockholm 2000, p. 151.

6 Statement by North Atlantic Council, 12 Sept. 2001. Communique PR/CP (2001) 124.

7 Declaration by the European Union, 12.09.01 – 16h25.SN 56/01.

deemed to have issued a de facto 'declaration of war' or even if the US sees itself as being 'at war', has no bearing on the right to take military countermeasures: It is the existence of an 'armed attack' within the meaning of the UN Charter which entitles a state to self-defence or, according to what might be a newly arisen interpretation, the existence of a large-scale international terrorist attack.

In any case, countermeasures will only earn the legitimation of international law if undertaken in self-defence and not as retaliation or revenge. Self-defence has a limited purpose – not the killing or punishment of enemies but the elimination of a threat to national security. Concepts such as retaliation and revenge suggest excessive force (forbidden by the principle of proportionality linked to self-defence) and indiscriminate attacks (forbidden by the laws of war).[8]

5.3.1 Self-defence against international terrorism

The World War II era drafters of the UN Charter did not foresee the need for counter-attacks against terrorist networks. Article 51 and its corresponding customary law assume that the perpetrator is known and that self-defence measures immediately follow the attack and are not subsequent and separate occurrences. (Delayed self-defence is however always possible to counter an unlawful occupation, as was the case with the liberation of Kuwait.) Thus far, most UN member states have been opposed to interpreting Article 51 as support for preventive self-defence, *i.e.*, military counter-actions in anticipation of an attack. The new exercise of the right of self-defence that emerged as a consequence of '9-11' can only be intended to prevent *new* ter-

8 The laws of war too, or international humanitarian law in armed conflicts, contain a principle of proportionality. Unlike the right of self-defence's comprehensive-strategic proportionality in the state-state relation (a *jus ad bellum* assessment), humanitarian law requires a tactical proportionality on the battlefield in the combatant-civilian relation (a *jus in bello* assessment). Under a mandatory norm of humanitarian law, the civil population shall be protected, since only military targets may be attacked. When such an attack occurs, the military value of the attack is measured against the risk of civilian casualties and losses ('collateral damage'). A certain level of 'collateral damage' is unavoidable in war, but attacks that result in disproportionately large civilian causalities are forbidden. See Article 51 (5) (b) of Additional Protocol I (1977) to the 1949 Geneva Conventions, which speaks of civilian victims and casualties that 'would be excessive in relation to the concrete and direct military advantage anticipated'.

rorist attacks, *i.e.*, it amounts to the kind of preventive self-defence which has not yet gained general acceptance. Whereas anticipatory self-defence is accepted to a certain extent, preventive self-defence is much broader and outside the scope of international law. Article 51 thus needs to be 'stretched' to make room for preventive self-defence against international terrorism.

On the other hand, it is clear under traditional international law, that states that harbour perpetrators of international terrorism cannot claim respect for their sovereignty or territorial integrity if and when countermeasures are undertaken.[9] It is not however clear just how much a state must aid and abet an armed terrorist attack in order for that state to subject its territory to military counter-measures (conducted in self-defence). The preamble of Security Council Resolution 1373 (2001) notes that the 1970 General Assembly Friendly Relations Declaration[10] recites a principle, reaffirmed in Security Council Resolution 1198 (1998), that every state must refrain from participating in or assisting terrorist acts in another state 'or acquiescing in organized activities within its territory directed towards the commission of such acts'. The Friendly Relations Declaration's reference to 'acquiescence' is directly linked to the fundamental prohibition of the use of force in Article 2(4) of the UN Charter, which, if violated, can trigger the right of self-defence. Thus, assuming that the Taliban regime in Afghanistan in this way violated the UN Charter's prohibition on force, then it also in the legal sense 'opened' its territory for legitimate and proportionate counter-attacks.

5.3.2 Earlier US practice concerning military counter-measures against terrorism

In 1986, President Reagan attempted, vis-à-vis Libya, to stretch Article 51 so as to include self-defence against terrorism, but the circumstances hardly sufficed to ensure support for such a construction at the time. A bomb outrage against a West Berlin discotheque (frequented by US soldiers) on 5 April 1986 was claimed to be the

9 See, *inter alia,* UN General Assembly Resolution 2625 (XXV) 1970.
10 *Op. cit.* note 9.

work of the Libyan regime,[11] *i.e.*, a case of state terrorism. A US solider and a Turkish woman were killed in the blast and some 200 persons (60 of whom were US citizens) were injured. On the night of 14 April some 40 US warplanes bombed five targets in Tripoli and Benghazi. Colonel Kadaffi's residence and headquarters incurred severe damage. Despite an effort to conduct precision bombing about 130 civilians died.

Immediately after the raid, President Reagan held a televised address to the nation in which he claimed that the action was conducted in self-defence and in conformity with Article 51. The action was said to be a preventive measure, which had greatly reduced Kadaffi's capacity to export terror. The following day, the President described the operation as 'a single engagement in a long battle against terrorism'.[12]

Article 51 stipulates that measures taken in self-defence shall be 'immediately reported to the Security Council'. The US ambassador to the UN, Herbert Okun, thus notified the Security Council in a letter of 14 April. The letter called the Libyan policy a breach of the prohibition on force under UN Charter Article 2(4). Libya's actions had precipitated 'the entirely justifiable response by the U.S'.[13]

The US line of argumentation was not however accepted by the Security Council. The non-aligned members presented a draft resolution condemning the action as violative of the UN Charter. The voting result for the draft was 9 to 5 in favour with 1 abstention. Three of the Council's permanent members, the US, France and Britain, exercised their right of veto, producing a 'triple veto' that prevented the opposition to the US line of argumentation from rising to the level of a condemnatory Security Council Resolution.

We may add with regard to the legal issue of 1986 that even if Libya was responsible for repeated acts of terror (an explosion on a TWA flight was cited in addition to the blowing up of the disco-

11 'German and American police had rather quickly ascertained the terrorists' identity. They were Libyan citizens who had received their terrorist training in one of the East German police's training camps.' Information from Sweden's then general consul in Berlin, D.M. Winter, in a letter to the editor of *Dagens Nyheter*, 7 Oct. 2001 [Translation ours].

12 32 Keesing's Contemporary Archives 1986, p. 34457. See generally, Bring, *supra* note 5, p. 176 ff.

13 UN Document S/17990, 14 April 1986.

theque), these acts did not constitute an armed attack on the US as such nor on the US armed forces, *i.e.*, there was no attack on a member state within the scope of the UN Charter. The bomb at the discotheque should thus have resulted in international police co-operation, not missiles. President Reagan's thesis on self-defence against international terrorism was not a statement of *lex lata*, but could of course be viewed as a *de lege ferenda* challenge.

More than 10 years later, in August 1998, President Clinton cited self-defence against terrorism after US embassies in Kenya and Tanzania were damaged by bomb-laden trucks, leaving 224 persons dead. That was probably the first time the general public heard the name Usama bin Laden. The US responded by conducting a missile attack on targets in the Sudan and Afghanistan, intended to knock out bin Laden's resources. On 20 August 1998, 60 cruise missiles were unleashed on bin Laden's tent and training camp in eastern Afghanistan. The missiles had been launched from warships in waters off the coast of Pakistan. At the same time, 13 missiles were fired at a pharmaceutical plant in Khartoum where chemical weapons were allegedly manufactured. The legality under international law of these attacks was problematic. The evidence that was to prove that the Sudanese plant produced chemical weapons never materialized, resulting in a certain international confusion. On the other hand, the missile attack on bin Laden's camp in Afghanistan was viewed with a certain understanding, at least in the West. The world's reaction on the whole was however doubtful and oscillating. The extensive interpretation of Article 51 posited by the US did not receive general support and state practice did not endow the missile attacks with legitimacy. No new *opinio juris* had emerged. On the whole, the world community appeared to view the bombs against the two US embassy buildings as ordinary, if serious, criminal acts requiring traditional police and law enforcement measures.

5.4 The new law on self-defence

After the recent dramatic reminders of international terrorism's presence in our world, the US appears to have received the support of the world community for an extended Article 51 interpretation, which it previously lacked. This is of course due to the sheer magnitude of the

9-11 catastrophe, which threatens open societies everywhere. The events prompted NATO members to activate the so called musketeer principle of Article 5 of the Washington Treaty: 'One for all and all for one'. Article 5 governs collective self-defence as follows:

> The parties agree that an armed attack against one or more of them in Europe or North America shall be considered an attack against them all; and consequently they agree that, if such an armed attack occurs, each of them, in exercise of the right of individual or collective self-defence recognized by Article 51 of the Charter of the United Nations, will assist the Party or Parties so attacked by taking forthwith, individually and in concert with the other Parties, such action as it deems necessary, including the use of armed force, to restore and maintain the security of the North Atlantic area.

The NATO Declaration represents a new *opinio juris* through which a group of states gave the right of self-defence a new meaning. The NATO countries accepted self-defence against terrorist networks when they declared that Article 5 is activated 'if it is determined that this attack was directed from abroad against the United States'.[14] They also accepted preventive self-defence. On 2 October 2001, NATO Secretary-General George Robertson stated that there was evidence that the attack had come 'from abroad', namely, from Usama bin Laden's al-Qaeda network. The evidence was 'clear and compelling'.[15] The *sine qua non* of Article 5 (an external armed attack) was thus fulfilled.

The European Union early leaned towards the same interpretation of the self-defence concept, even if its drafting style left all options open. The EU Council of Ministers stated on 21 September that: 'On the basis of Security Council Resolution 1368, a riposte by

14 Statement by the North Atlantic Council, 12 Sept. 2001. The following was also stated: 'The commitment to collective self-defence embodied in the Washington Treaty was first entered into in circumstances very different from those that exist now, but it remains no less valid and no less essential today, in a world subject to the scourge of international terrorism.'

15 Lord Robertson quoted by International Herald Tribune, 4 Oct. 2001, p. 8. Already on 15 Oct. 1999, the UN Security Council had sufficient evidence that Usama bin Laden (via Afghanistan) was behind the terrorist acts that occurred at that time. The Security Council, in its resolution 1267 (1999) condemned the Taliban's use of Afghan territory for the training of terrorists and for planning terrorist acts and demanded that bin Laden be extradited to a country where he was under indictment.

the U.S. is legitimate'.[16] At the UN General Assembly meeting on 1–4 October 2001, several EU member states elaborated on their view of the right of self-defence in the new situation. Sweden, among others, stated that the US was entitled to act in self-defence without the need for any additional Security Council Resolutions.[17]

Security Council Resolutions 1368 and 1373 have recognized the relevance of the right of self-defence in the (large-scale) terrorist context. When this theme was repeated in the latter Resolution, a pattern began to develop in which the Security Council did not expressly legitimate a unilateral US use of force, but did not close the door to such use either, cognizant of the fact that self-defence almost always begins unilaterally or in an alliance. Article 51 permits unilateral action and implicitly leaves the issue of possible proof to the acting state. All that is required under Article 51 is that the Security Council is immediately informed of measures taken and that those measures do not undermine the Security Council's latitude for action.[18] A decision that would censure US and British actions could not however be taken without the unlikely input of US and British delegates. The other veto-holding permanent members were, before the attacks on the Taliban forces in Afghanistan commenced, aware that the Security Council, through its resolutions, had opened the door for US unilateral or NATO collective self-defence and they did not appear to have any objections.

The concept of self-defence against (large-scale) international terrorism thus seems to be taking form and to be gaining acceptance in state positions (practice *in abstracto*). Not all debaters appreciate this development. One can probably assume that international lawyers and diplomats will be divided into two camps, which we can,

16 Conclusions and Plan of Action of the Extraordinary European Council Meeting on 21 September 2001. SN 140/01.

17 'My Government recognizes this right to take measures of self-defence to prevent a similar atrocity, and notes that any response would have to seek to avoid civilian casualties.' Ambassador Pierre Schori in an address before the UN General Assembly on 3 Oct. 2001.

18 The second sentence in Article 51 is worded as follows: 'Measures taken by Members in the exercise of this right of self-defence shall be immediately reported to the Security Council and shall not in any way affect the authority and responsibility of the Security Council under the present Charter to take at any time such action as it deems necessary in order to maintain or restore international peace and security.'

for the sake of simplicity, call traditionalists and evolutionists.[19] In the first camp, there is a desire to stick to the traditional interpretation of the right of self-defence even in situations where a terrorist attack has reached such dimensions that it constitutes an attack on a state as such. An attacked state would, according to this view, require a Security Council resolution in order to legitimate individual or collective military measures.[20] The evolutionist camp, for its part, cites the attacks as an event at the level of world history and as the first time a state as such has been attacked by transnational terrorism, and the attack is thus a new phenomenon requiring a new international law.[21] The evolutionists thus accept those expressions in state practice that embrace a new interpretation and broadening of Article 51.

A modification of current law would divest the classical *Caroline Case* of the decisive role it has played henceforth. US Secretary of State Daniel Webster claimed in 1842 in a statement that came to gain general acceptance that the right of self-defence could be exercised in situations where: [T]he necessity of that self-defence is

19 The website of the American Society of International Law (www.asil.org) begins with a discussion where Professor Fredrik L. Kirgis appears as a 'cautious evolutionist' who acknowledged a right of self-defence and Professor Gregory H. Fox as a 'clear traditionalist' who demanded the Security Council's acceptance of actions which the Security Council has not previously approved as self-defence. See ASIL Insights: *Terrorist Attacks on the World Trade Center and the Pentagon*, September 2001.

20 See *eg.*, Gregor Noll, *'USA utmanar folkrätten'*, Svenska Dagbladet 19 Sept. 2001 and Sverker Åström, *'Regeringen är otydlig'*, Dagens Nyheter Debatt 28 Sept. 2001. Åström cited the risk of unfortunate precedents that can be invoked by many states. 'Then we will have entered a world where the law of the jungle prevails and where the interests of small states are not worth a damn.' [Translation ours]. See also Said Mahmoudi, *'Sverige försvagar FN'*, Svenska Dagbladet Brännpunkt 24 Oct. 2001. On first blush, it also appears that an article by Katinka Svanberg & Diana Amnéus *'Invänta FN:s fulla stöd'*, Svenska Dagbladet Brännpunkt 29 Sept. 2001, belongs to the traditional category. The authors do however take somewhat of a middle position. Although they warn of the danger that an increased right of self-defence results in a situation where many states end up 'under a potential threat of armed attack', the authors do not appear to rule out that 'the newly born norm of self-defence in the world community' is upheld and moderated. [translation ours].

21 See Marie Jacobsson & Pål Wrange, *'Folkrätten förändras'*, Svenska Dagbladet Brännpunkt 22 Sept. 2001 & Per Ahlin, *'En nygammal svensk folkrätt'*, Dagens Nyheter 29 Sept. 2001, where Ahlin writes that 'international law is not, and ought not be, static' [Translation ours].

instant, overwhelming, and leaving no choice of means, and no moment for deliberation.[22]

Although this formulation has sometimes been cited as a basis of preventive self-defence in cases of imminent threat, it is not well adapted to situations where a terror attack against a state has ceased and military countermeasures to prevent renewed acts of terror are under consideration. And yet a new supplementary norm of self-defence (a *sui generis* norm) would leave the *Caroline Case* basically intact. Article 51 must continue (in 'normal' cases of interstate attacks) to be interpreted restrictively, entailing a prohibition on preventive self-defence and a requirement that self-defence is undertaken in direct response to the armed attack. It is only in connection with large-scale international terrorist threats that a right of preventive military measures could be exercised, and it is only then that targets within an accomplice state's territory could be attacked.

The future positions of state practice will demonstrate whether the *opinio juris* which was unfolding in the autumn of 2001 will gain acceptance as new international law. In assessing the state of the law, both the articulated positions of states but also their tacit consent will be of relevance. A new state of the law can enter the scene on the basis of what Bruno Simma and Andreas Paulus have called 'a modern positivist understanding of State practice',[23] *i.e.*, a crystallizing of norms in borderline areas between concrete acts of state and *opinio juris*, between activism and passivity, between support and tolerance.

The US-British missile attacks against targets in Afghanistan started on 7 October 2001. The following day, the fifteen foreign ministers of the EU declared their support for the operation ('support for the self-defence actions in accordance with the United Nations Charter and with resolution 1368 of the Security Council').[24] Russia's President Putin also indicated his support, as did China, if more implicitly.[25] UN Secretary-General Kofi Annan suggested in a commentary that the Security Council during its meeting of 8 October had confirmed the inherent right of individual or

22 Cited by Jennings, *supra* note 5, p. 89.
23 *Cf.* their formulations in *'Symposium on Method in International Law'*, American Journal of International Law, Vol. 93, 1999, pp. 302, 306.
24 EU Press Releases, Luxembourg 08/10 2001 (BELGA).
25 Dagens Nyheter, 9 Oct. 2001.

collective self-defence: 'The States concerned have set their current military action in Afghanistan in that context'.[26]

The Security Council did not adopt a new resolution but instead contented itself with US and UK reporting, as is required by states acting in self-defence under Article 51 of the UN Charter. The Security Council's chairman summarized it thus: 'The members of the Security Council were appreciative of the presentations made by the United States and the United Kingdom.'[27] An Arabic summit in Qatar on 10 October with 56 participating states issued a declaration signifying that the declarants had no objections to the legitimacy of the military campaign, but expressed the hope that the air missions would be executed so as to spare Afghanistan's civilian population. Many states were tolerantly passive vis-à-vis the air strikes, which they characterized as preventive self-defence against international terrorism. A new supplementary norm of self-defence had been established – an addition to UN Charter Article 51 (an Article '$51^1/_2$').

It was however unclear how the new norm's delimitation in time and space was to be dealt with, considering the international law requirements of proportionality and necessity in self-defence. State practice will have to provide the answer. Governments, diplomats and international lawyers thus have their work cut out for them. An amendment of the UN Charter requires big power consensus and reasonable precision and will not be attainable. One thing should be clear, though: The new possibility of preventive self-defence against international terrorism cannot be extended so as to allow a drawn-out military presence in a sovereign country (the target state). The concept of self-defence is linked to the existence of an international armed conflict and actions in self-defence can only continue for as long as the characteristics of such a conflict subsist. In Afghanistan the Taliban were defeated in December 2001 and the al-Qaeda terrorist threat from Afghan territory towards other countries was over. On 20 December the Security Council adopted Resolution 1386 (2001) which welcomed 'developments in Afghanistan that will allow for all Afghans to enjoy inalienable rights and freedom' and recognized that 'the responsibility for providing secu-

26 SG/SM/7985, AFG/149, 8 Oct. 2001.
27 Statement to the press by the President of the Security Council, 8 Oct. 2001.

rity and law and order throughout the country resides with the Afghans themselves'. From this point in time the US-UK military presence in Afghanistan could not rely on any right of self-defence, it had to rely on another legal ground. The one that presented itself was consent. US-UK military operations of some sort had to continue and they were consented to by the new provisional government in Kabul, the 'Afghan Interim Authority' as it was called in Resolution 1386. The Resolution also authorized the establishment of an International Security Assistance Force (ISAF), which made it possible for the UN and its member states to assist the Afghan Interim Authority in the maintenance of a secure environment, thereby supporting the peace-building efforts in Afghanistan.

Already before developments had reached that point, journalists and commentators all over the world wondered whether the new right of self-defence could be used towards other countries with an al-Qaeda presence, in a never-ending domino game mirroring the new US hegemony over international relations. The legal answer to that concern is that there is no carte blanche for further actions, labelled as self-defence, in the absence of clear evidence of a terrorist use of a certain territory, evidence which is convincing to the international community. Criteria for this will not be possible to inscribe in the UN Charter or any other treaty. Again, state practice will have to provide the answer in concrete cases. This is not an auspicious development for international law. Unavoidable and necessary, perhaps, but regrettable in its fuzziness, non-predictability and dependency on super power interpretations.

References

Books & articles

Ahlin, Per, *En nygammal svensk folkrätt*, Dagens Nyheter 29 Sept. 2001.
Amnéus, Diana & Svanberg, Katinka, *Invänta FN:s fulla stöd*, Svenska Dagbladet Brännpunkt 29 Sept. 2001.
ASIL Insight: *Terrorist Attacks on the World Trade Center and the Pentagon*, September 2001, www.asil.org.
Bring, Ove, *FN-stadgan och världspolitiken: Om folkrättens roll i en föränderlig värld*, 3rd ed., Norstedts Juridik, Stockholm, 2000.
Falk, Richard A., *What Future for the UN Charter System of War Protection?*, American Journal of International Law, Vol. 97, 2003, p. 592.
Jacobsson, Marie & Pål Wrange, *Folkrätten förändras*, Svenska Dagbladet Brännpunkt 22 Sept. 2001.
Jennings, Robert Y., *The Caroline and McLeod Cases*, American Journal of International Law, Vol. 32, 1938, p. 77.
Mahmoudi, Said, *International Use of Force: Quo Vadis?*, Juridisk tidskrift, 2003–04, p. 341.
Mahmoudi, Said, *Sverige försvagar FN*, Svenska Dagbladet Brännpunkt 24 Oct. 2001.
Noll, Gregor, *USA utmanar folkrätten*, Svenska Dagbladet Brännpunkt 19 Sept. 2001.
Symposium on Method in International Law, American Journal of International Law, Vol. 93, 1999, p. 302.
Walker, George K., *The Lawfulness of Operation Enduring Freedom's Self-Defense Responses*, Valparaiso University Law Review, Vol. 37, No. 2, 2003, p. 489.
Åström, Sverker, *Regeringen är otydlig*, Dagens Nyheter Debatt 28 Sept. 2001.

6 Human Rights and Terrorism

Iain Cameron

6.1 Introduction

The subject of terrorism and the law of human rights is vast and can be approached from a number of different perspectives. One can look at state denial of human rights as one, of many, *causes* of terrorism.[1] One can examine the *responsibility at international law of terrorist groups* for acts violating human rights.[2] One can examine the extent to which national *constitutional rights* place limits upon anti-terrorist measures – either national measures, or international arrangements.[3] Finally, one can take the perspective I do in this short article and look at the extent to which *applicable universal and regional human rights treaties* place limits on national and international anti-terrorist measures.[4]

1 Recall the preamble to the Universal Declaration of Human Rights (UDHR), UN Doc. A/811, 1948, where it is stated *inter alia* that 'it is essential, if man is not to be compelled to have recourse, as a last resort, to rebellion against tyranny and oppression, that human rights should be protected by the rule of law...'. This issue has not been studied so much by international lawyers, however it is touched upon by the rapporteur appointed by the Sub-Commission on Human Rights to look into the issue of terrorism. See Koufa, Kalliopi, *Terrorism and Human Rights*, preliminary report, second progress report, respectively, E/CN.4/Sub.2/1999/27 and E/CN.4/Sub.2/2002/35.

2 See, *e.g.*, Zegveld, Linda, *Accountability of Armed Opposition Groups in International Law*, Cambridge UP, Cambridge, 2002.

3 The literature on this is obviously considerable. There can obviously be an overlap with international human rights in that, in certain states, these can have constitutional status. For two national examinations of the impact of recent (UK and US) anti-terrorist legislation, see Walker, Clive, *Guide to the Anti-terrorism Legislation*, Blackstone Press, Oxford, 2002 and Gross, Emanuel, *The Influence of Terrorist Attacks on Human Rights in the United States*, North Carolina Journal of International Law and Commercial Regulation, Vol. 28, 2002, p. 1.

4 There are naturally other ways in which these two matters can interact, *e.g.* as factors to be taken into account in deciding whether or not to permit weapons exports. See the EU Code of Conduct for Export of Weapons, 5 June 1998, Council Doc. 8675/2/98 Rev. 2.

Within each perspective there are, in turn, a number of different issues. The term 'terrorism' refers essentially to a method by which an organisation seeks to achieve a goal, usually political, by means of violence and the creation of fear.[5] As such, it covers a multitude of different phenomena and different groups, everything, in fact, from small 'single issue' factions, using home-made bombs to force limited changes in government policy, to well-armed, organized and financed entities in control of territory, behaving as a quasi-government and aiming for the control of the state, or the creation of a new state.[6] The state responses to such tactics and groups will obviously vary. They can be *military* in nature, *i.e.* military force can be used against suspected terrorist groups. This subject involves discussion of the international law on the use of force and international humanitarian law. But the boundary between military and non-military responses to terrorism has now been, deliberately, obscured, and there is thus no clear dividing line between the applicable law of peacetime and wartime.[7] Anti-terrorist measures can take *economic* forms, both in the form of 'winning hearts and minds' of actual or potential terrorist supporters and in the form of unilateral and multilateral sanctions directed against the property of terrorist suspects (targeted sanctions) or against governments believed to be supporting terrorists.[8] Anti-terrorist measures can also be of a *law enforcement* character. They can create new offences and give increased police powers of, for example, arrest, detention, search and seizure. Finally, anti-terrorist measures can give increased *intelligence* gathering powers to security and intelligence agencies – in particular powers of surveillance and data-processing. All of these different types of measures can be combined as part of an overall anti-terrorism strategy.

States will usually unilaterally decide whether or not to take exceptional powers to deal with terrorism. However, various types

5 There is no agreement in doctrine as to what constitutes terrorism. See, *e.g.* Schmid Alex and Jongman Albert, *Political Terrorism: A new Guide to Actors, Authors, Concepts, Databases, Theories and Literature,* 2nd ed., North-Holland, Amsterdam, 1988.

6 Indeed, 'terrorism' need not be confined to non-state actors, but can cover even security forces using such methods, commonly called 'state terrorism'.

7 See below, note 24 and accompanying text.

8 See the Chapter by Fredrik Stenhammar in the present volume.

of duty to cooperate against terrorism, necessitating national legislation and measures, can be contained in universal or regional treaties. More recently, obligations on states in this field have come into being as a result of Security Council Resolutions.[9]

The first point as regards human rights I would like to make is the most important, namely that human rights are to be strictly complied with in dealing with terrorist threats.[10] States obviously sometimes have to take severe measures against terrorists but only if human rights are respected in the process is the struggle against terrorism legitimized. This might appear obvious, but the people responsible for formulating and implementing counter-terrorism measures are not usually the same people responsible for ensuring that the state complies with its international, and constitutional, duties as regards human rights. As states are usually prepared to push anti-terrorism measures to the limit of what is acceptable to public opinion, then these powers are likely to raise issues under many, if not all, constitutional rights at national law, and all the civil and political rights listed in the major universal and regional human rights treaties. Since this book is intended primarily for European readers, I will concentrate upon the most relevant rights existing under the European Convention on Human Rights (ECHR),[11] as it is interpreted in the case law of the European Court of Human Rights (ECtHR). I also refer on occasion to the International Covenant on Civil and Political Rights (ICCPR),[12] and the case law of the Human Rights Committee (HRC) interpreting this, as this is the human rights treaty setting out a catalogue of civil rights that is ratified by the majority of states in the world.

It should also be noted that there are three different groups of people whose rights are affected.[13] First, obviously, anti-terrorist measures can reduce, or take away, the human rights of terrorist suspects, for example, the freedom from torture or the right to a fair

9 See below, notes 26, 120–123 and accompanying text.

10 Among the many reminders of this see in particular Parliamentary Assembly of the Council of Europe Resolution 1271 (2002) Combating terrorism and respect for human rights, SC Res 1456, 20 January 2003, and GA Res 57/27, Measures to eliminate international terrorism, 15 January 2003.

11 ETS No. 5, 1950.

12 United Nations Treaty Series, Vol. 999, p. 71 (1966).

13 *Cf.* Warbrick, Colin, *The Principles of the ECHR and the Response of States to Terrorism,* European Human Rights Law Review, 2002, p. 287, at p. 288.

trial. Second, there can be 'collateral damage' in that people who may support the same general political ends as a targeted terrorist group (but who pursue these ends by peaceful means) can be lumped together with terrorists and have their rights limited in a variety of ways, for example, by secret surveillance. Thirdly, there can be what might be referred to as 'spillover' damage to 'ordinary' law enforcement: 'temporary' and 'exceptional' powers can become both permanent and the norm, thus threatening the rights of many people.[14]

In this short article, space constraints rule out looking at all the ways in which anti-terrorist measures can affect human rights. I only attempt to give an overview of terrorism and the rights to life, liberty and security of person and to a fair trial.[15] I have chosen these rights because they are among the most relevant to the issue of security – the theme of the present book. For the same reason I also look briefly at the subject of derogation (*i.e.* suspension) of rights during severe public emergencies. Before doing so, however, it is necessary to say something about the existing international regulation of terrorism and to take up some general issues regarding abuse of state power in this field.

6.2 The international regulation of terrorism

There is no universally accepted definition of terrorism among states, and there is no comprehensive treaty on terrorism in force.[16]

14 Ashworth, Andrew, *Human Rights, Serious Crime and Criminal Procedure,* Sweet and Maxwell, London, 2002, pp. 105–107.

15 I will not look at other rights often affected by anti-terrorism measures, such as the freedoms of expression, assembly and association, the protection of privacy (particularly important as regards data protection and secret surveillance), the protection against discrimination, the right of property, the freedoms from torture and of movement, thought, conscience and religion, and the right to an effective remedy before a national authority. For discussions of these rights under the ECHR from national security perspective, see Cameron, Iain, *National Security and the ECHR,* Iustus/Kluwer, Uppsala/the Hague, 2000.

16 The main UN actors in the field of terrorism are the Counter-Terrorism Committee established by the Security Council and the UN Office on Drugs and Crime which, so far, have been mainly working by identifying deficiencies in states' laws and practices and producing action plans and model laws. See the overviews of these bodies' work at www.un.org/Docs/sc/committees/1373 and www.unodc.org/unodc/en/crime_prevention.html.

However, in addition to bilateral treaties, there are twelve global multilateral treaties dealing directly with specific acts of terrorism[17] and nine regional treaties dealing with terrorism as a whole, or particular aspects of it.[18] Bearing in mind the fact that, especially in dysfunctional states, there can be a symbiotic relationship between organized crime and terrorism (the former can finance the latter, the latter can forward in different ways the goals of the former), the

17 The ICAO has adopted the following treaties, the Tokyo Convention on Offences and Certain Other Acts Committed on Board Aircraft, 1963, the Hague Convention for the Suppression of Unlawful Seizure of Aircraft, 1970, the Montreal Convention for the Suppression of Unlawful Acts against the Safety of Civil Aviation, 1971, the Protocol to the Montreal Convention for the Suppression of Unlawful Acts of Violence at Airports Serving International Civil Aviation, 1988 and the Montreal Convention on the Marking of Plastic Explosives for the Purpose of Detection 1991. The UN has adopted the following treaties, the Convention on the Prevention and Punishment of Crimes against Internationally Protected Persons, including Diplomatic Agents, 1973, the International Convention against the Taking of Hostages 1979, the International Convention for the Suppression of Terrorist Bombings 1997 and the International Convention on the Suppression of Financing of Terrorism 1999. The International Atomic Energy Agency has adopted the Convention on the Physical Protection of Nuclear Material, 1980. The International Maritime Organisation has adopted the Convention for the Suppression of Unlawful Acts against the Safety of Maritime Navigation 1988, and the Protocol for the Suppression of Unlawful Acts against the Safety of Fixed Platforms Located on the Continental Shelf, 1988. All these treaties can be accessed at untreaty.un.org/English/Terrorism.asp.

18 League of Arab States, Arab Convention on the Suppression of Terrorism, 1998, Organisation of the Islamic Conference, Convention on Combating International Terrorism, 1999, not yet in force, the Council of Europe Convention on the Suppression of Terrorism 1977, and amending Protocol 15 May 2003, not yet in force (conventions.coe.int/Treaty/EN/cadreprojets.htm), the OAS Convention to Prevent and Punish the Acts of Terrorism Taking the Form of Crimes against Persons and Related Extortion that are of International Significance, ILM, Vol. 10, 1971, p. 255, and the Convention Against Terrorism, ILM, Vol. 42, 2003, p. 19, the African Union (formerly Organisation of African Unity), Convention on the Prevention and Combating of Terrorism, 1999, not yet in force, the South Asian Association for Regional Cooperation, Regional Convention on Suppression of Terrorism, 1987, and the Commonwealth of Independent States, Treaty on Cooperation among the States Members of the Commonwealth of Independent States in Combating Terrorism 1999. Where another location is not indicated these treaties can be accessed at or via untreaty.un.org/English/Terrorism.asp. There are also a large number of EU arrangements of direct and indirect significance to terrorism, in particular the framework decision on terrorism, OJ L 164, 22 June 2002, and Common Position 2001/930/CFSP on Terrorism, OJ L 344, 28 December 2001, and Common Position 2001/931/CFSP on the Application of Specific Measures with a view to fighting terrorism, OJ L 344, 28 December 2001.

multilateral treaties creating criminal offences and providing for cooperation duties in relation to drugs, money laundering,[19] and organized crime generally are also relevant to terrorism. The International Criminal Court[20] was not given jurisdiction over terrorist offences,[21] although a review conference is expected to look again at this issue. Having said this, certain offences committed by groups, particularly non-state groups in control of territory, using terrorist methods can be of such a scale and intensity as to fall under the definition of 'crimes against humanity'.[22] The main treaties on international humanitarian law,[23] defining combatants and setting out prohibitions on methods of waging war, previously purported to determine both the issue of who is *not* a terrorist, and

19 Here one can also note certain important non-treaty based norms, *inter alia* the Financial Action Task Force (FATF) Special Recommendations on Terrorist Financing 31 October 2001 (at www.fatf-gafi.org). The efficacy of anti-money laundering methods against terrorism is highly doubtful. See Kichling, Michael, *A Magic Formula Which can do Away with Terrorism?*, Max Planck Research Bulletin, 1/2002.

20 *Rome Statute of the International Criminal Court*, UN Doc. A/CONF.183/9 (July 17, 1998), reprinted in ILM, Vol. 37, p. 999 (hereinafter Rome Statute). At the time of writing, the treaty has 90 parties and has been signed by a further 49 states. Ratification Status, at www.iccnow.org/countryinfo/worldsigsandratifications (2003-05-31).

21 For a discussion see Robinson, Patrick, *The Missing Crimes*, Cassesse, Antonio, *et al.* (Eds.), The Rome Statute of the ICC: A Commentary, volume 1, Oxford University Press, Oxford, 2002, pp. 510–521.

22 For a discussion of the practicalities, see, *e.g.*, Rubin, Alfred, *Legal Response to Terror: An International Criminal Court?* Harvard International Law Journal, Vol. 43, 2002, p. 65.

23 Geneva Convention (I) for the Amelioration of the Condition of the Wounded and Sick in Armed Forces in the Field 1949, United Nations Treaty Series, Vol. 75, p. 31; Geneva Convention (II) for the Amelioration of the Condition of Wounded, Sick and Shipwrecked Members of the Armed Forces at Sea 1949, United Nations Treaty Series, Vol. 75, p. 85; Geneva Convention (III) Relative to the Treatment of Prisoners of War 1949, United Nations Treaty Series, Vol. 75, p. 135; Geneva Convention (III) Relative to the Protection of Civilian Persons in Time of War 1949, United Nations Treaty Series, Vol. 75, p. 287; Protocol I additional to the Geneva Conventions of 12 August 1949 Relating the Protection of Victims of International Armed Conflicts 1977, United Nations Treaty Series, Vol. 1125, p. 3; Protocol II additional to the Geneva Conventions of 12 August 1949 Relating the Protection of Victims of Non-International Armed Conflicts 1977, United Nations Treaty Series, Vol. 1125 p. 513. As of 31 January 2003, the four Geneva conventions had 190 parties. Protocol I had 119 parties, and Protocol II 156 parties, see www.icrc.org/ihl.nsf/. See also the Convention on the Safety of United Nations and Associated Personnel, UN Doc. A/Res./49/59 (1995).

what are the permissible military responses to enemy combatants. But the advent of terrorists, which are not proxies of sponsor states, which operate as 'nomadic networks' with global or regional, rather than separatist, goals, has called this into question.[24] This has in turn created tensions between the US and other states, especially states whose nationals are caught up in a legal limbo; neither being regarded as having prisoner of war status, nor as being protected civilians, to which the laws of war apply nor as being ordinary criminals to which national laws (and applicable human rights standards) apply.[25] Finally, as already mentioned, there are obligations which exist as a result of customary international law and/or as authoritative interpretations of the UN Charter, in particular the obligation not to support or fund terrorists.[26] In the wake of the terrorist attacks of 11 September the Security Council adopted a number of Resolutions. Of special importance here are Resolutions 1373, of 28 September 2001, and 1390 of 16 January 2002. The former imposes obligations on all states *inter alia* to criminalize acts of financing of international terrorism, and to freeze and seize funds used for terrorism. It amounts, in effect, to an obligation to implement the operative provisions of the Convention on the Financing of International Terrorism. It contains no time limit. There is a reporting obligation, and a monitoring committee (the Counterterrorism Committee, CTC) is established with competence *inter alia* to review the reports submitted. The latter Resolution creates blacklists of terrorist suspects and imposes obligations to freeze the

24 For a recent useful survey see, Lippman, Mathew, *The New Terrorism and International Law,* Tulsa Journal of Comparative and International Law, Vol. 10, 2003, p. 297.

25 Hamdi v. Rumsfeld, 296 F.3d 278 (4th Cir. 2002). There are, after the US military actions against the Taliban/al-Qaeda in Afghanistan and Yemen, and incarceration of the 'illegal combatants' in Guautanamo in Cuba, a large number of Articles dealing with the problems of 'asymmetrical' war. See, *e.g.*, Paust, Jordan J., *Judicial Power to Determine the Status and Rights of Persons Detained Without Trial,* Harvard International Law Journal, Vol. 44, 2003, p. 301, Klabbers, Jan, *Rebels with a Cause?,* European Journal of International Law, Vol. 14, 2003, p. 299, and Jinks, Derek, *September 11 and the Laws of War,* Yale Journal of International Law, Vol. 28, 2003, p. 1. As mentioned already, I will not go into these issues which are discussed in other essays in the present volume.

26 See Declaration on Principles of International Law Concerning Friendly Relations and Co-operation between States in Accordance with the Charter of the United Nations, GA Res. 2625 (XXV), 1970 and Resolution on the Definition of Aggression, GA Res. 3314 (XXIX), 1974.

listed persons assets, imposes travel bans on them and criminalizes any attempts to provide them with financing or weapons. Resolution 1390 is directed against the al-Qaeda network, but it is 'open-ended' in that there is no connection between the targeted group/individuals and any territory or state.

The international regulation of terrorism is thus a patchwork. It has come into being, like the rest of international criminal law, in an *ad hoc* fashion; a major incident occurs, and diplomats rush to conclude a multilateral treaty, whereupon it is (more often than not) largely forgotten. Why is there no comprehensive framework and no universally applicable definition of terrorism? States are seldom sufficiently interested in a subject to devote the time and resources necessary to codify it, and this is a subject that is highly politically charged. Much of the problem in fact centres around states' difficulties in agreeing on a definition. The label of terrorism has a denunciatory function: it serves to delegitimize those who use such methods.[27] But states have different political systems (totalitarian, authoritarian, democratic and everything in between) and their governments have on occasion very different political goals, goals which they occasionally seek to achieve by using force and creating fear, or condoning the use of force and the creation of fear by others. Like-minded states naturally find it easier to agree on definitions, but any attempt among heterogenous states to criminalize non-state groups solely on the basis of the methods they use will run into the problem of outlawing groups pursuing goals which a state will on occasion want to support, plus risk outlawing methods of warfare which a state might on occasion want to use itself. It is not possible to produce a conceptually satisfactory definition which catches those one wants to catch (terrorists), and leaves untouched those one does not want to catch ('freedom fighters' and one's own military forces).[28]

Consequently states found it simpler, at least at the global level, to proceed by identifying those types of terrorist tactics and methods, such as hijacking, or taking of hostages, which are most disruptive of international relations, and to prohibit these. However, with

27 *Cf.* Warbrick, 2002, *op. cit.* p. 288.
28 For a recent discussion see, *e.g.*, Byford, Grenville, *The Wrong War,* Foreign Affairs, July/August, 2002, p. 34.

the end of the Cold War, it has become a bit easier to reach agreement, and the most recent global treaty, the Convention against the Financing of Terrorism defines terrorism (in Article 2) first by referring to the acts falling within nine specific global anti-terrorism treaties (hijacking, etc.), and second by referring to '[a]ny other act intended to cause death or serious bodily injury to a civilian, or to any other person not taking an active part in the hostilities in a situation of armed conflict, when the purpose of such act, by its nature or context, is to intimidate a population, or to compel a government or an international organisation to do or to abstain from doing any act'.[29] As mentioned, this definition was incorporated into Resolution 1373, and, at least as far as financing is concerned, it has become binding for all the states in the world.

The global treaties mainly provide for the creation of new criminal offences, the taking of extraterritorial jurisdiction over such offences, the inclusion of such offences in extradition treaties, the obligation to extradite or try suspected terrorist offenders and the obligation to cooperate as regards mutual legal assistance (MLA).[30] In particular, as regards MLA, some of the global, and regional, treaties have attempted to exclude the application to terrorists of what is called the 'political offence exemption', *i.e.* the rule that political offenders may not be extradited.[31] One can say that most of the existing global and regional treaties do not significantly involve human rights issues.[32] However, improved MLA treaties can raise such issues. MLA treaties have traditionally been designed to safe-

29 See also the definition employed in the EU framework decision and common position on terrorism, *op. cit.* which provide 'a terrorist act shall mean one of a listed series of acts committed intentionally, which, 'given its nature or its context, may seriously damage a country or an international organisation, as defined as an offence under national law, where committed with the aims of: i. seriously intimidating a population, or ii. unduly compelling a government or an international organisation to perform or abstain from performing any act, or iii. seriously destabilising or destroying the fundamental political, constitutional, economic or social structures of a country or an international organization'.

30 MLA covers such matters as the collection of evidence, the hearing of witnesses, the transfer of prosecutions, and convicted offenders as well as police and customs cooperation.

31 Wijngaert, Cristine van den, *The Political Offence Exemption to Extradition,* Nijhoff, Deventer 1980, Påle, Karin, *Villkor för utlämning,* Iustus, Uppsala, 2003.

32 Although *cf.* Boister, Neil, *Human Rights Protections in the Suppression Conventions,* Human Rights Law Review, Vol. 2, 2002, p. 199.

guard state sovereignty, and cumbersome, time-consuming arrangements are undoubtedly no longer suited to the global, and especially, regional, village of crime. But the double criminality and speciality rules, the refusal to extradite nationals and centralized procedures frequently requiring political consent often had the bi-product of safeguarding the human rights of suspects. Remove these obstacles, as the European Arrest Warrant[33] has done to a large extent for EU states, and one has to think seriously about harmonizing rules providing for minimum procedural safeguards for suspects, such as conditions of detention and maximum periods of detention awaiting trial. Improving mutual legal assistance as regards gathering of evidence is naturally desirable, but even here there can be problems, for example in equality of arms (where the prosecution has no duty to assist the defence in obtaining evidence). One can also note that unconditional extradition obligations can raise problems as regards torture and the death penalty. And treaties providing for intelligence exchange can raise a variety of issues relating to data protection.

6.3 When are states bound by the law of human rights when dealing with terrorism?

Obviously, a state has to be bound by a human right before one can say that a state's action against terrorism violates the right in question. The only general human rights catalogue binding upon *all* the states in the world is the Universal Declaration of Human Rights (UDHR) because it has entered into custom, and/or because it can be seen as an authoritative interpretation of the UN Charter obligations set out in Articles 1, 55 and 56.[34] However, the vagueness of the UDHR, mainly as a result of the general accommodation clauses, and the absence of international institutions with the power to make binding, or even persuasive decisions on its content, means

33 Framework Decision on the European Arrest Warrant, 18 July 2002, Official Journal L 190.

34 The customary nature of the UDHR was stressed by the Vienna Declaration of the World Conference on Human Rights, 1993, endorsed by the General Assembly in Res. 48/121 (1993).

that it is of limited use as a check upon state abuse of power. Thus, it is best if the state has made a treaty commitment to respect human rights. Obviously, this only binds the state *from the date of entry into force*, and only to the extent that the state has not made any (lawful) reservations, limiting its commitments.

6.4 What factors operate to induce compliance/ non-compliance?

While a state party will be bound vis a vis the other state parties as a matter of international law, the normal mechanism for ensuring compliance with bilateral commitments in international law, the fear that non-compliance will lead to similar behaviour by the other parties, does not operate so well as regards multilateral human rights commitments. To have any chance of persuading recalcitrant states to comply it is usually necessary to establish powerful supervisory bodies. The supervisory body, the Human Rights Committee (HRC) established by the main universal treaty providing for a general catalogue of rights, the ICCPR, has the power to adopt general comments, concluding observations on state reports, and, for those states which have ratified the first optional protocol to the ICCPR, the power to take decisions in individual cases.[35] The nature of the obligation undertaken by parties to the ECHR is stronger – involving a binding obligation to comply with judgments of the respective court. However, national security is the area where states are least inclined to be receptive to international criticism, and least inclined to make meaningful changes to national laws and practices.[36] This applies even in the context of the ECHR, where the 44 member states are, by and large, democracies, the informal peer group pressure to comply with the Convention and judgments of the Court is very strong, and where the economic power of the EU, both formally and informally, serves to strengthen states' inclinations to obey (a factor which works particularly well with EU candidate

35 These decisions, although not formally speaking binding, must be seen as highly authoritative interpretations of the states' obligations under the ICCPR, entailing, at least, a *prima facie* obligation on states to follow them.

36 See Cameron, 2000, *op. cit., passim*.

states). Some states obviously have more problems than others. Turkey has now had many judgments against it, finding anti-terrorist laws and practices to be in violation of the ECHR.[37] The first cases against Russia concerning the anti-terrorist/separatist conflict in Chechnya have recently been declared admissible.[38]

The built-in reluctance to comply in this area means that it is crucial that there is adequate follow-up to such judgments. States must often be pressured into making the necessary changes in laws and practices. This will often involve not simply repealing laws granting exceptional powers, but changing a 'culture of impunity', *i.e.* a deep-rooted practice of placing security forces above the law. This is not easy as it requires not simply commitment but also money, often large sums of money, *inter alia* to train and pay better soldiers, policemen, prosecutors, judges and prison-officers. And, where the root causes of terrorism are structural, based on for example poverty, serious inequalities in society, systematic discrimination or disenfranchisement of a minority, then simply making sure that the machinery of justice is operating reasonably well will naturally not end terrorism, but simply reduce the abuses in suppressing it.

The problem of 'the law on paper' not corresponding with the law in practice is multiplied as regards the ICCPR and, for that matter, the other two regional human rights treaties, the American Convention on Human Rights (ACHR)[39] and the African (Banjul) Charter on Human and Peoples Rights,[40] the state parties of which contain many authoritarian or only half-democratic regimes. Without sustained international pressure in different forms, economic, diplomatic etc., authoritarian regimes will ignore or belittle their international human rights obligations. And if terrorism gives liberal,

37 For discussion of the Turkish cases under Articles 2 and 10, see Cameron, 2000, pp. 261–265, 383–394.

38 Khashiyev v. Russia (no. 57942/00), Akayeva v. Russia (no. 57945/00), Isayeva v. Russia (no. 57947/00), Yusupova v. Russia (no. 57948/00), Bazayeva v. Russia (no. 57949/00) and Isayeva v. Russia (no. 57950/00) (16 January 2003). The applicants allege violation of their rights by the Russian military in Chechnya in 1999–2000. the Court declared admissible the applicants' complaints under Article 2 (right to life), Article 3 (prohibition of torture and inhuman or degrading treatment), Article 13 (right to an effective remedy) and Article 1 of Protocol No. 1 to the Convention (protection of property).

39 ILM, Vol. 9, 1969, p. 672.

40 ILM, Vol. 21, 1981, p. 59.

democratic states the excuse to limit human rights (indeed, national security nowadays is the only excuse accepted in secular states for limiting human rights), then this is doubly so for authoritarian regimes.[41] Protestors complaining about the political system, social injustice, economic mismanagement, corruption, rights abuses or environmental degradation can very easily be categorized as terrorists or 'terrorist supporters'. I would say that, apart from the casualties in Afghanistan and Iraq, one of the major tragedies (so far) of the post September 11 policies pursued by the present US government is the fact that human rights abuses by authoritarian states have largely been ignored, so long as the state in question supports the US line in dealing with al-Qaeda and other threats to the national security of the US. In my opinion, the great power of the US to pressure recalcitrant states into complying with human rights is not being used as it should be. I can add here that the same lack of concern can be seen in the work of the CTC, which, so far, has taken a narrow, effectivizing approach to terrorist cooperation.[42]

6.5 In what ways can terrorism be taken into account in limiting human rights?

One can argue that it is not possible to fight terror effectively while still respecting human rights. Terrorists who attack civilian targets or otherwise murder indiscriminately are certainly not restrained by any bleeding heart liberal notions of the Rechtstaat. And the security of the state may, at a time of panic, seem to be the overriding goal, capable of justifying anything,[43] even if this is fundamen-

41 As Lippman puts it, '[i]ronically, States which are engaged in the systematic violation of human rights are likely to have the most effective, if not totalitarian, mechanisms for controlling terrorism. The failure to provide even a loose definition of terrorism invites these countries to repress democratic elements under the guise of combating terrorism.' (*op. cit.* at p. 365).

42 The work of the OSCE shows that it is perfectly possible to have a security-oriented approach which nonetheless places respect for human rights at the centre of one's focus.

43 'Security is the most vital of all interests. On it we depend for our immunity from evil, and for the whole value of all and every good, beyond the passing moment.' Mill, John S., *Utilitarianism, on Liberty, Considerations on Representative Government,* Acton H.B. (Ed.), Dent, London, 1991, p. 56.

tally at odds with both the letter and spirit of international commitments to human rights. There are values that are higher than the security of the state. If the protection of the Rechstaat involves accepting the occasional obstacle to a short-term 'effective' measure, such as torture, then so be it.[44]

But there are relatively few absolute human rights. The case law of the most developed international supervisory system, the European Court of Human Rights (ECtHR), as well as that of the HRC shows that where there is an exceptional situation threatening public order, such as a wave of terrorist violence, then this background can be taken into account in determining the legitimacy of measures taken which allegedly infringe Convention rights.[45] Thus, states may take into account the terrorist context in relation to all rights, except those framed in absolute terms, and in practice subject them to implicit, more far-reaching, limitations.

There is naturally no *hard and fast* line between 'normal' terrorist situations and public emergencies. The factual situation can begin with political tension, moving on to sporadic internal disturbances to internal conflict to all-out civil (or international) war. The domestic legal response to this is also on a sliding scale, beginning with a situation in which existing legislation, particularly in the field of criminal procedure, is applied successively more severely, moving through to the *de facto* or *de jure* (promulgation) of a state of emergency whereby special legislation comes into operation by government decree or new legislation is passed. Ultimately, one

44 Here one can recall a statement regarding torture made by one of the delegates to the conference negotiating the ECHR, almost all of whom had personal experience of appalling tyranny, '[n]o cause whatsoever – not even ... the safety of an army or the security of the state – can justify its use or existence. I say that if a State, in order to survive, must be built on a torture chamber, then that state should perish.' See Council of Europe, *Collected edition of the travaux préparatoires to the ECHR,* 8 vol., Nijhoff, Dordrecht, 1975–1985, Vol. II, p. 40 (Mr. Cocks).

45 *E.g.* McVeigh, O'Neill and Evans v. UK, App. Nos 8022/77, 8025/77 and 8027/77, 20 DR 5 (1982), Brogan and others v. UK, 29 November 1988, A/145-B, para. 48, Fox, Cambell and Hartley v. UK, 30 August 1990, A/182, para. 32, Murray v. UK, 28 October 1994, A/300-A, paras. 90–92, Zana v. Turkey, 19 December 1997, paras. 59 and 60 and Incal v. Turkey, 9 June 1998, para. 58. For discussion see Warbrick, Colin, The ECHR and terrorism, International and Comparative Law Quarterly, Vol. 32, 1983, p. 82 and Warbrick, Colin, *The Prevention of Terrorism Act 1976 and the ECHR: the McVeigh Case,* International and Comparative Law Quarterly, Vol. 32, 1983, p. 757. As regards HRC case law see, *e.g.*, Kavanagh v. Ireland, No. 819/1998.

reaches a situation of chaos in which law is largely or totally ignored. Normal safeguards for civil and political rights could be put out of action long before the official proclamation of a public emergency. Similarly, the international law rules applicable vary depending upon the factual situation. The rules on humanitarian law and international human rights law can either apply successively, the former being seen as *lex specialis* to the latter, or in parallel, whereby the former are used to interpret the latter.[46] But, as already mentioned, what is not acceptable is that *neither* applies.

In any event, where 'normal' limitations are not enough, states are entitled to derogate from their human rights obligations. Derogation provisions can be found in the ECHR (Article 15) the ICCPR (Article 4) and the ACHR (Article 27).[47] The derogation clauses allow derogation only to the extent strictly required by the exigencies of the situation. The scrutiny of state measures is lesser in a public emergency – in other words they can get away with more – but there are naturally limits. For example, neither the ECtHR nor the HRC permit a derogation made only in respect of one geographical area to be applied to another area,[48] and both insist that the need for state measures to be 'strictly required' is not a formality.[49] Whereas there have been several situations in which a state has filed notices of derogation as regards anti-terrorist measures taken within its territory, so far, only one state has attempted to derogate from its obligations under the ECHR and ICCPR in relation to international terrorism. Following the ECtHR judgment in *Chahal* v.

46 For an example of the first situation, see the Advisory Opinion of the ICJ on the Use or Threat of Nuclear Weapons, ICJ Reports, 1996, para. 25. For an example of the latter situation, see the Abella case, Inter-American Commission on Human Rights, report No. 55/97, case No. 11.137 (Argentina) OEA/Ser/L/V/II.97 Doc. 38 at paras. 154–171. The 'gap' between the point at which normal human rights protection breaks down and the triggering point(s) for the application of humanitarian law has been the subject of considerable discussion. See, *e.g.*, the UN Commission on Human Rights, 57th session, *Fundamental Standards of Humanity*, Report of the Secretary-General submitted pursuant to Commission resolution 2000/69, 12 January 2001, E/CN.4/2001/91.

47 The African Charter has no derogation provision.

48 See Sakik and others v. Turkey, 26 November 1997, paras. 36–39, Cetin and others v. Turkey, Nos 40153/98 and 40160/98, 13 February 2003 and HRC General Comment No. 29, States Of Emergency (Article 4), CCPR/C/21/Rev.1/Add.11.

49 HRC General Comment, *ibid.* Cetin and Sakik, *ibid.* The ECtHR has approved a retroactive notice of derogation Brannigan and McBride v. UK, 25 May 1993, A/258-B.

UK,[50] it became clear that there is an unconditional obligation not to extradite or deport a terrorist suspect to a state where he or she can risk inhuman treatment (or, for parties to Protocol 6/13, the death penalty). Whereas the Convention Relating to the Status of Refugees admits of a degree of balancing between state security interests and individual rights,[51] the obligation contained in Article 3 ECHR and, presumably, Article 7 ICCPR, is unconditional.[52] As the option of deporting the person anywhere else often does not exist in practice, the alternative is to allow them to remain, and trying them, or subjecting them to special supervisory measures (residence requirement, reporting periodically to the police, increased surveillance, etc.). The UK, however, considers that terrorist suspects who cannot be deported, should be imprisoned without trial and has accordingly legislated to allow this in the Anti-Terrorism, Crime and Security Act 2001 (ATCSA) and filed a notice of derogation to ECHR Article 5. The English Court of Appeal found that this was not incompatible with the ECHR.[53] As of December 2002, thirteen people have been arrested under the ATCSA. Two have since been 'voluntarily' repatriated, while ten non-UK nationals are interned without trial in high security prisons and one in a mental hospital.[54]

6.6 Where is a state bound by human rights?

One also has to look at the spatial scope of application of human rights treaties. This is particularly relevant for national force contingents taking part in peace-keeping or peace-enforcement opera-

50 15 November 1996. See also the earlier case of Soering v. UK, 7 July 1989, A/161 and the HRC decision Kindler v. Canada, No. 470/1991, 18 November 1993.

51 United Nations Treaty Series, Vol. 189, p. 137 (1951). Article 1F can be interpreted to allow the exclusion of a terrorist from refugee status, Article 32 allows expulsion on national security grounds and the duty of non-refoulement in Article 33 is subject to a national security exception.

52 See Cameron, 2000, pp. 270-76.

53 A and others v. Secretary of State for the Home Department, Court Of Appeal (Civil Division) [2002] EWCA Civ 1502, [2003] 1 All ER 816. Both the Council of Europe Commissioner on Human Rights (opinion 1/2002, Doc CommHR(2002)7) and the Parliamentary Assembly (PA Resolution 1271, 2002) have criticized this.

54 Statewatch bulletin November–December 2002, Vol. 12 No. 6.

tions. The standard rule is that the treaty applies within a state's jurisdiction, which is usually the same as the state's territory. However, the question arises as to whether anti-terrorist action outside the territory of the state can entail state responsibility. The case law of the HRC provides that the protection of the ICCPR can apply in the case of military occupation of territory,[55] as well as in the situation when security forces, or 'irregulars' are sent outside the territory to commit anti-terrorist acts.[56] As regards the ECHR, the well-established case law of the ECtHR shows that there can be situations in which extraterritorial acts of state can give rise to responsibility under the Convention.[57] However, in the recent Bankovíc case,[58] which concerned the NATO bombing of the TV station in Belgrade during the Kosovo conflict, the ECtHR stated that 'the Convention operates in an essentially regional context ... [it] was not designed to be applied throughout the world, even in respect of the conduct of Contracting States. Accordingly, the desirability of avoiding a gap or vacuum in human rights' protection has so far been relied on by the Court in favour of establishing jurisdiction only when the territory in question was one that, but for the specific circumstances, would normally be covered by the Convention' (paragraph 80). This decision does not totally rule out Convention responsibility for anti-terrorist military operations carried out by member states of the Council of Europe, either as authorized by the Security Council, or as unilateral/regional initiatives, for example as

55 See, *e.g.*, Concluding Observations on Israel (1998) (CCPR/C/79/Add.93) 'the Covenant must be held applicable to the occupied territories and those areas of Southern Lebanon and West Bekaa where Israel exercises effective control'.

56 See Lopez Burgos v. Uruguay, No. 52/1979 and Celeberti v. Uruguay, No. 56/1979. The HRC also stated in its Concluding Observations on Iran (1993) (CCPR/C/79/Add.25 para. 9) that the *Fatwa* on Salman Rushdie and threats to execute it outside the territory of Iran entails state responsibility under the ICCPR. Thanks to Martin Scheinin for comments on this point.

57 See, in particular, Loizidou v. Turkey, 23 March 1995 (preliminary objections), A/310, Loizidou v. Turkey, 18 December 1996 (Merits). The ECtHR also consider that acts of *e.g.* police in a state party to the Convention (A) in arresting a suspect in another state, even a non-state party (B), can give rise to Convention responsibility, when the arrest is with the acquiesance etc. of B. See Öcalan v. Turkey, No. 46221/99, 14 December 2000.

58 Banković, Stojanović, Stoimenovski, Joksimović and Suković v. Belgium, the Czech Republic, Denmark, France, Germany, Greece, Hungary, Iceland, Italy, Luxembourg, the Netherlands, Norway, Poland, Portugal, Spain, Turkey and the UK, No. 52207/99, 12 December 2001.

part of a peacekeeping operation. However, it requires, at least, the exercise of a level of control over the territory analogous to that of a state.[59]

6.7 Some general issues regarding abuse of state power and anti-terrorist measures

It is obvious that the *Rechtstaat* faces a considerable risk for abuse of state power when dealing with terrorism. As one commentator has put it:

> [the] challenge is to secure democracy against both its internal and external enemies, without destroying democracy in the process. Authoritarian and totalitarian states do not have to face this challenge. In such countries there is no need to ensure that security agencies, whose techniques inevitably involve a great deal of secrecy, be accountable to an elected legislature. Nor is there a requirement in such states that all of their security measures be authorized or provided for by law and that none of their officials be above the law. Only liberal democratic states are expected to make sure that the investigation of subversive activity does not interfere with the freedoms of political dissent and association which are essential ingredients of a free society.[60]

Experience shows that when people are scared after a major incident and the executive encourages the police and intelligence agencies to 'wage war' against terrorism, then it is very easy for human rights, like truth, to become the first casualty of that war. The most important safeguard against misuse of power in the police and intelligence agencies is the 'internal' control at the individual and collegial level, in other words, their professionalism and integrity. When they are told, implicitly or explicitly, that a blind eye will be turned as long as results are produced, then this safeguard no longer operates effectively. And governments should not attempt to circumvent democratic scrutiny and control by encouraging the

59 See in this respect Ilascu v. Moldova and the Russian Federation, No. 48787/99, decision of 4 July 2001, currently pending before the Grand Chamber. For analysis, see Happold, Mathew, *Bankovíc v. Belgium and the Territorial Scope of the ECHR*, Human Rights Law Review, Vol. 3, 2003, p. 77.

60 Gross, 2002, *op. cit.* p. 12.

police and intelligence agencies to bypass the law by abusing existing delegated powers or demanding new ones unless this is strictly necessary. Nor should governments bypass scrutiny by agreeing to treaties that, in practice, risk that police or intelligence powers could be lifted out of existing parliamentary, judicial or administrative control mechanisms.

The legislature should resist the temptation to show that it is 'doing something' about terrorism, and should not be stampeded into enacting new laws quickly giving greater police powers. Laws, especially anti-terror laws, should only be enacted after long and careful consideration.[61] Politicians and the press have a responsibility not to whip up public emotions. The threat of terrorist use of weapons of mass destruction is obviously terrifying to most people and by portraying this as the likely, or standard, type of attack in the future, governments can secure powers which are far in excess of what is needed to deal with present and projected future terrorism.[62] The very starting point of criminal procedure – that it is better that a guilty person walk free than an innocent person be convicted – is called into question when terrorists are said to have weapons of mass destruction.[63] The rhetoric from politicians of a 'war against terror', like a 'war against crime' is thus very dangerous. Moreover, it blurs the dividing line between peacetime and wartime and misleads the public that total security can be achieved. Neither war can ever be 'won'. So, my view is that while severe or prolonged terrorism can create war-type situations, and so demand military

61 The ACTSA in the UK is a graphic example of what should not happen. The UK had already passed a law (the Terrorism Act) in 2000 specifically designed to give all the necessary powers to deal with international terrorism, even future threats. Notwithstanding this, 'gaps' were discovered which had to be filled, and the ACTSA was pushed through parliament with unseemly haste. The Swedish government has, correctly, resisted the temptation to legislate quickly. Legislation has been introduced as a result of the framework decision on terrorism (*op. cit.* note 18) and more can be expected as a result of the recommendations made by a recent Commission of Inquiry (Vår beredskap efter den 11 september, SOU 2003:32). Having said this, restraint at the domestic level has not been matched by restraint in the EU. Sweden and the other member states of the EU have adopted speedily – too quickly I would say – measures blacklisting terrorist groups which can create considerable human rights problems (see below, note 121)

62 See, *e.g.* Gearty, Conor, *Terrorism and Human Rights: A Case Study in Impending Legal Realities,* Legal Studies Vol. 19, 1999, p. 367 at p. 371.

63 Ashworth, *op. cit.,* p. 112.

responses, in general terrorism is to be dealt with by law enforcement and intelligence methods, but always by agencies *acting within the law.*

Secondly, international human rights standards are both a minimum level of protection, and an incomplete protection. It should not be forgotten that the international standards are subsidiary, or supplementary, to the national constitutional standards, which form the first, and most important, line of defence of the *Rechtstaat.* And the scrutiny of an international body, assuming a suitable case comes along, is absolutely not a substitute for proper democratic scrutiny of legislation. In many areas international standards are still rudimentary, such as data protection, or the construction of the administrative and constitutional mechanisms necessary to extert adequate democratic and judicial control over the police and intelligence agencies when they are engaged in secretive 'high policing'.[64] So, counter-terrorism measures can be doubtful or even a downright bad idea from the perspective of other values, such as democracy, accountability and transparency etc. but they may not infringe international human rights. Moreover, the ICCPR and ECHR, naturally enough, put few limits on states powers to criminalize in general, or to sentence offenders. One should thus not be content with the international standards, although, as already mentioned, in the 'legal limbo' of extraterritorial military action against, or internment of, terrorist suspects, national constitutional safeguards may not apply, and so there may be no other standards applicable.

Thirdly, as already mentioned as regards 'collateral damage', it is important to remember that giving the police and intelligence agencies greater powers, or encouraging them to use existing powers more freely, does not mean that these powers are used only against terrorists. For this reason, amongst others, the judiciary should be very vigilant in applying existing laws, in order to do what it can to buttress internal controls on misuse of power. A graphic illustration of this collateral damage is the wave of arrests of

64 For a valuable preliminary survey of the problems of oversight, see Council of Europe, Parliamentary Assembly, Committee on Legal Affairs and Human Rights, Control of internal security services in Council of Europe members states, György Frunda (rapporteur), Doc. 8301, 21 January 1999.

US aliens for simple misdemenours following the September 11 attacks, and the lengthy periods of detention that many suffered.[65] Terrorists operate in *secret*. In order to identify them, you have to subject many people to coercive measures (surveillance, arrest, questioning etc.) and open many files on suspects. A personnel management perspective on the work of collecting information is instructive here. It is much easier to identify and collect fat files on people who may be on the fringes of terrorism – those involved in political protest for example – especially when, it should be remembered, much intelligence comes from open sources such as newspaper reports. But 'soft' intelligence is unreliable, and many innocent peoples' lives can be affected by inaccurate intelligence which is used in some improper way. Moreover, much security intelligence (at least as far as internal security is concerned) comes from informers, who are not always volunteers. People in primarily immigrant communities, can be and are pressured into becoming informers by offering advantages (residence permits) or threatening disadvantages (deportation, prison, withdrawal of permits) for themselves, their friends and families. This sort of pressure may be necessary in the fight against terrorism, but we should not be hypocritical and say that only the guilty need fear extensive police powers.

Fourthly, more extensive police or intelligence powers can only go so far in defeating terrorism, which is crime with a political objective. Of course, the political objective can be totally unacceptable to the target state, and so perceived as impossible to negotiate over. Or the political injustice, which motivates terrorists can be, or become, only an excuse. The 'real cause' of violence can naturally be anthropological or economic in character.[66] Still, if the political injustice that is the root, or the excuse, for the violence is removed or ameliorated, then at the very least the supply of new recruits will be made more difficult.[67]

65 A US Justice Department report has severely criticized the measures taken. See New York Times, 2 June 2003.

66 Collier, Peter, *Economic Causes of Civil Conflict and Their Implications for Policy*, The World Bank, Washington, 2000. Collier identifies diasporas (and the sources of financing they entail) as a prime cause of continuing conflicts.

67 *Cf.* PA Resolution 1271, *op. cit.* note 10, which notes that higher levels of education, access to decent living conditions and respect for human dignity are the best instruments for reducing the support given to terrorism in certain countries.

6.8 The right to life and anti-terrorist operations

The ECHR's Article 2 and the ICCPR's Article 6 provide that the state is to protect the right to life.[68] Neither prohibits the death penalty, although protocols to both treaties do. Leaving aside the deliberate imposition of the death penalty and the extradition, or deportation, of a person from one state to a state where he or she can face the death penalty, the main issue of relevance which arises is the killing of terrorist suspects during police or military operations. Under ECHR Article 2(2)(a(c), deadly force can be used when 'absolutely necessary', in self-defence or to defend a person from a crime of violence, to arrest a suspected offender or prevent his or her escape or to quell an insurrection or a riot directed against a state institution. The exceptions in Article 2(2) are not limited to intentional killing, but are also intended to cover situations in which it is permitted to use force which may result, as an unintended outcome, to the loss of life.[69] The requirement of 'absolute necessity' imposes a higher standard than 'necessary in a democratic society' and means that force used must be strictly proportionate to the achievement of the aims set out in Article 2(2).[70] The factual situations covered by the exceptions to the Article will range, and have ranged, from a policeman accidentally killing a violent drunk with a baton, to major armed clashes involving aerial or artillery bombardments, tanks, etcetera.[71]

The first case in which the ECtHR found a violation of Article 2 was *McCann and others* v. *UK*.[72] The case concerned the killing in Gibraltar of three IRA terrorists by British soldiers. A narrow majority of judges on the Court (10 to 9) found a violation of Article 2 in that, even taking into account the terrorist context (*i.e.* the particular dangers involved in arresting suspected armed terrorists) the

68 There can theoretically be state responsibility for failure to protect against terrorist crimes which cause loss of life. However, the standard – knowledge of a 'real and immediate risk' to the victims – is set very high and will rule out such responsibility in practice. See Osman v. UK, 28 October 1998, at para. 121.

69 McCann and Others v. UK, 27 September 1995, A/324, para. 148.

70 *Ibid.* para. 149.

71 For an example of a case involving aerial bombardment (denied by the respondent government) see Isiyok v. Turkey, No. 22309/93, 91 DR 5 (1997) (friendly settlement).

72 *Op. cit.*

operation had been badly planned and implemented. There were a number of factors relevant to this decision. The authorities had had prior warning of the attack and time to plan their response, even if they were obviously not in possession of the full facts and had to work on the basis of hypotheses. The authorities had had the option of arresting them at the moment they entered Gibralter. The conjectures on which the arrest operation had been based had been presented in intelligence briefings to the participating soldiers as certainties. This meant that the use of deadly force became almost inevitable, as the slightest movement on the part of the suspects would be interpreted by the soldiers as an attempt to detonate a suspected bomb. Finally, the soldiers had received no training or instruction in variable responses to situations which might call for the use of deadly force. To put it another way: the soldiers could either have arrested the suspects or fired at them until they were dead. In practice, the planning of the operation meant that the former option had been excluded.[73]

The Court has reiterated the requirement that all operations that could involve the use of deadly force have to be carefully planned in later cases. In *Ergi* v. *Turkey*, the Court, while implicitly accepting that security forces could ambush terrorists, insisted that such a measure be planned and implemented in such a way as to avoid or minimize, to the greatest extent possible, risks to civilians, including risks caused by probable counter-fire from terrorists caught in the ambush. In the event, it considered that the Turkish forces had not fulfilled this requirement and found a violation.[74] The planning obligation is very important, as it incorporates Convention standards into decision-making.[75] It is not unreasonable in that it will obviously partly depend upon the time the responsible commander has available in which to plan his or her response.

One major problem that has become evident with the Turkish cases, all of which have, directly or indirectly, concerned the public emergency in the Kurdish areas in Eastern and Southern Turkey, is where the respondent government denies that state agents had

73 These factors are discussed by the Court at, respectively paras. 193, 205, 210 and 212.

74 28 July 1998, at paras. 79–81. See also Ogur v. Turkey, 20 May 1999.

75 Warbrick, 2002, *op. cit.* p. 292.

been responsible for the killing in question. Such cases necessitate on-site investigations and extensive hearing of witnesses, something that in turn has caused considerable practical and financial problems for the Convention organs. In some of these cases the Court found a state agent to be responsible, notwithstanding denials from the government.[76] In a number of other cases where this has been an issue the Court has found that state involvement could not be proven beyond a reasonable doubt, but nonetheless found violations of Article 2 because there was no, or no adequate, investigation following the killing.[77] The investigation requirement entails 'some form of independent and public scrutiny capable of determining whether the force used was or was not justified in a particular set of circumstances'.[78] Article 2 also requires the prosecution of a soldier or policeman who is suspected of having used excessive force.[79]

Two final points should be made in relation to Article 2. Claims have been made in the past that state agents involved in anti-terrorist campaigns occasionally 'contract out' killings of suspects to private individuals, or in some other way facilitate such killings. Sections of the security forces can be tempted to take the law into their own hands, particularly bearing in mind the difficulties involved in producing admissible evidence in court. In Northern Ireland, for example, allegations were persistently made that loyalist terrorists have been given information by people, or factions, in the British security forces. Such information has supposedly allowed them to identify and later murder republicans (suspected terrorists or otherwise). This was repeatedly denied. However, a recent government inquiry has revealed that there was substance to several of these

76 See, *e.g.*, Gülec v. Turkey, 27 July 1998 and Cakici v. Turkey, 8 July 1999. The Court also found that the investigation was ineffective.

77 See, *e.g.*, Kaya v. Turkey, 19 February 1998, Ergi v. Turkey, 27 July 1998, Yasa v. Turkey, 2 September 1998 and Tanrikulu v. Turkey, 8 July 1999.

78 See, *e.g.*, Kaya v. Turkey, para. 86, Ergi v. Turkey, para. 78. Although see Aytekin v. Turkey, 23 September 1998, where the Court accepted a two year delay in an investigation and prosecution of a fatal shooting.

79 See Yasa v. Turkey, para. 98, Ogur v. Turkey, para. 88. See also McShane v. UK, No. 43290/98, 28 June 2002 and Jordan, McKerr, Kelly and others and Shanaghan v. UK, No. 24746/95, 28883/95, 30054/96, 37715/97, 4 May 2001. For more detail on the investigation requirement, see Warbrick, 2002, *op. cit.* pp. 293–295.

allegations.[80] Such state involvement, if proved, would be enough to constitute a violation of Article 2 but the problem of proving state involvement should not be underestimated.

Another way of dealing with terrorist suspects is to 'disappear' them. The ECtHR had, until recently been largely spared the problem of having to decide if the state is responsible for disappearances, and if so, whether there is sufficient circumstantial evidence to be able to rule that the person in question has been murdered.[81] In the first Court case in which this issue arose, *Kurt* v. *Turkey*, the Court considered, on the basis of the Commission's fact-finding, and despite the denials of the respondent government, that the security forces were responsible for taking Kurt into custody.[82] It did not, however, feel able to rule that Kurt had been extrajudicially executed, which, in the circumstances was highly likely.[83] In the second Court case dealing with this issue, *Cakici* v. *Turkey*,[84] the Court found, again despite the denials of the respondent government, that the security forces had taken the applicant's brother into custody. However, it also proceeded to find the state responsible for extrajudicially executing him. The main reason for distinguishing the case from *Kurt* in this respect was that the respondent government had indirectly conceded that Cakici's brother was dead, by later claiming that his identity card had been found on a terrorist found dead after a gun battle with the security forces.[85] It can be

80 See the interim report by Sir John Stevens, HMSO, 17 April 2003.

81 The issue arose in the inter-state case of Cyprus v. Turkey. Res DH(92)12. The HRC has had several cases where the issue of disappearances has arisen. See, *e.g.* Bautista de Arellana v. Colombia, 563/93. Disappearance violations can be seen as being of a continuing character, see Varnava and others v. Turkey, Nos 16404-6, 16489873/90, 93 DR (1998).

82 25 May 1998. The Court ruled that there was a violation of Article 5, see below.

83 Cf. an earlier case before the Inter-American Commission, Fairén Garbi and Solís Corrales Case, Annual Report of the IACtHR 1989, which concerned the disappearance of two persons, allegedly killed in Honduras by government forces. After an extremely detailed examination, the Court stated: 'Although the government of Honduras has incurred in many contradictions, the failure to investigate this case ... is insufficient – in the absence of other evidence – to create a legal presumption that the Honduran Government is responsible for those disappearances' (para. 159). For a more recent example of how the Inter-American Court on Human Rights has handled the issue, see Casillo Páez Case, 3 November, 1997, HRLJ, Vol. 19, 1997, p. 219 (1998).

84 *Op. cit.*

85 *Op. cit.*, at paras. 85–87.

noted in conclusion on this point that the necessity for an investigation constitutes an important lightening of the burden of proof for the applicant as regards both disappearances and killings by persons unknown – or at least people who cannot conclusively be proved to be state agents – as a violation can be found notwithstanding the lack of conclusive proof of direct state involvement.

6.9 Arrest and detention

Article 5 ECHR and Article 9 ICCPR set out minimum rules applicable to arrest and detention. Underlying security concerns can affect the safeguards set out in these Articles, usually to dilute them.[86] The freedom from arbitary arrest and detention has a central position in the protection of human rights and this is reflected in the extensive ECtHR and HRC case law interpreting these Articles. In the following section, I will confine my remarks to the ECHR.

The grounds for detention set out in Article 5(1) are exhaustive.[87] This is inconvenient for states, as there can be situations in which the state wishes to detain someone on security grounds, but for one or other reason – most often an unwillingness to reveal intelligence received from an informer – it does not want to bring the matter before a criminal court. This is obviously particularly relevant in public emergencies, when there can be considerable pressure from the police and military to intern suspects. Article 5 does not permit this sort of preventive detention.[88] If a state wishes to intern terrorists it will have to derogate from the Convention.

86 There is much to be said for the view that a state faced with terrorist problems should derogate from its obligations under Article 5, rather than expecting the Court to temper Article 5 to meet its needs. And when the Court does so, it should expressly state that this is because of the special circumstances, so as to minimize the precedent effect of its judgment for ordinary crime. See Harris, David J., O'Boyle, Michael and Warbrick, Colin, *Law of the ECHR,* Butterworths, London/Dublin/Edinburgh, 1995, at p. 162.

87 A measure restricting movement not amounting to a deprivation of liberty will be considered under Article 2 of Protocol 4. See Guzzardi v. Italy, 6 November 1980, A/39.

88 Lawless v. Ireland, 1 July 1961, A/3. See also Ciulla v. Italy, 22 February 1989, A/148, which concerned an obligation on a maffia suspect to 'change his behaviour' (at para. 36).

The most relevant grounds for present purposes are Articles 5(1)(b), (c) and (f) – detention to 'secure the fulfilment of any obligation prescribed by law', on suspicion of having committed an offence and for the purposes of deportation. Article 5(1)(b) is of considerable use in gathering intelligence about terrorism, as it allows states to impose an obligation in law[89] and then to question people in connection with that obligation, without the need to suspect them of involvement in crime. For example, people entering a country may be required to 'submit to examination'[90] or people may be required to carry identification papers, and detained and questioned if they fail to do so.[91]

Article 5(1)(c) allows arrest and detention on 'reasonable' suspicion of having committed a 'crime'. Here one problem is vague offences such as 'being concerned with terrorism' or 'belonging to a proscribed organization'. Article 7 (the principle of legality) places only minimal requirements on the definition of offences. Proscription will thus allow arrest not simply for the offence of membership, but also offences of professing membership, of possessing articles for the purpose of terrorism (*e.g.* newsletters, the income of which goes to the organization) or fund raising for the organisation (*e.g.* by selling magazines).[92] There are obvious dangers for liberty, and such freedoms as expression and association, involved in proscription of organisations – not least because proscription tends to be by government decree. Moreover, issues arise of judicial control, effective remedies and the separation of powers because the national legislation

89 The obligation must be 'specific and concrete'. Engel and others v. Netherlands, 8 June 1976, A/22, para. 69.

90 McVeigh, O'Neill and Evans v. UK, *op. cit.*

91 See, *e.g.*, B. v. France, No. 10179/82, 52 DR 111 (1987) and Harris, O'Boyle and Warbrick, 1995, *op. cit.* p. 113.

92 See the UK case of R v. Secretary of State for the Home Department and another [2002] EWHC 2477 (Admin). This issue is discussed further in Cameron, Iain, *EU Anti-Terrorist Blacklisting,* Human Rights Law Review, Vol. 3, 2003, p. 225.

may be framed in such a way that the reasons behind the proscription may not be susceptible to judicial control.[93]

The test for what is 'reasonable suspicion' will vary with the circumstances. The Court stated in *Fox, Campbell and Hartley* v. *UK* that, in relation to terrorist crime less strict requirements as to 'reasonableness' can apply because of, first, the need to act speedily to avert terrorist violence, and second, the need to keep intelligence sources secret.[94] The Court nonetheless required that there be *some* objective evidence backing up the subjective belief that the applicants were terrorists. As the respondent government could not produce this evidence, the Court found a violation of Article 5(1)(c).

In the later case of *Murray* v. *UK* the applicant also alleged that she had been arrested, questioned and personal details about her recorded when there was no reasonable suspicion that she had committed an offence.[95] She argued that the purpose was instead 'low grade' intelligence gathering, primarily regarding what she knew about the whereabouts and activities of her brothers who *were* suspected of terrorist offences. In this case, the respondent government was able to produce some corroborative evidence, albeit fairly weak, that there had been a reasonable suspicion that the suspect had committed an offence. The Court considered that, in the circumstances, it had been legitimate to record and retain personal information on her.[96]

Article 5(2) requires the disclosure of the 'reasons for arrest and the charges against him'. However, the standards set in this regard are rather low. It follows from *Fox, Campbell and Hartley* v. *UK* that

93 *E.g.* section 302 of the US Antiterrorism and Effective Death Penalty Act (AEDPA) 1996, Pub. L. No. 104–132, 110 Stat. 1214 (1996) (codified as amended in various sections of 8, 18, 28, 40 & 42 USC) authorizes the Secretary of State to designate groups as 'foreign terrorist organizations'. In People's Mojahedin Organisation of Iran, v. United States Department of State, 182 F.3d 17 (D.C. Cir. 1999), the court concluded that the Secretary's finding that the organisation's activities threatened national security is nonjusticiable (at p. 23). For commentary, see Jinks, Derek P., *Case Report: People's Mojahedin Organisation of Iran v. United States Department of State,* American Journal of International Law, Vol. 94, 2000, p. 396.

94 30 August 1990, A/182, para. 32.

95 28 October 1994, A/300-A.

96 *Ibid.* at para. 93. As Harris, O'Boyle and Warbrick, 1995, *op. cit.* point out, the fact that the maximum period of detention was four hours was also material to the level of suspicion required (at p. 119).

little detailed information need be given in the circumstances of arrest for suspicion of having committed terrorist offences.[97]

Article 5(3) imposes a requirement that an arrested person be brought 'promptly' before a judge or other legal officer when he or she has been arrested on suspicion of having committed a crime. In *Brogan and others* v. *UK*,[98] the Court held that a delay of four days and six hours was a violation of the provision. The Court has not gone into detail as to why terrorist crime should entitle security forces to delay bringing a suspect before a judge. In *Brogan*, the respondent government had argued that more time was needed in order to obtain evidence which is usable and admissible. First, because terrorists are trained in anti-interrogation techniques, second, because scientific (forensic) evidence might need to be collected, and third, because information obtained in interrogations of a suspect needed to be correlated with information from other suspects and other security forces.[99] Where a foreign security agency has information that might corroborate or throw into doubt a suspect's version of events this will result in further delays. Another possible justification for delays in dealing with terrorist cases, particularly applicable to countries such as Turkey, is where suspects are arrested in remote regions. But the argument that terrorist offences can require extensive further inquiries can be admitted without accepting that there should be delays in bringing a suspect before a judge. In *Demir and others* v. *Turkey* the Court pointed out that the state can hardly insist that inquiries are completed before bringing a suspect before a judge: Article 5(3) is intended to apply precisely when inquiries or investigations are proceeding.[100] In fact, in terrorist cases, there are good reasons for demanding even *more* prompt appearance before a judge. An important reason behind this requirement is to minimize the risk of torture or illtreatment. Where too much time is allowed to elapse between arrest and being brought before a judge, the marks of illtreatment could heal.[101]

97 *Op. cit.* para. 41. See futher Harris, O'Boyle and Warbrick, 1995, *op. cit.* pp. 129–30.
98 29 November 1988, A/145-B.
99 *Op. cit.* at para. 56.
100 23 September 1998, at para. 52.
101 Harris, O'Boyle and Warbrick, 1995, *op. cit.* p. 132 and Aksoy v. Turkey, 18 December 1996, paras. 80 and 83.

The Court has allowed longer periods than four days when derogation has been made.[102] But even here there are limits to the period regarded as acceptable. In *Aksoy* v. *Turkey* and *Demir and others* v. *Turkey* the Court found violations of the provision where the applicants had been detained, respectively, for 14 days and periods varying from 16–23 days. And the Court is not willing to accept that medical examinations – limited to ascertaining whether suspects had been illtreated – is an adequate substitute for being brought promptly before a judge.

Article 5(4) requires that a detained person be able to challenge the lawfulness of his or her detention 'speedily' before 'a court'. As regards the 'speedily' requirement, there is an overlap with Article 5(3) as regards cases of arrest for suspicion of having committed an offence. And like the prompt requirement in Article 5(3), and the requirement of trial within a reasonable time in Article 6(1), there is no set limit to the detention. Instead, the Court takes into account all the circumstances of the case.[103] A terrorist context can serve to extend the period, although in *Sakik and others* v. *Turkey*, the Court found that that a delay of 12–14 days before the applicants had the possibility to challenge their detention was a breach of Article 5(4). The main issue arising under Article 5(4) once again concerns the revealing of security intelligence. Article 5(4) requires adversarial proceedings before a body of a judicial character, although the character of the body can vary depending upon the basis for the detention.

6.10 Fair trial

The right to a fair trial lies at the centre of traditional human rights protection. Anti-terrorist measures can limit this right in a number of ways.

6.10.1 Independent courts

When the security of a state is threatened, the independence of its system of justice also tends to be put under strain. There can be strong pressure from the military or sections of the executive to

102 See, *e.g.*, Brannigan and McBride v. UK, 26 May 1993, A/258-B.
103 Harris, O'Boyle and Warbrick, 1995, *op. cit.* pp. 156–57.

appoint specially vetted judges or courts to hear security cases, or to establish special security courts. One argument in favour of this, in states which have trial by jury, is the need to protect the jury, not just from pressure during the trial, but afterwards, perhaps years afterwards, from revenge from a terrorist group. Where there are many trials, there will be many jurors, all of whom might have to be protected.[104] This was one of the reasons for the US President's Military Order of 13 November 2001, providing that non-citizens can be tried by military commissions.[105]

Article 6(1) ECHR and Article 14 ICCPR both require that an accused receive a trial in an 'independent and impartial tribunal established by law'. The requirements of independence and impartiality are closely linked: a court that is not independent from the executive will not be impartial towards the parties, if one of them is the state.[106] The ECtHR stated in *Campbell and Fell* v. *UK* that the requirement of independence entails safeguards relating to 'the manner of appointment of judges, the duration of their office, the existence of guarantees against outside pressures and the question whether the body presents an appearance of independence'.[107] The requirement that the body be 'established by law' does not prohibit the establishment of special courts by government decree, as long as a statute provides for this.[108]

The HRC does not totally rule out trial of civilians by military courts, but considers that this 'should be very exceptional and take place under conditions which genuinely afford the full guarantees stipulated in Article 14'.[109] By contrast, the ECtHR clearly regards trials of civilians by courts, which consist wholly, or even partially,

104 See Wedgewood, Ruth, *The Case for Military Tribunals,* WSJ. Com 3 December 2001 (interactive.wsj.com/archive, 2002-20). For a different perspective see Gross, Emanuel, *Trying Terrorists – Justification for Different Trial Rules: The Balance Between Security Considerations and Human Rights,* Indiana University International and Comparative Law Review, Vol. 13, 2002, p. 1.

105 www.whitehouse.gov/news/releases/2001/11/20011113-27.html (2002-06-14).

106 Harris, O'Boyle and Warbrick, 1995, *op. cit.* p. 234.

107 28 June 1984, A/80, para. 78. See further, Council of Europe, Committee of Ministers Recommendation No. R (94) 1 on the independence, efficiency and role of judges.

108 X. and Y. v. Ireland, No. 8299/78, 22 DR 51 (1980), concerning the special criminal court, later examined again in the Eccles case, below.

109 HRC General Comment 13, Compilation of General Comments, HRI/GEN/1/Rev.5, 26 April 2001. See also Fals Borda et al v. Colombia, No. 46/79.

of serving military officers to be a violation of Article 6.[110] Extradition to states where military commissions try civilians is also probably forbidden.[111]

Nonetheless, it is certainly possible to have *special* courts with competence to try civilians for security offences, or to have special rules for deciding the composition of the court in security cases. And obviously with the majority of the parties to the ECHR being civil law states, jury trial is in any event not a requirement of Article 6. And where you do not have a jury, you do not need hearsay rules (another argument advanced for having military commissions). Some individual judges can obviously be more 'government friendly' than others, but the ECtHR will not see the mere fact that an ordinary, tenured judge has been specially selected before he or she is allocated cases with security implications as calling into question his or her independence. The significance of this point is increased bearing in mind the important role a judge can have in hearing security evidence, perhaps unsupervised by defence counsel, *in camera* (considered below). But it is not easy to show that an ordinary, tenured judge lacks impartiality.[112] It is more likely that special courts with *non-tenured* judges can raise an issue as to independence. But the Court will presumably be prepared to accept that the 'other guarantees against outside pressures' can be in practice, rather than in law.[113] And a fixed term of appointment (so as to avoid susceptibility to executive influence) is not seen as an absolute requirement of independence.[114]

110 Incal v. Turkey 9 June 1998. Ciraklar v. Turkey, 28 October 1998. This finding has been repeated in a large number of cases. See, *e.g.*, Atlay v. Turkey, No. 22279/93, 22 May 2001.

111 I can only say 'probably' because the Court has so far stated that extradition is only barred in relation to Article 6 where there is a risk of a 'flagrant denial of justice' (Einhorn v. France, op. cit.).

112 A 'sudden change' in the composition of the Spanish Audiencia National was one factor in the Court finding a lack of a fair hearing in Barberá, Messegué and Jabardo v. Spain, 6 December 1988, A/146.

113 Cf. Eccles, McPhillips and McShane v. Ireland, No. 12839/87, 59 DR 212 (1988). See further the discussion of this issue in the context of military courts martial in Findlay v. UK, 25 February 1997, Reports of Judgments and Decisions 1997-I and Morris v. UK, No. 38784/97, 26 February 2002.

114 Even in non-security cases, the standards of 'independence' set out by the Court in Campbell and Fell v. UK have been interpreted relatively liberally. *E.g.* judges with short periods of tenure (three years) have been allowed. See Harris, O'Boyle and Warbrick, 1995, p. 232.

6.10.2 Fair judicial proceedings and the problem of intelligence material

The use of intelligence material in court proceedings, and/or the circumvention of such proceedings altogether because of a refusal to reveal intelligence material, is a major challenge to the right of fair trial, in particular, the principle of 'equality of arms' between the prosecution and defence. There is little ICCPR case law on the issue of squaring fair trial with the need to conceal intelligence material,[115] but there have been a number of cases before the ECtHR. Generally speaking, the ECtHR has required there to be full court access to the material. And where the accused, or his/her lawyers, are not permitted access to material which is at the heart of the case against them, the ECtHR has required compensatory safeguards, such as a much more active role on the part of the trial judge, giving a sanitized version of the essence of the evidence to the defence and/or the provision of security cleared counsel to represent the interests of the accused.[116]

An important reason why we are willing to accept far-reaching police powers of data-matching, surveillance, arrest, search and seizure is because the necessity for, and proportionality of, these measures will eventually be authoritatively determined in a court. Thus, a criminal trial is a safeguard not only as regards the guilt or innocence of the accused, but also as a preventive measure, discouraging over-use of pre-trial coercive measures. However, police work in certain areas, particularly terrorism and organized crime, has become more intelligence-oriented (often called proactive policing) and the mandate of intelligence agencies in many states have, since the end of the Cold War, been expanded to encompass certain types of organized crime, and terrorism.[117] This has meant that the policing par-

115 For a general discussion, see Weissbrodt, David, *The Right to a Fair Trial under the UDHR and the ICCPR – Background, Development and Interpretation,* Kluwer, Boston/the Hague, 2001.

116 Sharpe, Sandra, *Article 6 and the Disclosure of Evidence in Criminal Trials,* Criminal Law Review, 1999, p. 273 and Cameron, 2000, *op. cit.* pp. 307, 320–323.

117 See, *e.g.*, Fijnaut, Cyril and Marx, Gary (Eds.), *Undercover: Police Surveillance in Comparative Perspective,* Kluwer, the Hague/London/Boston, 1995.

adigm has shifted somewhat from securing a conviction towards disrupting an ongoing criminal conspiracy. As far as organized crime is concerned, it may not ever be possible to kill the hydra, but at least you can take its money or make life difficult for it in other ways, so that it will go somewhere else. Dealing with terrorism is more difficult. It may not want to go anywhere else. It may not need a lot of money, and money certainly is not the main motivating force of the terrorist.

But as far as both organized crime and terrorism is concerned, there will be situations in which the police and/or the intelligence agencies will want to avoid a trial altogether. If charges *are* brought, then a means must usually be found of concealing the identity of informants and agents, and/or intelligence methods, for example by basing convictions wholly or largely on the testimony of crown witnesses, *penittenti*. This information has to be concealed not only from the public, which is not a problem, but also from the accused. It may even have to be concealed from the accused's lawyers.

Concealing evidence obviously causes particular problems for states that base their traditional conceptions of what is a 'fair hearing' on adverserial proceedings where the judge is expected to remain relatively passive. Where material has been excluded, in order to decide whether a defence hypothesis is correct – that the defendant was entrapped, or the evidential fruits were from a poisoned (illegally obtained) source – the trial judge can no longer rely on the issue being fairly debated, because the defence is at a great disadvantage. The trial judge will be put in the position of having to compensate for the inability of the defence to obtain enough information on which to question the prosecutor's case.[118]

The problem of revealing, or refusing to reveal, intelligence and proactive policing material in judicial proceedings obviously is not limited to fair trial in criminal cases, but can apply to deportation proceedings (Articles 2, 3, 8 and Protocol 7 ECHR, and Articles 6, 7 and 13 ICCPR). The ECtHR has required that mechanisms be in place to guarantee fair, quasi-judicial procedures in such cases.[119] It

118 Field, Stuart, and Pelser, Caroline, *Invading the Private: State Accountability and New Investigative Methods in Europe*, Dartmouth, Aldershot, 1998, p. 339.
119 Chahal v. UK, op. cit.

also applies to civil/quasi-criminal proceedings such as the freezing of assets of people suspected of involvement in terrorism (Article 6, Protocol 1 ECHR, Article 14 ICCPR). This last issue is particularly topical bearing in mind UN Security Council Resolutions 1267, 1333 and 1390 imposed on the Taliban and persons suspected of assisting al-Qaeda. The lack of protection in the US for the human rights of property and access to court as far as freezing of assets of foreigners is concerned is, from civil law European perspective, quite staggering.[120] The legality under EC law of sanctions imposed by the above Resolutions are currently being challenged before the European Court of Justice (CFI),[121] as is the legality of the EU's own sanction programs imposed by reference to Resolution 1373.[122] However, these issues involve so many different aspects that I cannot do justice to them in such a short article.[123]

6.10.3 The presumption of innonce and the privilege against self-incrimination

Terrorist offences can be formulated to provide for reversals of the onus of proof, or presumptions of law or fact which in effect make it easier, or much easier, to secure convictions. Such offences can obviously raise considerable problems. The ECtHR has not yet delivered any judgments dealing with such presumptions in rela-

120 See Fitzgerald, Peter, *'If Property Rights were Treated like Human Rights, they could never get away with this': Blacklisting and due Process in U.S. Economic Sanctions Programs,* (1999) 51 Hastings Law Journal, p. 73 and Judicial Review Commission on Foreign Assets Control, Final Report to Congress, January 2001, www.law.stetson.edu.

121 See Case T-306/01, Abdirisak Aden and others v. EU Council and EC Commission, Case T-315/01, Yassin Abdullah Khadi v. Council and Commission, Case T-318/01, Omar Mohammed Othman v. Council and Commission. For a detailed discussion, see Andersson, Torbjörn, Cameron, Iain and Nordback, Kenneth, *EU Blacklisting: The Renaissance of Imperial Power, but on a Global Scale,* European Business Law Review, Vol. 14, issue 2, 2003 p. 111.

122 Regarding Council Decision 2002/334, 2 May 2002 and the further implementing decision of 17 June 2002 blacklisting the PKK organisation – Osman Ocalan on behalf of Kurdistan Workers Party (PKK) and Serif Vanly on behalf of Kurdistan National Congress v. Council, Case T-229/02.

123 See Cameron, Iain, *Targeted Sanctions, Legal Safeguards and the ECHR,* Nordic Journal of International Law, 2003, Vol. 72, issue 2, p. 159.

tion to terrorist crime.[124] The ECtHR has found that Article 6(2) contains a prohibition against self-incrimination, *inter alia* in the *Funke* v. *France* and *Saunders* v. *UK* cases.[125] In *Heaney and McGuinness* v. *Ireland* and *Quinn* v. *Ireland*[126] the ECtHR applied this prohibition in relation to terrorist crime. The applicants in the cases had been requested by the police, acting under Section 52 of the Offences Against the State Act 1939, to give details about their movements at the time of a terrorist offence. Failure to answer such questions, where there is a reasonable suspicion that the suspect is involved with terrorism, is an offence punishable by imprisonment. They refused to answer any questions and each was convicted of failing to account for his movements and sentenced to six months of imprisonment. Heaney and McGuinness were acquitted of the substantive offence of which they were charged (membership of a paramilitary organization) whereas no such substantive charge was even brought against Quinn. The ECtHR unanimously found a violation of the presumption of innocence guaranteed by Article 6(2).

6.11 Concluding remarks

This chapter has dealt with some aspects of the relationship between terrorism and human rights. I can make two points in conclusion. The first is that, as regards extraterritorial action against terrorism, the blurring of the military and civilian responses to terrorism, and the consequent blurring of the applicable law, is a major challenge to human rights. The capacity of certain states, in particular the US, to affect the rights of foreign citizens outside of the territory of the state, is considerable. Secondly, as regards spe-

124 For example, see the offences of possession of items for the purpose of terrorism under sections 16A and 16B of the Prevention of Terrorism Act 1989 (now enacted in Terrorism Act 2000, section 57, as modified by the defence in section 118) and membership of proscribed organisations under section 11 of the Terrorism Act 2000. The compatibility of section 16A with Article 6 (2) of the Convention was considered by the English Divisional Court in R. v. DPP, Ex p. Kebilene and Others [2000] 2 AC 326 and the compatibility of section 11 was considered in Attorney General's Reference (No. 4 of 2002) [2003] EWCA Crim. 762.

125 Respectively, 25 February 1993, A/256-A, 17 December 1996.

126 Nos 34720/97 and 36887/97, 21 December 2000.

cial police and intelligence powers to deal with terrorist suspects, such powers should only be introduced when they are demonstratively necessary. They should be accompanied by effective safeguards designed to compensate for the increase in infringements in human rights they inevitably entail. Their application in practice must be kept under constant review, as experience shows that such powers tend to be used in other ways and against other targets than those the legislature intended. It is easy to whittle away hard-won rights in a series of measures designed to effectivize the struggle against terrorism. The *Rechtstaat* should of course be effective in fighting crime, but effectiveness is not the prime goal of the *Rechtstaat*. What is needed is a *satisfactory* level of effectiveness, no more. When total effectiveness is achieved, you no longer have a *Rechtstaat* left to defend.

References

Books & articles

Andersson, Torbjörn, Cameron, Iain and Nordback, Kenneth, *EU Blacklisting: The Renaissance of Imperial Power, but on a Global Scale,* European Business Law Review, Vol. 14, 2003, p. 111.

Ashworth, Andrew, *Human Rights, Serious Crime and Criminal Procedure,* Sweet and Maxwell, London, 2002.

Boister, Neil, *Human Rights Protections in the Suppression Conventions,* Human Rights Law Review, Vol. 2, 2002, p. 199.

Byford, Grenville, *The Wrong War,* Foreign Affairs, July/August 2002, p. 34.

Cameron, Iain, *EU Anti-Terrorist Blacklisting,* Human Rights Law Review, Vol. 3, 2003, p. 225.

Cameron, Iain, *National Security and the ECHR,* Iustus/Kluwer, Uppsala/the Hague, 2000.

Cameron, Iain, *Targeted Sanctions, Legal Safeguards and the ECHR,* Nordic Journal of International Law, Vol. 72, 2003, p. 159.

Collier, Peter, *Economic Causes of Civil Conflict and their Implications for Policy,* The World Bank, Washington, 2000.

Field, Stuart and Pelser, Caroline, *Invading the Private: State Accountability and New Investigative Methods in Europe,* Dartmouth, Aldershot, 1998.

Fijnaut, Cyril and Marx, Gary (Eds.), *Undercover: Police Surveillance in Comparative Perspective,* Kluwer, the Hague/London/Boston, 1995.

Fitzgerald, Peter, *'If Property Rights were Treated like Human Rights, They Could Never Get Away With This': Blacklisting and Due Process in US Economic Sanctions Programs,* Hastings Law Journal, Vol. 51, 1999, p. 73.

Gearty, Conor, *Terrorism and Human Rights: a Case Study in Impending Legal Realities,* Legal Studies, Vol. 19, 1999, p. 367.
Gross, Emanuel, *The Influence of Terrorist Attacks on Human Rights in the United States,* North Carolina Journal of International Law and Commercial Regulation, Vol. 28, 2002, p. 1.
Gross, Emanuel, *Trying Terrorists – Justification for Different Trial Rules: the Balance between Security Considerations and Human Rights,* Indiana University International and Comparative Law Review, Vol. 13, 2002, p. 1.
Happold, Mathew, *Bankovic v. Belgium and the Territorial Scope of the ECHR,* Human Rights Law Review, Vol. 3, 2003, p. 77.
Harris, David J., O'Boyle, Michael, and Warbrick, Colin, *Law of the ECHR,* Butterworths, London/Dublin/Edinburgh, 1995.
Jinks, Derek, *Case Report: People's Mojahedin Organisation of Iran v. United States Department of State,* American Journal of International Law, Vol. 94, 2000, p. 396.
Jinks, Derek, *September 11 and the Laws of War,* Yale Journal of International Law, Vol. 28, 2003, p. 1.
Kichling, Michael, *A Magic Formula which Can Do Away with Terrorism?,* Max Planck Research Bulletin, 1/2002.
Klabbers, Jan, *Rebels with a Cause? Terrorists and Humanitarian Law,* European Journal of International Law, Vol. 14, 2003, p. 299.
Koufa, Kalliopi, *Terrorism and Human Rights,* preliminary report, E/CN.4/Sub.2/1999/27.
Koufa, Kalliopi, *Terrorism and Human Rights,* second progress report, E/CN.4/Sub.2/2002/35.
Lippman, Mathew, *The New Terrorism and International Law,* Tulsa Journal of Comparative and International Law, Vol. 10, 2003, p. 297.
Mill, John S., *Utilitarianism, on Liberty, Considerations on Representative Government,* Acton H.B. (Ed.), Dent, London, 1991.
Paust, Jordan J., *Judicial Power to Determine the Status and Rights of Persons Detained Without Trial,* Harvard International Law Journal Vol. 44, 2003, p. 301.
Påle, Karin, *Villkor för utlämning,* Iustus, Uppsala, 2003.
Robinson, Patrick, *The Missing Crimes,* in Cassesse, Antonio, *et al.* (Eds.), The Rome Statute of the ICC: a Commentary, volume 1, OUP, Oxford, 2002.
Rubin, Alfred, P., *Legal Response to Terror: an International Criminal Court?* Harvard International Law Journal Vol. 43, 2002, p. 65.
Schmid Alex and Jongman Albert, *Political Terrorism: a New Guide to Actors, Authors, Concepts, Databases, Theories and Literature,* 2nd ed., North-Holland, Amsterdam, 1988.
Walker, Clive, *Guide to the Anti-terrorism Legislation,* Blackstone Press, Oxford, 2002.
Warbrick, Colin, *The ECHR and Terrorism,* International and Comparative Law Quarterly, Vol. 32, 1983, p. 82.

Warbrick, Colin, *The Prevention of Terrorism Act 1976 and the ECHR: the McVeigh Case,* International and Comparative Law Quarterly, Vol. 32 1983, p. 757.
Warbrick, Colin, *The Principles of the ECHR and the Response of States to Terrorism,* European Human Rights Law Review, 2002, p. 287.
Wedgewood, Ruth, *The Case for Military Tribunals,* WSJ. Com 3 December 2001 (interactive.wsj.com/archive, (20 December 2002).
Weissbrodt, David, *The Right to a Fair Trial under the UDHR and the ICCPR – Background, Development and Interpretation,* Kluwer, Boston/the Hague, 2001.
Wijngaert, Cristine van den, *The Political Offence Exemption to Extradition,* Nijhoff, Deventer, 1980.
Zegveld, Linda, *Accountability of Armed Opposition Groups in International Law,* Cambridge UP, Cambridge, 2002.

7 Anti-Personnel Landmines, Explosive Remnants of War and International Humanitarian Law

Anna Körlof

7.1 Introduction

When a person steps on an anti-personnel mine, a chain reaction starts. The mechanical pressure triggers a detonator, which ignites a booster charge of explosives. In its turn, the booster charge sets off a more powerful explosion of trinitrotoluene, better known as TNT. Shock waves then explode outward at high speed, driving metallic fragments, bacteria, earth and burning plastic into the victims' body.[1] The effects of an explosion caused by the moving of an unexploded cluster bomblet or a grenade are very similar to those of mines. But unlike most anti-personnel mines, which are designed to maim rather than kill, accidents involving other explosive ordnance are more likely to kill. A particularly insidious feature of many kinds of explosive ordnance, for instance cluster bomblets, is that they often look confusingly toy-like because they are frequently made in bright colours and shaped like soda cans or small metallic balls with toy-sized parachutes attached. In consequence, the victims are often children.

Modern armed conflicts leave behind hazardous remnants in the form of mines, sub-munitions from cluster bombs, artillery shells, grenades, mortars, rockets and missiles, which claim between 5,000 and 30,000 victims every year.[2] They often continue to inflict civil-

1 Cameron, Maxwell A., Robert J. Lawson and Brian W. Tomlin (Eds.), *To Walk Without Fear – the Global Movement to Ban Landmines,* Oxford University Press, Toronto, 1998, p. 2.

2 *Ibid.* See also International Campaign to Ban Landmines, *Landmine Monitor Report 2003: Toward a Mine Free World,* Human Rights Watch, New York, 2003, where it is estimated that on average 15,000–20,000 people are killed or injured by landmines in the world every year.

ian casualties decades after the actual conflict is over. Furthermore, socio-economic development, infrastructure restoration and the delivery of humanitarian assistance after the conflict are seriously hampered in areas where remnants are frequent. Tragic examples are Angola, Laos, Cambodia, Afghanistan, former Yugoslavia and Iraq.

Cases like these call for national and international rules prohibiting or restricting the use of weapons that may become hazardous remnants, as well as rules that make it possible to initiate clearing as soon as possible.

7.2 Definitions of anti-personnel landmines and ERW

Numerous kinds of weapons can become dangerous remnants of war. However, the focus of this article is on the rules of international law connected with anti-personnel landmines and explosive remnants of war (ERW), since they generally present the most serious humanitarian problems.

Landmines may be defined as 'mass-produced, victim-operated, explosive traps'.[3] The term 'landmine' includes, in the more strict sense, all mines for use in land warfare, that is, anti-personnel mines as well as anti-tank mines and anti-vehicle mines.[4]

The basic components of a mine[5] are a fuse and an explosive charge.[6]

The military use of anti-personnel landmines is either together with anti-tank or anti-vehicle mines to prevent their removal, or individually to protect infantry positions from enemy troops, or otherwise to obstruct enemy movement.[7] Anti-personnel land-

3 Croll, M., *The History of Landmines*, Leo Cooper, Barnsley, UK, 1988, p. ix.

4 Maslen, Stuart, *Anti-Personnel Mines under Humanitarian Law – A View from the Vanishing Point*, Intersentia Transnational Publishers, Antwerpen, Belgium, 2001, p. 3.

5 For a summary of categories of anti-personnel landmines, see for instance SIPRI, *Anti-Personnel Weapons*, Taylor and Francis LTD, London, 1978, table 7.1, pp. 182–187.

6 Cornish, P., *Anti-Personnel Mines, Controlling the Plague of Butterflies*, Royal Institute for International Affairs, London, 1994, p. 11.

7 SIPRI, p. 181. See *supra* note 5.

mines are defined in treaty law regulations. As stated by the classification in Article 2 of the Convention on the prohibition of the Use, Stockpiling, Production and Transfer of Antipersonnel Mines and their Destruction (the Ottawa Convention) and in Article 2 of the Protocol II[8] on Prohibitions or Restrictions on the Use of Mines, Booby-Traps and Other Devices as amended on 3 May 1996, a 'mine' is 'a munition placed under, on or near the ground or other surface and are to be exploded by the presence, proximity or contact of a person or a vehicle', and an 'anti-personnel mine' is 'a mine designed to be exploded by the presence, proximity or contact of a person and that will incapacitate, injure or kill one or more persons ...'

The term ERW is commonly used in the international debate in connection with the problem of remaining explosive ordnance.[9] At first glance, the expression 'explosive remnants of war' would appear to apply to remnants of all types of explosive weapons, including weapons of mass destruction if they contain explosives. However, the term is generally employed to describe explosive remnants generated exclusively by *conventional* weapons, that is, weapons *other* than weapons of mass destruction. (Weapons of mass destruction, WMD, is a term regularly used in security and foreign policy analyses for nuclear, chemical, and biological weapons. Occasionally, radiological weapons are also included. Contemporary international legal doctrine normally follows this definition of

8 Protocol II to the Convention on Prohibitions or Restrictions on the Use of Certain Conventional Weapons Which May be Deemed to be Excessively Injurious or to Have Indiscriminate Effects, Geneva, 10 October 1980.

9 Another term commonly used is 'unexploded ordnance', 'UXO'. NATO, for instance, normally uses this term. UXO is defined as '[e]xplosive ordnance which has been primed, fused, armed or otherwise prepared for action, and which has been fired, dropped, launched, projected or placed in such a manner as to constitute a hazard to operations, installations, personnel or material and remains unexploded either by malfunction or design or for any other cause'. See *e.g.* the *NATO Glossary of Terms and Definitions*, AAP-6, NATO Standardization Agreements, www.nato.int/docu/stanag/aap006/aap6.htm.

WMD.[10] Yet neither treaty law nor customary international law contains an authoritative definition of WMD).[11]

From the mine clearers' perspective it is for practical reasons often useful to include all explosives in or on the ground in the term ERW. A broad definition covering not only remaining explosive munitions, but also landmines, is therefore sometimes used by humanitarian organizations.[12] In this context the term may be used as to describe the explosive threat to the community in a region where the mines or munitions are present.[13]

In November 2003 the States Parties meeting of the UN regime of the 1980 Convention on Prohibitions or Restrictions on the Use of Certain Conventional Weapons which May Be Deemed to Be Excessively Injurious or to Have Indiscriminate Effects (CCW) adopted a new fifth Protocol annexed to the CCW. From a legal point of view, it was considered logical during the negotiations on the new Protocol to exclude from the term ERW, explosive remnants that were already the subject of explicit current international law regulations in order to avoid overlapping of rules. Hence, the Protocol V excludes from its scope of application all mines, booby-traps and other devices defined in Protocol II as amended on 3 May 1996. The discussions among the states parties, NGOs and military experts prior to the adoption of the Protocol resulted in a broad definition. According to the definition in Article 2, the term ERW includes unexploded ordnance and abandoned explosive ordnance. Unexploded ordnance means explosive ordnance that has been prepared and used, and should have exploded but has failed to do so. Aban-

10 Weapons of mass destruction are in general dealt with under the law of international security. Hence, the problems related to remnants of war in the shape of abandoned weapons of mass destruction ought to be, and is, considered to be under the auspices of disarmament and arms control regimes. For instance, the 1997 Chemical Weapons Convention contains regulations on abandoned chemical weapons. (See CWC Verification Annex, Part IV (B) C, Articles 8–18).

11 Fidler, D. P., *Weapons of Mass Destruction and International Law,* ASIL Insights, February 2003.

12 See for instance Herby, Peter, Nuiten, Anna R., *Explosive Remnants of War: Protecting Civilians through an Additional Protocol to the 1980 Convention,* International Review of the Red Cross, Vol. 83, No. 841, 2001, pp. 195–205. See also Moyes, Richard, Lloyd, Richard, and McGrath, Rae, *Explosive Remnants of War – Unexploded Ordnance and Post-Conflict Communities*, Landmine Action, British Library, London, 2002, p. 7.

13 See *Explosive Remnants of War (ERW) – Undesired Explosive Events in Ammunition Storage Areas,* Geneva International Centre of Humanitarian Demining, 2002.

doned explosive ordnance is ordnance that, instead of being used, has simply been left behind or dumped by a party to a conflict.

For the purposes of this article the term ERW is used as defined in CCW Protocol V, that is, munitions from conventional weapons other than those covered by Amended Protocol II to the CCW and the Ottawa Convention.

7.3 International law and the use and clearance of anti-personnel landmines and ERW

Since there is no precise scientific coherence in the system of international law, it is difficult to distinguish relevant areas and principles with regard to various issues relating to weapons. However, it may be useful to determine approximately the place occupied by the subject in the system of international law.

The rules of international law with respect to weapons may be subdivided roughly into two branches of law. The first branch covers peacetime disarmament, non-proliferation and arms control matters, such as the production, testing, stockpiling, destruction and export of weapons. Disarmament is sometimes said to represent an area of international security law, whereas arms control is partly a separate form of international regulation and partly connected with the issue of disarmament.[14]

The second branch is the law of armed conflict, in particular the international humanitarian law of armed conflicts (IHL), which primarily regulates the conduct of war. This branch of law provides a set of rules and principles relating to the use of weapons during an armed conflict. In addition to IHL, the law of armed conflict also includes the law of occupation, wich partly consists of IHL regulations and partly of rules related to international security, and the law of neutrality, since this area of law is partly related to armed conflicts.

Generally speaking, these two separate branches differ in terms of history and current relevance. The subject of this article is the rules and principles regulating the use of the weapons that may become

14 See Feldman, David, *The Place of Arms Control and Disarmament in the System of International Law,* The International Law of Arms Control and Disarmament – Proceedings of the Symposium Geneva 28 February–2 March 1991, Dahlitz, Julie & Dicke, Detlev (Eds.), United Nations, New York, 1991, pp. 35–43.

hazardous remnants (the 'in-conflict' perspective) and the rules regulating the clearance of the landmines and ERWs (the 'post-conflict' perspective). Disarmament, non-proliferation and arms control issues fall outside the scope of this article.

IHL has evolved over the past century to restrict or prohibit certain means or methods of warfare, and to provide legal protection for specific categories of persons not taking part in the actual hostilities, such as the civilian population, combatants *hors de combat*, medical personnel, UN personnel and the civil defence. The current rules are derived from customary law as well as treaty law. The traditional approach to IHL is that it regulates only the conduct of armed conflicts (*jus in bello*).[15]

IHL thus limits the application of its fundamental principles, such as distinction, precaution, proportionality, unnecessary suffering etcetera, to the de facto existence of an armed conflict. In consequence, the primary focus with regard to IHL in relation to weapons has been on their use in armed conflicts.[16] Questions concerning the deployment of weapons have either applied to prohibitions on certain specific weapons (*i.e.* means of warfare) or restrictions on the manner of deployment of weapons (*i.e.* methods of warfare).

The fundamental principle of restraint on means (weapons) of warfare is formulated in Article 22 of the Hague Regulations annexed to Hague Convention IV (confirmed in Article 35(1) of the 1977 Additional Protocol II to the 1949 Geneva Conventions). This Article states: '*the right of belligerents to adopt means of injuring the enemy is not unlimited*'. The Article can be understood as a reminder that violence in war is permitted only in so far as it 'serves the specific purpose of subduing the enemy'.[17]

15 On the importance of distinguishing the concept of 'ius in bello' from 'ius ad bellum', see *e.g.* Gill, T., *The Nuclear Weapons Advisory Opinion of the International Court of Justice and the Fundamental Distinction Between the Jus ad Bellum and the Jus in Bello,* Leiden Journal of International Law, Vol. 12, 1999, pp. 613–624.

16 For an overview of the international work that led to the adoption of the two Additional Protocols to the Geneva Conventions and eventually the CCW, see Blix, Hans, *Förbuden att använda vissa vapen,* Kungliga Krigsvetenskapsakademiens Handlingar och Tidskrift, 1980:6, pp. 283–292.

17 Blix, Hans, *Means and Methods of Combat,* Henry Dunant Institute, UNESCO, International Dimensions of Humanitarian Law, Martinus Nijhoff Publishers, 1988, p. 135.

Article 35 paragraph 2 of the 1977 Protocol I Additional to the Geneva Conventions of 1949 reflects the idea of Article 22 of the Hague Regulations: 'it is prohibited to employ weapons, projectiles and material and methods of warfare of a nature to cause superfluous injuries or unnecessary suffering'. This prohibition (although related only to 'unnecessary suffering') was also expressed in 1907 Article 23(e) of in the Hague Regulations.[18] The legal formula may be expressed as a restriction on means that entail suffering or injuries beyond what is necessary for achieving the military purpose.

According to the logic of customary law, a weapon shall be prohibited if it can be regarded as causing unnecessary suffering or superfluous injuries in relation to its military advantages. However, the general formulas of 'superfluous injury or unnecessary suffering' is not sufficient to allow definite conclusions with regard to new weapons. Some would argue that a specific weapon is not prohibited by the see general formulas unless there already exists an explicit regulation on the issue, in other words, that there has to be an agreement between states with regard to the specific weapon in question, where humanitarian imperatives are given precedence over military considerations.[19] Hence, the principles, prohibiting weapons of a nature to cause 'superfluous injury or unnecessary suffering' has been the basis of some codified treaty law regulations on certain specific weapons. Core questions regarding Article 35(2) of Additional Protocol I are the substance of the words 'unnecessary'

18 The English version of Article 23 (e) of the Hague Regulations reads: 'In addition to the prohibitions provided by special Conventions, it is especially forbidden [...] e) to employ arms, projectiles, or material calculated *to* cause *unnecessary suffering*'. The French version of the same Article reads: 'Outre les prohibitions établies par des conventions spéciales, il est notamment interdit [...] e) d'employer des armes, des projectiles ou des matières propres à causer des *maux superflus'* Since the English wording 'unnecessary suffering' does not fully cover the much broader meaning of the French 'maux superflus', it was generally considered necessary to render the French formulation by the two English expressions 'superfluous injuries and 'unnecessary suffering' in Article 35, para. 2 of the 1977 Geneva Protocol I.

19 Bring, Ove, Anderberg, Bengt, Wolbarsht, Myron L., *Blinding Laser Weapons and International Humanitarian Law*, Journal of Peace Research, Vol. 29, No. 3, 1992, pp. 287–297.

and how 'suffering' and 'injury' should be estimated.[20] Two prohibitions from the past are often mentioned to exemplify the principle. The first is the 1868 St Petersburg Declaration banning the use of projectiles weighing less than 400 grams. If they weighed less than 400 grams they would not have been effective against objects, such as buildings, but only against humans and would then cause injuries in excess of what was necessary to incapacitate an enemy. The other is the Hague Declaration of 1899, which prohibited the use of 'dum-dum bullets'. Here again it was considered that the kinetic energy of a "normal" piercing bullet had a sufficient disabling effect.[21]

Since civilians are not legitimate objects of attack it could be argued that these principles primarily relate to the effects of weapons in combatant-to-combatant situations. This viewpoint might also be inferred from the International Court of Justice's 1996 Nuclear weapons opinion. The ICJ states, referring to the 'cardinal principle', that 'it is prohibited to cause unnecessary suffering to combatants'.[22]

Regarding mines, some anti-landmine campaigners have suggested that the use of anti-personnel landmines should be restricted according to the basic norms and principles of humanitarian law, *i.e.*, that their use is inherently contrary to, *inter alia*, the prohibitions on the use of weapons of a nature to cause unnecessary suffering superfluous injuries.[23] The effects of an anti-personnel blast mine could reasonably be said to be more harmful than what is nec-

20 In 1974, the ICRC organized an international conference of government experts to examine the report entitled 'Weapons that may cause unnecessary suffering or have indiscriminate effects'. At the first session, which was held in Lucerne in 1974, it was expressed that 'injury' and 'suffering' comprised such factors as mortality, the pain or severe wounds, permanent damage and disfigurement. *'Conference of Government Experts on the Use of Certain Conventional Weapons: Report I'*, First session, Lucerne 1974, ICRC, Geneva, 1975.

21 The ICRC has undertaken in-depth research into the medical effects of weapons: 'the SirUS project'. The aim of the SirUS project was to determine customary law by settling the objective medical criteria to judge the relative injury and suffering inflicted by any weapon.

22 International Court of Justice, Advisory Opinion 'Legality of the Threat or Use of Nuclear Weapons', 8 July 1996 (Hereinafter Nuclear Weapons Advisory Opinion), para. 78.

23 See for instance the web pages of the ICBL (International Campaign to ban landmines) and the ICRC (International Committee of the Red Cross) under the sections on weapons/landmines and international humanitarian law.

essary to render a soldier *hors de combat,* since they are specifically designed to cause traumatic amputation and as a consequence inflict life-long disability (cf. Article 3(3) of Annexed Protocol II and Preamble of the Ottawa Convention).

However, state practice indicates, as a matter of customary law, that the use of anti-personnel landmines is recognized as legal. Each year between two and five million new mines are emplaced,[24] without any suggestion that they are illegal *per se*.[25] In other words, the present political reality shows that there is no consensus among states that anti-personnel landmines cause unnecessary suffering or superfluous injuries in the strict legal sense. Furthermore, the treaty law regulations regarding mines are aimed at the humanitarian problems relating to civilian victims, in particular the urgent post-conflict situation, rather than the effects of landmines *per se*.

As regards ERW, the problem is linked to the fact that they are remnants, and as such they come from a number of different weapons. Whether some of those weapons infringe the principles prohibiting weapons of a nature to cause unnecessary suffering and superfluous injuries, is not directly relevant as they have become remnants. Though once they have, the humanitarian problems connected with them are similar to the problems associated with mines.

Article 36 of Additional Protocol I constitutes an invitation to the states to take the IHL principles into account in the development of new weapon technologies. In other words, the states are under an obligation to consider whether the use of a new weapon would be inconsistent with the prohibition of means of combat that cause unnecessary suffering or superfluous injuries. They are also obliged to engage in *bona fide* negotiations concerning prohibitions or restrictions on the use of such weapons.[26] The rule of Article 36 is therefore relevant to the issue of whether a weapon should be banned by treaty law or not. Existing practice on this area indicates that an explicit treaty prohibition might be based on the unneces-

24 ICRC, *Anti-Personnel Landmines – Friend or Foe?: A Study of the Military Use and Effectiveness of Anti-Personnel Mines,* Geneva, 1996.

25 Polkinghorne, Michael, Cockayne, James, *Dealing with the Risks and Responsibilities of Landmines and their Clearance,* Fordham International Law Journal, Vol. 25, No. 5, June 2002, p. 1189.

26 *Ibid.*

sary suffering principle. This rule was, for instance, an important argument in connection with the 1996 CCW Protocol IV on the ban on use in warfare of anti-eye laser weapons.

Article 51 of the 1977 Geneva Protocol I outlines in some detail the general prohibition against making civilians the object of attack. The Article prohibits indiscriminate means as well as methods of warfare.

With respect to means, Article 51(4) prohibits the launching of an attack by employment of a 'means of combat which cannot be directed at a specific military objective' or a 'means of combat, the effects of which cannot be limited as required by this Protocol'. In the words of the ICJ: 'States must never make civilians the object of attack and must consequently never use weapons that are incapable of distinguishing between civilian and military targets'.[27] This brings attention to the question whether there exist weapons that are inherently indiscriminate, a view sometimes emphasized in the international debate. Could landmines and weapons that generate (a lot of) ERW be regarded as inherently indiscriminate?

The question whether there exist inherently indiscriminate weapons should probably be answered in the negative. One problem with the drafting of the Additional Protocol I was the meaning of the words expressed in Article 51(4). Many of the experts were of the view that the definition was not intended to indicate that there are means of combat that constitute an indiscriminate attack *per se*.[28] According to this opinion, the phrasing is meant to take account of the fact that weapons or methods of combat, which may be legal in some circumstances, can – in other circumstances – have indiscriminate effects.[29] Furthermore, the ICJ has endorsed this view in the *Nuclear Weapons Advisory Opinion* by stating that it could not conclude with certainty that the use of nuclear weapons would be illegal according to the principles and rules of IHL, owing to their inherent and total incompatibility with the law applicable in armed conflict.[30]

27 See *supra* note 22, Nuclear Weapons Advisory Opinion, para. 78.
28 Conference of Government Experts on the Use of Certain Conventional Weapons (Lucerne, 24 September – 18 October 1974). Report Published by the ICRC, Geneva, 1975, p. 10 para. 29.
29 Se also *supra* note 17, Blix, 1988, p. 145.
30 Nuclear Weapons Advisory Opinion, para. 95.

However, the different positions regarding inherently indiscriminate means do not extend to indiscriminate *methods* of warfare. A military commander must consider that a distinction must be made at all times between combatants and civilians[31] when choosing the means for launching an attack. In other words, the principle of distinction prohibits the indiscriminate use of weapons. On the subject of treaty law, Article 51(5)(a) of the Additional Protocol reflects this principle by prohibiting 'massive' bombardments or 'carpet bombing' in areas where civilian concentrations are located. Furthermore, Article 51(5)(b) bans attacks that may be expected to cause excessive incidental loss of civilian life in relation to the military advantage. Even so, under international humanitarian law some limited unavoidable civilian casualties or 'collateral damage' is tolerated, assuming that the commander in control has undertaken feasible precautions and proportionality considerations (see below). 'Collateral damage' may be defined as unavoidable and therefore permissible civilian casualties, however undesirable they be.

Two conditions for compliance with the principle of distinction are adequate identification of objectives before an attack (a matter of *targeting, i.e.* whether or not a specific object is a legitimate target or not) and the balancing of the humanitarian consequences against the military advantages so that the attack does not cause excessive civilian losses. These two conditions reflect two additional fundamental principles within the system of IHL: precautions in attack and proportionality.

The principle of proportionality involves a duty to balance the expected military outcome of an attack against the expected civilian losses or destruction of civilian objects. A workable interpretation of the principle of proportionality is to consider it as a sub-category of the principle of distinction.[32] Thus, article 51 (5) (b) may be said to reflect proportionality as an essential element in accordance with the principle of distinction.

With regard to precautions in attack, Articles 57 and 58 of the Additional Protocol prescribe *inter alia* that all feasible precautions must be undertaken with regard to the choice of means and meth-

31 See ICRC Resolution XXVIII, 1965.
32 See for instance Maslen, p. 195. See *supra* note 4.

ods of attack with the aim, as far as possible, of avoiding incidental civilian casualties. Constant care must also be taken to spare the civilian population, civilians and civilian objects. In other words, a military commander must take all necessary precautions to protect the civilian population, individual civilians and civilian objects under his or her control against the dangers resulting from military operations.

The principles of distinction, proportionality and precaution only apply direct the to armed conflict phase, although they are generally accepted as applicable in both internal and international armed conflicts.[33]

The legal demand for discrimination between military targets and the civilian population, proportionality and precautions in attack is of central significance as regards the use of weapons. With regard to weapons that generate ERW, as well as landmines, the military commander is clearly obliged, notwithstanding the view that they are not illegal *per se*, under the basic principles and rules of IHL to use them in a responsible and controlled way to avoid civilian casualties, and to take all feasible precautions to protect civilians from the effects of the ERW and landmines. If ERW from a certain weapon, for instance a cluster bomb, is likely to cause a disproportionate number of civilian casualties during an armed conflict, one may argue that the use of that specific weapon, at least if the civilian casualties occur shortly after an attack, would constitute a violation of the basic principles on methods of warfare. The same argument may also be applied to anti-personnel mines if they are emplaced in, or close to, civilian concentrations. It may as well be argued that responsibility to make reparation for injues, or to com-

33 See for instance the *Tadic Case*, where the ICTY Appellate Chamber held that customary law applicable in internal armed conflicts include 'protection of civilians from hostilities, in particular from indiscriminate attacks, protection of civilian objects, in particular cultural property, protection of all those who do not (or no longer) take active part in hostilities, as well as prohibition of means of warfare proscribed in international armed conflicts and ban of certain methods of conducting hostilities'. *The Prosecutor* v. *Dusko Tadic*, Appeals Chamber of the International Tribunal for the Prosecution of Persons Responsible for Serious Violations of International Humanitarian Law Committed in the Territory of Former Yugoslavia since 1991, No. IT-94-1-AR72, 2 October 1995, para. 127.

pensate the damage due to such irresponsible use of weapons during an armed conflict may arise under international law.[34]

It may also be relevant in this context to mention that if an attack is deliberately launched on civilians or a civilian object, or is launched in the knowledge that such attack will cause loss of life or injury to civilians, the giving of that order may constitute a war crime for which the military commander could be held individually responsible.[35]

There is today no clearcut answer as to how the basic principles of IHL should be interpreted and implemented in relation to ERW. This issue is part of the 2004 mandate of the states parties to the CCW regime. It is important in this context to examine how the IHL principles are applied by the states' military forces, in particular with regard to submunitions.[36]

As stated above, although the customary law stipulates restrictions on the use of any weapon in armed conflicts, it is difficult to draw the conclusion that there is a customary norm prohibiting the use of landmines or weapons that give rise to ERW *per se*. The rules prohibiting landmines, or regulating their use in detail, are therefore primarily laid down in *treaty obligations* undertaken with other state parties.

Two treaties regulate explicitly the use and clearance of landmines. The first treaty is the Amended Protocol II to the CCW and the second is the 1997 Ottawa Convention. The question of anti-personnel landmines was first raised by the ICRC in 1955, but it was

34 See for instance Article 3 of Convention (IV) Respecting the Laws and Customs of War on Land and its annex; Regulations concerning the Laws and Customs of War on Land, 18 October 1907, and Article 91 of Additional Protocol I.

35 Under Article 8 of the Rome Statute of the International Criminal Court 'war crime' is defined as the act of intentionally directing attacks against the civilian population as such or against individual civilians not taking direct part in hostilities; ... (iv) Intentionally launching an attack in the knowledge that such attack will cause incidental loss of life or injury to civilians or damage to civilian objects or widespread, long-term and severe damage to the natural environment which would be clearly excessive in relation to the concrete and direct overall military advantage anticipated; (v) Attacking or bombarding, by whatever means, towns, villages, dwellings or buildings which are undefended and which are not military objectives.

36 See working paper CCW/GGE/VII/WG. 1/WP. 2 "Proposal for the structuring of IHL/ERW discussions clearing CCW Experts Meetings in 2004" submitted by Sweden, March 2004.

only in the late 1980s that the medical personnel of the ICRC reported that the number of civilian victims due to anti-personnel landmines and other explosive ordnance was alarming.[37] In 1993 it was concluded in a report to Congress by the US Department of State that there were between 65 and 100 million emplaced and uncleared anti-personnel mines affecting 62 countries in the world.[38] The first explicit regulations on mines, booby-traps and other devices were adopted in 1980 in the shape of an annexed protocol to the CCW of 10 October 1980. Originally, three protocols were annexed to the CCW: the Protocol on Non-Detectable Fragments (Protocol I); the Protocol on Prohibitions or Restrictions on the Use of Mines, Booby-Traps and Other Devices (Protocol II); and the Protocol on Prohibitions or Restrictions on the Use of Incendiary Weapons (Protocol III).[39]

By the beginning of the 1990s many states held the view that the regulations of Protocol II were not sufficient to deal with the problems associated with landmines. In conflicts like those in Afghanistan, Angola, Cambodia and former Yugoslavia a large number of civilian victims were affected by anti-personnel landmines. To many, this was evidence of a humanitarian crisis out of control.

The first Review Conference of the CCW amended the regulations of Protocol II in 1996.[40] Today over 80 countries have ratified the Amended Protocol II, including China and the US. The Amended Protocol II does not contain a total ban on landmines, but compared to the 1980 Protocol II it provides much more restrictive regulations on the use of landmines. The protocol applies not only to anti-personnel mines, but also to anti-vehicle and anti-tank mines, and so called booby-traps and 'other devices'. A booby-trap is an object designed to kill or injure, but which looks apparently harmless, for instance a pen, a radio or a coffee-cup. 'Other devices'

37 See for example the Foreword by Cornelio Sommaruga in Maresca, L., Maslen, S., *The Banning of Anti-Personnel Landmines, the Work of the International Committee of the Red Cross 1955–1999*, Cambridge University Press, Cambridge, 2000, p. xvii.

38 US Department of State, *Hidden Killers: The Global Problem With Uncleared Landmines, A Report on International Demining*, Washington D.C., 1993.

39 In 1995 a fourth protocol on blinding laser weapons was adopted.

40 For further information on the history behind the CCW regime see Bring, Ove, Mahmoudi, Said, *Sverige och folkrätten*, 2nd ed., Norstedts Juridik, Göteborg, 2001, p. 144 *et seq.*

are defined as manually emplaced munitions and devices including improvised explosive devices designed to kill, injure or damage, which are actuated manually by remote control or automatically after a lapse of time.

Article 3 of the Protocol on general restrictions reflects the principles of general humanitarian law relating to unnecessary suffering or superfluous injuries, distinction, proportionality and precaution. Thus, it is prohibited to direct land mines against the civilian population or to use mines indiscriminately. Mines may only be targeted against legitimate military objectives. Moreover, 'all feasible precautions' must be taken to protect the civilian population from mines.

Amended Protocol II is the first treaty obliging its parties (including non-state parties covered by Additional Protocol II to the Geneva Conventions) to clear remnants, in this case landmines and other devices covered by the Protocol, 'without delay after the cessation of active hostilities'.[41] In other words, each party to an armed conflict is responsible for the mines emplaced by it. The state party also undertakes to clear, remove, destroy or maintain them under the terms of the Protocol.[42] Further, Amended Protocol II also includes compliance procedures.[43] The parties are required to take appropriate steps, including legislative and other measures, to prevent and suppress violations on their territory.

Article 8(1)(b) of Amended Protocol II may present problems in relation to landmine clearance. The Article prohibits states from transferring mines to recipients other than states or state agencies authorized to receive such transfers. The intention of the prohibition was to reduce the opportunities for armed opposition groups to acquire mines because these groups are often the worst violators of humanitarian norms. Article 2(15) defines 'transfer' to include not only the physical movement of landmines, but also the transfer of title and control. Read together, the two Articles could be construed to prohibit the transfer of 'title and control' from state parties to non-state agencies authorized to received such transfers. As

41 See Article 10.
42 In addition, detailed technical standards are imposed requiring landmines to be self-deactivating after a certain time. Ninety per cent of activated mines must be destroyed within thirty days after employment, and only one in 1,000 activated mines may still be explosive after 120 days. See the Technical Annex, p. 2.
43 See Article 14.

the terms 'state agency', 'title' or 'control' are not defined in the Protocol, the prohibitions may in fact restrict the capability (or justify the unwillingness) of states to subcontract landmine clearance work to experts, even though they often have better expertise in ordnance disposal than governments.[44] Probably this wording, however unfortunate it may be, has not actually limited the efficacy of the treaty undertakings in practice.

When the first Review Conference of the CCW was completed in Geneva on 3 May 1996, many of the participating states were apparently disappointed that no total ban on landmines had been achieved within the CCW regime. At the closing plenary of the review conference the Canadian delegation announced that Canada would host a meeting of pro-ban states later in the year, the purpose of which was to discuss ways of prohibiting anti-personnel mines. This led to a series of meetings in Ottawa and Oslo, which has subsequently come to be known as 'the 'Ottawa Process'. After about a year of discussion and negotiation, the Ottawa Convention was signed on 3 December 1997. It entered into force on 1 March 1999.[45]

The Convention provides not only IHL regulations banning the use of anti-personnel landmines, but also disarmament and arms control aspects, prohibiting or restricting the transfer, production and stockpiling of anti-personnel mines. Unlike Protocol II the Convention covers only anti-personnel mines, though it does include such anti-vehicle mines that are designed to function as anti-personnel mines too.

State parties undertake to destroy anti-personnel mines under their jurisdiction or control, in the case of emplaced mines within ten years from the entry into force of the Convention and in the case of stockpiled mines within four years. Extensions may be granted after the submission of a request to a meeting of the states parties explained landmine clearance efforts have already been undertaken and the circumstances that motivate an extension. The state parties undertake to 'make every effort' to identify mined areas and to clearly mark such areas, according to the standards set out in Protocol II to the CCW. Areas in which mines are known or sus-

44 Polkinghorne, Michael and Cockayne, James, p. 1191.
45 At the time of writing the treaty has been ratified by 141 states (notable absentees include China, Russia and the US).

pected to be emplaced must be perimeter-marked, monitored, and protected by fencing or other means to ensure that civilians are effectively kept out. States parties agree to retain control over mines.

Unlike Amended Protocol II the Ottawa Convention includes a precise exception permitting the transfer of mines for the purpose of destruction. (The other restrictions in the Amended Protocol II on transfer obviously still apply). The Convention calls upon its signatories to do their utmost to assist in the care, rehabilitation, and reintegration of mine victims. According to Article 6 paragraph 3, each state party is obliged to take all appropriate legal, administrative and other measures, including the imposition of penal sanctions, to prevent and suppress any activity prohibited to a state party under the Convention that is undertaken by persons or on territory under its jurisdiction.

After two years of negotiations the State Parties of the CCW in 2003 managed to agree on a new Protocol V, with the specific aim of reducing the considerable humanitarian with ERW. The threat relating to ERW had for a long time been given high priority by humanitarian organisations, such as the ICRC. The negotiating mandate included post-conflict measures of a 'generic nature'.[46] The status of the protocol remained an unsolved and uncertain question up to the very last meeting. A majority of the states were in favour of a new legally binding protocol, but many states, among those some 'key states', were in favour of a non-legally binding document. These states managed, however, to agree on a legally binding protocol at the last meeting.

Although the result was succesful, the protocol has been criticized, for example by many NGOs, for being vague in many respects. Examples of this are the numerous qualifiers, for instance among the core responsibilities set out in Article 3 and 4 of the Protocol (*cf.* Article 10 of amended Protocol II). The duty of the State

46 A few delegations, among those the delegations of Sweden, Norway, Austria, Canada and New Zealand, wanted the mandate also to include discussions on whether existing IHL rules are sufficient to cope with the problems of ERW, or whether they need to be further revised. However, no such agreement was reached at the meeting of the states parties in December 2002, at which the negotiation mandate was adopted. The IHL issue was instead moved to a 'second' section of the mandate, which meant that discussion on IHL could continue, but could not be included in the Protocol.

Parties to clear and remove ERW or undertake other measures to protect the civilian population and humanitarian missions from the effects of ERW is to be fulfilled after the cessation of active hostilities and "as soon as feasible" (Article 3). Similar wording are to be found with respect to the recording, retaining and providing of information on the use or abandonment of explosive ordnance to faciliate the clearing, marking, removal etc. of ERW. The obligation of State Parties and parties to an armed conflict shall be fulfilled to the maximum extent possible and "as far as practicable" (Article 4). Even though the regulations at large are very comprehensive, these and many other qualifiers may leave plenty of scope for subjective appraisal, and could notably provide signatory States and parties to a conflict with arguments to justify non-compliance.

The new protocol also contains a non-legally binding article on 'preventive generic measures' to encourage states to ensure that manufacturers and producers of munitions that may become ERW are subjected to qualify control measures, and, if possible, to reduce the number of ERW (Article 9). However, the experience of the 1980 Protocol II shows that vague formulations are often not respected in practice.

One of the most difficult issues to solve during the last session was the problem of distinguishing existing ERW. The Egyptian and Chinese delegations were in favour of a strong text on this matter from the beginning at the conference. The questions concerning the responsibility for ERW and landmines left over from the Second World War is an issue often raised by the states of North Africa.[47] But the majority of the participating states held the view that a new Protocol could not include retroactive rules. Existing ERW is therefore not subject to the same provisions on clearance, removal etc. as ERW that appears after the instrument's entry into force. With regard to existing ERW, the protocol includes provisions whose purpose is to encourage State Parties, on a voluntary basis, to assist in the clearing of existing ERW (Article 7).

47 For further reading on the subject see Partsch, K.J., *Remnants of War as a Legal Problem in the Light of the Libyan Case,* The American Journal of International Law, Vol. 78, Issue 2, 1984, pp. 386–401.

7.4 International law protecting the natural environment

The use of a weapon may also fall under the rapidly growing area of law protecting the natural environment. The treaty regulations of IHL that are most relevant to the weapon issue are expressed in Articles 35(3) and 55 of the 1977 Additional Protocol I to the 1949 Geneva Conventions. Another convention that has some relevance to the issue is the 1977 United Nations Convention on the Prohibition of Military or Any Other Hostile Use of Environmental Modification Techniques (the ENMOD Convention). The ENMOD Convention has a futuristic approach; rather than prohibiting the use of weapons *against* the natural environment, it prohibits the use of the natural environment *as* a weapon.

Article 35(3) of Additional Protocol I prohibits the employment of any methods or means of warfare that are intended, or may be expected, to cause widespread, long-term and severe damage to the natural environment. According to Article 55, under the section on the protection of civilian objects, care shall be taken in warfare to protect the natural environment against widespread, long-term and severe damage. This protection includes a prohibition of the use of methods or means of warfare which are intended or may be expected to cause such damage to the natural environment and thereby to prejudice the health or survival of the population.

The purpose of the quoted Article is not only to protect the environment from attacks intentionally directed against it,[48] nor just to protect humans from the suffering caused by the effects of severe environmental damage, but also to protect the natural environment itself.[49]

48 One of the historical experiences that brought about these provisions was the widespread environmental degradation caused during the war in Indochina by the use of extensive bombardments and herbicides (*e.g.* 'Agent Orange'), Approximately 80 million litres (20 million gallons) of herbicides were used in Vietnam between 1962 and 1971 to remove unwanted plant life and leaves which otherwise provided cover for enemy forces during the Vietnam Conflict.

49 See Pilloud, Claude, *et al., Commentary on the Additional Protocols of 8 June 1977 to the Geneva Conventions of 12 August 1949,* ICRC, Geneva, Martinus Nijhoff Publishers, Dordrecht, 1987, para. 1441.

The central question with regard to landmines and ERW is how the wording of Additional Protocol I long-term, widespread and severe should be measured or qualified. One first point is that the criteria are cumulative; that is, all of them must be fulfilled. The similar criteria of the ENMOD Convention are alternative, which is indicated by the word 'or' – 'long-term, widespread or severe'.[50]

It is, of course, difficult to find a generally accepted interpretation of the exact meaning of the criteria in Additional Protocol I. It has been suggested that 'widespread' means an area of more than several hundred square kilometres, 'long-term' is understood as a decade or more and that 'severe' refers to damage that is likely to endanger the continued survival of the civilian population or entails risk of major health problems.[51]

Anti-personnel landmines and ERW certainly appear to fulfil at least the criteria of 'widespread' and 'severe', given cases such as Indochina. The meaning of 'long-term' is obviously dependent on whether the mines and ERW can be cleared or not. However, it is very hard to find a consensus among states that these provisions should form a part of customary law.[52]

It is clear that environmental aspects must be considered by a military commander when using mines or weapons that generate ERW. Nevertheless, the exact meaning of the language of Additional Protocol I remains uncertain. Further praxis and research into the environmental aspects of mines and ERW in relation to international law would therefore be of great value.

50 As regards the meaning of this phrase, the Conference of the Committee on Disarmament (CCD) in Geneva came to the following understanding: the term 'widespread' signifies an area of several hundred square kilometres; 'long-lasting' means lasting for a period of months or approximately a season; and 'severe' represents serious or significant disruption of or harm to human life, natural and economic resources or other assets. However, the CCD stressed that these interpretations related exclusively for the ENMOD Convention. See Austin, Jay E., and Bruch, Carl E. (Eds.), *The Environmental consequences of War – Legal, Economic, and Scientific Perspectives,* Environmental Law Institute, Cambridge University Press, Cambridge, 2000, pp. 58–59.

51 Maslen, pp. 226–227.

52 Ibid, p. 226.

7.5 What will happen next?

Following the adoption of Annexed Protocol V, the CCW working group on ERW decided at the meeting of the state parties in November 2003 to continue its work in 2004. It will do so by considering the implementation of basic principles of IHL (distinction, precaution, proportionality etc.) and by further study, with the emphasis on meetings of military and technical experts, of the scope for improving the design of certain sub munitions, if possible, to reduce the risk of these munitions becoming ERW (preventive measures).[53]

The meeting of the state parties also adopted, after intense informal consultations, a mandate for the year 2004 regarding mines other than anti-personnel mines, MOTAPM (primarly anti-tank and anti-vehicle mines). The owner of the initiative was the US, together with Denmark. Anti-vehicle and anti-tank mines are, as well as anti-personnel mines, often the cause of considerable problems, directly for civilians and indirectly by hampering humanitarian aid and long-term economic and social development. The use of MOTAPM is today regulated in Amended Protocol II. However, it has often been pointed out, particularly by humanitarian organisations, that the existing rules with regard to MOTAPM are not sufficient to deal with the problems. The new mandate, to consider all proposals put forward with the aim of elaborating appropriate recommendations on MOTAPM,[54] leaves scope for different interpretions, it is, for example, a negotiation mandate for a new legally binding instrument or is it just a discussion mandate. A dialogue on proposals for regulating MOTAPM will be continued in 2004.

By way of conclusion, it must be emphasized that mines and ERW still put the lives of civilians at risk every day. The international community has adopted international regulations to prevent future landmines and ERW being emplaced or scattered and left uncleared. The problem with mines left over from past conflicts has to some extent been addressed by the provisions of the Ottawa Convention, which oblige states to clear minefields under their jurisdic-

53 Procedural Report of the Group of Governmental Experts of the State Parties to the CCW, 6th sessions, Geneva, 17–24 November 2003, CCW/GGE/VI/2, Annex III.

54 *Ibid.*, Annex IV.

tion and control. However, some 'key states' are not parties to the Ottawa Convention. Protocol V contains no similar rules concerning existing ERW, even though in some cases they present a greater humanitarian problem than mines (*cf.* Article 7 of Protocol V). The challenge of how to deal with the extensive damage already done remains crucial.

References

Books & articles

Austin, Jay E., Bruch, Carl E. (Eds.), *The Environmental Consequences of War – Legal, Economic, and Scientific Perspectives,* Environmental Law Institute, Cambridge University Press, Cambridge, 2000.

Blix, Hans, *Förbuden att använda vissa vapen,* Kungliga Krigsvetenskapsakademiens Handlingar och Tidskrift, 1980:6, pp. 283–292.

Blix, Hans, *Means and Methods of Combat,* Henry Dunant Institute, UNESCO, 'International Dimensions of Humanitarian Law', Martinus Nijhoff Publishers, 1988, pp. 135–151.

Bring, Ove, Anderberg, Bengt, Wolbarsht, Myron L., *Blinding Laser Weapons and International Humanitarian Law,* Journal of Peace Research, Vol. 29, No. 3, 1992.

Bring, Ove, Mahmoudi, Said, *Sverige och folkrätten,* 2nd ed., Norstedts Juridik, Göteborg, 2001.

Cameron, Maxwell A., Lawson, Robert J., Tomlin, Brian W. (Eds.), *To Walk Without Fear – the Global Movement to Ban Landmines,* Oxford University Press, Toronto, 1998.

Cornish, P., *Anti-Personnel Mines, Controlling the Plague of Butterflies,* Royal Institute for International Affairs, London, 1994.

Croll, Michael, *The History of Landmines,* Leo Cooper, Barnsley UK, 1988.

Feldman, David, *The Place of Arms Control and Disarmament in the System of International Law,* in 'The International Law of Arms Control and Disarmament' – Proceedings of the Symposium Geneva 28 February–2 March 1991, Dahlitz, Julie, Dicke, Detlev (Eds.) United Nations, New York, 1991, pp. 35–43.

Fidler, D. P., *Weapons of Mass Destruction and International Law,* ASIL Insights, February 2003.

Gill T., *The Nuclear Weapons Advisory Opinion of the International Court of Justice and the Fundamental Distinction Between the Jus ad Bellum and the Jus in Bello,* Leiden Journal of International Law, Vol. 12, 1999, pp. 613–624.

Herby, Peter, Nuiten, Anna R., *Explosive Remnants of War: Protecting Civilians Through an Additional Protocol to the 1980 Convention,* International Review of the Red Cross, Vol. 83, No. 841, 2001, pp. 195–205.

ICRC, *Anti-Personnel Landmines – Friend or Foe? A Study of the Military Use and Effectiveness of Anti- Personnel Mines,* ICRC publication, Commissioned by the International Committe of the Red Cross, Geneva, 1996.

International Campaign to Ban Landmines, *Landmine Monitor Report 2003: Toward a Mine Free World, New York,* Human Rights Watch, New York, 2003.

Maresca, L., Maslen, S., *The Banning of Anti-Personnel Landmines, the Work of the International Committee of the Red Cross 1955–1999,* Cambridge University Press, Cambridge, October 2000.

Maslen, Stuart, *Anti-Personnel Mines under Humanitarian Law – A View from the Vanishing Point,* Intersentia Transnational Publishers, Antwerpen, Belgium 2001.

Moyes, Richard, Lloyd, Richard, McGrath, Rae, *Explosive Remnants of War – Unexploded Ordnance and Post-Conflict Communities,* Landmine Action, British Library, London, 2002.

Partsch, K. J., *Remnants of War as a Legal Problem in the Light of the Libyan Case,* The American Journal of International Law, Vol. 78, No. 2, 1984, pp. 386–401.

Pilloud, Claude, *et al., Commentary on the Additional Protocols of 8 June 1977 to the Geneva Conventions of 12 August 1949,* ICRC, Geneva, Martinus Nijhoff Publishers, Dordrecht, 1987.

Polkinghorne, Michael, Cockayne James, *Dealing With the Risks and Responsibilities of Landmines and Their Clearance,* Fordham International Law Journal, Vol. 25, No. 5, June 2002.

SIPRI, *Anti-Personnel Weapons,* Taylor and Francis LTD, London, 1978.

Treaties

Convention (IV) Respecting the Laws and Customs of War on Land and its annex, Regulations concerning the Laws and Customs of War on Land, 18 October 1907.

Convention on the Prohibition of Military or any Hostile Use of Environmental Modification Techniques (ENMOD), 10 December 1976.

Convention on the Prohibition of the Development, Production, Stockpiling and Use of Chemical Weapons and on their Destruction, 13 January 1993.

Convention on the Prohibition of the Use, Stockpiling, Production and Transfer of Anti-Personnel Mines and on their Destruction, 18 September 1997.

Convention on Prohibitions or Restrictions on the Use of Certain Conventional Weapons Which May be Deemed to Be Excessively Injurious or to Have Indiscriminate Effects, 10 October 1980.

Protocol Additional to the Geneva Conventions of 12 August 1949, and relating to the Protection of Victims of International Armed Conflicts (Protocol I), 8 June 1977.

Protocol on Blinding Laser Weapons (Protocol IV), 13 October 1995.
Protocol on Explosive Remnants of War (Protocol V), 28 November 2003.
Protocol on Prohibitions or Restrictions on the Use of Mines, Booby-Traps and Other Devices (Protocol II), 10 October 1980.
Protocol on Prohibitions or Restrictions on the Use of Mines, Booby-Traps and Other Devices (Protocol II), as amended on 3 May 1996.
Rome Statute of the International Criminal Court, 17 July 1998.

Cases

The Prosecutor v. *Dusko Tadic,* Appeals Chamber of the International Tribunal for the Prosecution of Persons Responsible for Serious Violations of International Humanitarian Law Committed in the Territory of Former Yugoslavia since 1991, No. IT-94-1-AR72, 2 October 1995.
Advisory Opinion on the Legality of the Threat or Use of Nuclear Weapons, International Court of Justice, 8 July 1996.

UN documents

Declaration Renouncing the Use, in Time of War, of Explosive Projectiles Under 400 Grammes Weight, Saint Petersburg, 29 November/11 December 1868.
Declaration (IV, 3) concerning Expanding Bullets, The Hague, 29 July 1899.

Internet material

International Campaign to Ban Landmines, www.icbl.org
International Committee of the Red Cross, www.icrc.org
North Atlantic Treaty Organization Glossary of Terms and Definitions AAP-6, NATO Standardization Agreements, www.nato.int/docu/stanag/aap006/aap6.htm

Miscellaneous

Conference of Government Experts on the Use of Certain Conventional Weapons (Lucerne, 24 September–18 October 1974), ICRC, Geneva, 1975.
Explosive Remnants of War (ERW) – Undesired Explosive Events in Ammunition Storage Areas, Geneva International Centre of Humanitarian Demining, 2002.
Hidden Killers: The Global Problem With Uncleared Landmines, A Report on International Demining, US Department of State, Washington D.C., 1993.
ICRC Resolution XXVIII, of the 20th International Conference of the Red Cross, Vienna, 1965.
Proposal for the Structuring of IHL/ERW Discussions during CCW Experts Meetings in 2004, CCW/GGE/VII/WG. 1/WP. 2.

8 Computer Network Attacks and Public International Law

Cecilia Hellman

8.1 Introduction

> Expressing concern that these technologies and means can potentially be used for purposes that are inconsistent with the objectives of maintaining international stability and security, and may adversely affect the security of states.[1]

The unexpected end of the cold war some ten years ago opened the door for a new world order and consequently also for new threats to international peace and security. The risk of traditional attacks seems to have diminished whilst new non-traditional threats have started to surface. The conditions for a stable and secure world have therefore changed and new potential vulnerabilities are becoming evident.

The rapid growth of modern technology, with information systems at the forefront, has been an integral feature of the making of our western society during the last decade. Today the central infrastructure in our post-industrial society, such as telecommunications, finance and banking industries, water distribution and treatment systems, military command and control, the distribution of food, oil, gas and electricity, stable production at nuclear power plants and in industry and the health care sector, all rely on well functioning computers and computer networks. But, as the quotation above illustrates, we are now also becoming aware of the inherent weakness of our high-tech societies. These increasingly intertwined and interdependent networks are becoming our Achilles heel – both in times of peace and in conflict.

1 GA Resolution 53/70 (4 December 1998), *Developments in the Field of Information and Telecommunications in the Context of International Security*, para. 7.

Our reliance on information systems for social stability and order can be exploited by simple means. What are referred to as Computer Network Attacks (CNA) can shut down or alter critical parts of states' computerized infrastructure components, causing massive damage and destruction. Today, CNA capabilities are still in their infancy, but it is already possible to achieve similar effects by means of CNA as by traditional military attacks, the frightening difference being that the actors with the capability and tools to achieve the former are both more abundant and anonymous than those with the means to achieve the latter. Potential actors range from economic and political competitors to criminals, terrorists and enemy states. Non-state actors and states that would otherwise be unable to cause large-scale damage to an economically and militarily advanced state have found an asymmetrical advantage in CNA, which is cheap, effective and low-risk. Therefore, IT-warfare is no longer just a science-fiction scenario, it is already reality.

The technological advances we are witnessing are changing tomorrow forever, but legislation is usually based on our experience of yesterday. The question is how current public international law, partly based upon the divisions of the old world order, can prove itself capable of handling these new threats to national stability and order and international peace and security. Are the traditional laws and conventions concerning the use of force (*jus ad bellum*), conflict management and humanitarian law (*jus in bello*) applicable? The questions are many and difficult, and the answers are few and uncertain. This chapter will focus solely on the question of *jus ad bellum* in relation to CNA.

The term *jus ad bellum* means the right to resort to war and encompasses the situations that legally justify the use of force as means of settling disputes. The brutal and overwhelming effects of World War I and II demonstrated that this must be a heavily restricted right. Today the UN Charter allows for the use of force only in two situations: (1) pursuant to a mandate from the United Nations Security Council or (2) as part of the inherent right to unilateral and collective self-defence as stated in Article 51 of the UN Charter. Given the developments in modern technology and the possible effects of CNA, there is a need to analyse how the legal regime of *jus ad bellum* relates to CNA activities.

The key questions of this chapter are:

1 Would a large-scale CNA constitute a breach of the prohibition of use of force as found in Article 2(4) of the UN Charter?
2 Can we claim a right to self-defence in accordance with the UN Charter Article 51 against these new, perhaps non-physical, attacks, or
3 Should we, instead of trying to apply the old laws and conventions to CNA, adopt new approaches to regulating the activity?

8.2 The information age and *jus ad bellum*

In order to understand the impact that modern technology, specifically information and communications technology, has upon waging war and public international law it is helpful to start off with a brief historical account. This will make it apparent that public international law has been, and still is, under constant pressure to change and respond to developments in military affairs and to changes in society at large.

8.2.1 Transformation of warfare and public international law

Just as we can categorize the different eras and turning point events in civil society, such as the industrial and technological revolutions, we can do the same for different eras of war. When the nature of war fundamentally changes, this is referred to as a revolution in military affairs. Examples of such transformations of warfare are the advantages gained by the introduction of cavalry in the 15th century, the adoption of firearms for siege and open warfare in the 16th and 17th centuries, the introduction of the 'nation in arms' with a conscript army, the concept of 'mechanized warfare' and tank warfare, nuclear warfare and finally the current information age warfare.[2] When we talk today about the revolution in military affairs we are referring to the impact that information technology is having upon military affairs.

2 Gray, Colin S., *The Influence of Space Power upon History*, Comparative Strategy, Vol. 15, 1996, p. 297.

Another way of mapping this transformation of warfare is by categorizing the changes by the epochs in which they took place.[3] The military objectives and the means of achieving them are defined by the respective historical eras. For example, during the *agricultural* era the aim was to conquer land, the aim of warfare throughout the *industrial* era was to acquire industrial capacity and now the chief aim is superiority in *information* and information systems.

Linked to every transformation in warfare capabilities and conduct is a response in public international law. In order to stay relevant, public international law must react to the changes in the nature of warfare, either by applying old laws and conventions to the new activities or by adopting new ones. The early expressions of public international law naturally differ greatly from those of today. But one of the core principles in public international law, the objective of eliminating the worst and most meaningless suffering and destruction bestowed upon societies and individuals in times of imminent or ongoing armed conflict, can be discerned over the ages. Through this interaction between public international law and changes in warfare, public international law has managed to adjust to, and sometimes shape, the development of warfare. This inherent strength of public international law should be borne in mind when trying to address the new threats to public international law by CNA. As revolutionary or evolutionary the revolution in military affairs in the information age is, it is not changing the very essence of war. This is the reason why international law once again has the capability to succeed in addressing and containing the new CNA scenario.

8.2.2 War in the information age – information operations

All the transformations of warfare have made an immediate impact on the way wars are conducted, both with regard to the weapons at hand and, most interestingly, to the very focus of wars. The military

3 Toffler, Alvin and Heidi, *War and Anti-War*, Warner Books Inc, New York, 1995, p. 35.

use the term 'centre of gravity'[4] to explain this fundamental character of warfare. Since the late nineteenth century armed forces have had to rely on the industrial power of a nation to sustain them. During this era, the centre of gravity of a nation's military force shifted from success on the battlefield alone (as was the case during the agricultural era) to control of the cities where the industries were located. This started to blur the demarcation line between civilian and military targets, since civilians and civilian property were at the very heart of industrial production. Today, in the information age, the targets are information and information systems. In many cases the centre of gravity has become that which people value and what sustains them in a societal context.[5] This, together with the intertwined and interdependent nature of computer networks, has in many cases made the distinction between civilian and military targets nearly invisible[6] and highlights one of the challenges that face public international law today.

The information age has undeniably presented us with new challenges to international peace and security and is affecting the conduct of military operations. The term Information Operations (IO) is commonly used to explain warfare capabilities in the information age.

IO is defined as actions taken to affect adversary information and information systems, while defending one's own information or information systems.[7] The means and methods of conducting IO,

4 Centre of Gravity is defined as the characteristic(s), capability(ies), or source(s) of power from which a nation, an alliance, a military force or other grouping derives its freedom of action, physical strength or will to fight. It exists at the strategic, operational and tactical levels of operations. Joint Publication 1-02, *Department of Defence Dictionary of Military and Associated Terms*, 12 April 2001 (as amended up to 5 June 2003), p. 80. See www.dtic.mil/doctrine/jel/new_pubs/jp1_02.pdf. In other words, destruction or control of the centre of gravity (your own, friendly forces and opposing forces) is the key to success or failure in war.

5 Dearth, Douglas H, *Critical Infrastructures and the Humans Target in Information Operations*, Campen, Alan D., Dearth, Douglas (Eds.), Cyberwar 3.0: Human Factors in Information Operations and Future Conflict, AFCEA International Press, Virginia, 2000, p. 203.

6 Jacobsen, Mark R., *War in the Information Age: International Law, Self-Defense and the Problem of 'Non-Armed' Attacks*, Journal of Strategic Studies, Vol. 21, September 1998, pp. 1–23 at p. 5.

7 US Joint Doctrine for Information Operations, 9 October 1998 (Joint Pub 3-13), pp. 1–9.

both offensive and defensive, include, but are not limited to, psychological operations, operational security, military deception, electronic warfare and CNA.

CNA is seen as a subset of computer network operations (which includes computer network defence[8] and computer network exploitation[9]) and is defined as operations to disrupt, deny, degrade, or destroy information resident in computers and computer networks as well as the networks themselves.[10] Deploying CNA includes using such varied techniques as the spreading of viruses, logic bombs Easter eggs[11] or causing denial of service.

The unique, new character of CNA has presented our high-tech societies with a new array of ways to threaten national stability and order and international peace and security. We are confronted with new types of targets (computers and their networks) and with new means of carrying out an attack. Attacks no longer need be conducted by the deployment of traditional weapons[12] resulting in death and physical destruction, but by the transmission of electronic signals through cyberspace with the aim of shutting down/off computers and computer-dependent systems. These new means and methods of destabilizing society need to be addressed by appropriate public international law regimes.

As earlier stated, this chapter will not focus on all aspects of IO and public international law. Much of what is covered by the larger

8 Computer network defence is defined as measures taken to protect and defend information, computers and networks from disruption, denial, degradation or destruction (US Joint Information Operations Policy 6 November 1998 (CJCSI 3210.1)).

9 Computer network exploitation is defined as intelligence collection operations that access information resident in files or automated information systems and gain information about potential vulnerabilities, or access critical information resident within foreign automated information systems that could be used to benefit friendly operations. *Ibid.*

10 The distinction between computer network attacks and computer network exploitation may be difficult to make, especially for the targeted state. A single keystroke may be the only difference and their impact could be similar.

11 An Easter Egg is defined as a message hidden in the object code of a program as a joke orout of malice, intended to be found either by persons disassembling or browsing the code or as a response to some undocumented set of commands or keystrokes.

12 Traditional weapons are weapons in the normal sense of the word. This includes conventional weapons with explosive effects and weapons of mass destruction (*i.e.* nuclear, chemical and biological weapons).

definition of IO is not new to warfare (such as psychological operations) and CNA activity may very well already be controlled by and also violate many current legal obligations.[13] The analysis before us involves the possible effects of computer network attacks on the legal regime of *jus ad bellum*.

This question is difficult to address for several reasons. Let us start by identifying the five key issues:

1. Today, no part of the *jus ad bellum* legal regime deals specifically with CNA.
2. Our view of the use of force envisages primarily relates to *state*-sponsored actions implemented with *traditional weapons,* resulting in *death and/or destruction* of tangible objects and the *crossing of national borders* with physical objects. The intrinsically different character of CNA activity challenges these prerequisites and it is therefor difficult to make analogies to existing legal regimes.
3. To date, only a few officially acknowledged large-scale CNA have been carried out. There has been no public state response to CNA and therefore there is practically no material to review and draw conclusions about state practice from.
4. Progress in creating an international normative framework in this area is slow. The issues concerned are not yet well understood or explored. Many states have not started to address the issue of CNA in relation to the use of force.
5. The practical difficulties of tracing a CNA should not be underestimated. Being able to attribute an action to a certain actor, state or non-state, is the first dilemma for any legal analysis. This is especially true for questions relating to the use of force where the identity of the 'attacker' is crucial when it comes to determining if there has been an unlawful use of force. Or the problem may even be to determine whether *any* actor or malice at all lies behind the attack. The risk of accidents and innocent malfunctions is inherent in all computer systems. A frightening example of this is the software error in a Canadian nuclear reactor in 1990

13 Examples of current legal obligations that are applicable to CNA activity include telecommunications agreements and the International Telecommunications Satellite Organisation (INTELSAT) Agreement of 1973 that seeks to ensure that satellites are only used for peaceful purposes. It is, however, not clear to what extent they are applicable to CNA activity.

that caused thousands of litres of radioactive water to be released.[14] No enemy perpetrator, as was first thought, was guilty of this calamitous situation. Another illuminating example was the large-scale power failure of 14 August 2003 that darkened parts of eight US states and parts of Canada. These incidents show how dependent modern societies are on reliable power systems and how easily these systems are disrupted. The cause of the power failure is not yet fully known,[15] but regardless of whether it was due to computer failure, human error or foul play, it demonstrates the inherent weakness of computer-based systems. National criminal laws and the law enforcement mechanisms will play an instrumental part in the practical task of understanding the causes of computer-based malfunctions and identifying the perpetrator(s).

However, these five issues do not leave public international law in limbo. They just mean that until a legal regime evolves that can comprehensively address state and individual activities in cyberspace, conclusions and results must be well founded in relevant authorities and doctrines, and analogies to known phenomena must be carefully drawn.

8.3 The use of force – Article 2(4)

> All members shall refrain in their international relations from the threat or use of force against the territorial integrity or political independence of any state, or in any manner inconsistent with the Purposes of the United Nations. – UN Charter Article 2(4).

Today, more and more states are becoming aware of the possibilities and threats inherent in CNA activity, and some attempts have been made by the international community to address the issue.

14 Greenberg, Lawrence T., Goodman, Seymour E., Soo Hoo, Kevin J., *Information Warfare and International Law*, Institute for National Strategic Studies, Washington D.C., 1997, p. 61.

15 This article was completed in mid-August of 2003 and the cause of the power failure was then still under investigation.

Although progress is slow, we are moving down the path to establishing the legal boundaries for CNA activity.

Understanding and defining how CNA relates to international law on the use of force and armed attack is important for several reasons. First, it enables governments to avoid activities that might be regarded as breaches of international law. Second, states that are targets of CNA will know which remedies are accepted by international law – including the right to self-defence.

In the light of what we now know about the revolution in military affairs (RMA) in the information age, the character of public international law and the capabilities of information operations, is it not already possible to determine if CNA constitutes a use of force? The question would be easy to answer if there existed an established and clear-cut definition of the concept of 'use of force' as used in Article 2(4). Unfortunately, the Charter itself does not provide any such definition and to date no attempts on the part of the UN,[16] legal writings or state practice have succeeded in resolving the question. Without a clear-cut definition of the term 'use of force' we must adopt an alternative approach to the question. We must look back to the early practices of regulated warfare and to the steps taken towards the establishment of the UN Charter. This will perhaps help us better understand the intention and scope of Article 2(4).

8.3.1 The history of regulated warfare

Before the 20th century the right to wage war was a relatively unrestricted privilege of states. The earliest limitations date from the Roman era, when war and peace became legal terms and were defined as such. Legally justified reasons for waging war were

16 Attempts to address the issue can be found in the following resolutions: GA Resolution 2625 XXV (14 Oct. 1970), *Declaration on Principles of International Law Concerning Friendly Relations and Co-operation Among States in Accordance with the United Nations Charter*; GA Resolution 3314 XXIX (14 Dec 1974), the "Definition of Aggression", GA Resolution 42/22 (18 Nov.1987), *The Declaration on the Enhancement of the Effectiveness of the Principle of Refraining from the Threat or Use of Force in International Relations.*

required and it was the senate that had to decide when to go to war.[17] Later, during the Middle Ages, further restrictions developed. Here the subjective theory of *bellum justum* (stipulating that only just wars were legal) was formulated. It was developed by theologians and cannot be said to have been a valid rule of public international law, but shows that the right to wage war now had to be justified.[18]

The first formalized multilateral attempt to restrict the freedom to wage war evolved through the Hague Peace Conferences of 1899 and 1907. The second Hague Convention of 1907 prohibited recourse to war for the recovery of contractual debts and the third Hague Convention formalized the old notion of making a declaration of war. However, there was no general prohibition of the right to wage war.

World War I sadly demonstrated the shortcomings of these early attempts to regulate war. The wish and need for a more comprehensive attempt was expressed. The solution was the establishment of the League of Nations in 1920. The Covenant of the League is in fact Chapter I of the Treaty of Versailles[19] and was an attempt to prevent war and provide the world with an alternative dispute settlement regime. In the following years, further steps in this direction were taken. The Kellogg-Briand Pact from 1928 and the Saavedra-Lamas Treaty from 1933 condemned war as a solution to international controversies. But, as history sadly proved, all these efforts were insufficient to prohibit war. One problem was the lack of a system of sanctions linked to the prohibition. Another central flaw was that the restriction only covered 'war', not the use of force in general. This gave rise to military actions that were alleged not to be 'wars'.[20] The outbreak of World War II demonstrated the ultimate failure of these systems and spawned the genesis of the UN, simultaneously with the collapse of the League of Nations.

17 For a war not to be characterized as a criminal attack it had to be a response to an attack upon Roman territory, envoys, allies to the empire or Roman legations. Hence, all wars were wars of self-defence.

18 Simma, Bruno (Ed.), *The Charter of the United Nations – A Commentary,* 1st ed., Oxford University Press, Oxford, 1995, p. 109.

19 Green, Leslie C., *The Contemporary Law of Armed Conflict,* 2nd ed., Manchester University Press, 2000, p. 5.

20 This abuse was, for example, manifested extensively in 1931 and 1937 in the disputes between China and Japan.

8.3.2 The Charter of the United Nations

The brutal World Wars that caused 'untold sorrow to mankind'[21] and the lessons learned from the earlier attempts to out rule the resort to war laid the foundation for the establishment of the United Nations. The aim of Article 2(4) was an *absolute* (hence the wording 'or in any other manner inconsistent with the UN Charter'),[22] *extensive* (also covering mere threats to use force) and *effective* (ensured by the sanctions provided through Articles 39–51 prohibition on the use of force. The ultimate aim was to end all wars, finally, and to ensure a stable and peaceful world.

These broad and general principles of Article 2(4) do not help us to understand how CNA activity fits into this scheme. We need to know the *exact* meaning and scope of Article 2(4). There is no room for misunderstandings in the international arena of peace and security. Since its scope and intent was neither specifically defined at any of the preparatory conferences held prior to the adoption of the UN Charter, and neither the General Assembly, the Security Council[23] or the International Court of Justice has given it a definite meaning, we need to consider how the Article is best interpreted today.

The basis for interpreting treaties is found in the Vienna Convention on the Law of Treaties[24] from 1969. The Convention states in Article 31(1) that treaties are to be interpreted in 'good faith in accordance with the ordinary meaning to be given to the terms of the treaty in their context and in light of its object and purpose'. The Convention also specifies that subsequent practice shall be taken into account,[25] and as subsidiary means of interpretation the

21 Preamble of the UN Charter.

22 A remark by a US delegate to the San Francisco Conference gives an insight into how Article 2(4) was understood in 1945. 'The intention of the authors of the original text was to state in the broadest terms an absolute all-inclusive prohibition; the phrase "or in any other manner" was designed to insure that there should be no loopholes', Travaux Préparatoires to the UN Charter, UN Doc 784, I/1/27, 6 UNCIO Docs. 335 (1945).

23 In times of international instability the Security Council does not decide if Article 2(4) has been breached, only if the conditions laid down in Article 39 (threat to or breach of peace or act of aggression) have been met.

24 Vienna Convention on the Law of Treaties, United Nations Treaty Series, 1969, Vol. 1155, p. 331.

25 *Ibid.* Article 31(3) b.

preparatory works of the treaty and the circumstances of its conclusion may be consulted.[26]

Applying the provisions of the Vienna Convention is only helpful to a certain extent. A purely textual approach to defining Article 2(4) is not very useful. The 'ordinary meaning' of the word 'force' simply does not help us to understand the scope of Article 2(4). A subjective and contextual approach is perhaps more appropriate. We must focus on the intentions of the parties to the Charter and what they defined as the object and purpose of the Article.

8.3.2.1 Economic and political coercion

The *travaux préparatoires* of the UN Charter show that the definintion of 'force' was not a key question at the preparatory conferences, but there are statements and actions taken by delegates that shed light on the interpretation of what constitutes the use of force. One question that was, and still is, debated since the adoption of the UN Charter is whether economic and political coercion can amount to use of force, or are actions of this kind below the threshold of Article 2(4). This question is of particular interest in relation to CNA, since potential CNA activity will perhaps mainly make an impact on a state's economic and political sectors, similar to the impact of economic and political coercion.

During the Conference in San Francisco, Brazil's representative suggested that economic and political coercion should be included under Article 2(4). An amendment with this content was tabled, but was defeated by a vote of 26 to 2. This strongly supports the contention that Article 2(4) relates to *armed* force.[27] This position is also supported by the fact that the preamble of the Charter and Articles 41, 44 and 46 use the word 'force' in conjunction with the word 'armed'.

26 See *ibid.* at Article 32.

27 The US embargoes against Cuba since the early 1960s have not been deemed to constitute use of force, nor were the sanctions that were imposed on South Africa seen as a use of force.

In addition, the 1970 Declaration of Friendly Relations[28] also supports for a restrictive view of Article 2(4). There was considerable debate during the discussions before the adoption of this Resolution on what the term 'force' meant in Article 2(4). Two different views emerged. One side, supported by the Western and several Latin American states, mainly viewed 'force' as armed or physical force. On the other hand, African, Asian and Eastern bloc states supported the view that 'force' could be applied through all forms of pressure (including economic and political coercion). In the Declaration itself coercion is covered by the principle of non-intervention, not by the principle of the prohibition of the use of force.

From these remarks the conclusion may be inferred that there is no international consensus today that Article 2(4) also relates to economic and political coercion.[29] By the intentional elimination of economic and political coercion from the scope of Article 2(4), the notion of force must be understood as physical military force with death or destruction as its objective. Nevertheless, does this restrictive interpretation still hold true today?

At the time of the discussions of Article 2(4) in 1945 and again in 1970, the nature of what constituted economic and political coercion (trade sanctions, withholding economic benefits, unequal trading practices and interference with a state's external commercial relations) was entirely different from the potential CNA effects of today (shutting down banking systems, undermining the internal economic structures of a state). If CNA are viewed as a completely new and intrinsically different phenomenon, then the earlier debate on economic and political coercion may not be a good basis for analogy. At present there is no international consensus that this is how to understand the issue of CNA. Future UN attempts to address the question of the use of force and economic and political coercion may include a discussion of the impact that CNA activity can make.

28 GA Resolution 2625 XXV (14 Oct. 1970), *Declaration on Principles of International Law Concerning Friendly Relations and Co-operation Among States in Accordance with the United Nations Charter.*

29 Grove, Gregory D., Goodman, Seymour E., Lukasik, Stephen J., *Cyber-attacks and International Law,* Survival, The International Institute for Strategic Studies Quarterly, Vol. 42, No. 3, 2000, p. 93.

8.3.2.2 Physical force of a non-military nature

Even if it is supposed that CNA is different from previous understandings of economic and political coercion, we still do not know whether this means that it constitutes a prohibited use of force. Perhaps it is more fruitful to make analogies with acts of physical force of a non-military nature, for example the release of large quantities of water down a valley, the diversion of a river by an upstream state or causing fire to spread across a frontier.[30] If such activities amount to use of force under our current understanding of Article 2(4), then it seems difficult not to include CNA activity with similar effects under Article 2(4).[31]

International legal opinion is divided on this issue and no definitive authority exists. There is no consensus about how to view physical force of a non-military nature in relation to Article 2(4). Some legal scholars argue, 'any destructive state activity intentionally caused within the sovereign territory of another state is an unlawful use of force'.[32] This very broad interpretation of Article 2(4) would in the case also include physical force of a non-military nature. But given the restrictive view of the question of coercion and force, there is more support for the negative view. If acts of physical force of a non-military nature are included under the scope of Article 2(4), that would open up the possibility of including economic and political coercion in that provision as wll. Moreover, as has been argued earlier, this is clearly not the wish or intention of the international community.

In sum, it cannot be stated that acts of physical force of a non-military nature are included under Article 2(4). These actions could nonetheless constitute breaches of other areas of international law, such as the principle of non-intervention, but it seems awkward to argue that they constitute a use of force.

30 Brownlie, Ian, *International Law and the Use of Force by States*, Clarendon Press, Oxford, 1963, p. 363.

31 Wingfield, Thomas C, *The Law of Information Conflict, National Security Law in Cyberspace*, Aegis Research Corporation, Falls Church Virginia, 2000, p. 100.

32 Sharp Sr, Walter Gary, *CyberSpace and the Use of Force*, Aegis Research Corporation, Falls Church Virginia, 1999, p. 102.

8.3.3 CNA as weapons

The examples discussed above support a rather narrow interpretation of what acts constitute a use of force. Economic and political coercion and physical force of a non-military nature are acts that traditionally fall outside the scope of Article 2(4). Given current interpretation, it is difficult to see how CNA activity could be perceived as a potential breach of Article 2(4). However, in view of the devastating scenarios that might result from CNA activity, this appears to be an unsatisfactory result. The problem seems to lie in the common understanding that Article 2(4) relates to acts of *military armed* force. So, if use of force is synonymous with armed force, can it be argued that CNA can be considered as (military) weapons?

It should be borne in mind that considerable flexibility can be exercised in defining what constitutes 'military force'. As technological advances lead to the development of new types of weapons, the scope of Article 2(4) has grown to encompass new forms of military force. If it were not for this flexibility, all new forms of weapons after World War II would fall outside the scope of Article 2(4). Today we have no difficulty in classifying biological weapons, chemical weapons and laser weapons as tools of military force when used by states to cause intentional physical or property damage. Furthermore, the events of 11 September 2001 demonstrated the expansive potential of weapons categories. The highjacked and fuel-laden airplanes that were crashed into the World Trade Center buildings were referred to as *weapons* by the international community during the weeks following 11 September.

Can it then be claimed that CNA is a new type of weapon, and consequently a new type of military force? Several factors suggest that this is the case. First, the lack of any explosive effect or shock wave or heat in CNA should not disqualify them from being labelled 'weapons'. Biological and chemical weapons lack these properties, but are unquestionably weapons. [33] Second, CNA are commonly referred to as 'weapons' and even as weapons of mass destruction. Third, CNA *are* being used, or prepared for use, by armed forces today in military operations with the intention of destroying life and/or property. Last, if similar effects can be created

33 Brownlie, Ian, *supra* note 30, p. 362.

by both traditional military force and CNA, it seems strange not to define them both as force. For example, during both the Gulf War and the NATO intervention in Kosovo the US dropped special carbon fibres from aircraft onto electric power facilities, causing power outages.[34] This same type of effect can easily be caused by directed CNA, so why should similar effects be judged differently based on the means used to accomplish them?

Even if CNA are classified as weapons, it still does not completely answer the question if CNA constitute use of force. The mere fact that CNA are/could be classified as weapons does not mean that their deployment would represent an act of force, just as the firing of a single bullet is not. However, we now have a starting-point for what may be called an effect-based analysis.

8.3.4 Moving from instrument-based to effect-based analysis

Perhaps one reason for the difficulty of understanding the relationship between CNA and Article 2(4) is that our current method of evaluating whether an action is in breach of Article 2(4) is instrument-based (*i.e.* it concentrates on the means used). This is why the term 'armed' is so central to the analysis. This traditional instrument-based model simplifies the evaluative process by merely asking whether force has been used, rather than requiring a far more difficult assessment of the *consequences* of such use.[35] Hence we have today the unsatisfactory situation where a temporarily and spatially limited border incursion is in breach of Article 2(4), while the 1973–1974 Arab oil embargo was not. Yet such actions may very well constitute a greater threat to international peace and security than the first mentioned type of action.[36] This is the dilemma facing CNA.

If, instead, we adopted a method whereby the *effects* of an action were evaluateed, we could perhaps better understand the scope of Article 2(4). The focus should be on the consequences of a CNA, not

34 McIntyre, Jamie, *Secret Carbon Fibre Bombs Kill Power in Serbia,* CNN, 3 May 1999, www.cnn.com/US/9905/03/secret.weapon/.

35 Schmitt, Michael N., *Computer Network Attack and the Use of Force in International Law: Thoughts on a Normative Framework,* Columbia Journal of Transnational Law, Vol. 37, 1999, p. 887–937 at p. 911.

36 *Ibid*, p. 909.

on the means used or the act itself. This comprehensive and holistic approach might be more succesful when it comes to evaluating whether CNA constitute a breach of Article 2(4).

An effect-based analysis start on the assumption that economic and political coercion does not constitute use of force and that *armed* force does. Somewhere between these actions lies the demarcation line between actions that fall under Article 2(4) and ones that do not. Therefore, the question that must be asked is what is the difference between economic and political coercion and armed force? Professor Michael N. Schmitt,[37] one of the few public international law scholars who has penetrated the issue in depth, has developed a model for determining this difference on the basis of the following six criteria:[38]

1 Severity: Armed attacks threaten and cause physical injury or destruction to property and lives to a greater degree than other forms of coercion.
2 Immediacy: The effects of armed attacks usually occur with great immediacy whilst other forms of coercion take time to develop.
3 Directness: The consequences of armed force are directly tied to the act.
4 Invasiveness: With armed force there is a crossing of a border into the target state, whilst acts of economic and political coercion generally occur beyond the targets' border, causing a lesser intrusion into the rights of a state.
5 Measurability: Consequences of armed force are usually easy to determine; consequences of other forms of coercion are more difficult to measure.
6 Presumptive Legitimacy: Economic and political coercion are usually deemed legitimate absent some prohibitory law, whilst the opposite is true for armed violence.

If we apply these criteria to CNA we can see which acts of CNA would breach Article 2(4). Let us imagine two separate situations caused by CNA from a foreign state. The first example might

37 Michael N. Schmitt is Professor of International Law and Director, Executive Program in International and Security Affairs at George C. Marshall European Center for Security Studies, Garmisch-Partenkirchen, Germany.
38 Schmitt, Michael N., *supra* note 35, pp. 914–915.

involve CNA used to disrupt air traffic control systems causing mid-air collisions and plane crashes. In this example signals would have to be transmitted across borders and the consequences (the loss of life and destruction of property) would be immediate, severe and easily measured. Hence, according to the Schmitt analysis this constitutes a use of force.

The second example given by Schmitt is that of a university computer network destroyed CNA. The aim of the attack is to delete the military research conducted there with the long-term goal of diminishing future battlefield capability. The result (loss of data) is not *severe* and *is comparable* to that of traditional forms of military force. It is also difficult to assess and *measure* the consequences. Schmitt states that the desired outcome is both *remote* (the negative effects are not immediate) and *indirect* from the act. In sum, the example does not meet the criteria for use of force.

8.3.4.1 Are CNA use of force?

Schmitt's proposed criteria are indeed helpful in determining the difference between use of force and economic and political coercion. However, there are several flaws in the analysis when it is applied to CNA. On closer inspection it is perhaps only the criteria of *severity* that actually helps to differentiate between the two given examples.

Both examples relates to attacks caused by electronic signals sent across borders; hence they both meet the criteria of *invasiveness*. The fulfilment of the criteria of *directness* and *immediacy* is vague and leaves room for subjective interpretation. The question is *which* consequences of the CNA need to be immediate and directly linked to the act. In the second example, the effect of the loss of data is immediate and directly tied to the CNA activity. The secondary effects (potential damage to future battlefield capability) may be indirect, but then the analysis becomes a subjective matter of selecting which effects to assess. As for *measurability*, it is hard to see why the effects of the first example are more easily determined than the effects in the second example. Hence, the only clear difference between the two examples is the severity of the consequences of the CNA.

Using this logic, it then appears that the core principle in the analysis is the evaluation of the severity of the consequences. If physical injury or damage occurs as a direct consequence of CNA and it resembles the consequences resulting from traditional military weapons, then it may constitute a use of force. Unfortunately, this conclusion is unsatisfactory since it leaves the question of CNA and the use of force in a state of uncertainty. All we can establish at this point in time is that certain CNA are likely to constitute force under Article 2(4) whilst many others may not.

Unsatisfactory as the conclusion of the scope of Article 2(4) may be, there is a second analysis that follows. For a state that is subject to hostile CNA activity, an affirmative answer as to whether the CNA activity constitutes a use of force is not enough. The use of force must also be classified as an *armed attack*. This is because, under the the UN Charter, states only have the right to take counteraction in self-defence as a response to an armed attack.

8.4 The right to self-defence – Article 51

Article 51 of the UN Charter opens with the following words: 'Nothing in the present Charter shall impair the inherent right of individual or collective self-defence if an armed attack occurs against a Member of the United Nations.'

So far, the main focus of the international debate on public international law and CNA has been on the question whether CNA can constitute an unlawful *use of force*. As discussed in the previous sections, this is the case for obvious reasons. Article 2(4) is seen as the cornerstone of public international law and it is necessary to establish the demarcation line between lawful and unlawful *offensive* state activity.

But what about *defensive* state action: can a state claim the right to use military force to meet CNA? Just because CNA may be in breach of Article 2(4), it does not necessarily follow that the victim has a right to self-defence. There is a gap between the two terms. The right for a state to use military force in response to actions in breach of Article 2(4) is reserved for actions that amount to *armed attacks*. If one state fires some stray bullets over the border towards another state, there is a use of force, but not serious enough to amount to an armed attack. Hence, not every use of force involves an armed attack.[39] For example, the ICJ ruled in the *Nicaragua* Case[40] that the US *arming* and *training* of the *contras* constituted a threat or use of force against Nicaragua but not an armed attack.

In the light of the above, we need to examine which forms of CNA may constitute armed attacks that allow the attacked state to invoke the right to use force as a means of self-defence in accordance with UN Charter Article 51.

While missiles have specific objective and effect, CNA can have a multitude of effects. They span across the entire spectrum of intrastate activity, from causing mere inconvenience and annoyance to causing physical death and destruction. This makes it difficult to define CNA. However, it is not impossible to single out types of CNA that may be tantamount to an armed attack.

To start with, it is helpful to recall the three conditions that must be met before invoking the right to self-defence against traditional armed attacks.[41] First, there must be a claim of *necessity* to respond with military means, rather than by resolving the situation by more peaceful means. Second, the response must be *proportional* to the original armed attack, and, last, the response must be necessary in terms of *immediacy*. These three conditions should be taken into account when exploring the possibility of lawful responses to CNA under Article 51.

Once again, the UN Charter does not provide us with a clear-cut and unambiguous definition of armed attacks. At first glance it seems logical to examine the means used to carry out the attack. We are used to thinking in this way, as was mentioned in the analysis of Article 2(4), and the words themselves, *armed attack* (in French; *aggression armée*), encourages this way of thinking. However, there are two arguments that help to broaden the perspective.

First, the focus need not be on the 'weapon' used – traditional or electronic. This view is supported by the ICJ in the Nuclear Weapons Advisory Opinion of 1996, where the Court ruled that Article

39 Brownlie, Ian, *supra* note 30, p. 365.

40 Case Concerning Military and Paramilitary Activities in and against Nicaragua (*Nicaragua* vs. *U.S.*), ICJ Reports, 1986, p. 14.

41 These conditions were first formulated in the famous Carolina Case and are today part of customary international law. For further information on this case see Jennings, R. Y., *The Caroline and McLeod Cases*, American Journal of International Law, Vol. 32, No. 1, 1938, pp. 82–89 at pp. 82–232.

51 does not refer to specific weapons, but applies to any use of force regardless of the weapon employed.[42] This means that the fact that an attack was carried out electronically does not disqualify it from constituting an armed attack.

Second, an armed attack does not need to involve massive military action. A single engagement of a fighter plane can constitute an armed attack. These two arguments facilitate the following legal analysis. Again, we must look at the *consequences* of an attack.

Let us now apply the above mentioned arguments to the following example. If a CNA succeeded in creating a core meltdown in a reactor in a nuclear power plant by shutting down the control systems and its back-up systems, the consequences would be devastating. There would be countless casualties and widespread long-term effects as a result of radioactive materials being unleashed. If we focus on the consequences of this CNA, it is clearly imaginable that the same result could be caused by a missile targeting the power plant. Therefore, if the CNA was *intended* and *managed* to directly cause *physical damage* to *tangible objects* or injury to *human beings*, it could constitute an armed attack. As in the analysis of Article 2(4), the focus must be on the *consequences* of a CNA. A CNA that falls short of an armed attack may nevertheless be in breach of Article 2(4), and international remedies, other than the right to self-defence, would be called for.

If we can now claim with some certainty that some forms of CNA may constitute an armed attack, we must ask another question: Does it matter *who* the perpetrators are when it comes to invoking the right of self-defence?

8.4.1 The problem of state and non-state actors

In the Westphalian world order, it was states that were capable of severely harming societies through wars. Non-state actors simply did not have the means to carry out armed attacks. For this reason, the right of self-defence is traditionally reserved for putting an end to another state's unlawful behaviour.[43]

42 *Legality of the Threat or Use of Nuclear Weapons*, Advisory Opinion, International Court of Justice, 8 July 1996, para. 39.

43 Simma, Bruno (Ed.), *The Charter of the United Nations – A Commentary*, 1st ed, Oxford University Press, Oxford, (1995), p. 667.

Today, when CNA is a relatively cheap and simple tool, there is a wider range of actors who have the means and motives to cause devastating impacts on our societies. These include individual hackers acting on their own initiative, private corporations acting out of financial interest, terrorists, perpetrators of large-scale international terrorism,[44] state-sponsored terrorists (de facto state agents) and states.

If any one of these actors can potentially cause the effects of an armed attack, how should we view the question of self-defence? Does it follow that a state can claim the right of self-defence against a single individual?

In the best of worlds, the first three actors (individual hackers, private corporations and terrorists) are to be dealt with by civil law enforcement agencies. They are non-state actors and, as stated earlier, the right to self-defence is conferred upon states in order to meet armed attacks emanating from another state. Accordingly, military self-defence is not the proper immediate response for the affected state. Instead, the state from which the attacks were carried out should immediately take steps to end the attacks and assist the affected state in its effort to bring the offenders to justice under criminal law. Like other cross-border crimes, these situations are best dealt with by means of cooperative bilateral and multilateral extradition and mutual judicial assistance treaties.[45] This may appear to be an unsatisfactory solution for an affected state, but it would be both dangerous and difficult to undertake military operations to stop an individual hacker located in a foreign state. But of course, this is the problem: if the damage these actors can cause upon societies by CNA is as severe as state actors, shouldn't the response be similar? It cannot be ruled out that if, for example, the state from which the attack originated is either unwilling or unable to address the situation, other remedies must be sought by the affected state. One of these could be an armed self-defence response.

CNA conducted by the latter three actors (perpetrators of large-scale international terrorism, state-sponsored terrorists and states) are more in line with traditional views of actors that are capable of

44 The term large-scale international terrorism refers, for example, to the attacks of 11 September 2001.

45 Sharp, Sr. Walter Gary, *supra* note 32, p. 8.

carrying out armed attacks.[46] Accordingly, if these actors managed to launch a CNA that amounted to an armed attack, the responses to such an attack would include the right of self-defence. The response might be delivered by a CNA similar to the original attack or by traditional weapons. There is no principle or provision of public international law that says that the same weapon must be used in the counterattack. The only obligation that must be met is that the response may not be disproportionate to the original attack.

8.5 The efforts of the international community

One of the few UN attempts to date to address the issue of the risks of modern technology and public international law is a draft Russian resolution submitted in September of 1998 to the First Committee of the 1998 General Assembly.[47] Paragraph 3 of the draft resolution reads as follows:

> *Invites* all Member States to inform the Secretary-General of their views and assessments concerning ... advisability of developing international legal regimes to prohibit the development, production or use of particularly dangerous forms of information weapon[s][48]

Unfortunately, the proposal did not result in an intense debate about CNA and the legal regime of use of force. Only eight nations altogether submitted reports to the Secretary-General on the issue, and of these only Cuba and Belarus expressed support for the proposal to adopt legal regimes to limit information warfare capabilities. One problem with the Russian proposal was perhaps the forum in which it was offered. The First Committee deals with questions of disarmament and perhaps it would have been more appropriate and manageable to introduce this question in the Sixth Committee (the legal committee) instead.

46 After the events of 11 September 2001, the UN deemed terrorism to be a threat to international peace and security evoking the right to act in self-defence.

47 UN General Assembly, First Committee, Letter dated September 23, 1998, from the Permanent Representation of the Russian Federation to the United Nations to the Secretary General, concerning Agenda item 63, *Role of Science and Technology in the Context of International Security, Disarmament and other Related Fields*, A/C.1/53/L.17/Rev. 1, 30 September 1998.

48 *Ibid.*, para. 3.

Furthermore, the United States argued that it was premature to discuss negotiating an international agreement on information warfare. This argument was probably motivated by US interest in further exploring the military potential of CNA.[49]

This early attempt to regulate some forms of CNA was rejected and the Resolution that was finally adopted, *Developments in the field of information and telecommunications in the context of international security*, does not include the wording or meaning of the paragraph stated above.[50] Instead, the watered-down Resolution reads as follows:

> *Invites* all Member States to inform the Secretary-General of their views and assessments on the following questions ... advisability of developing international principles that would enhance the security of global information and telecommunications systems and help combat information terrorism and criminalit[y].[51]

8.5.1 The road ahead

Today, international legal opinion is divided on the issue of how to address and classify CNA activity. Several legal scholars would like to see a new normative architecture emerging for CNA activity. Unfortunately, there does not seem to be any agreement about the content.

The views about how to deal with CNA activity and the question of use of force and armed attacks span a broad spectrum. Some, as has been mentioned in the earlier sections of this chapter, argue that the current laws on the use of force may be interpreted as covering CNA activity. Others argue for an absolute prohibition of CNA activity.

Anthony D'Amato, Professor of Law at Northwestern University School of Law, argues that the US has far more to lose if US computer networks are attacked than it ever could hope to gain by attacking the computer networks of other countries. Therefore, he foresees

49 Doswald-Beck, Louise, *Computer Network Attack and the International Law of Armed Conflict*, Schmitt, Michael N. Schmitt, O'Donnell, Brian T. (Eds.), Computer Network Attack and International Law, Naval War College, International Law Studies, Vol. 76, 2002, p. 166.

50 GA Resolution 53/70 (4 December 1998), *Developments in the Field of Information and Telecommunications in the Context of International Security.*

51 *Ibid.* para. 10(c).

that an absolute prohibition of Internet disruption will be recognized as a foundational principle of international customary law.[52]

It does not seem to be too far-fetched to guess that human well-being, societal stability and international peace and security will increasingly depend on the stability and inviolability of computers and their networks. Given that a large-scale CNA attack would most definitely create cascading destructive effects far from its original impact, perhaps it does serve national long-term interests better to completely rule out the use of the Internet for anything other than peaceful purposes. [53] Maybe an absolute prohibition of CNA for any military or hostile use would also better safeguard the fundamental principles of the United Nations Charter, *i.e.* the maintainance of international peace and security.

On the other hand, it does not serve national or international interests if *states* are prohibited from using CNA at the same time as private individuals and other non-state actors have this opportunity. It would of course be possible to prohibit states from using CNA, but it would be much more difficult, if not impossible, to successfully prohibit, monitor and prosecute non-state actors.

Whatever path the international community chooses, there are pros and cons that need to be evaluated. Classifying CNA activity as an armed attack entails dangerous consequences that must be borne in mind. Such a classification might lead to an unnecessary escalation of a tense and fragile situation involving two opposing states. Since responses to a large-scale CNA may be carried out by deploying traditional weapons, we would risk increased resort to armed force that could perhaps be prevented.

However, ignoring the reality of the CNA threat also entails risks. If the right to self-defence was to be completely ruled out as means of dealing with a large-scale CNA, states might become increasingly vulnerable and susceptible to CNA activity.

52 D'Amato, Anthony, *International Law, Cybernetics and Cyberspace*, Schmitt, Michael N., O'Donnell, Brian T. (Eds.), Computer Network Attack and International Law, Naval War College, International Law Studies, Vol. 76, 2002, pp. 68–69.

53 Silver, Daniel B., *Computer Network Attacks as a Use of Force under Article 2(4)*, Schmitt, Michael N., O'Donnell, Brian T. (Eds.), Computer Network Attack and International Law, Naval War College, International Law Studies, Vol. 76, 2002, p. 94.

8.6 A Swedish perspective

Chapter 10, Article 9, of the Swedish Instrument of Government, includes the following provision: 'The Government may commit the Realm's armed forces, or any part of them, to battle in order to repel an armed attack upon the Realm.'[54]

From a Swedish perspective, the question of defining armed attack is pivotal. Being a small state with a history of neutrality in its foreign relations, it is a matter of crucial interest to whether we can legitimately use our military capability to respond to CNA.

According to the provision quoted above a condition for deployment of the armed forces is that Sweden must be under an armed attack. Given the uncertainty about the meaning of this term in international law it is interesting to see how Sweden interprets it. Must the attack be launched from and conducted by a foreign state? Without the answers to these questions Sweden will not know how to deal appropriately with CNA activity.

The Swedish Instrument of Government, together with the legislation supporting the Swedish Total Defence system, is based upon the traditional bi-polarized world order with its known (state) adversaries. The *travaux préparatoires* to the Instrument of Government clarify the intentions of the legislator in 1974[55] with regard to the meaning of armed attack in Chapter 10, Article 9. It becomes apparent that it is a traditional view of attacks and actors that is covered by the provision. For example, the heading of Chapter 10 reads 'Relations with other states'. If this means that Swedish Armed Forces are only to be deployed against traditional armed attacks by other states, should we conclude that CNA activity undertaken by non-state actors is a matter solely for the Swedish police to handle? A strict reading of the law leads to this rather unsatisfactory conclusion.

Today, Swedish law enforcement agencies are not manned, trained or equipped to handle large-scale CNA activity. Furthermore, since the Armed Forces are only to be used in the case of an armed attack, there is a legal lacuna regarding the protection of

54 The Swedish Instrument of Government (Regeringsformen) is one of the four fundamental laws that make up the Swedish Constitution.

55 The Swedish Instrument of Government law (SFS 1974:152) was passed in 1974.

Sweden and its interests. However, the law allows for some interpretation and leeway. There are two important factors that provide Sweden with the means to cope with large-scale CNA activity.

First, according to the *travaux préparatoires* to the Instrument of Government the understanding of the term armed attack should not differ from the UN interpretation of the same term. Thus, if the term armed attack is clarified by the UN and its organs, Sweden will follow this interpretation in the future. This adherence to the UN Charter can be seen in the Swedish Government Report 2003:32, Our Preparedness after September 11th.[56] In line with current UN interpretations of armed attack, the Commission proposes that the provisions contained in the Instrument of Government should now also be applied in the case of self-defence against certain attacks of a terrorist nature that do not emanate from a foreign state. This seems to open the door for a broader interpretation as to when the Swedish Armed Forces may be deployed.

Second, in the face of a large-scale CNA threatening our national security, it is ultimately up to the Swedish government to decide if the act constitutes an armed attack. It seems highly unlikely that we would place our national security and stability at risk for the sake of legal interpretation.

However, hopefully Sweden will state its position on this question beforehand. It lies in our best interests to establish a *Swedish* interpretation of the term 'armed attack'. Waiting for the international community to adopt one will most likely be a slow and protracted process and specific Swedish interests are not likely to be taken into account. Furthermore, it could be both dangerous and inefficient to wait until we are the subject of a CNA to determine its classification. As a society founded on the rule of law we attach great importance to the predictability and stability of the law and therefore it lies in our interests and historical tradition to clarify this matter in advance. There is also a practical side to this. In times of peace and stability we need to start equipping and training the agency or agencies that will deal with CNA activity and provide them with the legislative support they need.

56 In Swedish, SOU 2003:32 'Vår beredskap efter 11 september'.

When discussing these questions, one must also address the practical difficulty of gathering information about CNA activity. Today there is a lack of intelligence in this field. Since potential targets for CNA range from private companies to state authorities it is difficult (perhaps impossible) to acquire a comprehensive knowledge of CNA activities aimed towards a state. The goal of CNA might well be to cause long-term economic havoc and chaos, and this could be achieved by targeting private companies. Today it is not compulsory for Swedish private companies to report ongoing or past attacks on their systems and facilities. A single company may not see or understand the 'big picture' of well-organized CNA of which their problem could be just one part. Today, neither the policing agencies nor the armed forces can gather, individually or together, sufficient intelligence on CNA activity. Due to this lack of comprehensive intelligence the Swedish National Post and Telecom Agency has been given the task of establishing a Swedish IT Incident Centre (SITIC). Its object is to collect and compile information about IT-incidents[57] from private companies and state authorities in order to be able to issue warnings and give recommendations for appropriate responses. Unfortunately, all information provided to SITIC by companies is on a purely voluntary basis. Sweden lacks an updated and correct picture of CNA activity aimed at Sweden and Swedish interests. This, together with the fact that Sweden is a technology-dependent state, highlights the need for a national agenda on this issue. In order for us to be prepared to act properly against CNA activity, it is high time to start reviewing our legislation. We need to ensure that we have both adequate and just means of handling possible CNA activity.

57 IT incidents is a broader term than CNA. It encompasses all types of IT-activities, including purely incidental disturbances.

8.7 Conclusion

> Like the constitution of the United States itself, the Charter of the United Nations must not be static and inflexible, but must be adaptable to the changing conditions of progress- social, economic, and political- all over the world.[58] – US President Franklin D. Roosevelt.

The Charter of the United Nations, and its monopoly on the use of force, is the crowning of the quest for a prohibition of the right to wage war freely. It is today seen as the cornerstone of international peace and security. When it was drafted, in the aftermath of World War II, it was designed to be an absolute, extensive and effective prohibition of the use of force. It was intended to be able to stand the test of time and accordingly, as the quotation above emphasizes, adjust to developments in civil and military affairs without compromising its fundamental purpose – that of constituting a prohibition of wars and maintaining international peace and security.

Huge technological advances have been made since 1945, new types of weapons have been developed and new actors have entered the international arena. In order to be able to tackle these new situations and contingencies public international law has also developed and adjusted. Its flexibility and resilience is remarkable. And now, public international law is under pressure once again to demonstrate its capability for addressing the new questions posed by CNA with respect to the current understanding of *jus ad bellum* without compromising its fundamental purpose. Any attempt to understand new threats to international peace and security must be seen against this backdrop.

The international community is now becoming aware of the potential destructive effect of CNA activity. There have been some attempts to address the important question of how Articles 2(4) and 51 of the UN Charter apply to CNA activity. However, an international consensus upon this issue has still not been reached.

58 President Franklin D. Roosevelt was one of the principal architects behind the UN and his view expresses the flexible nature of the Charter that was intended. Opinion of the Department of Foreign Relations Concerning the Dumbarton Oaks Proposals of October 31, 1944, Doc. 2, G/7 (c), 3 U.N.C.I.O Docs. 74 (1945).

One approach is to argue that application of the prohibition of the use of force to CNA is a rather straightforward and uncomplicated task. The core question is whether the *consequences* of CNA are sufficiently similar the consequences of traditional weapons and wars (*i.e.* result in death and/or destruction of physical property). If the answer is in the affirmative, then it is seems possible that they may indeed constitute a use of force and, if severe enough, also armed attacks.

Another, diametrically opposite, approach is to take the stance that the fundamental purpose of the UN Charter is best served by an absolute prohibition against using CNA for any military or hostile use. Our technology-dependent society has far more to lose through the disruption of the Internet, computers and their networks than whe could ever hope to gain by military use of CNA.

Both these approaches entail practical difficulties and negative consequences. Even if it were possible to bind states to an absolute prohibition against CNA activity, this would only solve a part of the problem. Today's reality is that individuals and groups, not only states, are capable of launching large-scale CNA. A treaty-based prohibition would have to be accompanied by massive global efforts to strengthen and achieve uniformity in national criminal legislation and enhance law enforcement mechanisms. Without this, a prohibition might have counterproductive results that would make states more vulnerable than before.

On the other hand, caution is advisable when seeking to include CNA activity under Article 2(4) and 51. Such inclusion might lead to an unnecessary and otherwise preventable resort to armed force between two opposing states and thereby undermine the fundamental purpose of the UN Charter.

However this question is addressed, there are not likely to be any major codification or regulatory attempts in the near future. It will probably take some time before a decision from the international community can be expected on how to regulate CNA. Most nations need more time to determine what legal principles surrounding CNA activity best serve their long-term national interests. In the meantime, our best (and only) method of dealing with this new activity lies in a careful application of the current legal framework. This will prove difficult, but is by no means impossible.

References

Books & articles

Brownlie, Ian, *International Law and the Use of Force by States*, 1st ed., Clarendon Press, Oxford 1963.

D'Amato, Anthony, *International Law, Cybernetics and Cyberspace*, Schmitt, Michael N., O'Donnell, Brian T. (Eds.), Computer Network Attack and International Law, Naval War College, International Law Studies, Vol. 76, 2002.

Dearth, Douglas H., *Critical Infrastructures and the Humans Target in Information Operations*, Campen, Alan D., Dearth, Douglas (Eds.), Cyberwar 3.0: Human Factors in Information Operations and Future Conflict, AFCEA International Press, Falls Church Virginia, 2000.

Doswald-Beck, Louise, *Computer Network Attack and the International Law of Armed Conflict*, Schmitt, Michael N., O'Donnell, Brian T. (Eds.), Computer Network Attack and International Law, Naval War College, International Law Studies, Vol. 76, 2002.

Gray, Colin S. *The Influence of Space Power upon History*, Comparative Strategy, Vol. 15, 1996, pp. 293–309.

Green, Leslie C., *The Contemporary Law of Armed Conflict*, 2nd ed., Manchester University Press, Manchester, 2000.

Greenberg, Lawrence T., Goodman, Seymour E., Soo Hoo, Kevin J., *Information Warfare and International Law*, Institute for National Strategic Studies, Washington D.C., 1997.

Grove, Gregory D., Goodman, Seymour E., Lukasik, Stephen J., *Cyberattacks and International Law*, Survival, The International Institute for Strategic Studies Quarterly, Vol. 42, No. 3, 2000.

Jacobsen, Mark R., *War in the Information Age: International Law, Self-Defense and the Problem of 'Non-Armed' Attacks*, Journal of Strategic Studies, Vol. 21, September 1998, pp. 1–23.

Jennings, R. Y., *The Carolina and McLeod Cases*, American Journal of International Law, Vol. 32, No. 1, 1938, pp. 82–99.

McIntyre, Jamie, *Secret Carbon Fibres Bombs Kill Power in Serbia*, CNN 3 May, 1999, www.cnn.com/US/9905/03/secret.weapon/.

Schmitt, Michael N., 'Computer Network Attack and the Use of Force in International Law: Thoughts on a Normative Framework', Columbia Journal of Transnational Law, Vol. 37, 1999, pp. 887–937.

Sharp Sr., Walter Gary, *Cyberspace and the Use of Force*, Aegis Research Corporation, Falls Church Virginia, 1999.

Silver, Daniel B., *Computer Network Attacks as a Use of Force under Article 2(4)*, Schmitt, Michael N., O'Donnell, Brian T. (Eds.), Computer Network Attack and International Law, Naval War College, International Law Studies, Vol. 76, 2002.

Simma, Bruno (Ed.), *The Charter of the United Nations – A Commentary*, 1st ed., Oxford University Press, Oxford, 1995.

Toffler, Alvin and Heidi, *War and Anti-War*, Warner Books Inc, New York, 1995.
Wingfield, Thomas C., *The Law of Information Conflict, National Security Law in Cyberspace*, Aegis Research Corporation, Falls Church Virginia, 2000.

Treaties

The Charter of the United Nations, 1945.
Vienna Convention on the Law of Treaties, United Nations Treaty series, Vol. 1155, 1969, p. 331.

Cases

Legality of the Threat or Use of Nuclear Weapons, Advisory Opinion, International Court of Justice, 8 July 1996, para. 39.
Military and Paramilitary Activities in and against Nicaragua (*Nicaragua* v. *U.S.*), ICJ Reports, 1986, p. 14.

UN documents

Doc. 2, G/7 (c), 3 U.N.C.I.O Docs. 74 (1945), *Opinion of the Department of Foreign Relations Concerning the Dumbarton Oaks Proposals of October 31, 1944.*
GA Resolution 53/70 (4 December 1998), *Developments in the Field of Information and Telecommunications in the Context of International Security.*
GA Resolution 2625 XXV (14 October 1970), *Declaration on Principles of International Law Concerning Friendly Relations and Co-operation Among States in Accordance with the United Nations Charter.*
GA Resolution 3314 XXIX (14 December 1974), *the Definition of Aggression.*
GA Resolution 42/22 (18 Nov. 1987), *the Declaration on the Enhancement of the Effectiveness of the Principle of Refraining from the Threat or Use of Force in International Relations.*
Travaux Préparatoires to the UN Charter, UN Doc. 784, I/1/27, 6 UNCIO Docs. 335 (1945).
UN General Assembly, First Committee, Letter dated September 23, 1998, from the Permanent Representation of the Russian Federation to the United Nations to the Secretary General, concerning Agenda item 63, *Role of Science and Technology in the Context of International Security, Disarmament and other Related Fields*, A/C.1/53/3, 30 September 1998.

Miscellaneous

NATO Allied Joint Publication -01 (B) *Ratification Draft,* 1998, paragraph 0308.
SOU 2003:32 'Vår beredskap efter 11 september'.
The Swedish Instrument of Government (SFS 1974:152).
US Joint Doctrine for Information Operations, 9 October 1998 (Joint Pub 3-13).
US Joint Publication 1-02, *Department of Defence Dictionary of Military and Associated Terms,* 12 April 2001 (as amended through 5 June 2003).

9 The International Criminal Court and Collective Security

Inger Österdahl

9.1 Introduction

The International Criminal Court (ICC) is supposed to judge individuals for the most serious crimes of concern to the international community as a whole, according to the Statute of the Court.[1] The crimes that the ICC will consider are genocide, crimes against humanity, war crimes, and perhaps in a distant future the crime of aggression.[2] The jurisdiction of the ICC is dependent upon the ratification of the Statute by the state where the conduct occurred or the state of which the person accused of the crime is a national.[3] It is possible for a state that is not a party to the Statute to accept the

1 The Rome Statute of the International Criminal Court was adopted in Rome on 17 July 1998 and entered into force on 1 July 2002. At the time of this writing 92 states have ratified the Statute of the Court (including all current EU members), see www.icc-cpi.int. For information on the ICC see also www.iccnow.org.

2 Article 5 ICC Statute, further elaborated in Articles 6, 7 and 8 respectively. The crime of aggression is not elaborated further in the Statute.

3 Article 12 ICC Statute. On Article 12 (one of the most debated Articles in the Statute) see generally Triffterer, Otto, (Ed.), *Commentary on the Rome Statute of the International Criminal Court. Observers' Notes, Article by Article*, Nomos Verlagsgesellschaft, Baden-Baden, 1999, pp. 329–341; on the issue of the ICC Statute and third states, see for instance Gennady M. Danilenko, *The Statute of the International Criminal Court and Third States,* Michigan Journal of International Law, Vol. 21, 2000, pp. 445–494; *Cf.* also Klabbers, Jan, *The Spectre of International Criminal Justice: Third States and the ICC,* Zimmerman, Andreas (Ed.), International Criminal Law and the Current Development of Public International Law, Duncker and Humblot, Berlin, 2003, pp. 49–72; Mégret, Frédéric, *Epilogue to an Endless Debate: The International Criminal Court's Third Party Jurisdiction and the Looming Revolution of International Law,* European Journal of International Law, Vol. 12, 2001, pp. 247–268; La Haye, Eve, *The Jurisdiction of the International Criminal Court: Controversies Over the Preconditions for Exerciscising its Jurisdiction,* Netherlands International Law Review, Vol. 46, 1999, pp. 1–25; Morris, Madeline, *High Crimes and Misconceptions: The ICC and Non-Party States,* Shelton, Dinah (Ed.), International Crimes, Peace, and Human Rights: The Role of the International Criminal Court, Transnational Publishers, Ardsley NY, 2000, pp. 219–279.

jurisdiction by the Court also on a case-by-case basis,[4] and the Statute declares that the jurisdiction of the ICC shall be complementary to national criminal jurisdictions.[5]

This chapter will look at the ICC from the perspective of international security. It will deal with the relationship between the ICC and the collective security system of the United Nations (UN). The chapter is structured as follows. First, the relationship of the ICC with the Security Council of the UN will be dealt with. Secondly, the relationship of the ICC with the collective security system as a whole will be discussed. Third, the question will be raised whether the ICC is able to judge terrorists.

The chapter looks forward rather than backward. Thus there will be no discussion of the history of the ICC or of war crimes tribunals generally; nor will there be any discussion of substantive criminal law. It is the ICC's position and role within the UN system for collective security, which forms this chapter's frame of reference.

9.2 Links between the ICC and the UN Security Council

9.2.1 Referral

Under Article 13 of the Statute of the ICC, the UN Security Council may refer to the Prosecutor of the ICC for investigation a situation in which one or more of the crimes within the jurisdiction of the

4 Article 12(3) ICC Statute.

5 Article 1 ICC Statute. For a close investigation of the implications of complementarity, see Young, Simon N.M., *Surrendering the Accused to the International Criminal Court',* British Year Book of International Law, Vol. 7, Clarendon Press, Oxford, 2001, pp. 317–356; for a comparison between the *ad hoc* tribunals for the former Yugoslavia and Rwanda and the then draft ICC Statute, see Brown, Bartram S., *Primacy or Complementarity: Reconciling the Jurisdiction of National Courts and International Criminal Tribunals,* Yale Journal of International Law, Vol. 23, 1998, pp. 383–436; for a critical comment see Morris, Madeline, *Complementarity and its Discontents: States, Victims, and the International Criminal Court,* Shelton, Dinah (Ed.), *supra* note 3, pp. 177–201; see also generally Tallgren, Immi, *Completing the 'International Criminal Order',* Nordic Journal of International Law, Vol. 67, 1998, pp. 107–137.

ICC appears to have been committed.[6] When the situation is referred to the Court by the Security Council no additional ground for jurisdiction is needed in the form of a territorial link or one relating to the nationality of the accused.[7] The UN Security Council will make its referral acting under Chapter VII of the UN Charter, which seems to imply that the Council's reference of the situation to the ICC must take place after the Council has determined that the situation constitutes a threat to the peace, breach of the peace or act of aggression.[8] This in its turn would illustrate the close connection not only between the Security Council proper and the ICC, but also of the collective security system as a whole and the ICC. Referral of the situation to the ICC will then constitute one of several measures that may be taken to maintain or restore international peace and security under Article 39 of the UN Charter. This is in line with the emphasis by the Security Council on the respect for international humanitarian law in recent years in its resolutions adopted under Chapter VII of the Charter.[9] An encouraging aspect of Article 13 from the ICC's point of view is that the referral by the

6 Article 13(b). The others who may refer a situation to the Prosecutor are the states parties (Article 13(a)), and the Prosecutor may also initiate an investigation on his or her own initiative (Article 13 (c)). On Article 13 see generally *Commentary on the Rome Satute of the International Criminal Court. Observers' Notes, Article by Article, supra* note 3, pp. 343–351.

7 *Cf.* also Oosthuizen, Gabriël H., *Some Preliminary Remarks on the Relationship between the Envisaged International Criminal Court and the UN Security Council,* Netherlands International Law Review, Vol. 46, 1999, pp. 316–317.

8 *Cf.* Oosthuizen, *ibid.*, p. 320; Sarooshi, Danesh, *Aspects of the Relationship Between the International Criminal Court and the United Nations,* Netherlands Yearbook of International Law, Vol. XXXII, T.M.C. Asser Press, The Hague, 2002, pp. 33–34. On the relationship between the ICC and the Security Council in the context specifically of the crime of aggression in Article 5(1)(d) of the ICC Statute, see Müller-Shieke, Irina Kaye, *Defining the Crime of Aggression Under the Statute of the International Criminal Court,* Leiden Journal of International Law, Vol. 14, 2001, pp. 409–430.

9 See further below section 3, the enforcement of criminal responsibility could be likened to a targeted sanction; both constitute a kind of individualized punishment although the targeted sanction does not presuppose a violation of criminal law (or indeed of any law). Interestingly, the idea of targeted sanctions and of individual criminal responsibility (after the first post-World War II wave) have developed in parallel during the same period of time (*Cf.* the recent report Wallensteen, Peter, Staibano, Carina, Eriksson, Mikael (Eds.), *Making Targeted Sanctions Effective. Guidelines for the Implementation of UN Policy Options,* Results from the Stockholm Process on the Implementation of Targeted Sanctions, Uppsala University, Department of Peace and Conflict Research, Uppsala, 2003.)

Security Council of a situation to the Prosecutor is not compulsory for the Court. Article 13 states that '[t]he Court *may* exercise its jurisdiction (emphasis added)' *inter alia* if a situation is referred to the Prosecutor by the Security Council. Thus it is for the Court to decide, and not the Security Council, whether the case eventually shall be admissible or not before the Court.

Another distinguishing aspect of the Security Council's referral of a situation to the Prosecutor compared with the referral of a situation to the Prosecutor by a state party or the initiation by the Prosecutor of an investigation is the procedure relating to the possible deferral by the Prosecutor to a state's own investigation of the case. As we have seen earlier, the ICC shall be complementary to national criminal jurisdictions.[10]

When the situation is referred to the Prosecutor by a state party or the Prosecutor initiates the investigation, a procedure is foreseen whereby 'the Prosecutor shall notify all States Parties and those States which, taking into account the information available, would normally exercise jurisdiction over the crimes concerned'.[11] If a state has begun investigations, the Prosecutor of the ICC shall, if the state so requests, defer to the state's investigation unless the Pre-Trial Chamber of the ICC decides to authorize the investigation by the Prosecutor.[12] The deferral of the investigation is neither absolute nor definitive, but shows that the states have the first choice as to whether to take care of the investigations of the relevant crimes themselves or not. The procedure described strengthens the presumption in favour of national jurisdiction.

No similar procedure is foreseen when it is the Security Council who has initially referred the situation to the Prosecutor. Thus the jurisdictional position of the states is somewhat weaker when it is the Security Council who refers a situation to the ICC. The admissibility of a case before the ICC, however, is always eventually conditional upon the state having jurisdiction over it not investigating or

10 Article 1 of the ICC Statute.

11 Article 18(1) of the ICC Statute. The Article is entitled 'Preliminary rulings regarding admissibility'. On Article 18, see generally *Commentary of the Rome Statute of the ICC. Observers' Notes, Article by Article, supra* note 3, pp. 395–404.

12 Article 18(2) of the ICC Statute.

prosecuting the case itself.[13] Or, the state may have investigated the case but decided not to prosecute the person concerned, in which case the ICC is also prevented from admitting the case.[14] These conditions seem to apply as well when it is the Security Council who has referred a situation to the ICC; a referral by the Security Council does not overrun complementarity.[15]

The deferral to a state's own investigation or prosecution is conditional upon the state's genuine willingness and ability to investigate and prosecute the crimes concerned.[16] It is for the ICC to decide whether a state is willing and able to carry out the investigation and prosecution.[17]

The link between the Security Council and the ICC described so far strengthens the position of the ICC in that the Security Council is one more actor who may bring a situation before the Prosecutor. This would tend to increase the likelihood, at least in theory that more situations will reach the Prosecutor of the ICC. If the Security Council would refer a situation to the ICC this would also lend political support to the ICC, something which not all permanent members of the Security Council currently would like to see happen it seems.[18]

Perhaps the referral by the Security Council of a situation to the ICC would imply a certain political pressure on the ICC to also declare the case admissible, but in the end it is the Court that retains the right to decide on admissibility. The referral of a case to the ICC by the Security Council does not decrease the formal judi-

13 Article 17(1)(a) ICC Statute. On Article 17 see generally *Commentary on the Rome Statute of the International Criminal Court. Observers' Notes, Article by Article, supra* note 3, pp. 383–394.

14 Article 17(1)(b) ICC Statute.

15 *Cf.* Summers, Mark A., *A Fresh Look at the Jurisdictional Provisions of the Statute of the International Criminal Court: The Case for Scrapping the Treaty,* Wisconsin International Law Journal, Vol. 20, 2001, pp. 78–80; and Oosthuizen, *supra* note 7, p. 326. The particularly strict procedural regime in favour of national investigation laid down in Article 18 of the ICC Statute, however, does not apply to the cases referred to the Court by the Security Council (*Cf.* also Brown, Bartram S., *US Objections to the Statute of the International Criminal Court: A Brief Response,* New York University Journal of International Law and Politics, Vol. 31, 1998–1999, pp. 881–882).

16 Article 17(1)(a) and (b); 17(2); 17(3) ICC Statute.

17 Article 17(2) and (3) ICC Statute.

18 Of the permanent members, China, Russia and the US are not parties to the ICC Statute.

cial independence of the ICC.[19] If no cases are referred to the ICC by the Security Council, which would seem to be the most likely development for the foreseeable future, at least no harm is done to the ICC.[20] If, on the contrary, cases are referred to the ICC by the Security Council this could only be advantageous to the Court. The ICC thus would seem to have everything to win from the clause permitting the Security Council to refer situations to it.[21]

It is often pointed out that since the ICC is wholly dependent on the cooperation with the states parties in order for investigations to be carried out and criminals to be arrested – contrary for instance to the *ad hoc* tribunal for the former Yugoslavia which is backed up by the NATO-led SFOR in Bosnia-Herzegovina and KFOR in Kosovo – its chances of success are slight.[22] This is irrespective of the formal right of the ICC to claim jurisdiction if a state, which may also claim jurisdiction, is unwilling or unable to carry out the investigation or prosecution.[23] The ICC will be dependent on the willingness

19 *Cf.* Sarooshi, *supra* note 8, p. 29 *et seq.*, who, contrary to this author, seems to fear that neither the Prosecutor nor the Court will be able to resist the political pressure by the Security Council should the occasion arise. From a slightly different angle, *cf.* also Condorelli, Luigi and Villalpando, Santiago, *Can the Security Council extend the ICC's jurisdiction?*, Cassese, Antonio, Gaeta, Paola, Jones, John R.W.D. (Eds.), The Rome Statute of the International Criminal Court: A Commentary, Vol. 1, Oxford University Press, Oxford 2002, pp. 571–582. Sarooshi points out that the Security Council may threaten to create an *ad hoc* tribunal instead, if the ICC does not do as the Council wishes (*supra* note 8, p. 34). *Cf.* also Article 53(3)(a) ICC Statute.

20 *Cf.* Broomhall, Bruce, *International Justice and the International Criminal Court*, Oxford University Press, Oxford, New York 2003, p. 161.

21 Indeed, as argued by Morten Bergsmo, the ICC will most likely be dependent on referrals by the Security Council for a foreseeable future since the states who have ratified the ICC Statute so far are not likely to provide the ICC with cases (*Occasional Remarks on Certain State Concerns about the Jurisdictional Reach of the International Criminal Court, and Their Possible Implications for the Relationship between the Court and the Security Council,* Nordic Journal of International Law, Vol. 69, 2000, pp. 87–113); on the same note, see Berman, Sir Franklin, *The Relationship Between the International Criminal Court and the Security Council,* Herman, A.M., Lammers, Johan G. and Schukking, Jolien (Eds.), Reflections on the International Criminal Court, Essays in Honour of Adriaan Bos, von Hebel, T.M.C. Asser Press, The Hague, 1999, pp. 173, 180.

22 *Cf.* Part 9 ICC Statute on International Cooperation and Judicial Assistance. See further for instance Mochochoko, Phakiso, *International Cooperation and Judicial Assistance,* Lee, Roy S. (Ed.), The International Criminal Court. The Making of the Rome Statute – Issues, Negotiations, Results, Kluwer Law International, The Hague, London, Boston, 1999, pp. 305–317.

23 Article 17(1)(a) ICC Statute.

and ability of the individual state or states concerned to cooperate even if it is the ICC who carries out the investigation.[24] Undeniably, the inability or even unwillingness on the part of the parties to the ICC Statute to cooperate with the Court – not to speak of the non-parties – would constitute a considerable problem.

Under no circumstances will the ICC itself be able to force state parties to cooperate. As far as the use of force is concerned it is theoretically possible that the ICC would be assisted by the Security Council who could determine that the failure to cooperate with the ICC on the part of a state party – or even any state constituted a threat to the peace under Article 39 of the UN Charter and as a consequence authorize the use of military force in the last resort against the uncooperative state or states in order to assist the ICC.[25] In case a state party fails to co-operate and the matter was referred to the ICC by the Security Council, it is explicitly provided for in the ICC Statute that the Court may refer the issue of non-cooperation to the Security Council.[26] In case a non-party state that has entered into an *ad hoc* arrangement with the ICC[27] fails to cooperate, the Court may so inform the Security Council, according to the Statute, on condition as well that the matter had been referred to the Court by the Council.[28] Since only France and the UK among the permanent

24 *Cf.* Henquet, Thomas, *Mandatory Compliance Powers vis-à-vis States by the Ad Hoc Tribunals and the International Criminal Court: A Comparative Analysis,* Leiden Journal of International Law, Vol. 12, 1999, pp. 969–999.

25 *Cf.* Sarooshi, *supra* note 8, p. 36 *et seq.* Morten Bergsmo argues that due to the weak state co-operation regime of the ICC Statute, the ICC is in reality wholly dependent on the support of the Security Council in order to prepare and conduct trials effectively (Bergsmo, *supra* note 21, pp. 97–98, 110). *Cf.* also Oosthuizen, *supra* note 7, p. 340: '[T]hat the Court will founder or flourish on [its relationship with the Security Council] is clear.' Sarooshi again similarly states that '[t]here is an inextricable link between the effective operation of the ICC and an active role being played by the UN Security Council to support this fledgling institution' (Sarooshi, *supra* note 8, p. 52). *Cf.* also Gowlland-Debbas, Vera, *The Relationship Between the Security Council and the Projected International Criminal Court,* Journal of Armed Conflict Law, Vol. 3, June 1998, pp. 97–119.

26 Article 87(7) ICC Statute. On Article 87, see generally *Commentary on the Rome Statute of the International Criminal Court: Observers' Comments, Article by Article, supra* note 3, pp. 1055–1068.

27 Article 12(3).

28 Article 87(5)(b) ICC Statute. Oosthuizen points out that the ICC should reasonably be entitled to inform the Security Council of the non-party's non-cooperation even in the absence of an *ad hoc* arrangement or agreement (*supra* note 7, p. 339).

members of the Security Council have ratified the Statute of the ICC so far it seems unlikely that the Security Council would be able to unite on military measures in support of the work of the ICC, even if these measures were taken against states with which the permanent members did not sympathize.[29] A cooperative relationship between the Security Council and the ICC would be one of the best ways of strengthening the ICC – and perhaps in the long run the Security Council.

9.2.2 Deferral

Another link between the ICC and the Security Council which is less favourable not to say potentially destructive to the working of the Court finds expression in Article 16 of the ICC Statute which, contrary to Article 13, states that no investigation or prosecution may be commenced or proceeded with under the Statute for a period of twelve months after the Security Council, in a resolution adopted under Chapter VII of the UN Charter, has requested the Court to that effect.[30] The request may be renewed by the Council under the same conditions.[31]

Perhaps showing which of the two links between the ICC and the Security Council that will play the greatest role at least at short sight, Article 16 has already been used and was resorted to immediately upon the entry into force of the Statute of the ICC. On 12 July 2002, on the initiative of the US, the Security Council in Resolution 1422 requested that for a twelve-month period the ICC should not commence or proceed with investigation or prosecution of any case

29 *Cf.* Broomhall, *supra* note 20, p. 131.

30 On Article 16, see generally *Commentary on the Rome Statute of the International Criminal Court. Observers' Notes, Article by Article, supra* note 3, pp. 373–382. Morten Bergsmo and Jelena Pejic make the interesting reflection that by such a resolution, adopted under Chapter VII as it is, the Security Council acknowledges implicitly that ICC proceedings would be detrimental to international peace and security and they continue prophetically: 'In practice the costs of such an acknowledgement to Security Council credibility might prove very high.' (*Ibid.* pp. 381–382).

31 Yee, Lionel, *The International Criminal Court and The Security Council: Articles 13(b) and 16'*, Lee, Roy S. (Ed.), The International Criminal Court, The Making of the Rome Statue – Issues, Negotiations, Results, Kluwer Law International, The Hague, London, Boston, 1999, pp. 143–152, goes through the different versions of what was eventually to become Article 16 that were on the negotiating table.

involving current or former officials or personnel from a contributing state not a party to the ICC Statute concerning acts or omissions relating to a UN established or authorized operation.[32] The twelve-month period was to be counted from 1 July 2002.

In the same Resolution the Security Council also expressed the intention to renew the request each 1 July for further twelve-month periods for as long as may be necessary.[33] This intention was followed up by Resolution 1487 adopted by the Council on 12 June 2003.[34]

The connection between the ICC and international peace and security more generally finds expression in Resolution 1422 although in a negative way. The Resolution determines that it is in the interests of international peace and security to facilitate member states' ability to contribute to operations established or authorized by the UN Security Council.[35] The implicit message is that the risk of having one's citizens brought before the ICC will render it more difficult for member states, or certain member states in particular, not party to the ICC Statute to contribute to UN peace-keeping operations. Or inversely, that the absence of such a risk will facilitate the ability of the sceptic member state(s) to participate in UN

32 S.C. Resolution 1422 (12 July 2002) (15-0), operative (op.) paragraph (para.) 1. Marc Weller points out that although Resolution 1422 is explicitly adopted under Chapter VII of the UN Charter, it does not identify the threat to international peace and security justifying such action (*Undoing the Global Constitution: UN Security Council Action on the International Criminal Court*, International Affairs, Vol. 78, 2002, p. 707) Among a current total of 97 states contributing a total of 55,470 troops, military observers and civilian policemen to 16 UN operations, the US ranks twentyfourth with a total of 532 persons, www.un.org/Depts/dpko/dpko/contributors/index.htm (18 June 2004). Mark Zwanenburg argues convincingly that the US fears of ICC prosecution of American peacekeepers are largely unjustified, *The Statute for an International Criminal Court and the United States: Peacekeepers under Fire?,* European Journal of International Law, Vol. 10, 1999, pp. 124–143. On the relationship between the US and the ICC in general, see Sewall, Sarah B. and Kaysen, Carl (Eds.) *The United States and the International Criminal Court. National Security and International Law*, Rowman & Littlefield Publishers, Lanham, Boulder, New York, Oxford, 2000.

33 S.C. Resolution 1422 (2002), op. para. 2. It should be noted that ordinary voting rules apply in the Security Council also when the request is possibly renewed.

34 S.C. Resolution 1487 (12 June 2003) (12-0-3 (France, Germany, Syria). *Cf.* also S.C. Resolution 1497 (1 August 2003) (12-0-3 (France, Germany, Mexico)), op. para. 7 with respect to the Multinational Force and UN stabilization force in Liberia.

35 S.C. Resolution 1422 (2002), preambular (pre.) para. 7.

operations, which in their turn, according to the Resolution, are of great importance to international peace and security. Thus the Resolution hints a negative correlation between the activities of the ICC and international peace and security, which of course is bad for the image and status of the ICC.[36]

It can be noted that Article 16 in the ICC Statute, which allows for the exceptions to the jurisdiction initiated by the Security Council, mentions both investigation and prosecution as to what the Security Council may stop. In Resolution 1422 the Security Council is careful to hinder both investigation and prosecution of any case involving persons from a state not party to the ICC Statute. The Security Council Resolution also specifies that the ICC may neither commence nor proceed with investigation or prosecution, but considering that the Resolution and the ICC Statute came into effect the same day it is unlikely that the ICC would have initiated any investigation that it could 'proceed with' according to the resolution. In view of further renewals of the request for exceptions to the jurisdiction of the ICC by the Security Council the phrase 'proceed with' investigation or prosecution may be relevant, although if the ICC has never commenced any investigation against a person coming from a state not a party to the ICC Statute it is hard to see how the ICC may ever 'proceed with' such an investigation.

In theory but hardly in practice it is possible to imagine a situation where the Prosecutor of the ICC begins an investigation, finds that there are strong indications of crimes having been committed, submits a request for authorization of an investigation to the Pre-Trial Chamber which is granted, and then the Security Council intervenes with a resolution stopping the Prosecutor from proceeding with the investigation. Or, even worse, if the investigation is proceeded with to the point where the Prosecutor seeks trial against particular per-

36 *Cf.* also Smidt, Michael L., *The International Criminal Court: An Effective Means of Deterrence?,* Military Law Review, Vol. 167, 2001, pp. 156–240, who not only hints but argues explicitly that the ICC will lead to more international violence, not less. Smith, Thomas W., *Moral Hazard and Humanitarian Law: The International Criminal Court and the Limits of Legalism,* International Politics, Vol. 39, 2002, p. 189, is afraid precisely that humanitarian law will replace humanitarian intervention (simply speaking he fears less violence): '[P]rogress in humanitarian law should not weaken international resolve to use violence when necessary to stop human rights disasters.'

sons and then the Security Council stops the prosecution, or worse still if the Security Council intervenes to stop an on-going trial.

It would seem most likely that the Security Council would want to intervene as early as possible in the procedure, preferably before any investigation what so ever has been initiated, in order to avoid having to be ashamed of stopping the course of justice at a point where it is obvious that serious crimes have been committed and that the Security Council is aiming to protect those who are suspected of having committed these crimes. The worst would be if the Security Council adopted this kind of resolution in the middle of an on-going trial before the ICC, when the evidence against certain suspects became too convincing for instance.[37] It is theoretically possible under the ICC Statute that the Security Council would intervene in the procedure at this late stage, but for reasons of the public image of the Security Council in practice it is unlikely.[38] From the point of view of the ICC it is equally bad that the Security Council may hinder investigations from the very outset.

From the point of view of the Security Council and the states protected by the Resolution, Resolution 1422 was exemplary since it hinders anything to be done involving persons from states not party to the ICC Statute from the inception of the ICC.

A different but closely related situation to the hypothetic one described above when the Security Council intervenes with a resolution at a late state in the investigation or during the very trial before the ICC is where a permanent member of the Council who has ratified the ICC Statute initiates a hindering resolution when it becomes obvious that persons from that state risk being indicted with or convicted of serious crimes before the ICC.[39] If the perma-

37 *Cf. mutatis mutandis* the case of Libya when the Security Council adopted Resolution 748 of 31 March 1992, under Chapter VII of the UN Charter during the proceedings on provisional measures before the International Court of Justice (ICJ) (Questions of Interpretation and Application of the 1971 Montreal Convention arising from the Aerial Incident at Lockerbie (*Libyan Arab Jamahiriya* v. *United Kingdom/United States of America*), Provisional Measures, Order of 14 April 1992, ICJ Reports, 1992, p. 3).

38 *Cf.* Sarooshi, *supra* note 8, p. 39 *et seq.*, who discusses the hypothetical situation where the Council intervenes at an even later stage in the proceedings, when the trial has been completed and the judgment is pending or where a person has been convicted but not sentenced.

39 As we have seen, among the permanent members of the Security Council, France and the United Kingdom have ratified the ICC Statute so far.

nent member succeeds in convincing the other members of the Security Council that the resolution should be adopted there is on the one hand the ratification by the concerned state of the Statute of the ICC and on the other hand the resolution by the Security Council, under Chapter VII, stopping any further investigation or prosecution. It would seem as if the resolution by the Security Council would legally precede the ratification by the permanent member in this example of the ICC Statute due to Article 103 of the UN Charter.

Apart from the legal formalities, such a manoeuvre in order to avoid prosecution before the ICC would put the ratifying state to great shame, to the extent that the state would care. The same would apply to any other state party to the ICC Statute who would succeed in convincing the Security Council to take up its cause. Most likely it would be easier for a permanent member to convince the other members of the Security Council to engage in such an endeavour.

An alternative action for the state whose citizens risk being indicted before the ICC, and whose loyalty toward the Court is not entirely genuine, would be to withdraw from the Statute of the ICC. This is allowed under Article 127 of the Statute. The withdrawal, however, only takes effect one year after the receipt of the notification by the UN Secretary-General and does not discharge the state from the obligations arising from the Statute while it was a party.[40]

If looked upon from the point of view of the Security Council and individual states not favourably disposed toward the ICC, the possibility of having a Council resolution stopping investigation or prosecution before the ICC is a safety-clause in order both to avoid prosecution on the whole for crude political reasons and to avoid prosecution in case the ICC should turn out to be incompetent, biased or otherwise unable to carry out fair trials. Of course the latter is a matter of judgment to a high degree and may be used as a pretext for avoiding the jurisdiction of the ICC in a particular case.

From the point of view of the Security Council too and from the perspective of international peace and security generally the argument could be made that the possibility of stopping investigation or prosecution before the ICC could be a way of avoiding a disturbing

40 Article 127(1) and (2) ICC Statute.

trial during sensitive peace negotiations and thus a way of facilitating the achievement of a peace agreement, be it at the sacrifice of justice. Such an argument would seem old-fashioned, and little convincing, however, when much evidence would seem to point to the opposite conclusion *i.e.* that the proper course of justice facilitates the attainment of genuine peace and is indeed a prerequisite of lasting peace and security.[41] The question nowadays is no longer one of choosing between justice or peace but of necessarily having both or none, or considering the one to be the requisite of the other, not the opposite. The Security Council itself has strongly emphasized the connection between justice and peace in recent years. In numerous resolutions has the Council repeated that crimes against international humanitarian law constitute a threat to international peace and security or, inversely, that respect for international humanitarian law is a prerequisite of international peace and security. The Security Council has even gone so far as to hint that the lack of a credible justice system within a state in order to get to the bottom of suspected crimes against humanitarian law – in Sierra Leone as it were – constitutes a threat to international peace and security.[42] And of course, and not least, the Security Council has created two *ad hoc* tribunals – one for the former Yugoslavia and one for Rwanda – in order to bring suspected humanitarian criminals to justice which, if anything, should illustrate the belief of the Security Council in jus-

41 The closest one can come to an empirical investigation of this relationship to date is the study by Long, William J. and Brecke, Peter, *War and Reconciliation. Reason and Emotion in Conflict Resolution*, The MIT Press, Cambridge, Massachusetts, London, 2003. *Cf.* also Williams, Paul R. and Scharf, Michael P., *Peace with Justice? War Crimes and Accountability in the Former Yugoslavia*, Rowman & Littlefield Publishers, Lanham, Boulder, New York, Oxford, 2002; Neuffer, Elizabeth, *The Key to My Neighbor's House: Seeking Justice in Bosnia and Rwanda*, Picador, New York, 2001; Akhavan, Payam, *Justice in the Hague, Peace in the Former Yugoslavia? A Commentary on the United Nations War Crimes Tribunal*, Human Rights Quarterly, Vol. 20, 1998, pp. 737–816. In a thoughtful Article on the indispensable independence of the ICC, Sylvia de Bertodano argues that at least '[p]olitical interference ... does not necessarily achieve ... the political ends it seeks', *Judicial Independence in the International Criminal Court,* Leiden Journal of International Law, Vol. 15, 2002, p. 429. On a related ambiguous relationship, see Ratner, Steven R., *Democracy and Accountability: the Criss-Crossing Paths of Two Emerging Norms,* Fox, Gregory H. and Roth, Brad R. (Eds.), Democratic Governance and International Law, Cambridge University Press, Cambridge, 2000, pp. 449–490.

42 See further *infra* note 64.

tice as a measure to maintain or restore national and international peace and security. A belief it should be added which manifests itself more strongly in some cases than others.

What will be the likely significance to the ICC of Article 16? If in practice only the US is prone to make use of it the significance of Article 16 will be limited, although the US is not any country but the most powerful state in the world so that the consequences of the US unwillingness to cooperate with the Court will be considerable nevertheless. Still the situation would become even worse if more great powers practised the same hostile policy toward the ICC as the US.[43]

According to the way in which Security Council Resolution 1422 is drafted, however, no case relating to persons coming from any state not party to the ICC shall be dealt with by the ICC, thus not only US citizens, which means that the scope of the Resolution in fact becomes very wide although it was primarily the US who wanted the resolution to be adopted. Possibly other states not party to the ICC Statute finds it convenient to be protected by the Resolution as well even though they would not actively had sought for such a resolution themselves.[44] The states that are covered by the wording of the Security Council resolution although they may not wish to be so can always indicate to the Prosecutor of the ICC, once he or she is in place, that they would not mind their citizens being brought before the Court should the case arise.[45] Many states would probably hesitate to do this, however, once they have the option of shielding their citizens behind a Security Council resolution.

Also, it is not evident that individual states not party to the ICC Statute but not as unfavourably disposed toward the Court as the US are even allowed under UN Charter law to step out of the protec-

43 Judicial review by the ICC may narrow the scope of any resolution adopted by the Security Council under Article 16; *Cf.* Sarooshi, *supra* note 8, pp. 47–48; Condorelli, Luigi and Villalpando, Santiago, *Referral and Deferral by the Security Council, supra* note 19, pp. 627–655, pp. 650, 651, and 653. Incidentally, Condorelli and Villalpando seem to have largely underrated the destructive potential of Article 16 in practice. *Cf.* also Oosthuizen, *supra* note 7, pp. 331–334.

44 India sympathizes with the US concerns and China and Russia are conspicuously vague (UN Security Council, S/PV. 4568, 10 July 2002). In 2003 Pakistan expresses its support for the US concerns and China and Russia continue to make empty statements (S/PV. 4772, 12 June 2003).

45 As noted above, under Article 12(3) of the ICC Statue, a state which is not a party to the Statute may, by declaration lodged with the Registrar, accept the exercise of jurisdiction by the Court on an *ad hoc* basis.

tion granted them by the Security Council Resolution, and even if they would be, that the ICC would be allowed to investigate or prosecute cases involving persons from these countries even if the countries themselves agree to this. Again, according to the way the Resolution is drafted the ICC is in fact prevented from dealing with these cases without exception and the assent of one individual state would not seem to change this. The only exception provided for in the Resolution is if the Security Council decides otherwise, so that a state who is not party to the ICC Statute but who hypothetically would like the ICC to investigate or prosecute a case involving its citizens would have to persuade the Security Council to adopt a resolution exempting this state from the general protection by the Resolution. This would be to demand quite a lot from a state in order for the state to have its own citizens brought before an international court. Only the most convinced states would carry out this form of self-inflicted loss of face, as it appears to be, and if they are so convinced one may ask why they did not ratify the ICC Statute in the first place. Thus on the whole it is not likely that any state now covered by the Security Council Resolution will voluntarily abstain from this protection unless of course the state decides to ratify the Statute of the ICC.

If resolutions of the kind adopted by the Security Council upon the inception of the ICC continue to be as broadly formulated and many states, and big and important states in particular, wish to make use of this possibility then Article 16 may have a significant negative impact on the ICC. This impact will be greater the more states choose to remain non-parties to the ICC Statute. More ratifications on the other hand will probably, although not certainly, solve the problem of Article 16 and of the ensuing Security Council resolutions and of course generally be of crucial, positive, significance to the working of the ICC.

In the case of the current Security Council Resolution the only limitation to the ban on ICC involvement is that the acts or omissions which would otherwise have been the subject of investigation or prosecution relate to a UN established or authorized operation.[46] Thus if the suspected crimes have been committed outside the

46 S.C. Resolution 1422 (2002), op. para. 1.

framework of a UN operation the Resolution does not apply and the citizens of states not party to the ICC Statute may be the subject of investigation or prosecution before the ICC, provided that all other conditions are fulfilled relating to the jurisdiction of the Court.[47]

9.3 Links between the ICC and the collective security system as a whole

9.3.1 The *ad hoc* tribunals as enforcement measures

Since the end of the Cold War, *i.e.* since the beginning of the 1990s, a new and increasing emphasis on international humanitarian law and individual criminal responsibility has found expression in the practice of the UN Security Council under Chapter VII of the UN Charter.

The appearance of references to humanitarian law and individual criminal responsibility in the resolutions of the Security Council bears witness to the connection made by the Security Council between law and individual responsibility on the one hand and the maintenance and restoration of international peace and security on the other. Expressed in more general terms one could say that recently the Security Council makes an unprecedented connection, in the practice of the Council, between justice and order.

47 The US, however, is concluding so called 'Article 98 agreements' – surely unforeseen by the drafters of the ICC Statute – with as many states as possible in order to protect its citizens from being handed over to the ICC (see Article 98(2) ICC Statute (Article 98 is entitled 'Cooperation with regard to waiver of immunity and consent to surrender')). So far, the US has concluded such agreements with at least 79 states, www.iccnow.org (18 June 2004). For a critical comment, *cf.*, for instance Weller, *supra* note 32, pp. 708–709. *Cf.* also Council common position 2002/474/CFSP of 20 June 2002 amending common position 2001/443/CFSP on the International Criminal Court; Council common position 2003/444/CFSP of 16 June 2003 on the International Criminal Court; Council Conclusions, 30 September 2002 on the International Criminal Court, including the annexed EU Guiding Principles concerning Arrangements between a State Party to the Rome Statute of the International Criminal Court and the United States Regarding the Conditions to surrender of Persons to the Court. *Cf.* also Editorial Comment, *The European Union, the United States and the International Criminal Court,* Common Market Law Review, Vol. 39, 2002, pp. 939–944; US Congress, *Unilateral Enforcement of Immunity before the International Criminal Court (ICC),* American Servicemembers' Protection Act (ASPA), Entry into force 2 August 2002, quoted in Human Rights Law Journal, Vol. 23, 2002, pp. 275–279.

This trend is discernible also outside the framework of the Security Council, and is thus not limited to the collective security system of the UN.[48] In many countries where there has been civil unrest, truth and reconciliation commissions have been created in recent years in order to deal with the responsibility of individuals, legal or moral, as a means of furthering peace and security at the domestic level.[49]

With respect to the increased importance of humanitarian law and of individual criminal responsibility, the recent trend is also highly relevant according to which different kinds of state leaders are tried or demanded for extradition to foreign states for trial for alleged human rights and humanitarian law violations. The connection between justice and order in these cases rather concerns the domestic order in the countries in which the leaders originate; the international order is often disturbed by such demands for extradition at least initially.[50] Even if the attempts to have the state leaders tried in foreign countries do not succeed, the mere attempts arguably give evidence of a general trend to give more emphasis to humanitarian law and individual criminal responsibility.[51]

48 Payam Akhavan talks of 'the mainstreamning of criminal justice in international relations', *Beyond Impunity: Can International Criminal Justice Prevent Further Atrocities?,* American Journal of International Law, Vol. 95, 2001, pp. 7–31; against the backdrop, *inter alia,* of the development of the law of war and international criminal law Anne-Marie Slaughter and William Burke-White talk of the 'individualization' of international law, *An International Constitutional Moment,* Harvard International Law Journal, Vol. 43, 2002, pp. 1–21.

49 The U.S. Institute of Peace lists 25 truth commissions established since the 1980s (three were established in the 1980s), www.usip.org/library/truth.html#tc, (18 June 2004). One of the most interesting recent examples of alternative proceedings are the decentralized traditional trials in Rwanda called Gacaca; *Cf.* Cahiers du Centre de gestion des conflits, *Les juridictions Gacaca et le processus de reconciliation nationale,* Butare, Rwanda, 2001; Power, Samantha, *Rwanda: The Two Faces of Justice,* New York Review of Books, 16 January 2003, pp. 47–50.

50 For an analysis of the first in a row of cases, see for instance van Alebeek, Rosanne, *The Pinochet Case: International Human Rights Law on Trial,* British Year Book of International Law, Vol. 71, 2001, pp. 29–70; McLachlan, Campbell, '*Pinochet* Revisited', International and Comparative Law Quarterly, Vol. 51, 2002, pp. 959–966.

51 Although the judgment by the ICJ in the case of *Congo* v. *Belgium* is somewhat discouraging in this respect (*Case concerning the arrest warrant of 11 April 2000 (Democratic Republic of Congo* v. *Belgium*) judgement of 14 February 2002); see also *Case Concerning Certain Criminal Proceedings in France (Republic of the Congo* v. *France*) application filed on 9 December 2002.

The new emphasis by the UN Security Council on the important role of humanitarian law in the context of furthering international peace and security was first manifested in relation to the war in the former Yugoslavia. In 1993 the Council adopted the Resolution establishing the *ad hoc* tribunal for the former Yugoslavia.[52] In the Resolution the Security Council argues in favour of the establishment of an international tribunal and the prosecution of persons responsible for serious violations of international humanitarian law as a means of restoring and maintaining peace.[53] In order not to create a precedent, presumably, the Security Council is careful to point out that it is in the 'particular circumstances of the former Yugoslavia' and 'as an *ad hoc* measure' that the establishment of the international tribunal and the prosecution of the suspected criminals will contribute to the restoration and maintenance of peace.

The principled reasoning of the Security Council regarding the establishment of the *ad hoc* tribunal for the former Yugoslavia is worth quoting in greater detail since in the light of later resolutions the initial reasoning of the Council has turned out to have been of more general significance than the Council itself would perhaps like to admit. Also, since the creation of the *ad hoc* tribunal for Yugoslavia and then later for Rwanda paved the way for the eventual creation of the ICC, the reasoning of the Security Council with respect to the *ad hoc* tribunals is worth closer study.

First, the Security Council expresses its grave alarm at continuing reports of widespread and flagrant violations of international humanitarian law occurring within the territory of the former Yugoslavia.[54] Then the Council determines that 'this situation', most certainly alluding to the violations of humanitarian law, constitutes a threat to international peace and security.[55] Thereafter the Council expresses its determination to put an end to such crimes and to take effective measures to bring to justice the persons who are responsible for them.[56]

52 S.C. Resolution 827 (25 May 1993). The decision to establish an international tribunal was included in S.C. Resolution 808 (22 February 1993).
53 S.C. Resolution 827 (1993), pre. para. 6.
54 *Ibid.*, pre. para. 3.
55 *Ibid.*, pre. para. 4.
56 *Ibid.*, pre. para. 5.

Then comes the most important argument in principle from the point of view of the place of humanitarian law and individual responsibility in the collective security system, in spite of the fact that the Security Council tries to minimize the future effects of its argument by inserting the qualifications about the particular circumstances of the case of Yugoslavia that we just saw above. The Security Council states that it is convinced that, in the particular circumstances of the former Yugoslavia, the establishment as an *ad hoc* measure by the Council of an international tribunal and the prosecution of persons responsible for serious violations of international humanitarian law would enable the aim to be achieved of putting an end to the crimes and of taking effective measures against the perpetrators and *would contribute to the restoration and maintenance of peace.*[57]

In many later resolutions the Security Council has found that serious violations of international humanitarian law – and human rights – constitute a threat to the peace, and in some, but not as many resolutions, the Security Council has contributed to the establishment of tribunals in order to ensure that the suspected criminals are brought to justice.

The most obvious example of another tribunal created by the Security Council is the *ad hoc* tribunal for Rwanda established one and a half years after the tribunal for the former Yugoslavia.[58] The reasoning of the Council with respect to Rwanda is almost identical with its reasoning with respect to the case of Yugoslavia, which is not surprising in general since both Resolutions deal with the same kind of situation, but which is still somewhat surprising from what appears to be the Security Council's point of view not to create any precedent. Some paragraphs in the preamble of the Resolution on the Rwandan *ad hoc* tribunal are more or less the same word-forword as the corresponding paragraphs in the preamble of the Resolution on the tribunal for the former Yugoslavia.

In the central paragraph of the Rwandan Resolution, from the point of view again of the place of humanitarian law and individual responsibility in the collective security system, the Security Council states that it is convinced that in the particular circumstances of

57 *Ibid.*, pre. para. 6. (Not italicized in the Resolution.)
58 S.C. Resolution 955 (8 November 1994).

Rwanda, the prosecution of persons responsible for serious violations of international humanitarian law would enable the aim to be achieved of putting an end to the crimes and of taking effective measures to bring the responsible persons to justice and *would contribute to the process of national reconciliation and to the restoration and maintenance of peace.*[59]

In its Resolution on Rwanda the Security Council makes an interesting addition pointing out the significance of the national judicial system of Rwanda and the need for international cooperation to strengthen it, having regard in particular to the necessity for the Rwandan courts to deal with large numbers of suspects.[60] This must imply that the Security Council considers that the strengthening of the national judicial system of Rwanda would also contribute to the process of national reconciliation and to the restoration and maintenance of peace. Inversely and indirectly this must also imply that the lack of an effective national judicial system in Rwanda is considered by the Security Council to hinder national reconciliation and at least to aggravate an already existing threat to the peace, if not constituting a threat to the peace itself. Thus the Council concerns itself not only with international tribunals but also with national courts, should the occasion arise. This illustrates again the importance that the Security Council attaches to humanitarian law and to the prosecution of the suspected criminals.

The reasoning of the Security Council with respect to Rwanda is interesting also because the Council does not limit itself to propagating the prosecution of humanitarian law violators as a means of maintaining or restoring the peace most immediately, but it also argues that prosecuting the persons responsible would contribute to the larger process of national reconciliation in Rwanda.[61] Again this serves to illustrate the significance that the Security Council attaches to the trials of individuals as a way of consolidating the peace and facilitating the harmonious post-conflict development of the society, and as an element of the collective security system.

The national reconciliation element of the Council's Resolution on Rwanda is emphasized by the fact that by the time the Security

59 *Ibid.*, pre. para. 7. (Not italicized in the Resolution.)
60 *Ibid.*, pre. para. 9.
61 S.C. Resolution 955 (1994), pre. para. 7.

Council decided to establish the *ad hoc* tribunal the genocide and the civil war was already over so that the peace even if fragile had already been restored in Rwanda, when the tribunal was established (and the tribunal thus was not indispensable to the restoration of peace). The tribunal no doubt could help in maintaining the peace, which is also referred to in the Resolution, which comes close to what must be meant by the process of national reconciliation. Still, the decision was taken somewhat after the fact, which contributes to the impression that it was not the threat to the peace as such which was central to the Security Council, but rather the enforcement of the individual responsibility of those who had committed the genocide and other serious violations of international humanitarian law.[62]

Tellingly, contrary to the case of Yugoslavia where the Security Council expresses its alarm at the grave violations of international humanitarian law 'occurring' within the territory of the former Yugoslavia, in the case of Rwanda the Security Council expresses its concern at the genocide and other violations of international humanitarian law that 'have been committed' in Rwanda.[63] The *post factum* nature of the Resolution establishing the *ad hoc* tribunal for Rwanda brings out the importance of legal proceedings as such against humanitarian law offenders as a component of collective security, either there exists an immediate threat to the peace or not. It brings out the judicial element of collective security, just like the creation of the ICC does.

62 Some paragraphs in the preamble of Resolution 955 (1994) still are formulated as if the fighting was still going on in Rwanda when the Resolution was adopted: The Security Council determines that the situation continues to constitute a threat to international peace and security (pre. para. 5) and the Council states that it is determined to put an end to such crimes and to take effective measures to bring to justice the persons who are responsible for them (pre. para. 6). The Council is also convinced that the prosecution of the responsible persons would contribute to the restoration and maintenance of peace (pre. para. 7). The Council also states its belief that the establishment of the *ad hoc* tribunal will contribute to ensuring that such violations are halted and effectively redressed (pre. para. 8).

63 S.C. Resolution 827 (1993), pre. para. 3, and S.C. Resolution 955 (1994) pre. para. 4 respectively.

9.3.2 Continuing efforts at peace through individual justice

In a more recent case the Security Council returned to the issue of prosecuting those responsible for serious crimes against international humanitarian law. This time the Security Council was concerned with the aftermath of the civil strife in Sierra Leone and with the creation of the so called Special Court to deal with the serious crimes having been committed within the territory of Sierra Leone.[64] Incidentally, in Resolution 1315 the Security Council determined that the situation in Sierra Leone continues to constitute a threat to international peace and security, but no explicit reference is made to Chapter VII of the UN Charter.

In the preamble of the Resolution the Security Council speaks clearly of the importance of compliance with international humanitarian law and of the individual responsibility of those committing or authorizing serious violations.[65] The Council reaffirms solemnly that the international community will exert every effort to bring those responsible to justice in accordance with international standards of justice, fairness and due process of law.[66]

Then comes the central paragraph in the preamble with regard to the importance of individual legal accountability as an element of collective security. Just like in the cases of the former Yugoslavia and Rwanda the Security Council, for what it is worth, is careful to point out the particularity of the situation in Sierra Leone. The Security Council recognizes that, in the particular circumstances of

64 S.C. Resolution 1315 (14 August 2000), op. para. 10. The agreement on the Special Court was concluded between the UN and Sierra Leone on 16 January 2002. In 2003 a noteworthy indictment was issued by the Special Court against the incumbent President of Liberia, Charles Taylor. On the Court see further Cryer, Robert, *A 'Special Court' for Sierra Leone?,* International and Comparative Law Quarterly, Vol. 50, 2001, pp. 435–446; Linton, Suzannah, *Cambodia, East Timor and Sierra Leone: Experiments in International Justice,* Criminal Law Forum, Vol. 12, 2001, pp. 231–241; McDonald, Avril, *Sierra Leone's Shoestring Special Court,* International Review of the Red Cross, Vol. 84, No. 845, 2002, pp. 121–143; Schocken, Celina, *The Special Court for Sierra Leone: Overview and Recommendations,* Berkeley Journal of International Law, Vol. 20, 2002, pp. 436–460; Macaluso, Daniel J., *Absolute and Free Pardon: The Effect of the Amnesty Provision in the Lomé Peace Agreement on the Jurisdiction of the Special Court for Sierra Leone,* Brooklyn Journal of International Law, Vol. 27, 2001–2002, pp. 347–380. A Truth and Reconciliation Commission has also been established in Sierra Leone (Resolution 1315 (2000), op. para. 11).

65 *Ibid.*, pre. para. 6.

66 *Ibid.*

Sierra Leone, a credible system of justice and accountability for the very serious crimes committed there would end impunity and would contribute to the process of national reconciliation and to the restoration and maintenance of peace.[67] The way the Security Council includes the system of justice in its reasoning hints that it is not only the prosecution of those having committed serious human rights violations during the civil war which is important to national reconciliation and peace but the existence of a system of justice on the whole.

This impression is strengthened further by the recognition by the Security Council of the desire of the Government of Sierra Leone for assistance from the UN in establishing a strong and credible court that will meet the objectives of bringing justice and ensuring lasting peace.[68] And even more by the observation by the Security Council of the negative impact of the security situation on the administration of justice in Sierra Leone and the pressing need for international cooperation to assist in strengthening the judicial system of Sierra Leone.[69] Just like in the case of Rwanda the Security Council concerns itself with the national judicial system of Sierra Leone, and thus not only with the international tribunals, as one important factor in building a lasting peace.

If one stretches the argument of the Security Council a little, one could say that, inversely, the absence of a credible system of justice constitutes a threat to the peace, at least indirectly or potentially. If this understanding were correct, then the Security Council would have progressed in three steps with respect to its broader and broader interpretation of the concept of threat to the peace under Article 39 of the UN Charter.

First, serious crimes against human rights and humanitarian law were considered a threat to the peace. Then the lack of democracy was added to the threats to the peace. And now, perhaps, the absence of a credible system of justice is also considered a threat to the peace.[70]

67 *Ibid.*, pre. para. 7.
68 *Ibid.*, pre. para. 9.
69 *Ibid.*, pre. para. 11.
70 *Cf.* by this author, *Threat to the Peace. The Interpretation by the Security Council of Article 39 of the UN Charter*, Iustus förlag, Uppsala, 1998.

In the recent and similar case of East Timor, a Commission for Truth, Reception and Reconciliation was created within the framework of the comprehensive administration of East Timor by the UN.[71] Within the framework of the UN administration of East Timor a national criminal justice system was also created including the Special Panels for Serious Crimes at the District Court of Dili dealing with particularly serious crimes of the kind included in the Statute of the ICC.[72] The UN transitional administration in East Timor, and thus the national reconciliation commission created under its *aegis*, was created under Chapter VII of the UN Charter against the background of the situation in East Timor constituting a lingering threat to peace and security.[73]

In the Resolution prior to the one by which the Security Council established the UN transitional administration of East Timor, the Council stressed in a by now familiar way that persons committing serious violations of international humanitarian and human rights law bear individual responsibility.[74]

In Kosovo as well the efforts to strengthen the system of justice has made up an important part of the UN civilian administration of

71 *Cf.* Gorjão, Paulo, *The East Timorese Commission for Reception, Truth and Reconciliation: Chronicle of a Foretold Failure?,* Civil Wars, Vol. 4, 2001, pp. 142–162. For the larger framework, see S.C. Resolution 1272 (25 October 1999). Resolution 1272 states in op. para. 16 that the Security Council '*[c]ondemns* all violence and acts in support of violence in East Timor, *calls* for their immediate end, and *demands* that those responsible for such violence be brought to justice.' *Cf.* generally, Nordquist, Kjell-Åke, *East Timor – Intervention, State-Building, and Reconciliation,* Österdahl, Inger (Ed.), Is Intervention Humanitarian? Protecting Human Rights and Democracy Abroad, Department of Peace and Conflict Research, Uppsala University, Report No. 62, 2002, pp. 25–49.

72 *Cf.* Linton, *supra* note 64, pp. 202–230. The so called Extraordinary Chambers in the courts of Cambodia, established by Cambodian law in 2001, are considered to have been the model, so far unsuccessful, of both East Timor and Sierra Leone, *Cf.* Linton, *ibid.*, pp. 187–202; *Cf.* also Ratner, Steven R. and Abrams, Jason S., *Accountability for Human Rights Atrocities in International Law. Beyond the Nuremberg Legacy,* second edition, Oxford University Press, 2001, Part III: A Case Study: The Atrocities of the Khmer Rouge, pp. 267–328. Recently, the UN General Assembly has adopted a Draft Agreement between the UN and Cambodia concerning the Prosecution under Cambodian Law of Crimes Committed during the Period of Democratic Kampuchea, G.A. Resolution 57/228B (13 May 2003).

73 *Cf.* S.C. Resolution 1272 (1999), pre. para. 16.

74 S.C. Resolution 1264 (15 September 1999), pre. para. 13.

the province.[75] This is both in order to prosecute the persons who have already committed serious violations of international humanitarian law in Kosovo, and to build a lasting peace in the province and thereby rather to prevent future violations of international humanitarian law. The *ad hoc* tribunal for the former Yugoslavia also has the mandate to try individuals accused of serious violations of international humanitarian law in Kosovo. The Security Council specifically referred to violations of humanitarian law going on in Kosovo in one of its Resolutions preceding the intervention by NATO in Kosovo and the ensuing UN civilian administration of the territory.[76]

There have been a great number of cases in addition to the ones mentioned above in relation to which the Security Council has emphasized the role of compliance with international humanitarian law and, more recently, of individual responsibility and accountability. One could almost say that such a reference has become a standard one in the Resolutions of the Security Council dealing with threats to the peace under Chapter VII of the UN Charter, in most cases caused by civil strife.

In the case of Somalia in 1992, the Security Council expresses grave alarm at continuing reports of widespread violations of international humanitarian law occurring in Somalia.[77] In the same Resolution the Security Council authorizes, for the second time, the use of military force in order to establish a secure environment for humanitarian relief operations.[78]

75 *Cf.* S.C. Resolution 1244 (10 June 1999), op. para. 10. *Cf.* generally Brand, Marcus G., *Institution-Building and Human Rights Protection in Kosovo in the Light of UNMIK Legislation,* Nordic Journal of International Law, Vol. 70, 2001, pp. 461–488; Stahn, Carsten, *Constitution Without a State? Kosovo Under the United Nations Constitutional Framework for Self-Government,* Leiden Journal of International Law, 2001, pp. 531–561; Zimmerman, Andreas and Stahn, Carsten, *Yugoslav Territory, United Nations Trusteeship or Sovereign State? Reflections on the Current and Future Legal Status of Kosovo,* Nordic Journal of International Law, Vol. 70, 2001, pp. 423–460.

76 S.C. Resolution 1199 (23 September 1998), pre. para. 11.

77 S.C. Resolution 794 (3 December 1992), pre. para. 8.

78 *Ibid.*, op. para. 10. The first time the Security Council authorized the use of military force for purposes of securing the delivery of humanitarian assistance was with respect to the former Yugoslavia (Bosnia-Herzegovina) in August 1992 (S.C. Resolution 770 (13 August 1992), op. para. 2).

With respect to Burundi in 1996 the Security Council recalls that all persons who commit or authorize the commission of serious violations of international humanitarian law are individually responsible for such violations and should be held accountable.[79]

In the case of the Democratic Republic of Congo in 1996 the Security Council in general terms underlined the obligation of all concerned strictly to respect the relevant provisions of international humanitarian law.[80] Later on in 2000 the Security Council expressed its deep concern at all violations and abuses of human rights and international humanitarian law in particular in the eastern part of the Democratic Republic of Congo.[81]

In its Resolutions with respect to Afghanistan, the Taliban and the al-Qaeda network, the Security Council has referred to international humanitarian law and individual responsibility several times. In 1998 the Security Council reaffirmed that all parties to the then ongoing civil conflict were bound to comply with their obligations under international humanitarian law and in particular under the Geneva Conventions of 12 August 1949, and that persons who commit or order the commission of breaches of the Conventions are individually responsible in respect of such breaches.[82] In 1998 too, and on later occasions, the Security Council states that it remains deeply concerned at the continuing discrimination against girls and women and at other violations of human rights and of international humanitarian law in Afghanistan.[83]

Finally, in 2003 when the Security Council welcomed the deployment of ECOWAS (Economic Community of West African States) and French troops in Côte d'Ivoire and authorized them under Chapter VII to use force to protect their personnel and any civilians immediately threatened with physical violence, the Security Coun-

79 S.C. Resolution 1072 (30 August 1996), pre. para. 6.

80 S.C. Resolution 1080 (15 November 1996), pre. para. 5.

81 S.C. Resolution 1304 (16 June 2000), pre. para. 16; *Cf.* also S.C. Resolution 1484 (30 May 2003), op. paras. 5–7.

82 S.C. Resolution 1214 (8 December 1998), pre. para. 12. See also S.C. Resolution 1386 (20 December 2001), pre. para. 9.

83 S.C. Resolution 1193 (28 August 1998), pre. para. 13. See also S.C. Resolution 1267 (15 October 1999), pre. para. 3; S.C. Resolution 1333 (19 December 2000), pre. para. 12; S.C. Resolution 1386 (20 December 2001), pre. para. 9.

cil had emphatically condemned the violations of human rights and international humanitarian law taking place in Côte d'Ivoire, and almost even more importantly, stressed the need to bring to justice those responsible.[84]

In 2003, likewise, in its groundbreaking Resolution on the post-war administration of Iraq, the Security Council managed to include a preambular paragraph affirming the need for accountability for crimes and atrocities committed by the previous Iraqi regime.[85]

9.4 Will terrorists be prosecuted before the ICC?

If a terrorist action is serious enough to correspond to the crimes over which the ICC has jurisdiction – genocide, crimes against humanity and war crimes – there would seem to be nothing to prevent terrorists and other non-state perpetrators of crimes to be prosecuted before the ICC, if the situation is referred to the ICC by any of the actors entitled to refer cases to the ICC – a state party, the UN Security Council and the Prosecutor of the ICC.[86] The ICC would seem to be entitled to exercise its jurisdiction if the state where the terrorist acts were committed or the state of which the terrorists are nationals is party to the ICC Statute.[87] Judging from the way in which the prerequisites of the different crimes are laid out in the ICC Statute it would seem most likely that terrorists could be guilty of crimes against humanity, if the acts are sufficiently widespread or

84 S.C. Resolution 1464 (4 February 2003), op. paras. 8, 9 and 7 respectively. On international legal aspects of French interventions in Africa, *Cf.* also by this author, *La France dans l'Afrique de l'après-guerre froide. Interventions et justifications*, Document de recherche No. 2. Nordic Africa Institute, Uppsala, 1997.

85 S.C. Resolution 1483 (22 May 2003), pre. para. 11. *Cf.* also S.C. Resolution 1509 (19 September 2003), pre. para. 7 on Liberia; and S.C. Resolution 1529 (29 February 2004), op. para. 7 and S.C. Resolution 1542 (30 April 2004), op. paras. 7 III. (a) and 8 on Haiti.

86 *Cf.* Articles 6,7, 8 and 13 ICC Statute.

87 *Cf.* Article 12 ICC Statute.

systematic.[88] Perhaps genocide could also be carried out by terrorists or other non-state actors.

As far as war crimes are concerned it is specified in the ICC Statute that the Statute is applicable also in armed conflicts not of an international character, *i.e.* in civil wars.[89] Thereby members of guerrilla groups may make themselves guilty of war crimes under the ICC Statute.[90] The rules on war crimes in civil war situations, however, do not apply to situations of internal disturbances and tensions, such as riots, isolated and sporadic acts of violence or other acts of a similar nature so that domestic terrorist acts alone would not seem to be punishable as war crimes.[91] If terrorist acts are used by guerrilla groups as one means of fighting a civil war, the terrorist acts could most likely be prosecuted under the ICC Statute.

It should be added that crimes against the ICC Statute carried out on the territory of a state who is not a party to the Statute, by the state's own nationals, for instance within the context of a civil war will be out of reach of the ICC except if the situation is referred to the ICC by the Security Council.[92] This means that genocide, crimes against humanity or war crimes carried out by a government against its own citizens in such a country are in principle out of reach of the ICC (which illustrates the crucial importance of the Security Council for the proper working of the ICC).

88 *Cf.* Cassese, Antonio, *Terrorism is Also Disrupting Some Crucial Legal Categories of International Law,* European Journal of International Law, Vol. 12, 2001, pp. 994–995; Schrijver, Nico, *Responding to International Terrorism: Moving the Frontiers of International Law for 'Enduring Freedom'?,* Netherlands International Law Review, Vol. 48, 2001, p. 289; Roberts, Adam, *Counter-Terrorism, Armed Force and the Laws of War',* Survival, Vol. 44, 2002, p. 8; *Cf.* also Mettraux, Guénaël, *Crimes Against Humanity in the Jurisprudence of the International Criminal Tribunals for the former Yugoslavia and for Rwanda',* Harvard International Law Journal, Vol. 43, 2002, pp. 237–316.

89 Article 8(2)(c) ICC Statute. On the differentiation between international and non-international armed conflicts in the ICC Statute; see further Spieker, Heike, *The International Criminal Court and Non International Armed Conflicts,* Leiden Journal of International Law, Vol. 13, 2000, pp. 395–425; see also Fenrick, William J., *Should Crimes Against Humanity Replace War Crimes?,* Columbia Journal of Transnational Law, Vol. 37, 1998–1999, pp. 767–785.

90 *Cf.* further Zegveld, Liesbeth, *Accountability of Armed Opposition Groups in International Law,* Cambridge University Press, Cambridge, 2002.

91 Article 8(2)(d) and (f) ICC Statute.

92 *Cf.* Article 12(2) and 13 ICC Statute. On the extension of the ICC's jurisdiction by the Security Council; see further Sarooshi, *supra* note 8, p. 31; and Condorelli and Villalpando, *supra* note 19.

Whether *international* terrorist acts could be punished as war crimes under the ICC Statute is another matter. The most fundamental question would be whether there exists an armed conflict, according to a generally accepted definition of the term, as the result of one or several terror attacks and if so whether terrorist groups may at all be subject to the rules of the Geneva Conventions of 1949 pertaining to international wars.[93] It is stated in Geneva Convention IV, as in all the Geneva Conventions, that the parties to the Convention shall be bound by it in relation to a Power who is not a party to the Convention if the latter accepts and applies the provisions thereof.[94] Inversely and applied to a terrorist group it would seem as if a terrorist group could be bound by the rules of the Geneva Conventions if the group accepted and applied the provisions thereof. Since the methods of fighting used by terrorist groups almost by definition violate at least the Geneva Convention IV protecting civilians, it is unlikely that terrorists would accept and apply the provisions thereof.

Obviously, the Geneva Conventions would have to be considerably extended by interpretation in order to be applicable to international terrorist actions. From the point of view of the development of the law it would seem unlikely that international terrorist acts would be punishable as war crimes before the ICC in the foreseeable future.[95] From the point of view of real developments, one can only hope that international terrorism will not evolve in a way that would make the application of the Geneva Conventions to terrorism such a pressing issue before the ICC.

93 *Cf.* Article 2 of the Geneva Conventions (adopted in Geneva on 12 August 1949, entry inte force on 21 October 1950).

94 *Ibid.*

95 As far as the applicability on suspected terrorists of Geneva Convention III relative the Treatment of Prisoners of War is concerned, it can be noted that the US considers that the Convention does not apply to the al-Qaeda detainees at the US base at Guantanamo, Cuba, since al-Qaeda is not a state party to the Convention. As far as the Taliban are concerned, the US considers that they are covered by Geneva Convention III, since Afghanistan is a party to the Convention although the US never recognized the Taliban as the legitimate Afghan government, but that they do not qualify as prisoners of war. (Fact Sheet: White House on Status of Detainees at Guantanamo, 7 February 2002, usinfo.state.gov/topical/pol/terror/02020700.htm (18 June 2004).)

9.5 Conclusion

Since the trend recently both in the UN Security Council and on the national level has been to emphasize international humanitarian law and the individual responsibility for violations of it, as well as the respect for human rights generally, it would be strange if the ICC would not somehow benefit from this strong global ideological current. The ICC itself constitutes an emanation of this trend with the *ad hoc* tribunals for the former Yugoslavia and for Rwanda paving the way for the eventual creation of the permanent ICC. It would seem more likely than not that these developments would strengthen the ICC in the long run, and that the ICC in its turn will be able to strengthen them further. Considering the ideological background and the fact that the Security Council in many Resolutions has emphasized the importance of international law for international peace and security, a cooperative and mutually supportive relationship between the Security Council and the ICC would seem to be the most likely development, even if Resolutions 1422 (2002) and 1487 (2003) currently point in another direction.

If the attitude of the Security Council towards the ICC continues to be frosty this will disclose the shallowness of the Council's commitment to humanitarian law and the cynicism in particular of some of its permanent members, which is not surprising but would be unusually stark this time. The message would be that international tribunals for the prosecution of suspected war criminals are good for others but not for one's own citizens. The commitment of the Security Council to the international enforcement of humanitarian law only lasts as long as the citizens of some of its permanent members do not risk being the subject of such trials. This is a message that many other rogue states gratefully acknowledge.

References

Books & articles

Akhavan, Payam, *Beyond Impunity: Can International Criminal Justice Prevent Further Atrocities?,* American Journal of International Law, Vol. 95, 2001, pp. 7–31.

Akhavan, Payam, *Justice in the Hague, Peace in the Former Yugoslavia? A Commentary on the United Nations War Crimes Tribunal,* Human Rights Quarterly, Vol. 20, 1998, pp. 737–816.

van Alebeek, Rosanne, *The Pinochet Case: International Human Rights Law on Trial,* British Year Book of International Law, Vol. 71, 2001, pp. 29–70.

Bergsmo, Morten, *Occasional Remarks on Certain State Concerns about the Jurisdictional Reach of the International Criminal Court, and Their Possible Implications for the Relationship between the Court and the Security Council,* Nordic Journal of International Law, Vol. 69, 2000, pp. 87–113.

Berman, Sir Franklin, *The Relationship Between the International Criminal Court and the Security Council,* von Hebel, Herman A.M., Lammers, Johan G. and Schukking, Jolien (Eds.), Reflections on the International Criminal Court, Essays in Honour of Adriaan Bos, T.M.C. Asser Press, The Hague, 1999, pp. 173–180.

de Bertodano, Sylvia, *Judicial Independence in the International Criminal Court,* Leiden Journal of International Law, Vol. 15, 2002, pp. 409–430.

Brand, Marcus G., *Institution-Building and Human Rights Protection in Kosovo in the Light of UNMIK Legislation,* Nordic Journal of International Law, Vol. 70, 2001, pp. 461–488.

Broomhall, Bruce, *International Justice and the International Criminal Court,* Oxford University Press, Oxford, New York, 2003.

Brown, Bartram S., *Primacy or Complementarity: Reconciling the Jurisdiction of National Courts and International Criminal Tribunals,* Yale Journal of International Law, Vol. 23, 1998, pp. 383–436.

Brown, Bartram S., *US Objections to the Statute of the International Criminal Court: A Brief Response,* New York University Journal of International Law and Politics, Vol. 31, 1998–1999, pp. 855–891.

Cahiers du Centre de gestion des conflits, *Les juridictions Gacaca et le processus de reconciliation nationale,* Butare, Rwanda, 2001.

Cassese, Antonio, *Terrorism is Also Disrupting Some Crucial Legal Categories of International Law,* European Journal of International Law, Vol. 12, 2001, pp. 993–1001.

Condorelli, Luigi and Santiago Villalpando, *Can the Security Council extend the ICC's jurisdiction?,* Cassese, Antonio, Gaeta, Paola, Jones, John R.W.D. (Eds.), The Rome Statute of the International Criminal Court: A Commentary, Vol. 1, Oxford University Press, Oxford, 2002, pp. 571–582.

Condorelli, Luigi and Villalpando, Santiago, *Referral and Deferral by the Security Council,* Cassese, Antonio, Gaeta, Paola, Jones, John R.W.D. (Eds.),

The Rome Statute of the International Criminal Court: A Commentary, Vol. 1, Oxford University Press, Oxford, 2002, pp. 627–655.

Cryer, Robert, *A 'Special Court' for Sierra Leone?*, International and Comparative Law Quarterly, Vol. 50, 2001, pp. 435–446.

Danilenko, Gennady M., *The Statute of the International Criminal Court and Third States*, Michigan Journal of International Law, Vol. 21, 2000, pp. 445–494.

The European Union, the United States and the International Criminal Court, (Editorial Comment) Common Market Law Review, Vol. 39, 2002, pp. 939–944.

Fenrick, William J., *Should Crimes Against Humanity Replace War Crimes?*, Columbia Journal of Transnational Law, Vol. 37, 1998–1999, pp. 767–785.

Gorjão, Paulo, *The East Timorese Commission for Reception, Truth and Reconciliation: Chronicle of a Foretold Failure?*, Civil Wars, Vol. 4, 2001, pp. 142–162.

Gowlland-Debbas, Vera, *The Relationship Between the Security Council and the Projected International Criminal Court*, Journal of Armed Conflict Law, Vol. 3, June 1998, pp. 97–119.

Henquet, Thomas, *Mandatory Compliance Powers* vis-à-vis *States by the Ad Hoc Tribunals and the International Criminal Court: A Comparative Analysis*, Leiden Journal of International Law, Vol. 12, 1999, pp. 969–999.

Klabbers, Jan, *The Spectre of International Criminal Justice: Third States and the ICC*, Zimmerman, Andreas (Ed.), International Criminal Law and the Current Development of Public International Law, Duncker and Humblot, Berlin, 2003, pp. 49–72.

La Haye, Eve, *The Jurisdiction of the International Criminal Court: Controversies Over the Preconditions for Exerciscising its Jurisdiction*, Netherlands International Law Review, Vol. 46, 1999, pp. 1–25.

Lee, Roy S., *The Making of the Rome Statue – Issues, Negotiations, Results, Kluwer Law International*, The Hague, London, Boston, 1999, pp. 143–152.

Linton, Suzannah, *Cambodia, East Timor and Sierra Leone: Experiments in International Justice*, Criminal Law Forum, Vol. 12, 2001, pp. 185–246.

Long, William J. and Peter Brecke, *War and Reconciliation. Reason and Emotion in Conflict Resolution*, The MIT Press, Cambridge, Massachusetts, London, 2003.

Macaluso, Daniel J., *Absolute and Free Pardon: The Effect of the Amnesty Provision in the Lomé Peace Agreement on the Jurisdiction of the Special Court for Sierra Leone*, Brooklyn Journal of International Law, Vol. 27, 2001–2002, pp. 347–380.

Wallensteen, Peter, Staibano, Carina, Eriksson, Mikael (Eds.), *Making Targeted Sanctions Effective. Guidelines for the Implementation of UN Policy Options*, Results from the Stockholm Process on the Implementation of Targeted Sanctions, Uppsala University, Department of Peace and Conflict Research, Uppsala, 2003.

McDonald, Avril, *Sierra Leone's Shoestring Special Court,* International Review of the Red Cross, Vol. 84, No. 845, 2002, pp. 121–143.

McLachlan, Campbell, *Pinochet Revisited,* International and Comparative Law Quarterly, Vol. 51, 2002, pp. 959–966.

Mégret, Frédéric, *Epilogue to an Endless Debate: The International Criminal Court's Third Party Jurisdiction and the Looming Revolution of International Law,* European Journal of International Law, Vol. 12, 2001, pp. 247–268.

Mettraux, Guénaël, *Crimes Against Humanity in the Jurisprudence of the International Criminal Tribunals for the former Yugoslavia and for Rwanda,* Harvard International Law Journal, Vol. 43, 2002, pp. 237–316.

Mochochoko, Phakiso, *International Cooperation and Judicial Assistance,* Lee, Roy S. (Ed.), The International Criminal Court. The Making of the Rome Statute – Issues, Negotiations, Results, Kluwer Law International, The Hague, London, Boston, 1999, pp. 305–317.

Morris, Madeline, *Complementarity and its Discontents: States, Victims, and the International Criminal Court,* Shelton, Dinah (Ed.), International Crimes, Peace, and Human Rights: The Role of the International Criminal Court, Transnational Publishers, Ardsley, NY, 2000, pp. 177–201.

Morris, Madeline, *High Crimes and Misconceptions: The ICC and Non-Party States,* Shelton, Dinah (Ed.), International Crimes, Peace, and Human Rights: The Role of the International Criminal Court, Transnational Publishers, Ardsley NY, 2000, pp. 219–279.

Müller-Shieke, Irina Kaye, *Defining the Crime of Aggression Under the Statute of the International Criminal Court,* Leiden Journal of International Law, Vol. 14, 2001, pp. 409–430.

Neuffer, Elizabeth, *The Key to My Neighbor's House: Seeking Justice in Bosnia and Rwanda,* Picador, New York, 2001.

Nordquist, Kjell-Åke, *East Timor – Intervention, State-Building, and Reconciliation,* Österdahl, Inger (Ed.), Is Intervention Humanitarian? Protecting Human Rights and Democracy Abroad, Department of Peace and Conflict Research, Uppsala University, Report No. 62, 2002, pp. 25–49.

Oosthuizen, Gabriël H., *Some Preliminary Remarks on the Relationship between the Envisaged International Criminal Court and the UN Security Council,* Netherlands International Law Review, Vol. 46, 1999, 313–342, pp. 316–317.

Power, Samantha, *Rwanda: The Two Faces of Justice,* New York Review of Books, January 16, 2003, pp. 47–50.

Ratner, Steven R., *Democracy and Accountability: the Criss-Crossing Paths of two Emerging Norms,* Fox, Gregory H. and Roth, Brad R. (Ed.), Democratic Governance and International Law, Cambridge University Press, Cambridge, 2000, pp. 449–490.

Ratner, Steven R., and Jason S. Abrams, *Accountability for Human Rights Atrocities in International Law. Beyond the Nuremberg Legacy,* second edition, Oxford University Press, Oxford, 2001, Part III: A Case Study: The Atrocities of the Khmer Rouge, pp. 267–328.

Roberts, Adam, *Counter-Terrorism, Armed Force and the Laws of War,* Survival, Vol. 44, 2002, pp. 7–32.

Sarooshi, Danesh, *Aspects of the Relationship Between the International Criminal Court and the United Nations,* Netherlands Yearbook of International Law, Vol. XXXII, T.M.C. Asser Press, The Hague, 2002, pp. 27–53.

Schocken, Celina, *The Special Court for Sierra Leone: Overview and Recommendations,* Berkeley Journal of International Law, Vol. 20, 2002, pp. 436–460.

Schrijver, Nico, *Responding to International Terrorism: Moving the Frontiers of International Law for 'Enduring Freedom'?,* Netherlands International Law Review, Vol. 48, 2001, pp. 271–291.

Sewall, Sarah B. and Kaysen, Carl (Eds.), *The United States and the International Criminal Court. National Security and International Law,* Rowman & Littlefield Publishers, Lanham, Boulder, New York, Oxford, 2000.

Slaughter, Anne-Marie and William Burke-White, *An International Constitutional Moment,* Harvard International Law Journal, Vol. 43, 2002, pp. 1–21.

Smidt, Michael L., *The International Criminal Court: An Effective Means of Deterrence?,* Military Law Review, Vol. 167, 2001, pp. 156–240.

Smith, Thomas W., *Moral Hazard and Humanitarian Law: The International Criminal Court and the Limits of Legalism,* International Politics, Vol. 39, 2002, pp. 175–192.

Spieker, Heike, *The International Criminal Court and Non International Armed Conflicts,* Leiden Journal of International Law, Vol. 13, 2000, pp. 395–425.

Stahn, Carsten, *Constitution Without a State? Kosovo Under the United Nations Constitutional Framework for Self-Government,* Leiden Journal of International Law, 2001, pp. 531–561.

Summers, Mark A., *A Fresh Look at the Jurisdictional Provisions of the Statute of the International Criminal Court: The Case for Scrapping the Treaty,* Wisconsin International Law Journal, Vol. 20, 2001, pp. 57–88.

Tallgren, Immi, *Completing the International Criminal Order,* Nordic Journal of International Law, Vol. 67, 1998, pp. 107–137.

Triffterer, Otto (Ed.), *Commentary on the Rome Statute of the International Criminal Court. Observers' Notes, Article by Article,* Nomos Verlagsgesellschaft, Baden-Baden, 1999.

Weller, Marc, *Undoing the Global Constitution: UN Security Council Action on the International Criminal Court,* International Affairs, Vol. 78, 2002, pp. 693–712.

Williams, Paul R. and Scharf, Michael P., *Peace with Justice? War Crimes and Accountability in the Former Yugoslavia,* Rowman & Littlefield Publishers, Lanham, Boulder, New York, Oxford, 2002.

Yee, Lionel, *The International Criminal Court and The Security Council: Articles 13 (b) and 16,* Lee, Roy S. (Ed.), The International Criminal Court. The Making of the Rome Statue – Issues, Negotiations, Results, Kluwer Law International, The Hague, London, Boston, 1999, pp. 143–152.

Young, Simon N.M., *Surrendering the Accused to the International Criminal Court,* British Year Book of International Law, Vol. 7, 2001, pp. 317–356.

Zegveld, Liesbeth, *Accountability of Armed Opposition Groups in International Law,* Cambridge University Press, Cambridge, 2002.

Zimmerman, Andreas and Stahn, Carsten, *Yugoslav Territory, United Nations Trusteeship or Sovereign State? Reflections on the Current and Future Legal Status of Kosovo,* Nordic Journal of International Law, Vol. 70, 2001, pp. 423–460.

Zwanenburg, Mark, *The Statute for an International Criminal Court and the United States: Peacekeepers under Fire?,* European Journal of International Law, Vol. 10, 1999, pp. 124–143.

Österdahl, Inger, *La France dans l'Afrique de l'après-guerre froide. Interventions et justifications,* Document de recherche No. 2, Nordic Africa Institute, Uppsala, 1997.

Österdahl, Inger, *Threat to the Peace. The Interpretation by the Security Council of Article 39 of the UN Charter,* Iustus förlag, Uppsala, 1998.

Cases

Case Concerning the Arrest Warrant of 11 April 2000 *(Democratic Republic of Congo* v. *Belgium*), International Court of Justice, judgement of 14 February 2002.

Case Concerning Certain Criminal Proceedings in France *(Republic of the Congo* v. *France*), International Court of Justice, application filed on 9 December 2002.

Case Concerning Questions of Interpretation and Application of the 1971 Montreal Convention Arising from the Aerial Incident at Lockerbie (*Libyan Arab Jamahiriya* v. *United Kingdom/United States of America*), Provisional Measures, Order of 14 April 1992, ICJ Reports 1992, p. 3.

UN Documents

S/PV/4568, 10 July 2002
S/PV/4772, 12 June 2003
S.C. Res. 770 (1992)
S.C. Res. 794 (1992)
S.C. Res. 808 (1993)
S.C. Res. 827 (1993)
S.C. Res. 955 (1994)
S.C. Res. 1072 (1996)
S.C. Res. 1080 (1996)
S.C. Res. 1193 (1998)
S.C. Res. 1199 (1998)
S.C. Res. 1214 (1998)

S.C. Res. 1244 (1999)
S.C. Res. 1264 (1999)
S.C. Res. 1267 (1999)
S.C. Res. 1272 (1999)
S.C. Res. 1304 (2000)
S.C. Res. 1315 (2000)
S.C. Res. 1333 (2000)
S.C. Res. 1386 (2001)
S.C. Res. 1422 (2002)
S.C. Res. 1464 (2003)
S.C. Res. 1483 (2003)
S.C. Res. 1484 (2003)
S.C. Res. 1487 (2003)
S.C. Res. 1509 (2003)

Miscellaneous

US Congress, *Unilateral Enforcement of Immunity Before the International Criminal Court (ICC),* American Servicemembers' Protection Act (ASPA), Entry into force 2 August 2002', quoted in Human Rights Law Journal, Vol. 23, 2002, pp. 275–279.

10 Rethinking Security

Humanitarian Intervention in the Age of Human Security – A Responsibility to Protect?*

Diana Amnéus

10.1 Introduction

> The concept of security has for too long been interpreted narrowly: as security of territory from external aggression, or as protection of national interests in foreign policy or as global security from the threat of a nuclear holocaust. It has been related more to nation states than to people.[1]
>
> The international community in the next Century will have to redesign its institutions, including the UN to incorporate new concepts such as human security which have the potential to resolve the tragic flaw of the conflict between territorial integrity and individual integrity. To accomplish this the discourse of security will have to move to include not only rights, but duties and responsibilities.[2]

Human security is a relative new concept in foreign policy and the international security discourse and has evolved during the 1990s as an innovative tool to address in a holistic manner the sources of insecurity that affect people worldwide today. There is growing global recognition that approaching security in terms of national or territorial security alone is insufficient, and that the security of people or individuals should no longer be defined exclusively within the realm of states and merely as a consequence of state security.

* I would like to thank Professor Ove Bring, Senior Advisor Pål Wrange and the doctoral candidates Ebrahim Afsah, David Langlet and Fredrik Stenhammar for valuable comments on this chapter.

1 United Nations Development Programme, *Human Development Report*, Oxford University Press, New York, 1994, p. 22 (hereinafter HDR 1994).

2 Mendes, Errol, *Human Security, International Organisations and International Law: The Kosovo crisis exposes the 'tragic flaw' in the UN Charter*, 1999, p. 3, www.uottawa.ca/hrrec/publicat/bull38.html (2003-08-22).

Taking the human security approach seriously will make an impact on the discussion on the emerging international law of humanitarian intervention or a *responsibility to protect* people.

Humanitarian intervention has been described as the most extreme form of promoting human security,[3] and the NATO intervention in Kosovo has been labelled the '*first human security war*'.[4] Why was this considered a human security emergency and what implications does this intervention have for international law?

The first part of this contribution aims to introduce the reader to the concept of human security and new security thinking in what has been described as the Age of Human Security. An account will be given of the background to the concept, its key advocates in the international arena and the human security agendas created by states, coalitions and networks by way of introduction. I will also present the most commonly proposed definitions of human security and its linkages with the related concepts of state security and human rights.

The second part of the chapter deals with the connections between the development of the human security concept and the development of a responsibility to protect, *i.e.* a new ground for legitimising humanitarian intervention in extreme cases without a Security Council mandate. The Kosovo conflict and the NATO intervention will be described and analysed as the most recent and clear-cut example of acknowledgement in some sense of a collective responsibility to protect and react towards people's insecurity, even within the *domain reservé* of other states. In this context the legal constraints regarding the issue of a right to humanitarian intervention without a Security Council mandate will be described. The idea of a responsibility to protect introduced by the International Commission on Intervention and State Sovereignty (ICISS)[5] in response to the Kosovo conflict will be presented and discussed. The potential contribution of the concept of human security to the dilemma of state sovereignty and human rights is reviewed together with the challenges it poses to the interpretation of these concepts. A final

3 Banks, Kimberly, *Human Security and Canadian Foreign Policy*, af.3dgw.com/ smss/ pdf/banks_smss2001.pdf (2002-08-27), p. 8.

4 *Ibid.*, p. 10; Oberleitner, Gerd, *Human Security and Human Rights*, Occasional Paper Series, Issue No. 8, June 2002, European Training and Research Center for Human Rights and Democracy, Graz, p. 13.

aim of this contribution is to discuss a few of the implications for international law and international security of the human security concept and a responsibility to protect people.

10.2 The concept of human security

10.2.1 Background

The fall of the Berlin Wall symbolizes the great divide between the old world order and the emergence of a new world order. However, as Sadako Ogata, former United Nations High Commissioner for Refugees, admited in a speech, the period that followed betrayed everyone's optimism and euphoria about the coming of a more secure world.[6] In the changing political situation after the Cold War *new threats* to international peace and security emerged.[7] The nature of conflicts had changed from inter-state to intra-state; weak states and bad governance led to failed or collapsed states, with unforeseen security consequences for their citizens and for the international community. Gross violations of human rights and a culture of impunity in the aftermath of internal armed conflicts showed the world that the doctrine on national security can no longer claim to be the only guarantee of security to people and individuals. We saw that state security does not necessarily assume human security. Furthermore, globalization has created new vulnerabilities for all states, and brought with it transnational insecurity to people through terrorism, trafficking in drugs, arms and in people, the proliferation of HIV/AIDS, environmental degradation, international organized crime, extreme poverty, uncontrolled migration and refugee flows etcetera.[8]

5 Report of the Commission on Intervention and State Sovereignty, *The Responsibility to Protect,* International Research Centre, Ottawa, 2001 (hereinafter the ICISS Report). See also the Supplementary Volume to the Report of the Commission on Intervention and State Sovereignty, *The Responsibility to Protect, Research, Bibliography, Background,* International Research Centre, Ottawa, 2001 (hereinafter the ICISS Supplementary Volume).

6 Ogata, Sadako, *State Security – Human Security,* Fridtjof Nansen Memorial Lecture, Tokyo, 12 December, 2001.

7 Maybe many of these threats are not new in themselves, *e.g.* extreme poverty, but one could argue that renewed attention has been paid to them after the end of the Cold War.

8 See an almost exhaustive list of new threats to human security in Oberleitner, p. 11.

There is growing acknowledgement that such "non-military sources of instability in the economic, social, humanitarian and ecological fields have become threats to peace and security".[9] These *non-traditional* threats have become equally important security challenges today as the traditional inter-state concerns, and it is necessary to deal with them in order to ensure international security.

New legal and foreign policy instruments, not necessarily focusing on inter-state relations, but instead directed at mitigating threats to human security, have emerged during the last decade. To mention a few: the adoption of the Rome Statute establishing the International Criminal Court (ICC), the Ottawa Convention on Anti-Personal Landmines and the Optional Protocol to the Convention on the Rights of the Child on the Involvement of Children in Armed Conflicts.[10] The changing nature of global security has led to a shift of perspective in foreign policy itself, from state centrism and assumptions of the primacy of national security to a more peopleoriented discourse. The concept of human security, encompassing security beyond the protection of borders, has contributed to this paradigm shift in foreign policy – the *Copernican Revolution* of international security.[11]

10.2.2 Key actors and human security agendas

During the 1990s several actors – states, networks, organizations, universities and institutions – began to advocate the concept of human security in the international arena as a new form of diplomacy and as a contribution to the international security discourse.

9 A celebrated statement made by the President of the Security Council in 1992, quoted in UNHCR, *The state of the World's Refugees,* Oxford University press, New York, 1994. One example is the Security Council identification of hiv/aids as a threat to international peace and security, open debate, 10 January 2000. Seelye, Katharine Q., *Gore to Preside at Security Council Session on AIDS Crisis*, New York Times, January 9, 2000.

10 Rome Statute of the International Criminal Court (1998), Ottawa Convention on the Prohibition of the Use, Stockpiling, Production and Transfer of Anti-Personnel Mines and on their Destruction (1997); Optional Protocol to the Convention on the Rights of the Child on the Involvement of Children in Armed Conflicts (2000), A/RES/54/263.

11 Axworthy, Lloyd, *Introduction,* McRae, Rob, Hubert, Don (Eds.), Human Security and the New Diplomacy, McGill-Queen's University Press, Montreal, 2001, p. 15.

In this chapter a few of the most dominant actors and their respective human security agendas will be presented.

The United Nations Development Programme (UNDP) was first to use the terminology in its 1994 Human Development Report (HDR).[12] The report examines threats to human security under seven main categories: economic, food, health, environmental, personal, community and political security.[13] The UNDP's analysis focused mainly on human security in relation to human development,[14] while human security in violent conflict situations is only dealt with briefly under the category *personal security*. In the 1999 HDR, the UNDP applied the human security language again, and used it for an analysis of social fragmentation, world financial crisis and globalization.[15]

Canada began using the language of human security in the aftermath of the Cold War, when it became clear to them that a new foreign policy paradigm was needed to protect civilians from violence.[16] Under the leadership of Lloyd Axworthy (former Canadian Minister for Foreign Affairs) Canada has developed and advocated a human security agenda as a basis for a new way forward in thinking and acting multilaterally on security. Its agenda, which is regarded as complementary and not as an alternative to traditional foreign policy, identifies five priority issues: the protection of civilians, peace support operations, conflict prevention, accountability and public safety.[17] As a contrast to UNDP, Canada has focused its agenda around the *freedom from fear* aspect of human security, *i.e.* violent conflict concerns.

Furthermore, Canada has advanced the concept of human security by building a global network of like-minded countries associ-

12 See *supra* note 1.

13 *Ibid.* pp. 24–25.

14 See further work on the relationship between human security and human development in Ball, Nicole, *Linking Security and Development,* Report of a conference organized by the Programme for Strategic and International Studies, Graduate Institute of International Studies, Geneva, 15 April, 2001, www.humansecurity network.org/docs/report_may2001_3-e.php (2003-08-11).

15 HDR (1999) pp. 36–44, 100-107.

16 Axworthy, Lloyd, *Introduction,* McRae, Rob, Hubert, Don (Eds.), Human Security and the New Diplomacy, McGill-Queen's University Press, Montreal, 2001, pp. 3, 9.

17 Department of Foreign Affairs and International Trade (DFAIT), Canada, *Human Security Program,* www.dfait-maeci.gc.ca/foreignp/humansecurity/HS_program-.asp (2001-05-08).

ated with international organisations and NGOs.[18] Building on the momentum of the Ottawa Process on anti-personnel landmines to see if the winning formula could be replicated with other issues, the Canadian and Norwegian Foreign Ministers held a bilateral retreat in Lysøen, in May 1998. The meeting resulted in the Canada-Norway Partnership for Action: The Lysøen Declaration, stipulating an agenda covering nine areas of cooperation for the enhancement of human security.[19] This agenda too has a strong emphasis on *freedom from fear* issues.

The unwritten goal was to create a Humanitarian 8 (H-8), but the partnership expanded into the *Lysøen process* of twelve states and an observer state.[20] Their first meeting was held in Bergen, Norway, in May 1999, and the following year the *Lysøen group* became *The Human Security Network* (HSN), now including NGOs and experts from the civil society. Their agenda covers matters such as the ICC, protection of civilians in armed conflict, action against anti-personnel mines, education on human rights, conflict prevention, war-affected children and corporate citizenship. Their agenda is constantly being developed and further amplified.[21]

18 This is in accordance with the ideas of new multilateralism, consisting of non-traditional international coalition building, see Waschuk, Roman, *The New Multilateralism*, McRae, Rob, Hubert, Don (Eds.), Human Security and the New Diplomacy, McGill-Queen's University Press, Montreal, 2001, pp. 213, 220-1, and the discussion on the new diplomacy by coalitions of the willing, see McRae, Rob, *International Relations and the New Diplomacy*, pp. 250, 254.

19 Norway-Canada Partnership for Action: *The Lysøen Declaration*, Bergen, 11 May 1998. This is the first time the concept appears in an official agreement between Canada and another government. Small, Michael, *The Human Security Network*, McRae, Rob, Hubert, Don (Eds.), Human Security and the New Diplomacy, McGill-Queen's University Press, Montreal, 2001, pp. 231–235. The agenda deals with the ICC, landmines, human rights, humanitarian law, small arms proliferation, gender and peace-building, children and armed conflict, child labour and arctic and northern cooperation.

20 The idea of the 'Humanitarian 8' was to gather likeminded states around a human security agenda just as the G-8 has its economic agenda. See Waschuk and Small, *supra* note 18–19, pp. 219, 233. The states in the HSN are: Austria, Canada, Chile, Greece, Ireland, Jordan, Mali, The Netherlands, Norway, Slovenia, Switzerland and Thailand. South-Africa has observer status.

21 See Chairman's Summary, Second Ministerial Meeting, Lucerne, 11–12 May, 2000. See the following reports on their homepage: www.humansecuritynetwork.org (2003-08-11). Other issues that have emerged include *inter alia* hiv/aids, armed non-state actors, resources for development, 'women, peace and security', small arms and light weapons.

One of the purposes of the HSN is to play a catalytic role by bringing attention to new and emerging security issues. They have rotating annual ministerial meetings to review progress and priorities and to impart action, but also intersessional meetings focusing on specific human security issues.[22] In addition, it works as a thematic network in the UN (in the General Assembly, the Security Council and the UN Commission on Human Rights), where it acts in a coordinated voice on behalf of its members on issues under the human security umbrella.[23] The network has also initiated the publication of an annual Human Security Report, as a complement to the existing Human Development Report.[24] The purpose of the report is to map the incidence of global violence and analyze its causes, health and developmental consequences, as well as the community responses to this violence.

Canada's and Axworthy's strong commitment to the human security idea[25] has led to its proliferation into other international fora. He introduced the concept into the G-8 discourse in Cologne in 1999 at the Foreign Ministers' Meeting, and in the Organisation of American States (OAS) General Assembly in the summer of 2000.[26] The terminology also appears as a natural component of the analyses and theories forwarded in the ICISS report. The Commission was created by the Government of Canada together with a group of major foundations in September 2000 as a response to the debate on humanitarian intervention in the UN, following NATO's

22 There were ministerial meetings in Switzerland in 2000, Jordan in 2001, Chile in 2002, and Austria in 2003. *Ibid.*

23 In the Security Council, for example, they have made statements on children and armed conflict (14 January 2003), the protection of civilians (12 December 2002) and women, peace and security (28 October 2002). *Ibid.* Also personal interview with Jennifer Armstrong, Advisor (Political Affairs), Permanent Mission of Canada to the United Nations, New York, 11 April 2003.

24 The first issue will be edited by Human Security Press and published by Oxford University Press. It was planned to be published in December 2003 but has not yet been made available (May 2004). See Human Security Network News Bulletin, Vol. 2, Issue 2, March 2003, p. 4.

25 The motivating factor of the human security agenda is said to be 'crucial not only for the security of individuals, but also to maintain Canada's role as a leading voice on the world stage. See Axworthy, Llyod, *Introduction*, p. 9.

26 See G8 Foreign Ministers' Meeting, Cologne, 10 June 1999, Conclusions, para. 3; *Human Security: A Priority at the OAS General Assembly*, Canada World View, Issue 8, Summer 2000, www.dfait-maeci.gc.ca/foreignp/canada-magazine/wv_8/8t6-e.htm (2001-05-08).

intervention in Kosovo 1999. The connections between human security and the Commission's theories on a responsibility to protect will be further elaborated on in section 10.4.

Another state, alongside Canada, that has assumed a leading role in the area of human security is Japan, which has made human security a key perspective in the development of its foreign policy.[27] Japan has made substantial contributions to the Trust Fund for Human Security that was established at the UN in March 1999 on their initiative. Japan has no direct policy coordination with Canada or the HSN on human security, which could have to do with its more developmentoriented approach, but their like-mindedness on specific human security issues has led to convergence of interests in some international fora, for example G-8 and the UN.[28]

The Commission on Human Security (CHS), which was an initiative of the Government of Japan, was established in January 2001 after a meeting between the UN Secretary-General Kofi Annan, and Sadako Ogata.[29] The idea of an independent Commission of Human Security grew out of the UN Millennium Summit (2000), which focused on securing 'freedom from fear' *and* 'freedom from want'. The CHS secretariat has been located in New York, facilitating close contacts with the UN. Its main goals have been to promote public understanding and support for human security, to develop the concept as an operational tool for policy formulation and to propose a concrete program of action to address pervasive threats to human security.[30] Its final report, *Human Security Now: Protecting and Empowering People* (the CHS Report), was presented to the UN Secretary-General on 1 May 2003.[31] The next step is to set up an Advisory Board on Human Security to promote and follow up

27 *Sectoral Analysis of the International Situation and Japan's Foreign Policy,* Chapter II, Section 3 A. Overview-Human Security, www.mofa.go.jp/policy/other/bluebook/2000/II-3-a.html (2001-06-20).

28 *Ibid.*

29 See the CHS homepage: www.humansecurity-chs.org/index.html (2002-11-12). Sadako Ogata has been an active proponent of the concept in her position as the former High Commissioner for Refugees and in the CHS.

30 It has been co-chaired by Mrs. Sadako Ogata and Professor Amartya Sen, Nobel Laureate and Master of Trinity College, Cambridge.

31 Commission on Human Security, *Human Security Now: Protecting and Empowering People,* Communications Development Inc., New York, 2003.

the CHS Report and provide guidance on the criteria to be applied for the UN Trust Fund on Human Security.[32]

The CHS refrains from proposing an itemized list of what human security is made up of and believes that the concept must be dynamic and open to variations across individuals and societies.[33] Its approach to human security is, however, broader than the Canadian one, involving six main areas concerning both violent conflict and poverty; protecting people in conflicts and post-conflict situations, shielding people who are forced to move, overcoming economic insecurities, guaranteeing essential health care, and ensuring universal education. But compared to UNDP, the CHS Report places far more emphasis and weight on security issues connected with violent conflict situations. The CHS deliberately left out humanitarian intervention and its relationship with human security in their report due to the major work done in the area by the ICISS.[34]

Apart from being discussed in academic literature, newsletters, conferences, seminars and workshops, human security has also emerged as a new research projects at several universities and institutes.[35] Many of these programmes have inter-disciplinary approaches to security where development, human rights, conflict resolution and security are studied together. The Canadians have also created the Canadian Consortium on Human Security (CCHS) – an academic-based network promoting policy-relevant research on human security.[36]

32 *Human Security Now*, Remarks by Sadako Ogata at the fifth Ministerial Meeting of the Human Security Network, Graz, Austria, 8 May 2003. Also personal interview with Johan Cels, Liaison Officer, Commission on Human Security, New York, 11 April, 2003.

33 CHS Report, p. 4.

34 Personal interview with Johan Cels, CHS, see *supra* note 32.

35 A few examples: Harvard Program on Humanitarian Policy and Conflict Research (which is also in charge of the HSN's publication: Human Security Network News Bulletin), the Centre for Human Security at the University of British Columbia, Fletcher Institute for Human Security, Human Security and Global Governance at the Toda Institute for Global Peace and Policy Research (HUGG), the Human Security and Conflict Management Centre in Amman. See www.hsph.harvard.edu/hpcr/events/hsworkshop/related_research.pdf (2003-08-22) – a first attempt to list existing insitutions.

36 See its homepage: www.humansecurity.info/ (2003-08-11). The CCHS also issues the Human Security Bulletin, which is available at www.humansecurity bulletin.info/.

10.2.3 Human security – definitions[37]

> Human security has been described as many different things: a rallying cry, a political campaign, a set of beliefs about the sources of violent conflict, a new conceptualization of security, and a guide for policymakers and academic writers.[38]

There is no single authoritative definition but instead a variety of definitions of human security. For reasons of space I have chosen to present the definitions used by a few of the key actors. As shown above, it started out as a UN-inspired concept, and was developed under Lloyd Axworthy's leadership into a diplomatic initiative.[39] In the last two years it has flourished in many different fora and in academic works where it is continuously being developed and analyzed.[40]

However, a common feature of all the definitions is that human security is viewed as people-centred, reinforcing human dignity and containing two basic aspects: *freedom from want* and *freedom from fear* – the same *leitmotifs* of the United Nations at its creation in 1945.[41] These two fronts are interconnected and interdependent in a holistic view of the concept, but some actors have chosen to stress on one or the other aspect in their work.[42]

Some of the ideas embedded in the concept are, however, not really all that new. The notion that the protection of people is as

37 See a compilation on definitions of human security at www.hsph.harvard.edu/hpcr/events/hsworkshop/list_definitions.pdf (2003-08-14).

38 Paris, Roland, *Human Security: Paradigm Shift or Hot Air?* International Security, Vol. 26, Issue 2, Fall 2001, pp. 87–102, p. 6.

39 McRae, Rob, *International Relations and the New Diplomacy*, McRae, Rob, Hubert, Don (Eds.), Human Security and the New Diplomacy, McGill-Queen's University Press, Montreal, 2001, p. 251.

40 See *e.g.* the bibliography on human security compiled by the Harvard Program on Humanitarian Policy and Conflict Research: www.hsph.harvard.edu/hpcr/events/hsworkshop/bibliography.pdf (2003-08-14) and Edson, Sara, *Human Security: An Extended and Annotated International Bibliography*, Centre for History and Economics, King's College, University of Cambridge, June 2001.

41 The US Secretary of State stated at the time of the creation of the UN in 1945: 'The battle of peace has to be fought on two fronts. The first is the security front where victory spells freedom from fear. The second is the economic and social front where victory means freedom from want.'

42 UNDP and Japan are more freedom from want oriented although Japan adheres to both fronts, while Canada and the HSN focus their agendas on freedom from fear issues. The CHS appears to have an integrated approach to human security in this respect, dealing with violent conflict, health, education, economic security and refugee issues in its final report.

important as the sovereignty of states has achieved increasing recognition since the end of the Second World War with the creation and development of human rights and international humanitarian law, embedded in the UN Charter, the Universal Declaration on Human Rights (1948), the Genocide Convention, and the Geneva Conventions (1949) and their Additional Protocols (1977) etcetera.[43] Similar broad security concepts, such as common security and comprehensive security, can also be traced in earlier work, for example the reports from the Palme Commission, the Carlsson-Ramphal Commission, and in the Agenda for Peace.[44]

When the UNDP wrote about human security in the HDR (1994) (crafted by Mahbub ul Haq), it was the first time the concept of human security was introduced in a UN forum. The UNDP's definition of the concept remains one of the most widely cited and, according to Paris, the most authoritative formulation of the term.[45] The UNDP proposes that 'it means first, safety from such chronic threats as hunger, disease and repression. And second, it means protection from sudden and hurtful disruptions in the patterns of daily life – whether in homes, in jobs or in communities'.[46] Their definition and analysis of seven elements of human security are vast and all-encompassing and have been criticized for being so broad that is difficult to determine if anything might be excluded.[47]

The Canadian definition appears to be based on a more narrow approach, affirming that 'human security means safety for people from both violent and non-violent threats. It is a condition or state of being characterized by freedom from pervasive threats to peo-

43 Charter of the United Nations (1945), UNTS, Vol. 1, p. XVI; Universal Declaration on Human Rights (1948), GA Resolution 217 A (III); Convention on the Prevention and Punishment of the Crime of Genocide (1948), UNTS, Vol. 78, p. 277; see *supra* note 5 in Chapter 2 by Ola Engdahl for full reference to the Geneva Conventions and Additional Protocols.

44 Independent Commission on Disarmament and Security Issues, *Common Security, A Blueprint for Survival*, Simon and Chuster, New York, 1982; The Commission on Global Governance, *Our Global Neighbourhood*, Oxford University Press, New York, 1995; Boutros-Ghali, Boutros, *An Agenda for Peace*, second edition, with the new supplement and related UN documents, United Nations, New York, 1995. See also Oberleitner, p. 1, referring to the Brandt Commission and the Brundtland Commission.

45 Paris, p. 2.

46 HDR (1994), p. 23.

47 Paris, p. 2.

ple's rights, their safety, or even their lives'.[48] However, this definition has also been criticized for being sweeping and open-ended.[49]

The HSN has a greed on a similar definition, influenced by the Canadians: 'In essence, human security means freedom from pervasive threats to people's rights, their safety or even their lives'.[50] This statement too does little to clarify the meaning of the concept and its definitional boundaries.

The CHS's idea of human security, builds upon the idea of three pillars: the *human* elements of security, rights and development. According to the Commission human security means 'to protect the vital core of all human lives in ways that enhance human freedoms and human fulfilment. Human security means protecting fundamental freedoms – freedoms that are the essence of life'.[51]

For the ICISS Commission, human security means 'the security of people – their physical safety, their economic and social well-being, respect for their dignity and worth as human beings, and the protection of their human rights and fundamental freedoms'.[52]

In the academic field the definition, scope and utility of the concept of human security is contested and debated,[53] a central part of the debate centres on the inclusion or exclusion of threats from the human security agenda and their ranking, prioritization and placing on the agenda.[54] The concept is criticized for being too universalistic, containing conceptual flaws, comprising too many securi-

48 Department for Foreign Affairs and International Trade, *Human Security: Safety for People in a Changing World*, Toronto, April 1999, p. 5. For a more thorough comparison between the UNDP and the Canadian approach, see Bajpal, Kanti, *Human Security: Concept and Measurement,* Occasional Paper #19:OP:1, Kroc Institute, Notre Dame, August 2000, p. 20.

49 Paris, p. 2.

50 Human Security Network, *A Perspective on Human Security,* Chairman's Summary, Lysøen (Norway), 20 May 1999, p. 2.

51 CHS Report, p. 4.

52 ICISS Report, p. 15.

53 Academic analysis came mostly from the social sciences, international relations theory and security and peace studies. See *e.g.* Oberleitner, pp. 2–3, Paris, p. 5, Foong Khong, Yuen, *A Shotgun Approach to Alleviating Human Misery,* Global Governance, Vol. 7, 2001, pp. 231–236; Dorn, Walter, *Human Security: An Overview,* Pearson Peacekeeping Centre, 2001, www.rmc.ca/academic/gradrech/dorn24_e.html (2003-08-22), Osler Hampson, Fen, Hay, John, B., *Human Security. A Review of the Scholarly Literature,* draft manuscript, 2002, www.liucentre.ubc.ca/hsq/_Articles/Fen_fulldocument.pdf (2003-08-14).

54 Oberleitner, p. 11.

tized issues and therefore less useful as a foreign policy tool. At the same time, its proponents see it as a helpful expansion of traditional security concerns and consider it useful in foreign policy to group together a wide range of activities centred on people rather than states. Nonetheless, the concept has come to be regarded as a useful *chapeau* for a new field of academic security research concerned with non-military threats to the safety of societies, groups and individuals.[55]

Among the academic definitions, three main conceptions of human security have been identified, ranging from restricted concepts limited to a number of threats to broader understandings of security: 1) a narrow approach based on natural and human rights, 2) a humanitarian approach, seeing human security as an instrument preparing the ground for humanitarian intervention, and 3) the broad approach linking human security with globalization and the global economy.[56]

For the purpose of this chapter I will use the humanitarian approach to the concept, in order to analyze the emerging responsibility to protect people from a human security perspective. Hence, the important discussion of the relationship between human security and human development will not be dealt with here.

10.2.4 International security, state security and human security

International security has, since the Westphalian order was established in 1648, relied upon state security. The concept of state security has of course evolved during the centuries, but is today perceived as underpinned by the principles of state sovereignty, territorial integrity and non-interference, as formulated in the first chapter of the UN Charter. Its main focus has been on the defence of boundaries, national institutions and citizens from external aggression.[57] Since 1945, collective security – the offspring of national security in the form of an internationalized right to collec-

55 Paris, p. 5.

56 Hampson, Fen Osler *et al.*, *Madness in the Multitude, Human Security and World Disorder,* Oxford University press, Toronto, 2002, p. 5.

57 Lodgaard, Sverre, *Human Security: Concept and Operationalization*, Norwegian Institute of International Affairs, p. 1, www.hsph.harvard.edu/hpcr/events/hsworkshop/lodgaard/pdf (2003-08-22)

tively uphold international peace and security, dominates the international legal order. [58]

In the Post Cold War era, international security has been broadened by reluctantly including *inter alia* threats of internal violence in collective security activities.[59] The Security Council has inconsistently extended the interpretation of Article 39 and what constitutes a threat to international peace and security in order to meet the new security threats.[60] The present international legal order was not created to manage intra-state conflicts and failed states, and has therefore to some extent had difficulty in responding and adapting to these threats.

The introduction of human security into the security discourse was not meant to create a substitute for state security. Instead, acting as a complement to state security, its aim is better defined – namely to protect the people, and not an abstract entity.[61] Ultimately the beneficiary of security must be the individual human being.

State security and human security are interlinked in several ways: human security and state security are mutually supportive.[62] State security is a means for providing human security, and has historically been and still is the most effective instrument for protecting individual's security.[63] Improving the human security of people strengthens the legitimacy, stability and security of a state – 'if human security – then state security'.[64] But this axiom does not necessarily work the other way around, for two reasons – internal and transnational threats. Firstly, failed or dysfunctional states as well as repressive regimes fail in providing human security, and sec-

58 Oberleitner, p. 8.
59 *Inter alia* Somalia (1992), Bosnia (1992) and Rwanda (1993).
60 See the broadening of what constitutes a threat to international peace and security in Österdahl, Inger, *Threat to Peace, The Interpretation by the Security Council of Article 39 of the UN Charter*, Iustus förlag, Uppsala, 1998.
61 Oberleitner, p. 10. The concept of human security contributes to a perspective where the well being and the safety of the population are regarded as equally important goals.
62 See a discussion on the convergence of national and human security in Liotta, P. H., *Boomerang Effect: The Convergence of National and Human Security*, Security Dialogue, Vol. 33, No. 4, December 2002, pp. 473–488.
63 See more on the claim that states are the single most important macro-structure for individual security in Sørenson, Georg, *Individual Security and National Security: The State Remains the Principal Problem*, Security Dialogue, Vol. 27, No. 4, December 1996, pp. 371–386.
64 *Human Security: Safety for People in a Changing World*, see *supra* note 48.

ondly transnational threats to human security that go beyond the capacity of the state need to be managed at a global level.[65] In the Westphalian system the maintenance of international peace and security does not formally take these two other security perspectives into account to a sufficient extent. The new broadening *ad hoc* practice of the Security Council has led to tensions in the international community with regard to the interpretation of the foundational principles of the legal order. One reason why human security has not fitted easily into our traditional notions of security concerns is that many human security matters are within the domestic sphere and thus not traditionally an international concern.[66]

10.2.5 Human security and human rights

It is generally recognized that there is a close link between human rights and human security. The ultimate focus and bearer of both human rights and human security is the individual.[67] Security is a human right itself in the form of a right to personal security,[68] at the same time human rights constitute the core of, and a normative framework for, human security.[69] Human rights violations are often the root causes of conflict and insecurity and therefore respect for rights and freedoms promotes and reinforces human security.

But the concept of human security is wider than the concept of human rights. In conflict situations, human security is a concern not only with rights but also with the safety of civilians from violence.[70] Furthermore, it involves threats that human rights are not

65 Bajpai, see *supra* note 48, pp. 37–38.

66 McLean, George, *Instituting and Projecting Human Security: A Canadian Perspective*, Australian Journal of International Affairs, Vol. 54, No. 3, 2000, pp. 269–276, p. 271.

67 Oberleitner, p. 14. See a more elaborate analysis on the relationship between Human Security and Human Rights in *ibid.*, pp. 14–23. See also Seidensticker: *Human Security, Human Rights and Human Development*, Kennedy School, Harvard University, 2002, www.humansecurity-chs.org/doc/0206harvard.html (2003-08-14); Ramcharan, Bertrand G., *Human Rights and Human Security*, Martinus Nijhoff Publishers, The Hague, 2002, pp. 7–20.

68 Embedded in the right to life, liberty and security (see *e.g.* Article 3 in the Universal Declaration on Human Rights, GA Resolution 217 (III) (10 December 1948)).

69 Workshop on Relationship Between Human Rights and Human Security, San José, Costa Rica, 2 December 2001, www.humansecurity-chs.org/doc/sanjose-dec.html (2003-08-14), para. 2.

concerned with, for example, internal armed conflicts, terrorism, trafficking, transnational pollution, which are not covered by the many human rights instruments, and with actors not bound by human rights law. Human security encompasses threats that do not only emerge from the state, but also from non-state actors and global structural violence.[71] By putting people first, human security recognizes that their safety is integral in the promotion of international peace and security.[72]

With its broad security perspective, transgressing state borders and focusing on people's security, human security furthermore includes the issue of how to protect people from gross violations of human rights within a state and the issue of a possible international responsibility to protect and react in emergency cases.[73] Nowhere in the human rights instruments can an explicit right to use force to protect human rights be found, although many scholars have presented creative interpretations in the doctrinal debate so as to legitimate such internal involvement based on the UN Charter responsibility to promote human rights (Articles 55–56). See more on this below in section 10.3.2. The concept of human security provides further support for this standpoint and for the development of international law and global security in this regard. See also the discussion on human security, state sovereignty and human rights in section 10.5, and the implications on international law in 10.6.

70 McRae, Rob, *Human Security in a Globalized World,* McRae, Rob, Hubert, Don (Eds.), Human Security and the New Diplomacy, McGill-Queen's University Press, Montreal, 2001, p. 16.
71 *E.g.* poverty and cultural violence. See discussion on Johan Galtung, in Oberleitner, p. 22.
72 Axworthy, Lloyd, *Human Security and Global Governance: Putting People First,* Global Governance A Review of Multilateral and International Organizations, Vol. 7, 2001, pp. 19–23, at p. 20.
73 Oberleitner, pp. 22–23, 27.

10.3 Human security – a new imperative for humanitarian intervention?

10.3.1 The NATO intervention in Kosovo 1999

> The important consideration here is that the war against Serbia was a war of values, a war for human security and, once started, wars for values must be won or the values themselves are placed at risk.[74]

Why was the Kosovo case viewed as the first *human security war* or *humanitarian war*? The conflict in Kosovo has been termed a human security emergency,[75] in which NATO established a new benchmark – that humanitarian imperatives can be a *casus belli* for interventions.[76] Some people insist that the operation could not possibly be considered humanitarian because it caused so much humanitarian suffering, for example collateral damage, refugee flows, and destroyed infrastructure.[77] The concern for domestic crises as threats to international peace and security and the feeling that the UN Charter was originally not written to respond to such humanitarian challenges had been clearly articulated before the Kosovo challenge, but it was accentuated by the NATO response.[78] Was Kosovo then the first case in which real humanitarian motives were the driving force for action? There are those who claim that there were no political, strategic or military motives or interests other than true humanitarian ones – that it was a people-centred operation. Let's take a closer look at the Kosovo case and the NATO intervention to see what the arguments for action were and how the international community received them.

In 1974 Kosovo was granted full autonomy in Tito's People's Federal Republic of Yugoslavia (FRY), a status close to that of a constit-

74 Heinbecker, Paul, *Human Security: The Hard Edge*, Canadian Military Journal, Spring 2000, pp. 11–16, p. 15.

75 This was a statement by Canada, and Canada's role in the NATO bombings was justified in this manner, see McLean, pp. 274–275. Also in Heinbecker, Paul, MacRae, Rob, *The Kosovo Air Campaign*, MacRae, Rob, Hubert, Don (Eds.), Human Security and the New Diplomacy, McGill-Queen's University Press, Montreal, 2001.

76 Heinbecker, p. 16.

77 DiPrizio, Robert C., *Armed Humanitarians, U.S. Interventions from Northern Iraq to Kosovo*, The John Hopkins University Press, Baltimore, 2001, p. 145.

78 Kosovo Report, p. 185.

uent republic.[79] Fifteen years later in 1989, in a new wave of Serbian nationalism, the Serbian President Slobodan Milošević removed this autonomy and began a new deliberate and systematic policy aiming to change the ethnic composition of Kosovo *inter alia* through persecution and expulsion.[80] This provocation was countered by a declaration of independence in July 1990 by the ethnic Albanians in Kosovo. The government in Belgrade refused to recognize independence and the following years were marked by tension and civil unrest.

In January 1998, the first massacre of 45 Albanian separatists and Serb police occurred in Raçak. In February, another 58 persons were killed in Prekazi, marking the beginning of an internal armed conflict in FRY. US-sponsored peace negotiations between Milošević and Ibrahim Rugova (leader of the Democratic League of Kosovo) between February and May 1998 were not successful. The Security Council adopted Resolution 1160[81] in March, condemning the use of excessive force by the Serbian police against civilians as well as acts of terrorism by the Kosovo Liberation Army. The Resolution also imposed an arms embargo under Chapter VII and support for a peaceful resolution of the conflict involving an enhanced degree of autonomy and self-administration for Kosovo based on the territorial integrity of FRY. After the summer, fighting intensified and the security situation in Kosovo worsened, creating several hundred thousand refugees and internally displaced civilians. The Council passed Resolution 1199,[82] affirming that the deterioration of the situation in Kosovo constituted a threat to international peace and security and demanding that FRY implement a list of concrete measures to achieve a political solution, and decided to consider

79 Chesterman, Simon, *Just War or Just Peace, Humanitarian Intervention and International Law,* Oxford University Press, New York, 2001, p. 207.

80 Independent International Commission on Kosovo, *Kosovo Report, Conflict, International Response, Lessons Learned,* Oxford University Press, New York, 2000, pp. 1, 3, 164 (hereinafter the Kosovo Report). This pattern of Serb oppression included numerous atrocities that appeared to have the character of crimes against humanity.

81 Security Council Resolution 1160 (1998) 31 March, see preambular (pre.) paragraph (para.) 3, operative (op.) paras. 5, 8. The Council expressed its support for an enhanced status for Kosovo with a substantial degree of autonomy and self-administration within FRY.

82 Security Council Resolution 1199 (1998) 23 September, see pre. para. 14, op. paras. 4, 16.

further action and additional measures to maintain or restore peace and stability if the requests in Resolutions 1160 and 1199 were not conformed to.

In the beginning of October 1998, new massacres took place and in the following weeks Milošević was pressured to sign two agreements with the OSCE and NATO respectively,[83] *inter alia* establishing a Verification Mission in Kosovo to assess the developments on the ground and to verify the implementation of Security Council Resolutions. A strong and credible threat to use force by NATO was the key to achieving the agreements. NATO nevertheless took a decision on 13 October to use force if necessary and made it clear that it had the will and means to act on the situation if violence continued.

The issue of requesting the Security Council to authorize such a military operation resulted in Resolution 1203,[84] however at the end stripped from enforcement measures in the text. Russia and China abstained from voting and made clear statements that the Resolution did not directly or indirectly authorize use of force in FRY.[85] After the adoption of this Resolution it was clear that a military intervention was not going to be authorized by the Security Council, due to the expected Russian and Chinese vetoes. The Resolution endorsed the October agreements and demanded that FRY and Kosovar Albanians comply with the Verification Mission and earlier Resolutions.[86] The Council stated nevertheless that in the event of an emergency situation action might be necessary to ensure the safety of this mission, and furthermore re-emphasized the *need* to prevent the impending humanitarian catastrophe from happening.[87]

The parties did not comply with the demands and the humanitarian situation in Kosovo continued to deteriorate. Further peace negotiations in February and March 1999 in Rambouillet collapsed and FRY

83 Agreement of 15 October setting up an OSCE Verification Mission in Kosovo and agreement of 16 October establishing a NATO Air Verification Mission over Kosovo to complement the OSCE mission.

84 Security Council Resolution 1203 (1998) 24 October, see pre. paras. 3, 4. *Cf.* resolution 1199, pre. para. 10.

85 S/PV.3937, 24 October 1998.

86 See further on the legality of such agreements signed under the threat to use force and the violation of Article 2 (4) of the UN Charter, Chesterman, p. 209.

87 Security Council Resolution 1203, pre. para. 11, op. para. 9.

refused to sign any further agreements. By then over 1,000 civilians had been killed and 400,000 ethnic Albanians had fled their homes, and another 90,000 people left the country.[88] The situation strengthened NATO in its decision to take action to halt the violence and the violations of humanitarian law and human rights in Kosovo.[89]

Operation Allied Force began on 24 March 1999, with limited aerial bombardment in Kosovo and later Serbia. The campaign continued for eleven weeks, and thirteen out of nineteen NATO members contributed to the operation.[90] At the emergency session of the Security Council on 24 March several countries stated their opposition to the NATO campaign and declared it a violation of Article 2(4) of the UN Charter (*inter alia* Russia, China, Belarus and India).[91] The Security Council has the primary role and responsibility for international peace and security (Article 24) and the required authorization for regional organisations as demanded in Article 53 had not been observed. But the majority of states legitimated or acquiesced in the intervention. The EU declared through Germany that its members were under a moral obligation to ensure that indiscriminate behaviour and violence, as in the massacre at Račak, were not repeated.[92]

Russia, Belarus and India presented a draft resolution on March 26 condemning the military intervention as a violation of the UN Charter and demanding cessation of the use of force, which was turned down by 12 to 3 (Russia, China and Namibia supporting).[93]

88 Kosovo Report, p. 2. This can be compared to the 10,000 people who were killed, approximately 863,000 who were forced into refuge outside Kosovo, and another 590,000 internally displaced between March and June 1999. Heinbecker, Paul and McRae, Rob, *The Kosovo Air Campaign*, p. 124.

89 The intention was never to separate Kosovo from Serbia, only to bring Serbia out of Kosovo. See Secretary of State Madeleine Albright's Press Conference on Kosovo, October 8, 1998, www.secretary.state.gov/www.statements/1998/981008.html (2003-09-04).

90 Heinbecker and McRae, *The Kosovo Air Campaign*, p. 129.

91 See S/PV.3988, 24 March 1999.

92 *Ibid.*

93 Security Council Draft Resolution S/1999/328 (26 March 1999). See also S/PV.3989, 26 March 1999. See the discussion on the why this vote was historic in Wheeler, Nicholas, *Saving Strangers, Humanitarian Intervention in International Society*, Oxford University Press, Oxford, 2000, pp. 280-281.

FRY also brought the issue of legality of the use of force to the International Court of Justice, a case which is still pending.[94]

On June 10 the Security Council adopted Resolution 1244,[95] prepared by the G-8 – the "end of bombing package". It demanded the withdrawal of all FRY military and police forces from Kosovo and the guarantee of autonomy for Kosovo, and established a NATO-led international peacekeeping force in Kosovo (KFOR) and an interim civilian administration.[96] China abstained from the Resolution, claiming that the crisis was an internal matter for Yugoslavia alone. Still the Resolution added a sense of ex-post UN legitimacy to the NATO operation.[97]

NATO's official position seemed to reflect a fundamental division as regards the legal basis for the operation. NATO members avoided using the word humanitarian intervention by name and on the whole did not clearly or expressly invoke humanitarian intervention as a legal doctrine. Instead, many referred to a humanitarian catastrophe and the threat to international peace and security of the region.[98] The UK emphasized the need to protect Kosovar Albanian citizens, and argued that the action was legal and justified as an:

> ... exceptional measure to prevent an overwhelming humanitarian catastrophe. Under the present circumstances in Kosovo, there is convincing evidence that such a catastrophe is imminent ... Every means short of force has been tried to avert this situation. In these circumstances, and as an exceptional measure on grounds of overwhelming humanitarian necessity, military intervention is legally justifiable.[99]

94 See Case Concerning Legality of Use of Force (*Yugoslavia* v. *United States of America*), ICJ, 1999. FRY also asked the International Court of Justice for indication of provisional measures, but the request was turned down. See Press Release 99/33 International Court of Justice, 2 June 1999. For a resumé on the legal arguments presented by the NATO members in the Court, see Gray, Christine, *International Law and the Use of Force*, Oxford University Press, New York, 2000, pp. 35–42.

95 Security Council Resolution 1244 (1999) 10 June.

96 The resolution created a unique institutional hybrid, which was a UN protectorate with unlimited power whose purpose is to prepare the province for autonomy and self-government in the framework of FRY.

97 Kosovo Report, p. 163. The resolution terminating the war has been argued to implicitly validate the NATO decision to intervene when the Security Council was unable to, see Heinbecker and McRae, *The Kosovo Air Campaign*, p. 132.

98 Chesterman, p. 214; Gray, p. 32.

99 S/PV.3988, 24 March 1999.

It is, however, clear that the Security Council Resolutions prior to the operation did not provide a legal basis for the action. Several NATO states claimed that the action was taken in support of or consistent with Security Council Resolutions – they were relied on to provide political justification.[100] The three Resolutions may justify the claim that NATO was in fact acting in pursuance of the aims of the international community, but the majority of states have not been willing to accept a doctrine of *implied authorization*, which the US, the UK and other NATO allies relied on as part of their justification.[101] The Security Council thus came to play a purely formal role, rather than operating as a source of legal authority when intervening in Kosovo.

The view among the NATO members was that the Kosovo case was exceptional and should not have any precedential effects.[102] The US emphasized that it is important not to overdraw the various lessons that come out of the Kosovo case and later the UK stressed the exceptional nature of the air campaign.[103]

Other NATO representatives have argued that its actions were based on its changed conception of security, not on any traditional notions of defence or national interest.[104] From a Canadian point of view, the Kosovo intervention was seen as an instrument of human security, driven as much or more by values than by interests: 'The crisis in Kosovo, and the Alliance's response to it, is a concrete expression of this human security dynamic at work.'[105]

100 Chesterman, pp. 214, 218. See this argumentation from *e.g.* Canada, in Heinbecker and McRae, *The Kosovo Air Campaign*, p. 123.
101 Gray, pp. 37–38, 193–195.
102 Chesterman, p. 216.
103 Byers, Michael, Chesterman, Simon, *Changing the Rules about Rules? Unilateral Humanitarian Intervention and the Future of International Law,* Holzgrefe, J.L., Keohane, Robert O. (Eds.), Humantarian Intervention, Ethical, Legal, and Political Dilemmas, Cambridge University Press, Cambridge, 2003, p. 199.
104 McKenzie, Mary M., *The UN and Regional Organizations,* Newman, Edward, Richmond, Oliver P. (Eds.), The United Nations and Human Security, Palgrave publishers Ltd, New York, 2001, p. 163. Policy differences between the NATO allies led to a 'lowest common denominator' approach to achieving the military objectives.
105 Axworthy, Lloyd, *NATO's New Security Vocation*, NATO Review, Vol. 47, No. 4, Winter 1999, pp. 8–11 at p. 5, in which he argues that the new concept of human security is central to the new NATO, www.nato.int/docu/review/1999/9904-02.htm (2003-09-04). See also Heinbecker and McRae, *The Kosovo Air Campaign*, p. 125.

But there were other interests as well involved in the campaign. For the US, regional stability and the credibility of NATO were as important as the humanitarian concerns.[106] A regional conflict or instability that the situation in Kosovo could have developed into would undermine NATO's credibility as guarantor of peace and stability in Europe. The fundamental US national interest in ensuring that Europe remained prosperous, secure and free were as compelling as the sense of guilt in the West for failing to stop the genocide and ethnic cleansing in Bosnia and other recent internal crises.

The controversy over the legality of the NATO intervention raised a wave of further debates on the issue of humanitarian intervention and human security in the Security Council and the General Assembly's session in the fall of 1999.[107] The dividing line between supporters and opponents more or less followed the North-South division. The position of many of the G-77 countries is that humanitarian intervention, in particular without a Security Council mandate, is a form of neo-colonial western imperialism. The Non-Aligned Movement and the Organisation of African Unity made it clear that no matter how noble the pretext, unilateral intervention is not acceptable and that the NATO intervention was indeed illegal.[108]

The Independent International Commission on Kosovo[109] concluded in its Report that the NATO military intervention was illegal but legitimate – illegal due to its lack of prior approval from the Security Council, but nevertheless justified because all diplomatic avenues had been exhausted and it had the effect of liberating the eth-

106 DiPrizio, Robert C., see *supra* note 77, pp. 135, 139–144. Albright's strong rhetoric and commitment to human rights as well as Clinton's wish to divert attention from the Monica Lewinsky affair are also mentioned as factors contributing to the US lead in the NATO decision to intervene.

107 See *e.g.* the Swedish statement on the Secretary-General Report on the Work of the Organization, by Ambassador Hans Dahlgren, Permanent Mission of Sweden to the United Nations, 8 October 1999.

108 Schnabel, Albrecht, Thakur, Ramesh, *Kosovo and the Challenge of Humanitarian Intervention, Selective Indignation, Collective Intervention and International Citizenship*, Policy Brief: Lessons from Kosovo Conflict, p. 2, www.unu.edu/p&g/kosovo_full.htm (2003-08-28); Gray, p. 195.

109 The purpose of the Commission was to examine the background to the conflict, the human rights violations, options to meet the crisis, the diplomatic efforts, the military intervention and the adequacy of present norms in international law and bring together the lessons learned. See Kosovo Report, p. 331, *supra* note 80.

nic Albanians from oppression.[110] Furthermore, the Commission stated that the international community failed to take sufficient preventive action and that much more effort needed to be devoted to the prevention of conflicts, but also to increased funding for post-conflict operations.[111] Far more attention and money was spent on Kosovo during the intervention than before or after.[112] Military intervention should remain 'a poor second best' strategy of last resort.[113]

10.3.2 Humanitarian intervention without a Security Council mandate[114]

Extensive work and analysis has been done on the illegality and legitimacy of the NATO intervention in Kosovo, and the purpose of this section is not to summarize all the opinions and arguments supporting or opposing the intervention,[115] nor to mention the vast literature on the issue of humanitarian intervention *per se*.[116] This chapter will highlight a few important legal points and thus establish a legal context for the understanding of the Kosovo debate and provide a legal framework for the issue for the purposes of the subsequent discussions in this paper.

110 Kosovo Report, pp. 4–5, 7. Nonetheless, the Report concluded that the war was neither a failure nor a success. The intervention failed to prevent another massive (reverse) ethnic cleansing, the Serbian people were considered the main losers of the war, and Serbia suffered considerable economic losses and destruction of civilian infrastructure. See the Commission's criticism of the NATO intervention, p. 289.

111 Kosovo Report, pp. 1–2, 8.

112 *Ibid.*, p. 11.

113 *Ibid.*, p. 295.

114 Chapter 3 in this book, *The Security Council as a Law Enforcer and a Legislator*, elaborates on the issue of authorized humanitarian interventions by the Security Council.

115 See *e.g.* Simma, NATO, *The UN and the Use of Force: Legal Aspects*, European Journal of International Law, Vol. 10, 1999, pp. 1–22; Cassese, Antonio, *Ex iniuria ius oritur: Are We Moving towards International Legitimation of Forcible Humanitarian Countermeasures in the World Community?*, European Journal of International Law, Vol. 10, 1999, pp. 23–30; Henkin, Louis, *Kosovo and the Law of 'Humanitarian Intervention'*, American Journal of International Law, Vol. 93, No. 4, October 1999, pp. 824–828; Schnabel, Albrecht, Thakur, Ramesh (Eds.), *Kosovo, and the Challenge of Humanitarian Intervention*, The United Nations University Press, Tokyo, 2000.

> [H]umanitarian intervention ... is the threat or use of force across state borders by a state (or group of states) aimed at preventing or ending widespread and grave violations of the fundamental human rights of individuals other than its own citizens, without the permission of the state within whose territory force is applied.[117]

The existence of a right to humanitarian intervention, in particular without Security Council mandate, is a longstanding controversy among states and legal scholars. The historical roots of the doctrine date back to the classical works on international law on just war (*bellum justum*) in the 16th and 17th centuries.

The legal limitation in international law today for interventions without authorization, is primarily[118] found in the prohibition of the use of force in Article 2(4) of the UN Charter, which stipulates only two possible exceptions, the right to self-defence under Article 51 or enforcement measures decided by the Security Council under Chapter VII. The *travaux préparatoires* of the UN Charter on the interpretation of Article 2(4) make it quite clear that there was no intention to allow for the existence of any other exceptions to use force than those explicitly provided for in the Charter. The International Court of Justice also embraced the position in the *Corfu*

116 A few recent works are: Holzgrefe, J.L., Keohane, Robert O., *Humantarian Intervention, Ethical, Legal, and Political Dilemmas*, Cambridge University Press, Cambridge, 2003; Wheeler, see *supra* note 93; Chesterman, see *supra* note 79; Téson, Fernando R., *Humanitarian Intervention, An Inquiry into Law and Morality*, Transnational Publishers, New York, 1997; Danish Institute of International Affairs, *Humanitarian Intervention, Legal and Political Aspects,* DUPI, Copenhagen, 1999; Keren, Michael, Sylvan, Donald, *International Intervention, Sovereignty versus Responsibility*, Frank Cass, London, 2002; Wallensteen, Peter (Ed.), *International Intervention: New Norms in the Post-Cold War Era?,* Report No. 45, Department of Peace and Conflict Research, Uppsala University, 1997. For a comparative analysis on the ICISS Report, the DUPI Report and the Kosovo Report, see Newman, Edward, *Humanitanian Intervention, Legality and Legitimacy*, The International Journal of Human Rights, Vol. 6, No. 4, 2002, pp. 102–120.

117 Holzgrefe, J.L., *The Humanitarian Intervention Debate*, Holzgrefe & Keohane (Eds.), Humanitarian Intervention, Ethical, Legal and Political Dilemmas, *supra* note 116, p. 18.

118 Other legal limitations in customary international law relevant for the evolvement of such a norm is the principles on non-intervention, the territorial integrity of states, state sovereignty and the equality of states (flowing from Article 2 (1) of the UN Charter and the General Assembly Resolution on Principles of International Law concerning Friendly Relations and Co-operation among States in Accordance with the Charter of the United Nations (1970), GA Resolution 2625 (XXV)).

Channel case that no implicit exceptions to Article 2(4) are acceptable.[119] Moreover, the prohibition of the use of force is also a *jus cogens* norm, which means that it is accepted and recognized by the international community of states as a whole as non-derogable and universally binding on all states.[120] Only a subsequent *jus cogens* norm of a peremptory nature can modify the content of this rule.[121] As far as I know, there is still no recognized peremptory norm that has modified the prohibition on the use of force.

Nevertheless there are many lawyers who argue for a right to humanitarian intervention both within the UN Charter framework and outside it, as an emerging norm in customary international law. The legal foundations for a right of member states to use force in order to protect human rights are claimed[122] through a contextual interpretation of the UN Charter – reading Article 56, which requires member states to take joint and separate action in co-operation with the UN to promote human rights according to Articles 1(3) and 55, together with an *e contrario* interpretation of Article 2(4), in which humanitarian intervention is seen as not 'directed against the territorial integrity or political independence of a state or in any other manner inconsistent with the purposes of the UN'. This line of thinking has, however, been refuted by the International Court of Justice in the *Nicaragua* case.[123] It may be the case, however, that new state and UN practice during the post Cold War period has changed or is influencing a change in *opinio juris* on whether the use of force is an appropriate method for monitoring or ensuring respect for human rights.

The existence of a right, or an emerging right, to humanitarian intervention in customary international law, as a supplementary

119 Corfu Channel Case, ICJ Reports, 1949, p. 35.

120 It is a universal *jus cogens* norm, which cannot be contracted out of even at the regional level. See Simma, p. 3, *supra* note 118.

121 See Article 53 of the Vienna Convention on the Law of Treaties (1969), UNTS, Vol. 1155, p. 331. Chesterman, p. 60.

122 See Bring, Ove, *FN-stadgan och världspolitiken, Om folkrättens roll i en föränderlig värld,* fourth edition, Norstedts Juridik, Stockholm, 2002, pp. 140-141.

123 Military and Paramilitary Activities in and against Nicaragua, ICJ Reports, 1986, para. 268. The Court stated that '[i]n any event, while the United States might form its own appraisal of the situation as to respect for human rights in Nicaragua, the use of force could not be the appropriate method to monitor or ensure such respect.'. There are lawyers who have attempted to intrepret the case narrowly, see *e.g.* Tesón, pp. 308–309.

regime to the UN Charter, is also extensively debated. However, an amendment of the UN Charter by subsequent practice must in the case of Article 2(4) in any case reach the level of a *jus cogens* norm, as explained above.[124] There is little or no evidence that there existed such a rule or even a regular customary rule, either before the adoption of the UN Charter, mainly due to the Briand-Kellogg Pact (1928),[125] or during the Cold War, because of the practically non-existent state practice regarding humanitarian intervention. In the post-Cold War period there are only three genuine cases of humanitarian intervention without Security Council mandate: Liberia (1990), Northern Iraq (1991) and Kosovo (1999).[126] It is doubtful whether these cases constitute persistent practice, and since they have been criticised as regards the legality of intervention, the emergence of a new *opinio juris* on humanitarian intervention in these cases could as well be contested. Moreover, since much support was given both by states and the UN, and there was no condemnation by the Security Council but instead *post factum* endorsement, it is possible to argue that theses cases may represent evidence of a greater acceptance of the fact that humanitarian intervention may be morally justifiable in extreme cases.[127] But unless the rules on the formation and change of customary law have changed,[128] there is still a lack of consistent and substantial evidence for the emergence of a customary rule on a right to humanitarian intervention without the authorization of the Security Council.[129]

NATO did not present any legal justification for its intervention that was based on the UN Charter.[130] All the arguments, except those submitted by the UK (see above section (note 10.3.1)), were

124 Chesterman, p. 60.

125 The international customary rule prohibiting the use of force was further codified in 1928 in order to remedy some of the gaps in the Treaty of the League of Nations, and the right to humanitarian intervention became practically non-existent. See Bring, pp. 69–70, 143. As a result, any existent Just War tradition became extremely circumscribed.

126 The Economic Organisation of West African States intervened in Liberia, the US, the UK and France in Iraq, and NATO in Kosovo. See DUPI, p. 90.

127 DUPI, p. 93.

128 See Byers, Michael, Chesterman, Simon, *Changing the Rules about Rules? Unilateral Humanitarian Intervention and the Future of International Law, supra* note 103.

129 Chesterman, *supra* note 79, p. 87.

130 Cassese, *supra* note 115, p. 24.

political and moral arguments, in other words *de lege ferenda* arguments, which could be argued to be similar to elements of the old 'just war doctrine'. There is still a gap between the legality and the legitimacy of such actions. The following section offers a contribution towards closing this gap between the legality and legitimacy of humanitarian intervention without Security Council authorization. The following presentation and subsequent analyses also belong to the *lege ferenda* sphere.

10.4 'The responsibility to protect' and human security

> One of the virtues of expressing the key issue in this debate as 'the responsibility to protect' is that it focuses attention where it should be most concentrated, on the human needs of those seeking protection or assistance.[131]

The ICISS was a response to the call by the UN Secretary-General to the international community to find a new consensus on how to approach and respond to situations of massive violations of human rights and humanitarian law within a state.[132] Its main aim was to look into the legal, moral, operational and political questions in the debate on humanitarian intervention. The report, which was released in December 2001, is based on extensive research, wide and global consultations and more than ten regional roundtables.

Internal security situations in which the Security Council has not been able to act are still problematic from a human security perspective. The literature discussing this dilemma is vast, as explained in section 10.3.2, and the lists suggesting new norms and criteria

131 ICISS Report, p. 15.

132 Kofi Annan has argued that *individual sovereignty* must enter the calculations and not merely state sovereignty. Annan, Kofi, *Two Concepts of Sovereignty*, The Economist, 18 September 1999. Just as the Brundtland Commission on the Environment and Development coined the term 'sustainable development' as a response to the apparently irreconcilable issues of development and environmental protection, there was hope that the ICISS Commission would be able to find new ways to reconcile the concepts of intervention and state sovereignty. See ICISS Report, p. 81.

for humanitarian interventions are as manifold as there are states and writers. The ICISS initiative that will be presented here is therefore only one among several proposals. However, the ICISS's ideas and analysis are unique in the way they connect the concept with human security, upon which the responsibility to protect explicitly rests. In the 'responsibility to protect language' the Commission has managed to merge two fields – the need for a broader security perspective and the need for the international community to act under certain circumstances to protect people's security, even when the Security Council fails to take action.

The principal idea that the Commission introduces in its report is a change of terminology,[133] away from the highly controversial right to humanitarian intervention to a responsibility on the part of states to protect not only their own citizens from security threats, but also a responsibility for the international community of states to do so if another state is unwilling or unable to, or is itself the perpetrator. It is believed that this may constitute a more effective basis for encouraging state action.[134] The change of language has three other big advantages:[135] it focuses on those who need support instead of on states that want to intervene; it implies that the primary responsibility rests with the state concerned and that only if it fails will the international community take its place; and finally it is an umbrella concept which is much broader than just a right to intervene for humanitarian purposes. The concept of responsibility to protect encompasses three elements: the responsibility to prevent, react, and rebuild, and thus not just the responsibility to intervene (react). In this chapter I will, however, only deal with one element – the responsibility to react.

The Kosovo Report also contains language on duties and responsibilities and proposes the adoption of a General Assembly Resolution on the Right and Responsibility of Humanitarian Intervention in order to facilitate an emergent doctrine of humanitarian inter-

133 ICISS Report, p. XI. Prevention is the single most important dimension according to the Commission.

134 ICISS Supplementary Volume, p. 148.

135 Evans, Gareth, Sahnoun, Mohamed, *The Responsibility to Protect*, Foreign Affairs, Vol. 81, No. 6, November- December 2002, p. 101. Evans and Sahnoun cochaired the ICISS.

vention and close the gap between legality and legitimacy.[136] In this respect, the ICISS has built its ideas upon the ideas of the Kosovo Commission and developed them further. The ICISS doctrine on responsibility to protect is thus a continuation of a line of thinking that had already been pursued.

The ICISS's core principle is that state sovereignty implies responsibility. The ICISS argues that the foundations of a responsibility to protect as an emerging guiding principle for the international community are inherent in the concept of sovereignty and can be found in a miscellany of legal provisions in human rights and humanitarian law as well as in state practice and in Security Council practice.[137] The Commission acknowledges that it is premature to claim the existence of such a rule now, but nevertheless presents an analysis of how such a responsibility could evolve and what it could contain.

The ICISS's idea of sovereignty as responsibility involves both internal and external duties – a state's internal duty to protect the safety of its citizens, but also an external duty owed to the international community through membership of the UN, and a responsibility for state actions or omissions (what we would traditionally call state responsibility).[138] It is argued that this way of viewing responsibility as sovereignty is being strengthened by the ever-increasing impact of human rights norms and of the concept of human security in international discourse.[139]

136 Kosovo Report, p. 187. The declaration should deal with the duties on behalf of the UN and other collective actors in the international community to act effectively for the implementation of human rights and the prevention of humanitarian catastrophes, balanced by respect for sovereign rights. The Kosovo Commission also states the need to close the gap between legality and legitimacy by incorporating a more flexible view of legitimacy – an international moral consensus. See Kosovo Report, pp. 10, 164, 186. See pp. 10, 192–197 on the Kosovo Commission's framework for humanitarian intervention.

137 ICISS Report, p. XI, 50. See also the chapter 'From Rights to Responsibilities' in the ICISS Supplementary Volume, pp. 147–150, (*supra* note 5), which explains the idea of complementing the individual's right to protection with a correlative collective duty or responsibility in order to realize the rights. This suggestion of a residual responsibility for the international community, multilateral bodies and ultimately 'everyone', when the state does not fulfil these obligations, is a *lege ferenda* argument. See *ibid.* p. 148.

138 *Ibid.*, p. 13.

139 *Ibid.*

The decision to intervene with military means to protect people is suggested to be limited to certain kinds of emergencies – extreme cases which genuinely "shock the conscience of mankind" or which present such an obvious and imminent danger to international security that they call for coercive military intervention.[140] In order to identify such exceptional cases the Commission proposes a set of criteria that must be fulfilled before the decision to intervene is taken, which it calls the *just cause threshold*. These are situations of 1) large-scale loss of life or 2) large-scale ethnic cleansing is taking place. However, the Commission deliberately gives no definition of what constitutes *large-scale*. Furthermore it states that these circumstances can be either actual or apprehended (imminent), so that an intervention can be carried out either to halt or avert such a situation. Consequently, the ICISS formula for humanitarian intervention[141] legitimizes anticipatory measures in response to clear evidence of *probable* large-scale killing, as explained in the report in order to "avoid the morally untenable position of having to await the beginning of a genocide before being able to stop it".[142]

There is also a demand for *right authority* regarding the actor(s) authorizing or carrying out the intervention. The general idea is that the Security Council is the appropriate body to authorize military interventions, and such authorization should always be sought. But if the Security Council rejects a proposal or fails to deal with it within a reasonable time, the Commission proposes alternative options. In such cases the matter could be considered under the 'uniting for peace' procedure in the General Assembly, and by regional organisations under Chapter VIII of the UN Charter, subject to their seeking a Security Council mandate.[143]

The Commission's perception of the responsibility of the Security Council and the international community is rooted in a human security perspective. The responsibility of the Security Council for

140 *Ibid.*, p. 31.

141 Four precautionary principles for military intervention are also included in the criteria, demanding a) a right intention of the interveners, b) that the intervention is applied as a last resort, c) that proportional means be used when the operation is carried out, and d) the existence of reasonable prospects of achieving the intended results. *Ibid.*, see pp. XII-III, 31–37.

142 ICISS Report, pp. 32–33.

143 *Ibid.*, pp. XIII, 47–55.

international peace and security, laid down in Article 24 of the UN Charter, is also assumed to involve clear and responsible leadership of the Council to protect people 'when significant loss of human life is occurring or is threatened, even though there may be no direct or imminent threat to international peace and security in the strict sense'.[144] This is a call to the Security Council to adopt a broader security agenda than has traditionally been the case.

The Commission also believes that if the Security Council *fails* to discharge its responsibility to protect in 'conscience-shocking situations crying out for action', the Council should take into account that it is unrealistic to expect concerned states to rule out other means or forms of action to meet the security emergency.[145] In such situations alternative means of discharging the responsibility to protect cannot be entirely discounted, and pressure for interventions by *ad hoc* coalitions or even by individual states acting without a Security Council mandate will increase and find wide favour.[146] Furthermore, it is pointed out that if an *ad hoc* coalition of individual states fully observes and respects the criteria identified in the report and succeeds in getting the support of world public opinion, this may have serious consequences for the credibility of the UN itself.[147]

This acknowledgement of a subsidiary role and responsibility of states for protecting international peace and security when the Security Council is unable to fulfil its responsibilities has been called the 'link theory'.[148] This theory has no legal basis in the UN Charter, which only refers to the subsidiary roles of other UN organs. The conditioning of the prohibition of the use of force with the effectiveness of the collective security system under Chapter VII, in particular since it is a peremptory norm, has no legal foun-

144 *Ibid.*, p. 52.

145 At the same time the Commission stresses that the creditbility of the UN may suffer as a result, and that the task is not to find alternatives to the Security Council but to make it work much better than it does at present. See p. XIII, 49, 55.

146 *Ibid.*, pp. 53–54. The Commission warns the Security Council that this will always involve a risk of abuse. An *ex post facto* authorization may offer a way out of the dilemma, if a situation like the intervention in Kosovo should ever occur again.

147 *Ibid.*, p. 55.

148 DUPI, p. 82. The link theory was first developed by Jessup, *A Modern Law of Nations*, 1948.

dation. These arguments are merely *de lege ferenda* arguments about how the law *should be*. Nonetheless, the argument that the Security Council had primary but not *exclusive* responsibility for maintaining international peace and security was used by one of the NATO members to justify the intervention in Kosovo, and may be used again in similar situations.[149]

The proposal of a responsibility to protect for states, the UN and the international community thus involves a new way of looking at security, state sovereignty and human rights. The Commission also recognizes that there is much more to human security than humanitarian intervention, and displays an awareness that protecting people is not only a question of military intervention in a conflict, actual or apprehended. The additional demands and expectations created by human security in relation to the way states treat their people have been creatively used by ICISS to develop a *de lege ferenda* conceptual framework for international action.[150] The responsibility formula is intended to reconcile the urge for humanitarian intervention with the persisting reality of state sovereignty.[151]

The UN Secretary-General has described it as an extraordinary and eloquent report, a remarkable accomplishment and the most comprehensive and carefully thought out response to date to the challenge of humanitarian intervention.[152] The added value of this initiative is that it encapsulates the element of international solidarity as well as taking into account the prevention and follow-up assistance components of external action.[153] The report has been received with concern as well, *inter alia* as regards the prospect of consistency in real world application and the risk of serving as a justification or pretext for inappropriate interventions.[154]

149 Heinbecker and McRae, *The Kosovo Air Campaign*, p. 124.
150 *Ibid.*, pp. 6, 11.
151 Thakur, Ramesh, *Intervention, Sovereignty and the Responsibility to Protect*, Security Dialogue, Vol. 33, No. 2, September 2002, p. 325. Thakur was one of the twelve members of the ICISS Commission.
152 Remarks made to the International Peace Academy seminar on The Responsibility to Protect in New York, 15 February 2002, quoted in Thakur, p. 338.
153 *Ibid.*, p. 328.
154 A thorough analysis and critique on the assumptions and controversies of the findings in the ICISS Report, see Welsh, J., Thielking, C., Macfarlane, N.S., *The Responsibility to Protect, Assessing the Report of the International Commission on Intervention and State Sovereignity*, International Journal, Vol. 57, No. 4, pp. 489–512.

The ICISS was demand-driven in its work – "looking for consumers" – which is probably why the report has been welcomed in political circles.[155] Thomas Weiss, co-head of the ICISS research directorate, believes that the idea of a responsibility will be mainstreamed in the next four or five years. The next step has been to induce the UN General Assembly to adopt a resolution affirming the just cause criteria and the four precautionary principles presented by the ICISS, but has failed until now.[156] For more discussion of the explanations for this, see below, section 10.6.

10.5 Human security, state sovereignty and human rights

> Human security is best guaranteed in the sovereign state which is governed under the rule of law with full respect for the human rights and the fundamental freedoms of those who reside in its territory.[157]

This is a 'best of worlds formula' for how human security, state sovereignty and human rights should interlink and cooperate to fully serve the interests of mankind. However, in countries that suffer from internal strife, bad governance and repression, state sovereignty is the only principle that is upheld by international law – at the expense of human security and human rights – when the Security Council is unable to take action under Chapter VII. Differences within the Security Council in the Kosovo case reflect the lack of consensus in the international community over how to achieve a proper equilibrium between respect for and protection of state sovereignty and human rights.[158]

There is a long debated dilemma between the potentially conflicting conceptions embedded in the UN Charter: the principle of sovereignty, implying protection of the territorial integrity of the state

155 Canadian Consortium on Human Security, *The Responsibility to Protect: Intervention and State Sovereignty*, Peacebuilding and Human Security After September 11th Conference Report, Session 7, pp. 1, 3, www.humansecurity.gc.ca/finalreport-en.asp (2003-08-04).

156 Thakur, p. 338.

157 Corell, Hans, *From Territorial Sovereignty to Human Security*, Address to the Annual Conference of the Canadian Council of International Law, 1999, www.un.org/law/counsel/ottawa.htm (2003-08-22).

158 DUPI, p. 37.

and non-intervention, and on the other hand the protection of human rights.[159] The UN Charter explicitly affirms the supremacy of maintaining international peace and security in Article 1(1) over the protection of human rights in Article 1(3). Promotion of human rights thus has a subordinate position among the purposes of the UN.

> The question which of the two principles should prevail when they are in conflict which each other has been answered in favour of territorial integrity and non-intervention in the times of the cold war. The last decade has brought along significant changes and has led to a new, yet fragile balance between the two concepts.[160]

The concept of human security supports the idea of stronger emphasis on human rights and hence challenges state sovereignty by demanding that the security of citizens become an international concern at times of great emergency. At the same time, human security has been presented as a concept with the potential to reconcile these two conflicting principles of the UN Charter, by finding a new balance between them.[161] The values behind territorial integrity and the protection of human rights have been declared compatible – the security of the state has to be seen alongside the security of the individual.[162] Its advocates also claim that the concept combines the essential values behind territorial integrity and political independence where they are compatible with international humanitarian law and human rights.[163]

Nonetheless, a greater adherence to the idea of protecting human security may lead to a need both to reformulate the concept of state sovereignty and the role of human rights in international law. It has in fact been acknowledged that the promotion of human rights and human security naturally leads to a reconsideration of sovereignty in all its aspects, a reconsideration that is part of the broader process of globalization.[164]

159 See *e.g.* the discussion in Reisman, Michael W., *Sovereignty and Human Rights in Contemporary International Law*, American Journal of International Law, Vol. 84, 1990, pp. 866–876; and Thakur, *supra* note 151, pp. 324–325.
160 Oberleitner, p. 9.
161 Mendes, p. 3.
162 Oberleitner, p. 9.
163 Mendes, p. 3.
164 McRae, Rob, *Human Security in a Globalized World*, p. 16.

The idea of regarding sovereignty as both an internal and external responsibility implies a shift and a departure from a sovereignty as the perception of right to exercise supreme power over a state's territory free from outside interference. The most significant implication of this reconceptualization is that it provides a new paradigm for consideration of the long-standing norm of non-intervention.[165] The concept of human security suggests that the principle of non-intervention should yield to an international responsibility to protect in situations where a population is suffering serious harm and the concerned state is unwilling or unable to avert it.[166] The rights and responsibilities of sovereigns therefore become equally important.

10.6 Implications for international law and international security

The implications of human security for international law could be said to be 'largely a reinforcement of a paradigm shift which has been under discussion in the international debate long since. Human security means that the international order can no longer rest on state sovereignty as the overriding concept of international law, but that the individual has to be in the centre'.[167] Its normative underpinnings, perceived as a departure from state security, challenge the state-centric order of international law. By shifting the focus from territory to people, it clearly challenges fundamental concepts of international law such as territorial integrity, state sovereignty and non-intervention. It is not surprising that international law has been reluctant as a discipline to respond to the emergence of the concept of human security.

As demonstrated in the previous chapter, some of the underlying problems which the concept of human security addresses are not unknown to international law and it has, through state and UN

165 Posteraro, Christopher Clarke, *Intervention in Iraq: Towards a Doctrine of Anticipatory Counter-Terrorism, Counter-Proliferation Intervention*, Florida Journal of International Law, Vol. 15, Fall 2002, pp. 151–213, pp. 196, 201.
166 *Ibid.*, p. 196.
167 Oberleitner, p. 29.

practice, been subject to a certain degree of development and legislation in the area of human rights, humanitarian law, refugee protection and humanitarian intervention.[168] But there is still much more to do in order to accommodate the concept of human security properly in international law and the security discourse. This will require further reinterpretation of traditional concepts as well as the development and creation of new norms that address human security concerns.

There is also reluctance within the UN, in particular among the G-77 states, to embrace the concept due to its close connection to humanitarian intervention.[169] Nevertheless human security is increasingly influencing international decision-making and global governance. The concept is believed to have effects on the institutional aspects of international law as well, due to its challenges to international security institutions – first and foremost with regard to the future of the Security Council. A Security Council applying the concept of human security will look different from the Security Council we know today, with regard to decision-making processes, operating methods, available tools, transparency and accountability.[170] Human security adherents have gone as far as to propose the creation of an Economic Security Council which can address the social, economical and ecological security threats to international peace and security.[171]

The ICISS initiative for a responsibility to protect explores the human security arguments and rationale for allowing the use of force in order to protect human rights. The question remains whether this formula will succeed in strengthening international security and the world order or will instead weaken the Security

168 The concept brings together these fields that have traditionally been kept separate. Oberleitner, pp. 28–29.

169 Personal interview with Johan Cels, see *supra* note 32. In Dorn, p. 2, the author explains that one a reason why the Security Council has never used the concept of human security in a binding resolution, although it has been used in statements by the Council President and in reports of the Secretary-General, is the great powers' reservations about a *duty* to intervene.

170 Oberleitner, p. 25. *Cf.* Ramcharan, pp. 21–29, which deals with the practice of the Security Council with regard to human rights and human security.

171 ul Haq, Mahbub, *New Imperatives for Human Security*, UNDP, New York, 1994, p. 7; McLean, p. 273, *supra* note 66. The outlook for the creation of such a Council is extremely bleak, in particular since the already existing UN reform proposals for the Security Council are very hard to realize.

Council and pose a threat to the foundations of international law. As an *ad hoc* strategy it will continue to be directed towards keeping the Security Council in focus, while at the same time allowing for improved protection for individuals.[172] If supported by the international community as a whole it could in time modify the existing norms of the UN Charter by establishing a legal doctrine of a subsidiary right of humanitarian intervention outside Security Council auspices. Such a development will, however, be affected by the problem of selectivity that accompanies the right to humanitarian intervention, and which would still exist with 'the responsibility to protect formula':

> The issues of consistency and capacity to act are important to any definition of interests and responsibilities ... At the same time as ethical principles should ideally be applied uniformly, it would be foolish to ignore the reality that such an obligation ultimately depends on the operational ability to carry it out. Because of the difficulty in saving all the victims all the time, should we not resort to trying to save some of the victims some of the time?[173]

For the formula to gain universal acceptance and eventually succeed in modifying the rules on the prohibition of the use of force, it is necessary that people's lives are equally valued around the world, and that the scope of interventions be extended to include 'forgotten places'. But, at the same time, if responsibility to react without the Security Council becomes is invoked too often, this could lead towards the establishment of a legal exception[174] to the prohibition of the use of force, thus severely testing the credibility and legitimacy of the UN. This seems to be an insoluble dilemma.

Since the terrorist attacks on September 11 the human security agendas and the Millennium Summit goals have partly and temporarily been pushed aside from the political agenda. In the war against terrorism, national and state security in the traditional sense have been revitalized. International commitment to humani-

172 DUPI, pp. 128–129. *Cf.* DUPI's four strategies for humanitarian intervention: the status quo, *ad hoc*, exception and general right strategy, pp. 27, 111–120.

173 ICISS Supplementary Volume, pp. 149–150. This problem is openly admitted and taken into consideration by the ICISS.

174 In other words an exception to the UN collective security system similar to that provided in exception in Article 51. See the discussion in Cassese, p. 29.

tarian intervention has reclined, and will probably occur in the future if and when the humanitarian interests are reinforced by strong national or other interests.[175] On the other hand, it may be a matter of time for the responses to international terrorism to merge with the emerging human security agenda.

As the international community moves forward in its struggle against terrorism, the increasing focus on human security is influencing and shaping international security policy and practice. Indeed, September 11 appears to have catapulted the post-Cold War period into a new phase of the world's unfolding history: "the Age of Human Security".[176]

10.7 Concluding remarks

The years ahead will prove whether the concept of human security is useful as a new instrument to meet new security challenges or whether it is too vague and incoherent and impossible to use as a practical guide in academic research or governmental policy-making. Although the definition of human security suffers from theoretical incoherence and is far from becoming a legal concept, there are those who believe it is on the way to changing institutions as well as the practice of global governance by 'becoming a new organizing principle of international relations and international law'.[177] The Kosovo case shows us that international action based on human security is increasingly becoming legitimate. The trend is indisputably moving towards a broader perspective on international security in the interdependent world that we inhabit, and

175 Reiter, Howard L., *September 11 and the Prospects for Humanitarian Intervention by the US*, Österdahl, Inger (Ed.), Is Intervention Humanitarian, Protecting Human Rights and Democracy Abroad, Report No. 62, Department of Peace and Conflict Research, Uppsala University, 2002, p. 93: 'From the vantage point of late 2001, however, it appears that the United States is not likely to be in the forefront of most acts of humanitarian intervention.' See a discussion on whether the Iraq war can be regarded as a humanitarian intervention in the next paper by Marie Jacobsson.

176 Ayton-Shenker, Diana (Ed.), *A Global Agenda, Issues Before the 57th General Assembly of the United Nations,* Rowman & Littlefield Publishers, Inc., Oxford, 2002–2003, p. xiii.

177 Axworthy, *Introduction*, p. 10; Heinbecker, p. 16; Oberleitner, p. 28.

human security could function as a positive catalyst for changes in the way we understand security.

An increased commitment to human security will change the role and position of human rights in international law, elevating its role in the maintenance of international peace and security at the expense of state sovereignty. By securitizing gross and systematic violations of human rights in international security and foreign policy, human security could become the leverage that is needed to push this development forward. The maintenance of international peace and security and the promotion of human rights do not necessarily have to be viewed as conflicting goals, but instead as mutually reinforcing. In the framework of the *responsibility to protect* these two fundamental purposes of the United Nations could merge and thus contribute to the closing of the gap between the legality and legitimacy of humanitarian interventions. Ultimately the concept of human security will influence how we view international security and national security, our understanding of threats to international peace and security, and the means we employ to achieve and maintain peace.

References

Books & articles

Annan, Kofi, *Two Concepts of Sovereignty,* The Economist, 18 September 1999.

Axworthy, Lloyd, *Human Security and Global Governance: Putting People First,* Global Governance A Review of Multilateral and International Organizations, Vol. 7, 2001, pp. 19–23.

Axworthy, Lloyd, *Introduction,* McRae, Rob, Hubert, Don (Eds.), Human Security and the New Diplomacy, McGill-Queen's University Press, Montreal, 2001.

Axworthy, Lloyd, *NATO's New Security Vocation,* NATO Review, Vol. 47, No. 4, Winter 1999, pp. 8–11.

Ayton-Shenker, Diana (Ed.), *A Global Agenda, Issues Before the 57th General Assembly of the United Nations,* Rowman & Littlefield Publishers, Inc., Oxford, 2002–2003.

Bajpal, Kanti, *Human Security: Concept and Measurement,* Occasional Paper No. 19:OP:1, Kroc Institute, Notre Dame, August 2000.

Bring, Ove, *FN-stadgan och världspolitiken, Om folkrättens roll i en föränderlig värld,* fourth edition, Norstedts Juridik, Stockholm, 2002.

Byers, Michael, Chesterman, Simon, *Changing the Rules about Rules? Unilateral humanitarian Intervention and the Future of International Law,* Holzgrefe, J.L., Keohane, Robert O. (Eds.), Humantarian Intervention, Ethical, Legal, and Political Dilemmas, Cambridge University Press, Cambridge, 2003.

Cassese, Antonio, *Ex iniuria ius oritur: Are We Moving towards International Legitimation of Forcible Humanitarian Countermeasures in the World Community?,* European Journal of International Law, Vol. 10, 1999, pp. 23–30.

Chesterman, Simon, *Just War or Just Peace, Humanitarian Intervention and International Law,* Oxford University Press, New York, 2001.

Commission on Human Security, *Human Security Now: Protecting and Empowering People,* Communications Development Inc., New York, 2003.

Danish Institute of International Affairs, *Humanitarian Intervention, Legal and Political Aspects,* DUPI, Copenhagen, 1999.

Department for Foreign Affairs and International Trade, *Human Security: Safety for People in a Changing World,* DFAIT, Toronto, April 1999.

DiPrizio, Robert C., *Armed Humanitarians, U.S. Interventions from Northern Iraq to Kosovo,* The Johns Hopkins University Press, Baltimore, 2001.

Evans, Gareth, Sahnoun, Mohamed, *The Responsibility to Protect,* Foreign Affairs, Vol. 81, No. 6, November/December 2002.

Foong Khong, Yuen, *A Shotgun Approach to Alleviating Human Misery,* Global Governance, Vol. 7, 2001, pp. 231–236.

Gray, Christine, *International Law and the Use of Force,* Oxford University Press, New York, 2000.

Heinbecker, Paul, *Human Security: The Hard Edge*, Canadian Military Journal, Spring 2000, pp. 11–16.
Heinbecker, Paul, McRae, Rob, *The Kosovo Air Campaign*, McRae, Rob, Hubert, Don (Eds.), Human Security and the New Diplomacy, McGill-Queen's University Press, Montreal, 2001.
Henkin, Louis, *Kosovo and the Law of 'Humanitarian Intervention'*, American Journal of International Law, Vol. 93, No. 4, October 1999, pp. 824–828.
Holzgrefe, J.L., Keohane, Robert O., *Humantarian Intervention, Ethical, Legal, and Political Dilemmas*, Cambridge University Press, Cambridge, 2003.
Human Security Network, *A Perspective on Human Security*, Chairman's Summary, Lysøen, Norway, 20 May 1999.
Independent International Commission on Kosovo, *Kosovo Report, Conflict, International Response, Lessons Learned,* Oxford University Press, New York, 2000.
Liotta, P. H., *Boomerang Effect: The Convergence of National and Human Security,* Security Dialogue, Vol. 33, No. 4, December 2002, pp. 473–488.
McKenzie, Mary M., *The UN and Regional Organizations,* Newman, Edward, Richmond, Oliver P. (Eds.), The United Nations and Human Security, Palgrave publishers Ltd, New York, 2001.
McLean, George, *Instituting and Projecting Human Security: A Canadian Perspective,* Australian Journal of International Affairs, Vol. 54, No. 3, 2000, pp. 269–276.
McRae, Rob, Hubert, Don (Eds.), *Human Security and the New Diplomacy,* McGill-Queen's University Press, Montreal, 2001.
McRae, Rob, *Human Security in a Globalized World*, McRae, Rob, Hubert, Don (Eds.), Human Security and the New Diplomacy, McGill-Queen's University Press, Montreal, 2001.
McRae, Rob, *International Relations and the New Diplomacy,* McRae, Rob, Hubert, Don (Eds.), Human Security and the New Diplomacy, McGill-Queen's University Press, Montreal, 2001.
Oberleitner, Gerd, *Human Security and Human Rights,* Occasional Paper Series, Issue No. 8, European Training- and Research Center for Human Rights and Democracy, Graz, June 2002.
Ogata, Sadako, *State Security – Human Security,* Fridtjof Nansen Memorial Lecture, Tokyo, 12 December 2001.
Paris, Roland, *Human Security: Paradigm Shift or Hot Air?* International Security, Vol. Vol. 26, Issue 2, Fall 2001, pp. 87–102.
Posteraro, Christopher Clarke, *Intervention in Iraq: Towards a Doctrine of Anticipatory Counter-Terrorism, Counter-Proliferation Intervention,* Florida Journal of International Law, Vol. 15, Fall 2002, pp. 151–213.
Ramcharan, Bertrand G., *Human Rights and Human Security,* Martinus Nijhoff Publishers, The Hague, 2002.
Reisman, Michael W., *Sovereignty and Human Rights in Contemporary International Law,* American Journal of International Law, Vol. 84, 1990, pp. 866–876.

Reiter, Howard L., *September 11 and the Prospects for Humanitarian Intervention by the US*, Österdahl, Inger (Ed.), Is Intervention Humanitarian, Protecting Human Rights and Democracy Abroad, Department of Peace and Conflict Research, Report No. 62, Uppsala University, Uppsala, 2002.

Report of the Commission on Intervention and State Sovereignty, *The Responsibility to Protect,* International Research Centre, Ottawa, 2001.

Seelye, Katharine Q., *Gore to Preside at Security Council Session on AIDS Crisis,* New York Times, 9 January 2000.

Simma, NATO, *The UN and the Use of Force: Legal Aspects,* European Journal of International Law, Vol. 10, 1999, pp. 1–22.

Small, Michael, *The Human Security Network,* McRae, Rob, Hubert, Don (Eds.), Human Security and the New Diplomacy, McGill-Queen's University Press, Montreal, 2001.

Supplementary Volume to the Report of the Commission on Intervention and State Sovereignty, *The Responsibility to Protect, Research, Bibliography, Background,* International Research Centre, Ottawa, 2001.

Swedish statement on the Secretary-General Report on the Work of the Organization, by Ambassador Hans Dahlgren, Permanent Mission of Sweden to the United Nations, 8 October 1999.

Sørenson, Georg, *Individual Security and National Security: The State Remains the Principal Problem,* Security Dialogue, Vol. 27, No. 4, December 1996, pp. 371–386.

Téson, Fernando R., *Humanitarian Intervention, An Inquiry into Law and Morality,* Transnational Publishers, Inc., Irvington-on-Hudson, New York, 1997.

Thakur, Ramesh, *Intervention, Sovereignty and the Responsibility to Protect,* Security Dialogue, Vol. 33, No. 2, September 2002.

ul Haq, Mahbub, *New Imperatives for Human Security,* UNDP, New York, 1994.

United Nations Development Programme, *Human Development Report,* Oxford University Press, New York, 1994.

Wallensteen, Peter (Ed.), *International Intervention: New Norms in the Post-Cold War Era?,* Department of Peace and Conflict Research, Report No. 45, Uppsala University, Uppsala, 1997.

Waschuk, Roman, *The New Multilateralism,* McRae, Rob, Hubert, Don (Eds.), Human Security and the New Diplomacy, McGill-Queen's University Press, Montreal, 2001.

Wheeler, Nicholas, *Saving Strangers, Humanitarian Intervention in International Society,* Oxford University Press, Oxford, 2000.

Österdahl, Inger, *Threat to Peace, The Interpretation by the Security Council of Article 39 of the UN Charter,* Iustus förlag, Uppsala, 1998.

Treaties

Charter of the United Nations (1945), UNTS, Vol. 1, p. XVI.

Convention on the Prevention and Punishment of the Crime of Genocide (1948), UNTS, Vol. 78, p. 277.

Optional Protocol to the Convention on the Rights of the Child on the Involvement of Children in Armed Conflicts (2000), A/RES/54/263.

Ottawa Convention on the Prohibition of the Use, Stockpiling, Production and Transfer of Anti-Personnel Mines and on their Destruction (1997).

Rome Statute of the International Criminal Court (1998).

Vienna Convention on the Law of Treaties (1969), UNTS, Vol. 1155, p. 331.

Cases

Case Concerning Legality of Use of Force (*Yugoslavia* v. *United States of America*), ICJ Reports 1999.

Corfu Channel Case, ICJ Reports 1949, p. 35.

Military and Paramilitary Activities in and against Nicaragua, ICJ Reports 1986.

UN documents

Friendly Relations and Co-operation among States in Accordance with the Charter of the United Nations (1970), GA Resolution 2625 (XXV).

Universal Declaration on Human Rights, GA Resolution 217 (III) (10 December 1948).

Security Council Resolution 1160 (31 March 1998).

Security Council Resolution 1199 (23 September 1998).

Security Council Resolution 1203 (24 October 1998).

Security Council Resolution 1244 (10 June 1999).

Security Council Draft Resolution S/1999/328 (26 March 1999).

Internet material

Axworthy, Lloyd, *NATO's New Security Vocation*, NATO Review, 47 4, Winter 1999, 8–11, www.nato.int/docu/review/1999/9904-02.htm (2003-09-04).

Banks, Kimberly, *Human Security and Canadian Foreign Policy*, af.3dgw.com/smss/pdf/banks_smss2001.pdf (2002-08-27).

Canadian Consortium on Human Security, www.humansecurity.info/ (2003-08-11).

Canadian Consortium on Human Security, *The Responsibility to Protect: Intervention and State Sovereignty*, Peacebuilding and Human Security After September 11th Conference Report, Session 7, www.humansecurity.gc.ca/finalreport-en.asp (2003-08-04).

Corell, Hans, *From Territorial Sovereignty to Human Security*, Address to the Annual Conference of the Canadian Council of International Law, 1999, www.un.org/law/counsel/ottawa.htm (2003-08-22).

Department of Foreign Affairs and International Trade, *Human Security Program*, Canada, www.dfait-maeci.gc.ca/foreignp/humansecurity/HS_program-.asp (2001-05-08).

Dorn, Walter, *Human Security: An Overview*, Pearson Peacekeeping Centre, 2001, www.rmc.ca/academic/gradrech/dorn24_e.html (2003-08-22).

Harvard Program on Humanitarian Policy and Conflict Research, www.hsph.harvard.edu/hpcr/events/hsworkshop/bibliography.pdf (2003-08-14); www.hsph.harvard.edu/hpcr/events/hsworkshop/list_definitions.pdf (2003-08-14); www.hsph.harvard.edu/hpcr/events/hsworkshop/related_research.pdf (2003-08-22).

Human Security: A Priority at the OAS General Assembly, Canada World View, Issue 8, Summer 2000, www.dfait-maeci.gc.ca/foreignp/canada-magazine/wv_8/8t6-e.htm (2001-05-08).

Human Security Bulletin, www.humansecuritybulletin.info/ (2003-08-14).

Human Security Network, Chairman's Summary, Second Ministerial Meeting, Lucerne, 11–12 May, 2000, www.humansecuritynetwork.org (2003-08-11).

Lodgaard, Sverre, *Human Security: Concept and Operationalization*, Norwegian Institute of International Affairs, www.hsph.harvard.edu/hpcr/events/hsworkshop/lodgaard/pdf (2003-08-22).

Mendes, Errol, *Human Security, International Organisations and International Law: The Kosovo crisis exposes the 'tragic flaw' in the UN Charter*, 1999, pp. 1–3, www.uottawa.ca/hrrec/publicat/bull38.html (2003-08-22).

Osler Hampson, Fen, Hay, John, B., *Human Security. A Review of the Scholarly Literature*, draft manuscript, 2002, www.liucentre.ubc.ca/hsq/_articles/Fen_fulldocument.pdf (2003-08-14).

Schnabel, Albrecht, and Thakur, Ramesh, *Kosovo and the Challenge of Humanitarian Intervention, Selective Indignation, Collective Intervention and International Citizenship, Policy Brief: Lessons from Kosovo Conflict*, www.unu.edu/p&g/kosovo_full.htm (2003-08-28).

Secretary of State Madeleine Albright Press Conference on Kosovo, 8 October, 1998, www.secretary.state.gov/www.statements/1998 981008.html (2003-09-04).

Sectoral Analysis of the International Situation and Japan's Foreign Policy, Chapter II, Section 3 A. Overview-Human Security, www.mofa.go.jp/policy/other/bluebook/2000/II-3-a.html (2001-06-20).

Workshop on Relationship Between Human Rights and Human Security, San José, Costa Rica, 2 December 2001, www.humansecurity_chs.org/doc/sanjosedec.html (2003-08-14).

Miscellaneous

Conclusions from the G-8 Foreign Ministers' Meeting, Cologne, 10 June 1999.

Human Security Network News Bulletin, Vol. 2, Issue 2, March 2003.

Human Security Now, Remarks by Sadako Ogata at the fifth Ministerial Meeting of the Human Security Network, Graz, Austria, 8 May 2003.

Independent International Commission on Kosovo, *Kosovo Report, Conflict, International Response, Lessons Learned,* Oxford University Press, New York, 2000.

Iraq: Legal Basis for the Use of Force, Legal Background paper, Brittish Foreign Affairs Committee, 2003. President Bush Address to the Nation, 17 March 2003.

Press Release 99/33 International Court of Justice, 2 June 1999.

S/PV.3937, 24 October 1998.

S/PV.3988, 24 March 1999.

S/PV.3989, 26 March 1999.

Statement made by the Secretary-General of the UN in Paris,14 June 1993.

Statement made by the UN Secretary-General Kofi Annan at the Inaguration of the International Criminal Court on March 2003 in the Hague, Archives of the Swedish Ministry for Foreign Affairs. S/PV. 4625 (16–17 nov. 1998).

11 The Use of Force and the Case of Iraq

Marie Jacobsson

11.1 Introduction

Since the start of the Iraqi aggression against Kuwait in August 1990, the use of military force against Iraq has been controversial and debated. It should be recalled that even though the very first military measures against Iraq were sanctioned by United Nations Security Council Resolutions, there were those who questioned the legality of the military action. The reason was that the character of the mandate to use force, namely, the 'delegation' to a coalition of willing states to enforce the Resolutions, was exceptional, but not unprecedented, in the history of the Security Council.[1] For those lawyers who argued that there were actually two bases for the use of force against Iraq in 1990–1991, *i.e.* collective self-defence based on Kuwait's request and a Security Council Resolution, doubts expressed about the mandate seemed odd elements in the debate.[2] Yet they were present.

Throughout the subsequent decade, force was used against Iraq on several occasions and every time force was used, a debate arose. The fundamental legal questions to be answered were: Did those countries that used force have a mandate to do so? How long did the mandate to use force in Resolution 678 last, and were there other legal grounds for resorting to force?

1 The first example of mandated force was the case of Korea in 1950, see UN Security Council Resolutions 82, 83 and 84 (1950). The Security Council recommended in Resolution 84 that the forces were made available to a unified command under the USA.

2 The controversy is reflected in the writings of many lawyers; see for example the debate between Bring and Falk, in Juridisk tidskrift 1991–92. As to the discussion on innovative interpretation of Chapters VI to VIII of the UN Charter, see *e.g.* Bring, Ove, *From Suez to Kosovo: A Dynamic View of Chapters VI–VIII of the UN Charter*, Broms, Bengt, Liber Amicorum, Finnish Branch of the International Law, Helsinki, 1999. For a recent reference, See also Gray, Christine, *International Law and the use of Force*, Oxford University Press, Oxford, 2000, pp. 153–154.

In parallel to the discussions on Iraq, the Security Council developed its own praxis as regards 'mandated' force. Few lawyers would today question the right of the Security Council to give a coalition of willing, often regionally or politically connected states, a mandate to intervene to maintain or restore international peace and security.[3] There is nothing in the Charter that prevents the Security Council from taking such measures. On the contrary, it is often claimed that this, in fact, reflects the idea of the role of regional arrangements referred to in Chapter VIII of the United Nations Charter. Furthermore, such delegation of power to take enforcement measures after a decision by the Security Council is welcomed and most often considered financially and politically cost-effective – especially since the Military Committee procedure has never functioned in the manner foreseen in the Charter. At the same time, concern has been raised in relation to the entrustment of the use of force to a limited group of states, since it could have 'a negative impact on the Organization's stature and credibility'.[4]

The decade also experienced a revival of another legal debate, namely, the debate on humanitarian intervention. This renewed debate was primarily caused by the Halabja chemical massacre, the genocide in Rwanda and the threat to the existence of the Kosovo-Albanians. Was there a right to use force to prevent humanitarian catastrophes even without a mandate from the Security Council?[5]

It is against the above-sketched background that the debate on the United States and United Kingdom-led military coalition against Iraq during the spring of 2003 should be viewed.

Contrary to the Kosovo case, the US and UK use of force against Iraq did not initially cause a particularly significant *legal* debate

3 See the formulation in Article 39 of the UN Charter. For an analysis of Article 39, see Österdahl, Inger, *Threat to the Peace. An Interpretation by the Security Council of Article 39 of the UN Charter*, Iustus förlag, Uppsala, 1998.

4 These are the words of former UN Secretary General, Boutros Boutros-Ghali, *An Agenda for Peace*, 1995, p. 29. Boutros-Ghali also expresses concern that this model may cause the states participating in the operation to 'claim international legitimacy and approval for forceful actions that were not in fact envisaged by the Security Council when it gave its authorization to them', *ibid.*

5 See the contribution in this volume by Diana Amnéus.

among international *lawyers* since most of them seemed to agree that the use of force was contrary to the wording of the UN Charter.[6] As a logical consequence, it then followed that the use of force was not legal. Yet the use of force caused a significant *political* and *philosophical* debate, since many participants in that debate considered the use of force *legitimate.* The discussion was often pseudo-legal though disguised in legal terms, particularly at the height of the debate.

The kind of legitimacy referred to (directly or indirectly) depended on the background of the participant, the aim of the argumentation or the time of intervention in the debate.[7] Initially the dominant argument was a welcoming of the fall of Saddam Hussein since his reign was a threat to international peace and security. Saddam's weapons of mass destruction should be eradicated since they constituted a threat to international peace and security. The United Nations had failed to tackle this threat and it was wel-

6 It took time before any scholarly article that argued in favour of the US-UK legal argumentation was published, see *infra*. The 'normal' differences in views on the issue of 'use of force' among international lawyers did not surface. Shortly before the outbreak of the war, Professor Anne-Marie Slaughter, USA, was interviewed by Bernard Gwertzman, consulting editor for Council of Foreign Relations. The interview was published by The New York Times, 4 March 2003 (www.nytimes.com visited on 6 March 2003). She expressed a belief that 'eight out of 10 international lawyers' as well as 'legal advisers of most other countries in the United Nations' would say that a US-invasion of Iraq without a specific Security Council resolution would violate international law. The prediction proved to be highly relevant.

7 It is well known that the content of the concept of legitimacy varies. Any lawyers that address or use the concept are faced with this complication. For a recent example, see Fassbender, Bardo, *Uncertain Steps into a Post-Cold War World: The Role and Functioning of the Security Council after a Decade of Measures against Iraq,* European Journal of International Law (EJIL hereinafter), Vol. 13, No. 1, 2002, p. 292. After having made the compulsory references to the writings of Thomas Franck, Fassbender pertinently refers to the much earlier writings of Carl Schmitt (1932) on *Legalität und Legitimität*. Debaters sometimes use the word 'legitimacy' without giving it a specific meaning and rather refer to a situation when 'legitimate' could be replaced by 'justified' or simply 'right'. This is often the case with non-legal debaters, but this more relaxed use of legitimate can also be found in legal writings, such as by Robert Howse, when he, in the same volume of EJIL, p. 91, formulates his sentence: 'Now it is legitimate to ask....'. Howse, Robert, *The Road to Baghdad is Paved with Good Intentions*, EJIL, Vol. 13 (2002), pp. 89–92. This colloquial use of 'legitimacy' here is far from the working definition of legitimacy, proposed by Franck, Thomas, *The Power of Legitimacy Among Nations*, Oxford University Press, New York, 1990.

come that the United States and the United Kingdom assumed responsibility for eliminating this peril.[8]

After a while, another kind of argumentation surfaced and became dominant. Saddam was a dictator whose respect for human rights was nil. The Iraqi people needed assistance in order to liberate themselves from this tyrant. A *jus gentium* that cared more about the regime of the tyrant than about the human rights of individuals was not to be respected.

Some international lawyers tried to point to the fact that human rights were part of *jus gentium*, but that the principle of sovereignty and the UN Charter restricted the possibilities to act. Let us then replace the sovereignty of states with 'human rights', responded some critics, enthusiastically.

Those who argued against the legality of the military intervention in Iraq referred to the wording of the UN Charter. The Security Council had not given a mandate to use force and this was not a situation where the right to self-defence could be invoked. Resolution 678 was not applicable and Resolution 1441 did not contain the code words for a mandate to use force ('all necessary means'). Admittedly, the human rights situation of the people in Iraq was appalling, but it did not amount to the type of acute situation often claimed to be a prerequisite for a humanitarian intervention.[9]

Representatives of the US and the UK and their coalition claimed that the use of force was not only legitimate, but also legal. This is natural since no state that resorts to force would be prepared to admit that it does so contrary to international law. A legal basis must be found, whether or not this basis is strong or weak or indeed

8 In particular, US-based lawyers have been critical of the UN management of the question of Iraq. Many represent a group of lawyers that, from the beginning, thought it was naïve to believe that Saddam Hussein would yield to the pressure imposed by the sanctions and claimed that those who suffered were the people of Iraq. The remedies suggested for the suffering were either to suggest the lifting of sanctions (the 'idealists'), or to get rid of Saddam Hussein (the 'realists'). Robert Howse provides a short and concentrated argument reflecting the 'realist' approach in EJIL, Vol. 13, 2002, pp. 89–92. Howse's argument is interesting since it was written before the Iraqi war in 2003. Yet it contains in concentrated form, the reoccurring and relevant arguments.

9 See also note 76.

whether or not it exists at all.[10] The main legal argument on the part of the US and the UK was that the mandate to use force as found in Resolution 678 was still in force since Iraq was in material breach of a series of UN Resolutions.

11.2 The legal and political context

As indicated above, the US-led military intervention in Iraq has a history not to be neglected.

Iraq invaded Kuwait on 2 August 1990. The Security Council condemned the invasion the same day in Resolution 660 and demanded that Iraq immediately withdraw its forces.[11] When Iraq did not respond accordingly, the Security Council sharpened its demands and imposed sanctions through Resolution 661 adopted on 6 August 1990.[12] Although Kuwait's inherent right of individual and collective self-defence in response to the armed attack by Iraq was affirmed in the latter Resolution's preambular paragraph, none of the Resolutions contained a mandate to use force independent of this right to self-defence.[13] This means that the Security Council

10 Mary Ellen O'Connell claims that there is still 'a strong case that states are committed to international law on the use of force', *Re-leashing the Dogs of War* (Review Essay), AJIL, Vol. 97, 2003, p. 456.

11 The voting figures were 14 to none. Yemen did not participate in the vote.

12 Voting figures: 13 to none and two abstentions (Cuba and Yemen).

13 Gray, *supra* note (2000) indicates that one of the reasons for the inclusion of the right of Kuwait to self-defence was an initiative by the United Kingdom. It wanted to prevent an interpretation of the Resolution whereby it was argued that the right to individual or collective self-defence had elapsed since the Security Council had imposed sanctions (*i.e.* taken measures), pp. 93–94. This touches upon the perpetual problem of when the right of individual and collective self-defence ceases, which arises from the wording of Article 51 of the UN Charter that nothing in the Charter 'shall impair the inherent right of individual or collective self-defence if an armed attack occurs against a Member of the United Nations, *until the Security Council has taken measures necessary to maintain international peace and security'* (author's emphasis).

The affirmation of Kuwait's right of individual and collective self-defence in response to the armed attack by Iraq (preambular paragraph 5) should be compared with the reference to the inherent right to individual or collective self-defence in Resolution 1368 (2001), *i.e.* the resolution adopted as a result of the large-scale terrorist attacks against the United States in 2001. Resolution 1368 recognises (preambular paragraph 3) the right to individual or collective self-defence, but contains no reference against whom or where to such self-defence should be directed.

took measures and acted in accordance with its responsibility, but it leaves open the question whether the Security Council had taken sufficient measures to maintain international peace and security.[14]

The US declared its intention to implement the Resolution based on the request expressed by the Government of Kuwait to assist Kuwait in conducting its right to self-defence, and informed the Security Council in accordance with the obligation in Article 51 of the UN Charter. Given the fact that the US did not need a Security Council resolution to assist the Government of Kuwait to make use of its right to individual self-defence, it seemed odd when the then Secretary-General of the UN, Peres de Cuellar, signalled that the measures were not appropriate, since Resolution 661 lacked a use-of-force mandate.[15]

Iraq still did not respond according to the demands of the Security Council, and therefore the Security Council adopted Resolution 665 on 25 August 1990. The Resolution calls upon those member states that are co-operating with Iraq and which are deploying maritime forces in the area 'to use such measures commensurate to the specific circumstances as may be necessary' to ensure the strict implementation of the provisions in Resolution 661 (*i.e.* the Resolution imposing sanctions) relating to shipping. Hence, the states concerned were given an enforcement mandate that went beyond the mere right to individual and collective self-defence according to Article 51 of the UN Charter in that they were asked to enforce the implementation of Resolution 661 (the Sanctions Resolution) through inspection and verification of cargoes. Although the laws of naval warfare give the belligerents quite extensive rights to inspect and verify cargoes of neutral shipping, they are not obliged to do so. In contrast, Resolution 665 imposes (calls upon) the 'Kuwaiti coalition' to act. This formulation and mandate covered the grey-zone areas between the laws of naval warfare and the UN Charter law that otherwise would have existed. The effect was that the legal gap between the *jus in bello* and the *jus ad bellum* rules was closed, and the legal conditions for a practical management of the

14 Compare the wording in Article 51 and see the comments in note 13, *supra*.
15 Statement made in Lima on 16 August 1990, obtained from the Press Centre at the United Nations. The statement must therefore be regarded as an expression of a political (and not legal) position.

situation were established. The Resolution places a restriction on the self-defence coalition in that the measures need to be 'commensurate'. Given *inter alia* the principle of proportionality, such a restriction was legally redundant, but sent a political signal. After having made a dutiful reference to the role of the Military Staff Committee, the Security Council then only requested the states concerned to report to the Council and to the sanctions committee.[16]

When Iraq, almost one-and-a-half months after its invasion of Kuwait, still had not complied with the demands expressed in the Resolutions, the Security Council pronounced, for the first time, a *de facto* threat of more concrete and forceful measures by Resolution 667.[17] The threat is further enhanced in Resolution 670, in which the Security Council underlines that non-compliance by Iraq 'could lead to further serious action'.[18] Since the sanction regime was further sharpened by this Resolution, there was no doubt that the threat was related to the use of military force.

On 29 November 1990 the Security Council expressed (in Resolution 678) its determination to to 'secure full compliance with its decisions', and authorized Member States co-operating with Iraq 'to use *all necessary means* to *uphold and implement resolution 660* (1990) and *all subsequent relevant resolutions* and to restore international peace and security in the area', unless Iraq on or before 15 January 1991 fully implemented the previous Resolutions adopted by the Security Council (emphasis added).[19]

The Resolution gave Iraq a chance to withdraw and comply, but it also contained a trigger mechanism. It gave the coalition a three-pronged mandate: to make sure that the Iraqi forces were with-

16 Resolution 665, op. para. 4. This obligation gave a signal that the Security Council wanted to keep the issue under its control, and prevent a repetition of the Korean case, when the mandated forces under the US in reality acted without a continuous Security Council control, once it had been given a mandate. For description in Swedish of the Korean case, see Bring, Ove, *FN-stadgan och världspolitiken*, Norstedts juridik, Stockholm, 1992, pp. 309–314.

17 Adopted unanimously on 16 September 1990. The Security Council decides to consult to take 'further concrete measures' as soon as possible. The first measures had already been taken by Resolution 661.

18 Adopted on 25 September 1990. Cuba voted against the resolution.

19 Resolution 678 was adopted by 12 votes to 2 (Cuba and Yemen) and one abstention namely, the permanent member China.

drawn from Kuwait, to implement all subsequent relevant Resolutions, and to restore international peace and security in the area. The coalition rapidly fulfilled the first element of the mandate, *i.e.* to make sure that the Iraqi troops were withdrawn from Kuwait.

Whereas it was clear from the purposes of the Resolution (including its negotiating history) that the authorization to use 'all necessary means' meant a mandate to use force, there were other, possibly unforeseeable ambiguities in the Resolution. It is primarily the formulation 'all subsequent relevant resolutions' that has caused interpretation problems in relation to the military measures adopted after the liberation of Kuwait (from 1991 and onwards).[20] Clearly the formulation intended to contain a threat to use force, but was it meant to formulate a mandate to enforce *all* resolutions that were to be adopted *after* Resolution 678?[21]

In the course of the full decade that followed, military force was used against Iraq a number of times. It is as impossible to list all occasions, as it is impractical to list all UN Security Council Resolutions.[22] However, a few situations should be recalled.

The first relates to the 'no-fly-zones'. The background was an intensified severe security situation in Southern Iraq. There had been clashes between Iraqi and Kuwaiti soldiers, Iraq had moved missiles to the southern no fly zone and undertaken several incur-

20 Szasz, Paul, argues that there are even grammatical reasons for why the phrase 'all subsequent resolutions' must be read in the context of the reference to 'the above-mentioned resolutions', see his argumentation in ASIL Proceeding 1998, p. 140.

21 It should be noted that the third element of the mandate was to restore (not maintain) international peace and security in the area. That indicates that the mandate had a time limit, compare the formulation in Article 39 of the UN Charter. This interpretation is supported by op. para. 6, which includes a demand to withdraw its own forces from the demilitarised zone and by the formulation in Resolution 686, op. para. 8. Molander, Johan, *The United Nations and the Elimination of Iraq's Weapons of Mass Destruction: The Implementation of a Cease-Fire Condition*, United Nations, New York, 1992, takes the view that military action in support of Resolution 687 'could certainly not take the massive character required to end Iraq's occupation of Kuwait' but that it could 'comprise air-strikes to destroy sites where Iraq opposes the demolition of prohibited items....', p. 137.

22 Numerous articles and books have been written on the development of the UN management of the question of Iraq. For an easy reference to occasions between 1991–1999 on which force has been used, see Graham-Brown, Sarah, *Sanctioning Saddam. The politics of intervention in Iraq*, Tauris in association with Association, MERIP, London, 1999. Appendix.

sions into the demilitarized area. Furthermore, Iraq refused the weapons inspectors permission to fly to Baghdad.[23]

When the US, the UK and France, on 13 January 1993, undertook a raid in the area, the then Secretary-General of the UN, Boutros Boutros-Ghali, made a statement. He declared that the forces had 'received a mandate from the Security Council, according to Resolution 678 and the cause of the raid was the violation by Iraq of Resolution 687 concerning the cease-fire'.[24] Even if the statement could not give legal sanction to the military operations, it certainly gave them political legitimacy. The content of the statement was blurred by the additional comments by Mr. Sills, a UN Press Spokesman, when he said that '"a no fly zone" in Iraq was not specifically authorised by a United Nations resolution, but he understood that the Member States involved felt that there was authorization within the overall framework of the relevant resolutions, specifically Resolution 688 (1991) which dealt with humanitarian aid'. The use of force for the purpose of assisting the population was a far more delicate matter for the majority of states, than the use of force to make Iraq comply with its obligations.

The problem with the latter interpretation is of course that there is no reference to the use of force in Resolution 688.[25] Yet it did send an important signal that the appeal in Resolution 688 to all member states and all humanitarian organisations to contribute to the humanitarian relief efforts meant something more than a traditional plea to act.

The Iraqi obstruction worsened in 1997 and 1998 when Iraq attempted to break (partially or completely) its co-operation with the UN. The US and the UK signalled already at an early stage that they wanted to have a renewed mandate to use force in Iraq, while at the same time stressing that they did not need a new authorization since they already had one. It was clear from the beginning that the other permanent members of the Security Council, France, Russia and China, were against any formulation that came close to something that could be interpreted as a mandate to use force. The

23 Graham-Brown, Id., under 1993.

24 UN Press Release: Statement made by the Secretary-General of the United Nations in Paris, 14 January 1993.

25 For an analysis of this and similar situations see Gray (2000), *supra* note 2, pp. 28–31.

three countries believed that a use-of-force mandate no longer existed and they were not prepared to give one. Intense consultations between the two groups were conducted throughout the first two months of 1998 in order to reach agreement on texts of resolutions that could be adopted by consensus.

The discussion came to a large extent to focus on whether or not to spell out in a forthcoming resolution that Iraq was in material breach of it obligations. The discussion on 'material breach' dates back to Resolution 707 (1991), in which Iraq was condemned for its

> 'serious violation of a number of its obligations under section C of resolution 687 (1991) ... which constitutes a material breach of the relevant provision of that resolution which established a cease-fire and provided the conditions essential to the restoration of peace and security in the region'.

Contrary to some other resolutions, Resolution 707 contains no threat of further action by the Security Council.[26]

'Material breach' is a treaty law term. The Vienna Convention on the Law of Treaties provides in Article 60 that a material breach (*violation substantielle*) entitles parties to a multilateral treaty to suspend the operation of the treaty in whole or in part or to terminate it. 'Material breach' is further defined for the purpose of the Vienna Convention. A material breach of a bilateral treaty has similar consequences but the legal context is of course less complicated since there are fewer parties involved. Given the perceived seriousness in situations of material breach, it is somewhat odd that another treaty term, fundamental breach, was not used. A fundamental breach in treaty law context is more serious than a material breach. It is worth noticing that whereas the International Law Commission was of the view that a material breach could generate a right to retorsion or reprisals, there was no agreement on at what stage such a right can be resorted to (armed reprisals were excluded under any circumstances since they would fall under the prohibition of the use of force in Article 2(4) of the UN Charter).

26 Compare for example the wordings in Resolution 1134 (1997), Resolution 1137 (1997), Resolution 1154 (1998) and Resolution 1194 (1998).

The concept found its way into the Iraq case through the curious feature of Resolution 687 that has been likened to a 'semi-treaty' or a contractual provision.[27]

Reference to 'material breach' was a sensitive matter and there were good reasons for such sensitiveness. Five years earlier, the President of the Security Council had made a Presidential Statement on 11 January 1993, declaring Iraq to be in material breach of its obligations.[28] Two days later, the US, the UK and France launched a strike against Iraq.[29] It was in this context that the UN Secretary-General made the statement (referred to *supra*) that the forces had 'received a mandate from the Security Council, according to Resolution 678 and the cause of the raid was the violation by Iraq of Resolution 687 concerning the cease-fire'.[30]

That certainly established a connection between a reference to 'material breach' and the use of force, and although it appears as if none of the members of the Security Council took the view that a reference to 'material breach' would in itself authorize or sanction use of force, many were politically concerned about making such a reference. One country, in particular, did not want to see the combination of a reference to 'material breach' and 'serious consequences' since such a combination could be viewed as a new code expression for a use-of-force mandate. In addition, there was a clear negative attitude on the part of some members of the Council, as regards whether or not force should be used at all. Furthermore, countries did not want to build in any kind of automaticity between the reference to Iraq's violations and possible consequences of such violations.

27 Much has been written about this semi-contractual provision and there is no need to go further into this in this article, see *e.g.* the articles by Pål Wrange referred to in the Reference section, pp. 410–411. Molander, *supra* note 21, analyses the resolution from a more historical perspective, but concludes that Resolution 687 'constitutes a complete novelty', p. 156.

28 UN Doc S/25091 (11 Jan. 1993).

29 Strikes were undertaken on 13, 17 and 18 January 1993.

30 UN Press Release: Statement made by the Secretary-General of the United Nations in Paris, 14 January 1993.

On 2 March 1998, the Security Council adopted Resolution 1154, which stressed that Iraq must accord immediate, unconditional and unrestricted access to UNSCOM and IAEA and that 'any violation would have severest consequences for Iraq'.[31] The formulation reflects the disagreement between the five permanent members. There is no reference to 'material breach', there is no authorization to use 'all necessary means' and there is no 'automatic resort' to further steps in the Resolution. However, the Security Council recalls 'all its previous resolutions' (without specifically mentioning Resolution 678), and declares that is will 'remain actively seized of the matter' in accordance with 'its responsibilities under the Charter' so as to 'ensure implementation of this resolution, and to secure peace and security in the area'. It was clear that this was a compromise formula where the reference to 'all its previous resolutions' was inserted to meet the demands of the US and the UK, as was the reference to 'severest consequences'. The opposing view was reflected in the reference to the ambition of the Council to remain '*actively* seized', its responsibilities under the Charter, and not least to the lack of references to 'material breach' and 'all necessary means'.

Clearly, the disagreement gave Iraq an incentive to continue to refuse to submit to its obligations, and as a peak in a series of decisions and obstructive measures, Iraq decided on 1 November 1998 to halt its co-operation with UNSCOM and IAEA, *i.e.* the weapons inspectors.

By then the US and UK had lost patience, both with Iraq and apparently also with their fellow member states on the Security Council. A massive military, but in time and to a geographically extent limited, operation against Iraq was undertaken from 16 to 19 December 1998. Both countries took the view that they had a mandate within the context of the 'cease fire Resolution' (687). None of them took the view that a mere reference to 'material breach' could serve as a use-of-force mandate.

Other members of the Security Council declared that the use of force against Iraq had required a new and clear mandate from the Security Council. The Russian President and the Russian Foreign

31 Security Council Resolution 1154 (1998).

Minister stated that they considered the attack as a flagrant violation of the UN Charter and universally accepted principles of international law. The same was said by China. There can be no doubt that there was a clear disagreement among the members of the Council as regards the mandate to use force against Iraq. This showed that the Council had distanced itself from the use-of-force mandate in Resolution 678 and that there was no agreement that a breach of Resolution 687 by necessity would be a 'Sleeping Beauty kiss' that would automatically awake the mandate to use force in Resolution 678.[32] Irrespective of the post-facto 'acceptance' of the use of force in 1993, the situation was now different and the disagreement among the members of the Council showed that there was no implied consent. Any development in the direction of acceptance of a 'continuous mandate' was certainly discontinued.[33]

11.3 The run-up

The relationship (if it is at all possible to express it in such terms) between the US and Iraq worsened severely after the terrorist attacks on targets in the US on 11 September 2001. In addition, Saddam Hussein had continued to use the UN sanctions against Iraq as a political tool. Iraqi citizens were de facto deprived of the benefits of the refined system of sanctions (under the so called *oil-for-food* mechanism), there were no UN inspectors in Iraq despite the establishment in 1999 of UNMOVIC,[34] and Saddam Hussein sat even steadier in the saddle. The situation was far from safe and sound. The US, and to a lesser extent the UK, signalled that they wanted action against Iraq. This became even clearer after the state-

32 The discussions on 'automaticity' resembled the discussions in the context of Resolution 1441. On the one hand, it was important to give Iraq a clear signal that force might be used. On the other hand, it was important to give Iraq an incentive to change its obstructive behaviour.

33 There is no space to discuss the relevant, but not necessarily crucial, question of whether Resolution 687 established a contractual relation between Iraq and the coalition or between Iraq and the Security Council. See also note 27.

34 The United Nations Monitoring, Verification and Inspection Commission, UNMOVIC, replaced UNSCOM through a decision by the Security Council in 1999, see Resolution 1284 (1999). UNMOVIC was led by Dr. Hans Blix from Sweden.

ment President Bush delivered at the general debate of the UN General Assembly in 2002.

Throughout the work during the autumn of 2002 that finally led to the adoption of Resolution 1441 on 8 November 2002,[35] there was a clear reluctance on the part of many members of the Security Council to adopt a resolution that authorized the use of force against Iraq. Instead, they wanted a step-by-step approach, including an enhanced inspection regime. Yet it was obvious that many states did not exclude the use of force when all other means were exhausted. The difference lay between those who thought that the UN-track (enhanced, improved and increased UN inspections) was a viable way and those who were unconvinced. Many countries also expressed political and legal concern about action without a clear mandate.[36]

11.3.1 Interpretation of Resolution 1441

After difficult and long negotiations the Security Council managed to agree on Resolution 1441 on 8 November 2002. It is an extensive Resolution but its crucial point is the decision by the Security Council that 'Iraq has been and remains in material breach of its obligations under relevant resolutions, including resolution 678 (1991)...'. The Security Council decides to afford Iraq 'a final opportunity to comply with its disarmament obligations' and decides to set up an enhanced inspection regime. It also decides that Iraq shall provide UNMOVIC and the IAEA 'immediate, unimpeded, unconditional and unrestricted access'. The Resolution recalls that the Council had repeatedly warned Iraq that 'it will face serious consequences as a result of its continued violations of its obligations'.[37]

The negotiating history of Resolution 1441 provides clear evidence that attempts (primarily on the part of the US, but also the

35 For a description of the Resolution, see Kirgis Frederic L., *Security Council Resolution 1441 on Iraq's Final Opportunity to Comply with Disarmament Obligations,* ASIL Insights, 14 November, 2002.

36 This is evidenced by the official records of the Council, see *e.g.* the summary of the Security Council Debate on Iraq at the request of the Non-Aligned Movement 16–17 November 2002, SC 4625th Meeting.

37 Resolution 1441 (2002).

UK) failed to have a clear reference to enforcement measures (to use 'all necessary means') in Resolution 1441. Russia, China and France stated on the day of the adoption that Resolution 1441 'excludes any automaticity in the use of force'.[38] The phrase carried two messages: firstly, that the Resolution alone did not give a mandate to use force against Iraq, and secondly, that the issue had to be returned to the Security Council before use of force was undertaken. The slightly blurred formulation reflects both the disagreement among the five permanent members of the Council, and the intention not to exclude military enforcement measures should Iraq fail to meet its responsibilities. But there was no trigger mechanism as in Resolution 678. The five permanent members had to tackle their divergence in opinions while, at the same time, upholding the authority of the Security Council and the enhanced inspection regime under Dr. Hans Blix, UNMOVIC and Dr. El-Baradei, IAEA.

Also the Permanent Representative of the US, Ambassador John D. Negroponte, signalled in his explanation of vote in the Security Council, that the Resolution contained no 'hidden triggers' and no 'automaticity with respect to the use of force.'[39] Negroponte stressed that Iraq was and remained in material breach of its disarmament obligations. In case of further Iraqi breach, the matter was to be returned to the Security Council. That did not necessarily imply that the Security Council must take a new resolution with a new and clear enforcement mandate, according to the implicit view of the US (which is a view fully consistent with previous positions taken.) Furthermore, a failure 'to act decisively ... does not constrain any member from acting to *defend* itself against the *threat posed* (but not yet undertaken) by Iraq, or to enforce relevant UN resolutions and protect world peace and security', declared Negroponte.[40] In an elusive manner, he thereby also touched upon the connection between the US perception of a connection between the Iraqi threat and the right of (pre-emptive) self-defence (see below).

38 www.accessatlanta.com/ajc/news/1102/09interpretation.html (11 November 2002) (outprint on file with the author).

39 www.un.int/usa/02_187.htm (13 November 2002) (outprint on file with the author).

40 www.un.int/usa/02_187.htm (13 November 2002) (outprint on file with the author).

The Permanent Representative of the UK, Ambassador Greenstock, declared in his explanation of vote that Iraq was in 'material breach of Security Council Resolution 687'. In addition, Ambassador Greenstock assured that there was no automaticity in the Resolution and that the matter would return to the Council for discussions in case of further Iraqi breach of its disarmament obligations.[41] Unlike the statement by the US representative, the British Ambassador did not mention the possibility of unilateral acts against Iraq.

It should be underlined that although 'automaticity' (or lack of 'automaticity') does not *in itself* mean that force is triggered, the word itself had a history, since it was used in the context of the Kosovo case. Russia argued in relation to the adoption of Resolution 1203 (1999) that the Resolution did not contain an enforcement mandate and, as a result, there was no automatic use of force.[42]

11.3.2 Renewed efforts to get an enforcement mandate

Dr. Blix's team commenced its inspections, as did Dr. El-Baradei's. Both reported back to the Security Council. Iraq was considered to have cooperated, but not to the extent required. The need to bring the matter back to the Security Council for a discussion of the consequences of Iraq being in material breach and to negotiate an enforcement mandate surfaced more and more clearly. At the same time, it became clear that the prospects of a new resolution with a clear mandate to use force were very small. France and Russia threatened to veto a resolution, and China gave a similar signal.

Contrary to the situation in 1998, the debate was not a debate on whether or not to use force. It was a debate about if, and when, the Security Council might decide to use force against Iraq as a consequence of Iraq's obstruction. It was a split between those states that believed that inspectors from UNMOVIC and IAEA should be given more time and those that believed the inspections were meaningless. It became a question of legality, legitimacy and credibility.

41 www.ukun.org/xq/asp/SArticleType.17/Article_ID.516/qx/Articles_show.htm (13 November 2002) (outprint on file with the author).

42 Gray (2000), *supra* note 2, p. 193.

11.4 The decision to engage in military operations and the differences in views

By mid-March 2003 it became entirely clear that the attempts to reach an agreement on a text to be adopted by the Security Council had failed. On 17 March 2003 the US advised El-Baradei and Blix to pull out their weapons inspection teams.

11.4.1 The US argument

The US and the UK decided to act on their own and President Bush delivered an ultimatum to Saddam Hussein. Three days before the commencement of the operations, President Bush delivered an address to the nation on 17 March 2003 in which he gave Saddam Hussein and his sons 48 hours to leave Iraq and stated: 'The United Nations Security Council has not lived up to its responsibilities. So we will rise to ours'. He then presented the US argument for the use of force against Iraq.[43] He made few references to the previously adopted UN Resolutions. Although it was apparent that he wanted to direct the listeners' thoughts towards the Resolution, the argument was more associative than legal.

President Bush asserted that Resolution 678 and 687 were 'both still in effect'. He also stated that the United States and its allies 'are authorized to use force in ridding Iraq of weapons of mass destruction'.

There is no legal causality connection between those two assertions.[44] Bush notes in his statement that the Security Council passed Resolution 1441 (according to which Iraq was in material breach of its obligations) unanimously and vowed 'serious consequences' in case Iraq did not disarm 'fully and immediately'. At the same time, President Bush notes that there was a risk that some permanent members of the Security Council would veto a resolution compelling the disarmament of Iraq.

The attack was launched on 21 March 2003, and shortly thereafter, the United States reported to the Security Council. The letter was construed in more legal terms than President Bush's statement. It is claimed that the military actions are authorized under existing

43 President Bush's Address to the Nation, 17 March 2003.
44 The type of causality reasoning found in the British argument is lacking.

Security Council Resolutions, including Resolutions 678 and 687. (The word 'including' clearly indicated that also other Resolutions were considered relevant). It is argued that a material breach of the cease-fire established under Resolution 687 removes the cease-fire and revives the authority to use force under Resolution 678. It is furthermore argued that this has been the basis of use of force in the past, accepted by the Security Council, and claimed to be evidenced 'by the Secretary-General's public announcement in January 1993' (see above).

11.4.2 The United Kingdom's argument

The United Kingdom delivered a more formalistic argument, perfectly construed as a syllogism.[45] It is argued that 'Resolution 678 authorized force against Iraq, to eject it from Kuwait and to restore peace and security in the area', and that resolution 687 'suspended but did not terminate the authority to use force under Resolution 678'. It is stated that a 'material breach' of Resolution 687 revives the authority to use force under Resolution 678, and that Resolution 1441 determines that Iraq has been and remains in material breach of Resolution 687. 'Thus, the authority to use force under resolution 678 has revived and continues today'.

The fact that Resolution 687 does not contain any reference to material breach,[46] nor contains any procedural structure for the administration of a violation of the conditions in Resolution 687, is not commented upon. There is no doubt that the use-of-force mandate could be revived, but the question was now (as on previous occasions): could a revival be made by one or two members of the Security Council, or would the Council *in corpore* have to decide to revive the mandate? The questions posed show that it can be difficult to interpret a Security Council resolution. It is perhaps worth

45 The answer was given in the British Parliament (Foreign Affairs Committee) by the Attorney-General, Lord Goldsmith, in reply to a question (regarding the legal basis for the use of force by Iraq) posed by Baroness Ramsay of Cartvale. Annexed to the reply in a legal background paper: *'Iraq: Legal Basis for the Use of Force'*. The documents are on file with the author. The quotations are from Lord Goldsmith's answer, unless otherwise indicated.

46 The first time 'material breach' was used was in Resolution 707 (1991).

recalling the wise words from the Legal Adviser of the Foreign and Commonwealth Office, Michael Wood:

> 'In the case of SCRs, given their essentially political nature and the way they were drafted, the circumstances of the adoption of the resolution and such preparatory work that exists may often be of greater significance than in the case of treaties.'[47]

The British Attorney-General Lord Goldsmith does not rely on Resolution 1441 (2002) as an independent basis for the use of force. It is emphasized in the legal background paper that there is a reference to Resolution 678. Such reference confirms that the resolution is still in force. It is argued that the reference to material breach in the 1990s served to revive the authorization of force in Resolution 678.[48]

This does not seem to be entirely correct. Iraq was indeed condemned in Resolution 707 for its material breach of some specific elements of Resolution 687, but since then the term did not appear until 2002. There had been no prospects of including a reference to 'material breach'. While it is true that a reference to material breach was included in 1441, the negotiating history clearly showed that this did not mean a revival of the mandate without further discussion and decision by the Council.[49]

The view that there existed an ongoing mandate since the adoption of Resolution 678 was not new, as shown above. Evidence of this can be found in the arguments put forward in 1998 by a former legal adviser to the State Department, Mr. Matheson.[50] While Matheson admits that the question remains whether the Security Council would have to authorize the use of force, or whether member

47 Wood, Michael C., *The Interpretation of Security Council Resolutions,* Max Planck Yearbook of International Law, Vol. 2, 1998, pp. 1–23, p. 23.

48 See Legal Background paper, *supra* note 45, para. 9. The British argument stresses the fact that it is the Security Council (and not the individual states) that has determined that Iraq is and continues to be in material breach.

49 Such a decision did not necessarily need to materialize in the form of a Resolution. But there had to be some kind of expression of will, and that 'expression' had to be communicated.

50 See the debate at the 1998 ASIL Proceeding, Wedgewood (1998) takes a similar position to that of Matheson.

states of the coalition could act on their own, he declares that the US position is that members of the coalition can act on their own. He continues to say that it would be 'acceptable and useful' to have the Security Council reiterate such authority.[51] Mr. Matheson's argument preceded the attacks on Iraq in December 1998. The position expressed by Matheson was strongly opposed by Szasz and Franck.[52]

11.4.3 Views on the use of force in relation to Iraq 2003

The US claimed that forty-nine countries are members of the coalition that had contributed to the military operations against Iraq.[53] That is indeed an impressive number, although the criteria for being placed on the list are both vague and wide. They range from direct military participation to political support, over-flight rights and humanitarian aid. At least as many countries as 'the 49' have been directly negative or critical, either for legal or political reasons or for both. The Arab League adopted a Resolution on 24 March 2003, condemning the action as a breach of the UN Charter and international legal principles. A similar statement was made by the Non-Aligned Movement (116 member states).

As to the three remaining permanent members of the Security Council (France, Russia and China), they were all critical and not prepared to support the US-led coalition. Russia stated that the action was contrary to principles and norms of international law and the Charter of the UN, China expressed serious concern in almost identical words to those of Russia. France embedded its legal critique in elegant words, but it was the negative attitude taken by France that caused much irritation in the US.

Even Secretary-General Kofi Annan expressed doubts with respect to the questions of legality and legitimacy. In response to a ques-

51 *Ibid.*, p. 141. He also claims that it is not necessary that the Council decides if there is a material breach or not, since this is an 'objective fact'.

52 It is interesting to note that the discussion also focused on the concept of self-defence, *ibid.*

53 www.whitehouse.gov/infocus/iraq/news/20030327-10.html, (28 August 2003) (outprint on file with the author).

tion posed to him at the inauguration of the International Criminal Court on 19 March 2003 in The Hague, he said, '[i]f the US and others were to go outside the Council and take military action it would not be in conformity with the treaty'.[54]

Indeed, it is primarily the actions or attitudes of states (rather than law professors) that develop international law or prevent further development of international law. At this stage in time, it is far too difficult to estimate whether one could seriously make a list of states that were in favour or against the military action. The figures of those listed to be in support of the war and those that have participated in manifestations against military force do not add up, mathematically speaking.[55] It is particularly for these reasons that this article will not address the issue of what kind of legal value the statements have. Yet it would be difficult to argue that the member states of the international community have either given an implied consent or expressed acquiescence.

11.4.4 The doctrine

There are not that many scholars that have argued in favour of the US-UK legal argument regarding the legality of using force. The most prominent are Ruth Wedgewood (US) and Christopher Greenwood (UK), and possibly Ivan Shearer (Australia).

US Professor and member of the Secretary of State's Advisory Committee on Public International Law Ruth Wedgewood published an article in a Swedish newspaper already on 22 March 2003. Wedgewood argued that Resolution 687 is the foundation for the demands (by the international community) on Iraq since 1991 and the previously adopted Resolution 678 gives the allies the right to force Iraq out of Kuwait and use force with the support of all 'relevant subsequent resolutions' in order to maintain peace and security in the region.[56] She implies that the US did not need another

54 Archives of the Swedish Ministry for Foreign Affairs.

55 The total number of individually counted states would then far exceed the number of UN member states.

56 *'Attacken är helt legal'* (The Attack is Perfectly Legal) Svenska Dagbladet, 22 March 2003, published on the so called *Brännpunkt*-page. The text was published in Swedish but must have been written originally in English. There is an obvious problem with translating the text back into English, but this is the only possibility since Wedgewood's text only appeared in Swedish.

resolution to use force. UN Security Council Resolutions are forceful tools and do not cease to exist just because the UN elects a new Secretary General, wrote Wedgewood (who apparently had more confidence in Boutros-Ghali's statements than those by Kofi Annan). She quoted the UN Secretary-General's statement that use of force against Iraq would be contrary to the UN Charter, but argued that the UN Charter has never functioned in the way in which the founding fathers thought it would function. She implicitly raised the issue of humanitarian intervention and concluded that the credibility of the UN will be questioned if dictators that murder their own people and invade neighbouring countries are not forced to comply with the UN Charter.

It is most likely that an editor has shortened the original article by Wedgewood which contains a mixture of legal and political arguments.[57] Irrespective of this, it shows her legal conviction, namely, that the action was not only legitimate but also legal. She differs here from her American colleague Professor Anne-Marie Slaughter who has argued that there were good reasons for going around the UN and that the action was legitimate, but not legal.[58]

Two professors of international law, Sam Blay and Ryszard Piotrowicz, have argued that Resolution 1441 did not need to reiterate the wordings of Resolutions 678 and 687 since the Security Council did not need to adopt 1441 in the first place. They conclude that 'in the context and the history of the Resolution, "serious consequences" has to mean measures that will actually achieve the core purpose of the Resolution, namely, securing disarmament by Iraq in compliance with its obligations under Resolution 687'. Such measures, they argue, mean enforcement measures under Article 42 of the Charter.[59]

57 There is of course nothing wrong with such a mixture, but it is difficult for a non-lawyer to categorize the argument as legal or political. This is of course the purpose with the mixture and it is not only a rhetoric trick, but rather reflects a policy-oriented legal method.

58 Slaughter, Anne-Marie, *Good Reason for Going Around the UN,* International Herald Tribune, 19 March 2003.

59 Blay, Sam and Piotrowicz, Ryszard, *The Use of Force and the Force of Law in Iraq*, Australian Law Journal, Vol. 77, 2003, *op. cit.* p. 287. Blay and Piotrowicz are working in Australia and Wales respectively.

It is far easier to find lawyers that author legal arguments in opposition. Critical lawyers have raised their voice in the UK[60] where the issue was particularly sensitive since the deputy legal adviser Elizabeth Wilmhurst is reported to have resigned as a result of the position taken by the Government.[61] Two former legal advisers, Sir Franklin Berman and Sir Arthur Watts, expressed regrets that the Government had abandoned the search for express Security Council endorsement, and add that the Government and its allies 'naturally bear the burden of justifying its legality and dealing with the numerous consequential issues that will arise in the aftermath of an armed conflict without such express endorsement'.[62]

One prominent lawyer, Professor Christopher Greenwood, is reported to have said that he considered that there existed authority to use force. Such 'existing authority [derives] from resolutions 678, 687 and 1441'.[63] He also added that 'a lost' second resolution would not 'taint' the legal authority of existing Resolutions since the Security Council is not a court, but a political body.

60 See *e.g.* the article: *War Would be Illegal*, the Guardian, 7 March 2003, by Ulf Bernitz, Dr. Nicolas Espejo-Yaksic, Agnes Hurwitz, Vaughan Lowe, Ben Zaul, Katja Ziegler, James Crawford, Susan Marks, Roger O'Keefe, Christine Chinkin, Gerry Simpson, Debora Cass, Matthew Craven, Phillippe Sands, Ralph Wilde and Pierre-Marie Dupuy from various universities in the United Kingdom and France. The law firm Matrix Chamber in London has issued two legal opinions. The first analysed the draft US/UK Resolution, published on 23 February 2003. The second analyses the legality of the use of force against Iraq. Both legal opinions were made at the request of the Campaign for Nuclear Disarmament (CND) and written by Rabinder Singh QC and Charlotte Kilroy of Matrix Chambers. Information about the CND can be found on www.cnduk.org.

61 This was reported in several newspapers; see *e.g.* The Guardian, 22 March 2003.

62 Berman, Franklin and Watts, Arthur, *Implications of Acting against Iraq Without UN Sanction*, Financial Times, 20 March 2003. They also write that 'the Government and its allies must accept the responsibility of accounting for their actions to the international community in whose name they claim to act'.

63 www.timesonline.co.uk/newspaper, (18 March 2003) (outprint on file with the author).

Lawyers in Australia were also critical (on legal grounds) of the Australian position to commit troops to the coalition against Iraq.[64]

Those lawyers (and representatives) of states that argued that there were no legal grounds for the use of force relied on the fact that the Security Council had not adopted a new resolution with a clear and unequivocal formulation that allowed for the use of force against Iraq. There was simply no new resolution with the formula 'all necessary means'. Resolution 1441 was considered not to have given a mandate and the previous mandate in Resolution 678 cannot reasonably last forever. A contrary interpretation would have meant a blank check for the US and its coalition partners to use force any time it considered that Iraq was in breach of its obliga-

64 See *e.g.* the similar manifestation by a considerable number (43) of lawyers, including the most prominent international lawyers in Australia, see the Article: *Coalition of the Willing? Make that War Criminals*, Herald, 26 February 2003. It should be noted that the most renowned Australian international lawyer, Professor and Judge Ivan Shearer, did not sign the Article. He is reported to have criticised the conclusion on a specific issue regarding war crimes, see Albrechtsen, Janet, *Academics fail Court Examination,* The Australian, 5 March 2003, but apparently not on the issue of the use of force. This corresponds to the view that Shearer expressed on a website under the Sunday Morning Herald, www.smh.com.au (6 March 2003). Shearer criticises the authors of the article in The Herald for adhering to 'a static view of the meaning of the UN Charter'. He claims that the Charter can and must be interpreted in the light of changing conditions and dangers. He claims that there is room in Article 2(4) to allow force to be used, for example, by way of humanitarian intervention. A 'failure of the Security Council to act decisively cannot in the end deprive states, especially those acting collectively and with transparent motives, from using armed force to advance the wider objectives of the charter, especially the protection of human rights'. Given the context of the contribution, Shearer thereby signals that he does not exclude that the use of force would be consistent with the UN Charter, but he does not go the whole hog and claim that it is legal.

It should be recalled that Australia has been present in the Persian Gulf with maritime forces since the Iraq-Kuwait war. Also the Labour Party (in opposition) was critical to the position of the Howard Government and claimed that the decision to go to war was not legal, whereas such unlawful action does not expose the Australian troops to legal action, either home or abroad, Statement by the Leader of the Opposition the Hon Simon Crean, MP, Canberra, 20th March 2003. The position is based on a legal opinion by Professor George Williams and Devika Howell, Director of the International Law Project. Grant Nieman has written a legal opinion addressing the possible exposure of the Australian troops to legal action.

tions under the Resolutions adopted. The debaters most often deny that the doctrine of pre-emptive self-defence has a basis in international law.[65]

The two major questions that arose were, as has been shown: Was the basic mandate to use force in Resolution 678 still in force, and was the determination that Iraq was in material breach of Resolution 1441 a legal basis for resorting to the use of force?[66]

Those who argue that the use-of-force mandate in Resolution 678 was still valid at the time of the 2003 military measures against Iraq tend to disregard the persistent objection by other members of the Security Council, primarily the three permanent members: France, Russia and China. Mass media has reported that both Russia and France were prepared to use their veto (whether or not they would have done so remains an unanswered question, but their attitude certainly hinted their position).

Given the assumption that a mandate by the Security Council to use force against a state does not last forever, but only as long as the reason for the mandate exists or as long as the Security Council has not terminated the mandate, it seems difficult to argue that the explicit rejection of the US-UK interpretation by the other permanent members can be neglected. Although the praxis of 'exit clauses' in resolutions is quite new (and a result of the problem with interpreting Resolutions 678 and 687), absence does not necessarily mean that it is up to a limited number of members of the coalition

65 The Guardian, 7 March 2003. A similar position has been taken in an Article in La Civiltà Cattolica, where it is claimed that international law does not accept pre-emptive wars. It is likely that this Article reflects the position of the Vatican. The Article might have caused the US representative to the Holy See to invite the controversial catholic theologian Michael Novak, who argued that the war against Iraq would be a continuation of the war from 1991.

66 The debate over these issues continues, see for example the section entitled *Agora: Future Implications of the Iraqi Conflict,* AJIL, Vol. 97, 2003, pp. 553–642, and the contributions by *e.g.* the Legal Adviser for Political-Military Affairs of the United States Department of State, Todd F. Buchwald (pp. 557–563), Professor Ruth Wedgewood (pp. 576–585), Professor Richard Falk (pp. 590–598), and Miriam Sapiro (pp. 599–607) – just to mention a few of the contributors to this section. See also Lowe, Vaughan, *The Iraq Crisis: What Now?* ICLQ, Vol. 52, October 2003, pp. 859–871.

to auto-interpret the conditions. The mandate to use force is the most serious decision that the Security Council can take and any resolution containing such a mandate must be interpreted restrictively. This means that termination of a mandate can be made explicitly or de facto.[67]

11.5 Is just war returning to the scene?

11.5.1 The 'Bush doctrine'

President Bush's argument in defence of the use of force against Iraq can be seen against the background of the so called 'National Security Strategy' of the United States.[68] The National Security Strategy reflects the US security thinking after the September 11 attacks that were directed at the heart of the United States financial, military and political centres. Although the ideas in the National Security Strategy do not solely emanate from the Bush administration (many of the ideas emanate from the thinking of the Clinton administration), it was President Bush that made a strategy out of them.[69]

There are many positive elements in the National Security Strategy – regrettably often neglected. Two examples are its focus on the need for international, including regional, cooperation and the view on development assistance. At the same time, the elements of the National Security Strategy of direct legal relevance for this arti-

67 There are also other arguments relating to the mandate in Resolution 678. They relate to the question of for what purpose force could be used. It is not possible to address this issue in this article.

68 The National Security Strategy of the United States of America, September 2002, can be obtained through www.whitehouse.gov/nsc/nss.html, (28 August 2003) (outprint on file with the author).

69 The National Security Strategy hardly touches upon security matters relating to nuclear weapons. Such matters were already dealt with by the Nuclear Posture Review that was published during spring 2002. Another strategy (National Strategy to Combat Weapons of Mass Destruction) was made public on 10 December 2002 (but dated 17 September 2002). The three 'strategies' must be read together.

cle, primarily the discussions of the right to intervene by force but also the references to human dignity rather than human rights, also need to be examined.[70]

A broad coalition is gathering, declared President Bush in his statement on 17 March 2003, 'to enforce the just demands of the world'. A similar formulation is to be found in the National Security Strategy: 'The reasons for our actions will be clear, the force measured, and the cause just.' The similarity to the philosophical and religious reasoning for *just war* is obvious.

The Security Council has not lived up to its responsibilities, continued the President. The reason for acting now is that the risk of not acting is greater. The National Security Strategy declares: 'The greater the threat, the greater is the risk of inaction.'

Bush also raised the issue of pre-emptive self-defence (without using the words) against terrorists. He uses a phrase so often heard among US international lawyers that it deserves to be labelled 'classic': 'responding to such enemies only after they have struck first is not self-defense, it is suicide.' This formulation is also recognizable from the National Security Strategy, that declares: 'We cannot let our enemies strike first.'

It is sometimes said that the discussion on the use of force had little or nothing to do with the Bush doctrine, yet it is impossible to disregard the fact there is a close connection between the ideas in the doctrine and the extensive, but legitimate, right of the United States to defend itself from perceived security threats, wherever they may appear. One example is the view expressed by Professor Kenneth Anderson: 'Of course it is legal, it is absolutely legal. The U.S. is entitled to go forth and defend its national security in a case, as here, where there's nothing contrary to law or morality.'[71] The view resembles the one expressed by Ambassador Negroponte when

70 The references to human dignity and the lack of reference to human rights (except on four instances) will not be addressed in this article.

71 Interview by Jan Crawford Greenburg, Washington Bureau, The Chicago Tribune, 20 March 2003, www.chicagotribune.com/archives (outprint on file with the author). Professor Anderson is a professor at the American University in Washington.

he stated that a failure 'to act decisively ... does not constrain any member from acting to *defend* itself against the *threat posed* (but not yet undertaken) by Iraq, or to enforce relevant UN resolutions and protect world peace and security' (see above). With this argument, he defends the US action not as an action under the laws of the collective security system, but under the rules of the inherent right to self-defence.

11.6 Where do we go from here?

A debate about the conditions for the use of force, taking as its starting point the Iraqi war, cannot be meaningfully undertaken by a group of more or less agreeing international lawyers. But nor can it be meaningfully undertaken without them. What is at stake is the skeleton of the system of international law, namely, state sovereignty, and that is clearly within the legal sphere.

A clear distinction appeared between experts on security policy from the realist school and non-realist international lawyers. Realists often regard international law as a highly irrelevant element in power politics. This view holds that other factors (primarily military and economic power) generate influence – international law is but a decoration and its existence is justified only as long as it can be used for political purposes.

Both realists and romantics tend to care about human rights. The conflicting view appears first when human rights are to be implemented and the tools for implementing the rules need to be strengthened. Can it be done by unconstitutional means and methods? Can a great power force democracy and human rights upon another power? Or must people drive the transformation to democracy? Or can it happen through the UN? Does the end justify the means?

Against the realist view, there exists a romantic view on international law. People with a strong international engagement tend to rely on the UN collective rather than on individual states as troubleshooters. The presumption is that international law is 'just', and there can be no 'just wars' unless decided on by the Security Council.

There is a related and classical debate about the discrepancy between the 'laws of politics' and morality. The German author Hans Magnus Enzensberger addresses this issue in his critical view of the position of the pacifist movement with regard to the then ongoing war against Iraq.[72]

As a result of the debate on the 2003 Iraq war, many international lawyers were reminded that it is insufficient to hide behind the existence of a rule and thereby avoid the discussion of legality versus legitimacy, and legality versus morality.[73] Part of the reluctance to discuss the dichotomy or overlap between the concepts might be caused by a concern not to 'mix' morality and law. The Kosovo Commission has formulated this as a 'gray zone of ambiguity between an extension of international law and a proposal for an international moral consensus', which 'goes beyond strict ideas of legality to incorporate more flexible views of legitimacy'.[74]

There is a risk that the US-led action in Iraq will prevent further discussions on an unrestricted and non-prejudicing debate about the necessity to act to protect people in emergency situations – situations in which military force might be needed. Such interventions will be made, but they will be made *ad hoc* and by states that have the political and military ability to act on their own. Western states will not feel threatened by such intervention. For them it is rather a matter of principle and loyalty towards the UN system. Non-democratic developing countries and states ruled by dictators will most likely wave 'the principle of sovereignty' as a protective shield. By doing so, they will attempt to avoid a burdensome debate about the legitimate right of other states (or UN-representatives) to point out deficiencies in their management of democracy and human rights.

Some Western representatives will most likely continue to defend what they consider a 'moral right' of removing a regime that does not allow individuals to make use of their human rights. It is a misperception to believe that 'regime change' is an idea that was introduced by the present President of the United States. Regime changes and removal of distrusted sovereigns have always been

72 See Enzensberger, Hans Magnus, *Pacifism and Hypocrisy (Pacifismen och hyckleriet),* translated from German and published in the Swedish newspaper Dagens Nyheter, 27 April 2003.

73 Some lawyers are prepared to discuss, see Franck, especially pp. 174–191.

74 Independent International Commission on Kosovo, *Kosovo Report, Conflict, International Response, Lessons Learned,* Oxford University Press, New York, 2000, p. 164.

undertaken – legally or illegally, through political alliances or subversive intrusion.[75] In addition, the Security Council has removed sovereigns. Closely connected is the issue of legal pressure on a government to adjust to human rights and democracy as an entrance ticket for membership in a political alliance, such as the European Union's demands on Turkey and other states that want to become members, or similar requirements by the African Union.

Few states – if any – are prepared to criticize the US because it managed to get rid of the terror regime of Saddam Hussein. The criticism is focused on the fact that the UN track had not been fully tested when violence was used and the fact that weapons of mass destruction have not yet been found. There is still no stability in Iraq. It is sometimes claimed that the Governing Council was not representative and constituted prolonged arm of the US, despite the fact that it was endorsed by, for example, the United Nations.

The great challenge for the international community is how to tackle the balance between the principle of sovereignty and the protection of human rights in practical terms. The idea that sovereignty implies responsibility is not new in itself, but the implications of such responsibility as expressed by the International Commission on Intervention and State Sovereignty (ICISS) are certainly welcome.[76] However, there is a risk that the positive elements of the proposals made in the report of the Commission, 'Responsibility to Protect', will again be set aside and not even be debated among states despite the fact that the 'criteria' for a military intervention described in the report would not have been fulfilled in the case of Iraq 2003. One of the Co-Chairs of the International Commission on Intervention and State Sovereignty, Gareth Evans, argued that

75 One might even quote Oppenheim from 1905 when he stated that when a state treats its citizens with such a cruelty that humanity staggers, the great powers ought to restore the legal order the extent necessary to guarantee its citizens living conditions appropriate for a modern civilization, Oppenheim, *International Law*, 1905, p. 347.

76 ICISS Report, *Responsibility to Protect*, p. 13.

'it would be deeply depressing – and utterly counterproductive for those working for a more decent international order – if the view were to take hold that this war was justified on humanitarian grounds.'[77]

Just war theories have been controversial and they continue to be so.[78] Resorting to just war theories can be a way to avoid the law. In conducting a political and legal discussion on possible situations in which, on humanitarian grounds, states might need to use military force against other states, 'just war' must not be mentioned. The ICISS Report is very quiet on the resemblance between the 'criteria' put forward in the Report and Thomas Aquinas's ideas on just war criteria. The choice to avoid reference to the 'just war' concept or to one example of 'just war', namely humanitarian intervention, is a good choice for political reasons. However, avoiding politically loaded concepts like "just war" and "humanitarian intervention" will not solve anything. The issue of international morality and non-interventionism will remain. A balance is needed. Values transform into politics and political decisions formulate new legal norms. It is no longer possible to compartmentalize discussions on national security, human security, the right to use force, human rights and moral and political considerations.

77 Evans, Gareth, *Humanity did not Justify this War,* Financial Times, 15 May 2003. See also the ICISS Report, *Responsibility to Protect, supra* note 76, *e.g.* p. 32 where the Commission lists the relevant decision-making criteria for a military intervention: right authority, just cause, right intention, last resort, proportional means and reasonable prospects, pp. 54–55 for the implications of inaction of the Security Council, and p. xii regarding the so called 'just cause threshold'.

78 For an excellent discussion with historical illustrations on the issue of just wars, see Walzer, Michael, *Just and Unjust Wars,* third edition, Basic Books, New York, 2000. The book, originally published in 1977, lacks a gender perspective, as does most other literature on 'just wars'. For a feminist perspective on the use of force, see Charlesworth and Chinkin, especially pp. 250–274. Chinkin also discusses the 'just war' concept in her article *Peace and Force in International Law,* 1993.

References

Below follows a very limited list of references. The list is unbalanced and subjective. There are several reasons for this. The first is that there is so much written on use of force in general and the question of Iraq in particular that it is impossible to make a fair *and* limited reference list. The second is that up to October 2003 there were few academic articles discussing the aspects of *jus ad bellum* and the 2003 Iraqi war. Finally, the list below contains references to quite a few Swedish authors. This is a way of acquainting students with the thinking of Swedish lawyers, whose articles will, in turn, contain references to the writings of lawyers based outside Sweden. I hope that this will give students incentives to search for other sources on their own. Looking for sources, articles and books – preferably in a library – is indeed, part of academic work, and it is fun, stimulating and inspiring.

Finally, a 'disclaimer' must be added: since there are few traditional academic articles in print I also used newspaper interviews as sources. This is a great risk because anyone who has been interviewed knows that newspaper 'quotations' rarely reflect what is actually said. They are often simplified and lack part of the argumentation, and therefore it is reasonable to believe that misquotations regularly occur.

Books & articles

Albrechtsen, Janet, *Academics Fail Court Examination,* The Australian, 5 March 2003.

ASIL Proceedings, *Legal Authority for Use of Force Against Iraq,* American Society of International Law, 1998, pp. 136–150.

Blay, Sam and Piotrowicz, Ryszard, *The Use of Force and the Force of Law in Iraq,* Australian Law Journal, Vol. 77, 2003, pp. 283–289.

Boutros-Ghali, Boutros, *An Agenda for Peace,* second edition with the new supplement and related UN Documents, United Nations, New York, 1995.

Bring, Ove, *FN-stadgans folkrätt,* Norstedts juridik, first edition, Stockholm, 1992.

Bring, Ove, *From Suez to Kosovo: A Dynamic View of Chapters VI to VIII of the UN Charter,* Broms, Bengt, *Liber Amicorum,* Finnish Branch of the International Law, Helsinki, 1999, pp. 12–38.

Bring, Ove, *Reflections on Richard Falk's Article on the Gulf War: Should a Functional Approach to the UN Charter be Considered Unconstitutional?* Juridisk Tidskrift, No. 2, 1991–92, pp. 375–378.

Buchwald, Todd F., Wedgewood, Ruth, Falk, Richard, Sapiro, Miriam, *Agora: Future Implications of the Iraqi Conflict,* AJIL, Vol. 97, 2003, pp. 553–642. Legal Adviser for Political-Military Affairs of the United States Department of State, 2003.

Byers, Michael, *The Shifting Foundations of International Law: A Decade of Forceful Measures against Iraq,* EJIL, Vol. 13, No. 1, 2002, pp. 21–41.

Charlesworth, Hilary and Chinkin, Christine, *The Boundaries of International Law. A Feminist Analysis,* Melland Schill Studies in International Law, Manchester University Press, Manchester, 2000.

Chinkin, Christine M., *Peace and Force in International Law,* Dallmeyer, Dorinda G, Reconceiving Reality: Women and International Law, Studies in Transnational Legal Policy, No. 25, American Society of International Law, 1993, pp. 203–230.

Enzensberger, Hans Magnus, *Pacifism and Hypocrisy (Pacifismen och hyckleriet),* translated from German and published in the Swedish newspaper Dagens Nyheter, 27 April 2003.

Evans, Gareth, *Humanity did notJustify this War,* Financial Times 15 May 2003.

Falk, Richard, *Reflections on the Gulf War Experience: Force and War in the United Nations System,* Juridisk Tidskrift, No. 1, 1991–92, pp. 181–193.

Falk, Richard, *What Future for the UN Charter System of War Prevention,* AJIL, Vol. 97, 2003, pp. 590–598.

Fassbender, Bardo, *Uncertain Steps into a Post-Cold War World: The Role and Functioning of the Security Council after a Decade of Measures against Iraq,* EJIL, Vol. 13, No.1, 2002, pp. 273–303.

Franck, Thomas M., *The Power of Legitimacy Among Nations,* Oxford University Press, New York, 1990.

Franck, Thomas M., *Recourse to Force. State Action Against Threats and Armed Attacks,* Cambridge University Press, Cambridge, 2002 (reprinted 2003).

Graham-Brown, Sarah, *Sanctioning Saddam. The politics of intervention in Iraq,* Tauris in association with Association, MERIP, London, 1999.

Gray, Christine, International Law and the Use of Force, Oxford University Press, Oxford, 2000.

Gray, Christine, *From Unity to Polarization: International Law and the Use of Force against Iraq,* EJIL, Vol. 13, No. 1, 2002, pp. 1–19.

Howse, Robert, *The Road to Baghdad is Paved with Good Intentions,* EJIL, Vol. 13, No. 1, 2002, pp. 89–92.

Independent International Commission on Kosovo, *Kosovo Report, Conflict, International Response, Lessons Learned,* Oxford University Press, New York, 2000.

Lowe, Vaughan, *The Iraq Crisis: What now?* ICLQ, Vol. 52, October 2003, pp. 859–871.

Mahmoudi, Said, *International use of Force: Quo Vadis?* Juridisk Tidskrift, No. 2, 2003–04, pp. 341–358.

Molander, Johan, *The United Nations and the Elimination of Iraq's Weapons of Mass Destruction: The Implementation of a Cease-Fire Condition,* Tanner,

Fred (Ed.), From Versailles to Baghdad: Post-War Armament Control of Defeated States, United Nations, New York, 1992, pp. 137–157.

Murphy, Sean D. (Ed.), *Use of Military Force to Disarm Iraq,* American Journal of International Law, Vol. 97, 2003, pp. 419–432 (in the section: Contemporary Practice of the United States Relating to International Law).

O'Connell, Mary Ellen, *Re-leashing the Dogs of War* (Review Essay), American Journal of International Law, Vol. 97, 2003, pp. 446–456.

Oppenheim, Lassa, *International Law: a treatise,* Vol. I, Peace, Longmans & Co, London, 1905.

Report of the International Commission on Intervention and State Sovereignty (ICISS), *Responsibility to Protect,* Ottawa, 2001, see also www.iciss-ciise.gc.ca.

Sapiro, Miriam, *The Shifting Sands of Preemptive Self-Defense,* AJIL, Vol. 97, 2003, pp. 599–607.

Singh, Rabinder and Kilroy, Charlotte, *In the Matter of the Potential Use of Armed Force by the UK against Iraq and the Draft US/UK Resolution,* Matrix Chambers, London, 23 February 2003. (Legal Opinion, 3 March 2003, dated 15 November 2002); In the matter of the legality of the use of force against Iraq and the alleged existence of weapons of mass destruction (Legal Opinion, 6 June 2003). The legal opinions are written at the request of the Campaign for Nuclear Disarmament (CND). Information about the CND can be found on www.cnduk.org.

Slaughter, Anne-Marie, *Good Reason for Going Around the UN,* International Herald Tribune, 19 March, 2003.

Taft, William H. and Buchwald, Todd F., *Preemption, Iraq and International Law,* AJIL, Vol. 97, 2003, pp. 557–563.

Walzer, Michael, *Just and Unjust Wars,* third edition, Basic Books, New York, 2000.

Vaughan, Lowe, *The Iraq Crisis: What now?* ICLQ, Vol. 52, October 2003, pp. 859–871.

Wedgewood, Ruth, *Attacken är helt legal* (The Attack is Perfectly Legal), Svenska Dagbladet 22 March 2003, published under the so called *Brännpunkt*-page.

Wedgewood, Ruth, *The Enforcement of Security Council Resolution 687: The Threat of Force against Iraq's Weapons of Mass Destruction,* AJIL, Vol. 92, No. 4, 1998, pp. 724–728.

Wedgewood, Ruth, *The Fall of Saddam Hussein: Security Council Mandates and Preemptive Self-Defence,* AJIL, Vol. 97, 2003, pp. 576–585.

Wood, Michael C., *The Interpretation of Security Council Resolutions,* Max Planck Yearbook of International Law, Vol. 2, pp. 1–23.

Wrange, Pål, *Reflections on Law, Schizophrenia and the Gulf Crisis,* Juridisk Tidskrift, No. 2, 1991–92, pp. 378–381.

Wrange, Pål, *De brittiska och amerikanska bombningarna av Irak,* Juridisk Tidskrift, No. 3, 1998–1999, pp. 620–638.

Wrange, Pål, *The American and British Bombings to Iraq and International Law,* Scandinavian Studies in Law, Vol. 39, Stockholm, 2000, pp. 491–514.

Österdahl, Inger, *Threat to the Peace. An Interpretation by the Security Council of Article 39 of the UN Charter,* Iustus förlag, Uppsala, 1998.

Internet material

Anderson, Kenneth, interview by Jan Crawford Greenburg, Washington Bureau, The Chicago Tribune, 20 March 2003, www.chicagotribune.com/archives (outprint on file with the author).
Christopher Greenwood, interviewed by Jan Crawford Greenburg, Washington Bureau, The Chicago Tribune, 20 March 2003, www.chicagotribune.com/archives.
Coalition Members, www.whitehouse.gov/infocus/iraq/news/20030327-10.html.
Kirgis, Frederic L., *Security Council Resolution 1441 on Iraq's Final Opportunity to Comply with Disarmament Obligations,* ASIL Insights, 14 November 2002, www.asil.org.
Shearer, Ivan, Contribution to the website debate, under the Sunday Morning Herald, www.smh.com.au (6 March 2003).
The National Security Strategy of the United States of America, September 2002, www.whitehouse.gov/nsc/nss.html.
www.whitehouse.gov/infocus/iraq/news/20030327-10.html, (28 August 2003.

Miscellaneous

President Bush, Address to the Nation, 17 March, 2003, Legal Background Paper, Foreign Affairs Committe, *"Iraq: Legal Basis for the Use of Force",* (on file with the author).
Statement by UN Secretary General Kofi Annan at the inauguration of the International Criminal Court on March 2003 in the Hague, Archives of the Swedish Ministry for Foreign Affairs.

Latin–English vocabulary

ab initio (inito)	from the beginning
ad hoc	temporary; for a particular purpose
bellum justum	just war
bona fide	done in good faith; honest intent
bona fides	good faith
cf. (confer)	compare
contra legem	against the law
de facto	in fact; in reality
de jure	by right; by force of law
desuetude	disuse; obsolescence
domaine reservé	domaine reservé (reserved domain); subject to domestic jurisdiction, *i.e.* not to international law
e contrario	on the contrary
et seq. (et sequens, et sequentes)	and the following one/ones
hors de combat	out of the fight; non-combatant
ibid. (ibidem)	in the same place (book, chapter etc.)
inter alia	among other things; among others
infra	below

jus cogens	peremptory norms of international law that must be observed by all states
jus ad bellum	law governing states' resort to force
jus in bello	rules governing the conduct of warfare
jus gentium	the law of nations; international law
lex lata (de lege lata)	established, binding law, the law as it exists
lex ferenda (de lege ferenda)	the law as one would want it to be
mala fide	in bad faith
mala fides	bad faith
mutatis mutandis	with the necessary changes
op. cit. (opere citato)	in the work cited
opinio juris	the conviction that certain behaviour is required by law
pacta sunt servanda	agreements must be honoured
per se	by or in itself
post factum (facto)	after the fact
quid pro quo	something given or received in exchange for something else
sine qua non	something that is indispensable
stare decisis	to stand by that which was decided; abide by precedent
supra	above
teleological	an approach to interpretation based on the purpose rather than the letter of legislation

travaux préparatoires	all the documentation drawn up during the preparation of a statute; legislative history
usus	usage; state practice
uti possidetis	the doctrine according to which the borders of newly sovereign states are defined on the basis of previous administrative borders

Diana Amnéus in cooperation with Robert Crofts and Annelie Gunnerstad

Index